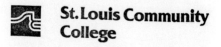

THE SHIP IN THE MEDIEVAL ECONOMY, 600-1600

The Ship in the Medieval Economy 600-1600

Richard W. Unger

CROOM HELM   LONDON

McGILL-QUEEN'S UNIVERSITY PRESS
MONTREAL

©1980 Richard W. Unger
Croom Helm Limited, 2-10 St John's Road, London SW11
ISBN 0-85664-949-X

McGill-Queen's University Press
1020 Pine Avenue West, Montreal H3A 1A2

ISBN 0-7735-0526-1

Legal deposit 3rd quarter 1980
Bibliothèque Nationale du Québec

Printed and bound in Great Britain by
Redwood Burn Limited Trowbridge & Esher

CONTENTS

ILLUSTRATIONS

ACKNOWLEDGEMENTS

I am grateful to the following for allowing me to reproduce the illustrations in this book:

1. Rosenkilde and Bagger for Figures 17 and 18 of pp. 54 and 55 in Olaf Hasslöf, Henning Henningsen and Arne Emil Christensen Jr (eds), *Ships and Shipyards, Sailors and Fishermen* (1972).
2. Bibliothèque Nationale, Paris, for Ms. Parisinus Graecus no. 510, fol. 367 verso.
3. Dr R. Pohl-Weber, Director of the Focke-Museum, Bremen for no. 60, page 108 from Siegfried Fliedner, ' "Kogge" und "Hulk" . . .' in *Die Bremer Hanse-Kogge* (1969) (top) and Detlev Ellmers, *FHMN*, p. 55, no. 37 (bottom).
4. Detlev Ellmers, *FHMN*, p. 56, no. 39.
5 , 7, 8. University Museum of National Antiquities, Oslo, Norway, which also holds the copyright.
6 , 12. Ole Crumlin-Pedersen, the former appearing in *AB*, p. 217, no. 144 and the latter in T. Andersson and K. O. Sandred (eds), *The Vikings*, p. 38, no. 5.
9. Detlev Ellmers, *FHMN*, p. 39, nos. 17-18.
10. Walter De Gruyter and Co., Berlin, from Ekkehard Eickhoff, *Seekrieg und Seepolitik zwischen Islam und Abendland* (1966), p. 8.
11. John Dotson and the Editor of *The Mariner's Mirror*, the Quarterly Journal of the Society for Nautical Research, from J. E. Dotson, 'Jal's *Nef X* and Genoese Naval Architecture in the 13th Century', *MM*, LIX (1973), p. 164.
13 (top), 14. VEB Hinstorff Verlag Rostock, from Herbert Ewe, *Schiffe auf Siegeln* (1972), p. 122, no. 41, p. 210, no. 217 and p. 165, no. 127, respectively. Drawings by Gerda Nützmann.
13 (bottom). George G. Harrap and Company Limited, from Romola and R. C. Anderson, *The Sailing-Ship* (1926), plate III.
15. Detlev Ellmers, Director, Deutsches Schiffahrtsmuseum.
16 (left), 17, 18. F. C. Lane, from his *Navires et Constructeurs à Venise pendant la Renaissance* (1965), pp. 40, 21 and 8, respectively.
16 (right). Dr R Pohl-Weber, for p. 99, no. 23 from Siegfried Fliedner, ' "Kogge" und "Hulk". . .'
19,24. By permission of the archive, the city of Dordrecht, Holland. On

these drawings see R. W. Unger, 'Four Dordrecht Ships of the Sixteenth Century', *MM*, LXI (1975), pp. 109-16.

20,23. José Maria Martinez-Hidalgo, from his *Columbus' Ships* (1966), pp. 88 and 50, respectively.

21. National Maritime Museum, London, from *AB*, p. 291, no. 204.

22. By permission of the editors of *The Mariner's Mirror*, the Quarterly Journal of The Society for Nautical Research, from R. Morton Nance, 'The Ship of the Renaissance', *MM*, XLI (1955), no. 20.

25,26. Dover Publications Inc., from H. Arthur Klein, *Graphic Worlds of Peter Bruegel the Elder* (1963), pp. 63 and 59 respectively.

27. Vereeniging Rijksmuseum Nederlandsch Historisch Scheepvaart Museum.

The seals at the beginning of each chapter are taken from Herbert Ewe, *Schiffe Auf Siegeln*, drawings by Gerda Nützmann, nos 60, 10, 155, 194, 242 and 245 respectively, and are reproduced with the permission of VEB Hinstorff Verlag Rostock.

A NOTE ON ILLUSTRATIONS

It is impossible adequately to illustrate all the changes in the history of European ship design described in this book. A small sample of pictures and drawings shows some of the major developments. To supplement the illustrations included here there is a second system of citation used throughout the book. Small roman letters refer to notes which list sources of pertinent illustrations. Some citations refer to the same picture in different books. It is impossible to keep all of the 23 books cited for their illustrations, not to mention the relevant numbers of the three journals, handy at all times. Two or three of the most commonly cited books should be enough, especially since often the same picture or drawing, if it is highly informative, is used in more than one of the works. Other publications besides the two or three more convenient can be consulted for specific design changes or types of vessels. Björn Landström's *The Ship* contains many extremely helpful drawings based directly and as fully as possible on medieval illustrations. It contains many drawings which are directly relevant to the developments described in this book. He later published a shorter work, *Sailing Ships*, which has many of the same drawings plus a few others. In the notes to illustrations *The Ship* is cited if a drawing appears in both works and *Sailing Ships* only when that is the one place it can be found. All books mentioned for their illustrations are marked with an asterisk in the bibliography. The ultimate collection of illustrations of classical and medieval ships is Friedrich Moll's *Das Schiff in der Bildenden Kunst*. Unfortunately it is so massive that it is difficult to use but remains the final authority for depictions of medieval vessels. It can be used as the final source for the pictorial evidence which is the basis of the observations in this book.

ABBREVIATIONS

AB	Basil Greenhill, *Archaeology of the Boat* (A. and C. Black Limited, London, 1976).
AN	*The American Neptune.*
FHMN	Detlev Ellmers, *Frühmittelalterliche Handelsschiffahrt in Mittel- und Nordeuropa* (Karl Wachholtz Verlag, Neumünster, 1972).
HSUA	George F. Bass (ed.), *A history of Seafaring based on Underwater Archaeology* (Thames and Hudson, London, 1972).
	pp. 65-86: Peter Throckmorton, 'Romans on the sea'.
	pp. 113-32: Peter Marsden, 'Ships of the Roman period and after in Britain'.
	pp. 133-58: Frederick van Doorninck, 'Byzantium, mistress of the sea: 330-641'.
	pp. 159-80: Arne Emil Christensen, 'Scandinavian ships from earliest times to the Vikings'.
	pp. 181-204: Ole Crumlin-Pedersen, 'The Vikings and the Hanseatic merchants: 900-1450'.
	pp. 205-24: Enrico Scandurra, 'The Maritime Republics: Medieval and Renaissance ships in Italy'.
	pp. 225-52: Alexander McKee, 'The influence of British naval strategy on ship design: 1400-1850'.
	pp. 253-80: Mendel L. Peterson, 'Traders and privateers across the Atlantic: 1492-1733'.
IJNA	*The International Journal of Nautical Archaeology and Underwater Exploration.*
MAB	*Marine Academie van België, Mededelingen (Académie de Belgique, Communications).*
MM	*The Mariner's Mirror.*
TCHM, I	Michel Mollat (ed.), *Travaux du Première Colloque (International) d'Histoire Maritime* (1956) (SEVPEN, Paris, 1957).
TCHM, II	Michel Mollat (ed.), *Travaux du Deuxième Colloque (International) d'Histoire Maritime* (1957) (SEVPEN, Paris, 1958).
TCHM, III	Michel Mollat (ed.), *Travaux du Troisième Colloque*

International d'Histoire Maritime (1958) (SEVPEN, Paris, 1960).

TCHM, IV   Michel Mollat (ed.), *Actes du Quatrième Colloque International d'Histoire Maritime* (1959) (SEVPEN, Paris, 1962).

TCHM, V   Michel Mollat (ed.), *Actes du Cinquième Colloque International d'Histoire Maritime* (1960) (SEVPEN, Paris, 1966).

TCHM, VI   Michel Mollat (ed.), *Travaux du Sixième Colloque International d'Histoire Maritime* (1962) (SEVPEN, Paris, 1964).

TCHM, VIII   Michel Mollat (ed.), *Actes du Huitième Colloque International d'Histoire Maritime* (1966) (SEVPEN, Paris, 1970).

FOR MY PARENTS

PREFACE

Knowledge about the design of European ships in the middle ages and the Renaissance is increasing rapidly. The changes necessary in this manuscript over the last two years show the pace of learning. Most of the new information comes from the work of archaeologists who are excavating the boats themselves. The impetus in northern Europe was given in the 1960s by the investigation under Ole Crumlin-Pedersen and others of five ships from about 1000 at Skuldelev near Roskilde in Denmark. In the Mediterranean the use of SCUBA gear since the 1940s has made possible a whole new range of work. Recently the Institute of Nautical Archaeology at Texas A & M University under the direction of George Bass has undertaken a number of significant digs.

It is perhaps foolhardy to attempt a summary of the history of European ship design just at the point when the understanding of that history is undergoing continuing revision. Yet there is a danger in that growth of knowledge. It can become uncontrolled and so it may prove difficult to identify what is important and what is not. Above all, the function of this book should be to place in the context of the economic history of Europe those developments in ship design. Often the data produced from archaeology yield a mass of technical information obscure and unintelligible to any but the initiated. It is easy to fall into the trap of concern for the data itself, in large part because shipwrights solved their various problems in many different and fascinating ways. At times this book may have succumbed to that fascination for obscure technical detail. On the other hand the study does not discuss ship design and technological change for their own sake. There is instead an effort to show how changes in ships were critical to certain major changes in the social and political development of Europe. In some cases the connections are obvious but in many instances it has been possible only to suggest how new types of ships led to social change.

Like all books — and many medieval ship types — this book will be superseded as more is learned about the ships themselves. Until it passes out of use perhaps this book can serve as a guide to marine archaeologists, maritime ethnologists and more generally maritime historians to suggest where they might find productive avenues of investigation. A more valuable contribution would be to convince historians of the middle ages and the Renaissance not to look on ships simply as objects for antiquarian interest. The argument throughout the book is that the development of ships made a significant contribution to a broad range of developments in European society, that for medieval and early modern Europe it was technical change in sea transport which had a most pervasive and enduring influence on society. There is one final contribution which this book might make and that is to show that ships were more than the fine craftmanship of skilled workers in wood. They were part of the solution to the economic problem of scarcity. As such, European shipbuilders were not immune from economic pressure in making decisions about how to build ships. It was in fact precisely those economic pressures which generated over the millennium discussed in this book the vehicle for European commercial and military success throughout the world.

The economic theory of induced innovation and its application to history is not in a stable state. Controversy has centred on the nineteenth and twentieth centuries but the discussion is equally relevant to the eleventh and twelfth. A simple causal relationship between factor costs and the character of innovation is not accepted here. On the other hand, where evidence broadly supports such a connection it is firmly asserted. It is difficult to document any such relationship since the factor use of innovations is almost as imperfectly known as the factor costs at any point in time. Unfortunately this leaves a great deal of latitude. Speculation has of necessity played a role in defining the social changes attributable to changes in ship design. Given the goals of this book it was decided to suggest potential connections rather than opt for describing short-term and immediate results of innovation in shipbuilding.

Long lists of individuals and institutions which have helped in the production of books fill many prefaces. It is only after going through the preparation of a work even as limited as this one that it becomes clear to what an extent such lists only begin to reflect how much help in fact is needed. In the case of this book the process of writing has been a long one which has served to lengthen the list. Financial support has come from the American Council of Learned Societies in the form of a Grant-in-Aid. The Humanities and Social Sciences Grants Committee of the University of British Columbia has three times awarded me sums to help with typing the manuscript and for travel. The University of British Columbia has also given me a year of study leave to write the book.

In gathering data on illustrations, bibliographical information and general material on ships I owe a debt to the directors and staffs of a number of maritime museums throughout Europe. Especially helpful have been the staffs at the Maritiem Museum Prins Hendrik in Rotterdam and the Rijksmuseum Historisch Scheepvaart Museum in Amsterdam and Messrs D. DeVries and J. P. Puype, respectively librarians of the two museums. Leo Akveld and Elly Bos at the Rotterdam maritime museum were always helpful in my many visits there.

Elsewhere in Europe my thanks go to Per Lundström (Stockholm), Sven Molaug (Oslo), Lauritz Pettersen (Bergen), Henning Henningsen (Elsinor), Göran Sundström (Göteborg), Jürgen Hoika (Schleswig), Jürgen Meyer (Hamburg, Altonaer Museum), Ole Crumlin-Pedersen (Roskilde), Rosemarie Pohl-Weber and Siegfried Fliedner (Bremen), Detlev Ellmers (Bremerhaven), Arne Grønningsæter (Molde), D. W. Waters (Greenwich), Peter Marsden (London), J. van Beylen (Antwerp), Hervé Cras (Paris), Manuel Maia (Lisbon), José Massó (Bueu), Alm. Morales (Madrid), José M. Martinez-Hidalgo and Laureano C. Relat (Barcelona), G. B. Rubin de Cervin (Venice), among many others in those maritime museums. I am also grateful to G. D. van der Heide, former director of excavations in the Ijsselmeerpolders in the Netherlands for information about his work and to his successor, Mnr. Reinders. The library staff at the University of British Columbia, especially of the Interlibrary Loan Office, have been of great help. I owe thanks to the staff of the Bibliothèque Nationale in Paris and especially to the staff of the Provincial Bibliotheek in Middleburg, Zeeland, for assuming many an extraordinary task.

At various times I have had a chance to present some of my views about the evolution of medieval ship design to conferences. I am grateful to the organisers and to the participants at the Sixth Annual Meeting of the Medieval Association of the Pacific held at Stanford University, the Third Naval History Symposium at Annapolis, Maryland and the Eighth Medieval Workshop of the Committee for Medieval Studies, University of British Columbia. In correspondence and in conversation I have benefited from the criticisms of Tom Glasgow, Jr, John Dotson, Barbara Kreutz, Paul Meyvaert, Arne Emil Christensen, Peter van der Merwe, Tim Runyan, and especially Frederic C. Lane and Ole Crumlin-Pedersen. Lynn T. White Jr. has been a continual source of support to me as he has to all of us working in the history of medieval technology. The manuscript has been read in earlier stages by Archibald R. Lewis, Detlev Ellmers and D. W. Waters, who have deftly steered me away from many errors. Jaap Bruijn as always was a helpful guide.

Bob Goudswaard, Maryse Ellis and Faith Bateman typed the manuscript. Bob Jemison as well as the staff of Audio-Visual Services at the

University of British Columbia helped to prepare the illustrations. Lee and Belia Gordenker gave me the opportunity of enjoying the solitude of their house for thinking and writing. Piet van der Veen and Emily DeJosselin DeJong offered their kind support and friendship while I was working on this book. The greatest support came, as always, from my wife. Tolerance came from my daughter. My deepest debt of gratitude, though, remains that to my parents. Even in times of trouble they have continued to make sacrifices on my behalf. This book is as much a product of their effort as of mine.

INTRODUCTION
THE ECONOMY AND TECHNICAL CHANGE

Writers on the history of ship design usually take one of two approaches. They are interested in the ship as a thing of beauty, as an artistic expression of man's creative powers, or they are interested in the ship as a machine with complex equipment to deal with technical problems. A ship is and was always more than that. It was above all a way to move goods and people. It was an instrument for solving the economic problem of scarcity. Success in dealing with that problem was always a crucial consideration for the men who built and operated ships. The goal here is to show the connection in the middle ages between the economy and changes in ship design and simultaneously to explain some of the economic and social results of those changes.

By the seventh century the political situation in the Mediterranean Sea and throughout Europe formed the basis for novel commercial relationships divorced from the pattern of the classical past. One thousand years later commerce and those commercial relationships had changed as much as European society. In that millennium the changes in ship design were even more dramatic. In 600 ships were small. Their voyages were of limited distances. They tended to stay close to shore. They carried few goods. In 1600 the seagoing ship was the major vehicle of transport for all kinds and types of goods, moving those goods over unprecedented distances. There were regular shipping services not only in Europe but also from Europe to the New World and India. There were vessels of specialised design made for certain tasks and an almost complete separation of warships from merchant vessels.

The middle ages was by no means a period of stagnant technology. Through a mass of experiments European shipbuilders laid the basis for the development of sailing ships which were the vehicles of the international economy up to and through the Industrial Revolution. Shipbuilders supplied capital goods to shippers and in that form the ships were a source of economic growth and also of change in European society. By 1600 the improvements made by designers affected not only European society but also the relative position of Europe in the world. The superiority of European ships both for commercial and for naval uses made possible the domination by westerners of societies in the Orient and the New World.[1]

21

Better shipping services created opportunities, largely economic but also political and social, for Europeans. The possibilities for action expanded with lower costs, with the more efficient movement of goods and of men. Ships always enjoyed an advantage over land transport from the days of the first dugouts because in the water there is less friction to overcome than on land. But it was the progressive improvements and the exploitation of those improvements which expanded the range of potential action. That range was itself chosen or, rather, limited by the specific choice of design changes made by shipbuilders. The shipwrights too were constrained in their choices of improvements by the advantages which could be gained from specific innovations. They were usually faced with a choice among many possible adjustments in design. They had to decide which would prove the most profitable, and profitable in the broadest sense. The system was by no means fully determined. The economy did not dictate certain profit opportunities which then were taken up by shipbuilders which in turn led to a set of social changes. At each step of the historical process there was a variety of options open to individuals.

It was not the economy alone which placed constraints on technical change. The list of other forces is finite but lengthy. Social change, though bounded by techniques in use, still is never fully determined by those techniques. Indeed, in the chain between the economy, technical change and change in society, for each step it is a question of establishing sufficient conditions, the basis for or preconditions for some adjustment, rather than demonstrating an obvious and necessary causal connection. For example, both economic theory and the study of the economy of the nineteenth and twentieth centuries have failed to establish a direct, consistent and immutable connection between the economy and technology.[2] For the history of medieval ship design, given the scarcity and the character of the evidence, it is not even possible to attempt such a demonstration. In fact it is difficult enough to show where sufficient conditions for technical change may have existed.

Knowledge about shipbuilding changed surprisingly little from 600 to 1600. There were certainly some inventions but change usually came in the form of new combinations of existing features or greater emphasis on already known features. It is a commonplace of the history of medieval technology that developments occurred at least 50 years before the date of the earliest known evidence. For changes in ship design the time span is even greater.[3] The effect of the study of the history of ship design has consistently been to erode categories and periods for that history which were established by earlier writers. It has been done with the discovery of new evidence which usually in turn makes possible a reinterpretation of existing evidence. For medieval shipbuilders, though not everything was possible, still there was a broad range of ways for them to go about building a ship. There were many building techniques and designs and approaches known in western Europe at any one time and these were used on vessels of different sizes and in different places. Knowledge of those designs was easily diffused, and still more easily as time passed and the vessels made voyages of even greater distances. Shipbuilders themselves travelled on board ships visiting harbours throughout Europe and seeing the types in use. [4] Merchants made extensive voyages as well and they carried information about ships. So the possibility existed for European shipwrights to know about almost all potentially useful methods of wooden boat construction. There were exceptions of course. But it would be wrong, as has been traditional, to see shipbuilders as confined to one method of working and waiting until by some odd chance information reached them from some other place about an alternative.[5] On the one hand diffusion of knowledge of shipbuilding techniques did take place and took place easily. On the other it was not diffusion on which the introduction, development and use of new techniques necessarily depended. Within a relatively narrow geographic area builders could find all the new ideas they wanted or could use.

Faced with a choice from among a large number of known techniques and designs shipwrights could then allow economic considerations to weigh heavily in their decisions. Technical improvement by definition means increased output from the same inputs. Saving in the use of factors of production will, except in the most extreme of circumstances, lead to a reduction in costs. So for buyers, in this case shippers and shipowners, almost any technical change is gladly accepted. Their concern is for a lowering of total costs. Relative factor costs and especially expectations about capital and labour costs appear to have historically directed the character of innovation. Perceived cost patterns can and have affected the sequence and the timing of combinations of technical features.[6] Technical change has been apparently biased to save more of that factor which was expected to rise relatively in price. There is no reason to believe shipbuilders in medieval Europe escaped such bias.

The pattern of demand as well has dictated technical limits for producers which in turn have suggested directions for technical change. The extent and the nature of demand and the size of saving which in turn is a result of relative factor costs, both present and anticipated, will affect the degree and speed of adoption of any new method. The economic drive – that is, to save effort no matter the method – leaves technicians open to pursue improvement within a broad range. The choice of direction is also a function of the expectations of success. For medieval shipbuilders those expectations were to a large degree defined by past experience. Technical change in ship design did have some life of its own, a history and development which was cumulative. Immediate past practice did after all present the various design features from which the shipwright chose most if not all parts of his new design. The essential body of information about the performance of vessels in the water did not change over the millennium. No new possibilities were suddenly created by some increase in knowledge of the physical world. As a result builders throughout the years from 600 to 1600 faced similar technological constraints in attacking their basic problem. This left them to respond to economic pressures within that framework of knowledge giving those economic pressures greater significance than in conditions where an increase in theoretical understanding might lead them to concentrate on exploiting what was new rather than what at the moment seemed most economical.[7]

There could be technical retrogression. Knowledge of design could be lost over time as builders, having abandoned a certain method, feature or approach, would first lose familiarity with a technique and then forget about it. The loss might only be in one district or region and in that case diffusion could serve to jog the collective memory. But the loss of technique is probably the hardest aspect of the history of technology to identify and to demonstrate. At best the evidence can only be negative. The widespread diffusion of technique in the middle ages certainly mitigated against such loss. The loss may have been aided by the shape of demand and by the levels of factor prices over time. Despite retrogression and despite stagnation in theoretical knowledge of ship performance and despite a lack of learning about ship design, it does not appear that ignorance of boat-building techniques was the effective constraint for medieval European shipwrights.

Constraints on shipbuilders were of a different sort. Design changed slowly. The choice was usually to adhere to what had been done in the past for a certain type of vessel. Large ships would retain features even though an improved method could be adopted from the design of smaller vessels produced in the same place and perhaps even by the same ship carpenters. This has led to the common accusation of excessive conservatism on the part of shipwrights. Ship carpentry and boat building have been called the most traditional of all trades where techniques are jealously guarded secrets to be handed down from father to son as a valuable legacy.[8] Since knowledge of relative factor costs, especially among historians, is so imperfect, the tendency is to place emphasis on irrational resistance to technical change. Adherence to past practice among medieval shipwrights was not dictated by traditionalism, by a desire to maintain stability or by some kind of socially imbued abhorrence of change. There were cost problems. A change in the design of a ship type increased the risk of losing the vessel. Such risk was always high in the middle ages. With no theory, no science of shipbuilding to guide them, shipbuilders could not predict the outcome of design changes. Moreover, with only some intuitive feeling of the potential which would be embodied in the change, shipwrights could not demonstrate the advantages of experiment to buyers. The arguments of the innovative would have had little force. Both buyers and builders faced an unchanging sea. So techniques which had worked in the past were likely to work again. The logic of conservatism could only be refuted by some marked change in demand or in costs.

Builders were at the same time constrained by the equipment they used. Their tools and the character of materials available to them set extreme limits on their capacity to innovate. For example, designing ships on the basis of the exact measurements of the ship was meaningless if the tools were not good enough to make parts to fit those measurments. Extreme changes in hull shape were not possible unless some material more malleable and resilient than wood was found. Major innovations in shipbuilding, innovations which had a massive effect like those of the nineteenth century as a result of having a reliable steam engine and large quantities of quality iron easily available, depended on technical change outside of shipbuilding. Shipping too was confined by other technologies. The most important in the middle ages was navigation. Without better navigational techniques at any point in time the opportunities for using any ship were limited. The advisability of increasing the capabilities of ships through design improvements was certainly affected. Ship design had to conform to limiting conditions set by other technologies as well as by the limited knowledge of physical forces acting on ships.

The problems of designing a ship could not be dealt with simply by compromise. The increase of carrying capacity, speed and security, three common goals, put sharply conflicting demands on design. It was in most cases impossible to trade off one against the other so there was instead a complex groping for solutions which would satisfy all three goals at once.[9] Shipbuilders then retained strong loyalty to traditional designs and practices and for good reasons. Other than that underlying aversion to risk, the principal source of influence on the actions of ship carpenters was demand for shipping services. Their ability to respond to that demand depended on the state of related technologies and on the economics of operating ships. Shipbuilders were interested in satisfying demands made on them in an efficient way and not in some vague maximisation of the economic potential of the ship. They typically set out to satisfy certain immediate requirements and otherwise proceeded in a traditional manner.

Economic forces and pressures were transmitted to shipbuilders by buyers, by people willing to invest in what for the middle ages was a sizeable capital good. Buyers would invest only with the expectation of some reward, almost invariably an economic one. In the early middle ages governments too were looking for economic rewards. Economics and politics were inseparable. Merchant ships were always built to serve an economic function. Governments, at least until the sixteenth century, were interested generally in warships which would be the most efficient form of defence and attack for the state. Orders for commercial vessels depended on the existence of trade, the presence of goods produced in one place and a market for precisely those goods in another. Those conditions were almost always present. Also needed – and this was by no means always present – was a vehicle which could carry the goods over the distance at a cost which would make trade pay for itself.

It was then the responsibility of the shipbuilders to produce vessels which would keep costs down and make the expansion of trade profitable. The major costs faced by shippers were labour – that is the pay and maintenance of the crew during the voyage – and the ship itself. The latter included not only the original outlay but also repairs and replacement of parts over the life of the vessel and also the risk, the chance that the ship would be lost because of either weather or hostile action. As far as buyers were concerned, once the ship had been bought their capital was invested and the original price did not matter. They were locked into their position unless they chose to sell the ship in the second-hand market. The presence of such a market, and there usually was one, might affect the original decision to buy a ship. But prices in that market did not nor could they change the size of the investment. For the economy as a whole and over the long term, capital costs, taken in the broad sense of total expenditure in all forms on the ship, were a significant component of transport costs. Technical change embodied in the ship, created and introduced by shipbuilders, could and did act on both labour and capital costs. Shipbuilders could by the design of the ship embody certain labour requirements. Indeed, the essential features of design fixed minimum requirements and therefore minimum labour costs. Manning ratios, the number of crew members for each ton carried, could and often did exceed the minimum in the interests of defending the ships against pirates and privateers. Shipbuilders to a limited degree had control over that component of costs too by building, for example, for defensibility or for speed. Shipwrights could by the design of the ship embody certain capital requirements. Through the use of types of wood, of different sail plans and different raw materials, they set not only the original outlay but also minimum risks and minimum repair costs. The shipbuilder by his choice also determined the maximum speed of the vessel at sea. Costs to the shipper and to society were affected by the time goods spent in transit. The shipbuilder on the other hand had only limited control, through his design, over the period the ship would spend in port waiting for a cargo.

Shipwrights then, in the form of their product, set limits for shippers. But those limits were chosen by shipbuilders because of demand — the needs of men who wanted to move goods at a profit. Shipping was subject to numerous other constraints set by government action, by the quality of communications, by business methods, constraints which in turn dictated the final form of ships built. Probably the most important economic constraint on shippers though was the potential for a round trip with the ship where there was a paying cargo in both directions. The presence of supply in one place and demand in another was often enough to establish a trading connection. But if shippers could find a back cargo, that is some goods which could be carried in the opposite direction, the cost of the principal voyage would fall, in the extreme case by 50 per cent. The volume and value of the back cargo would fix the percentage saving in shipping costs.[10] Again, to some degree ship carpenters were in a position to influence the use of ships to carry back cargoes by the form and features incorporated into the ships.

For moving bulk goods — that is, good with low value per unit volume — cost of transport was crucial. Generally these were commodities which could be produced in most parts of Europe, and imports were a supplement to local output. Small changes in the delivered price of such goods meant in general better than equivalent percentage changes in demand and therefore greater demand for shipping services. It was here that the greatest potential for over-all growth, if not of profits, for shippers lay. For luxury goods, or more precisely those of high value per unit volume, transport costs were less of a factor in determining delivered prices. These were scarce goods for which the place of production was usually determined by geography or climate.[11] Once a certain threshold of transport costs was reached and this was a high threshold, then technical change in ships had little effect on the volume of luxuries shipped. Such goods were often a sign of the status and income of consumers. Their ability to devote income to such ostentation made a greater difference to the movement of luxuries than did marginal changes in the cost of carriage.

The technical change in ship design from 600 to 1600 made it possible to ship bulk goods in ever greater quantities. Over time, shippers increasingly found that they could make a profit on the movement of such goods in the absence of artificial market conditions such as government subsidies or imposed systems for the movement of goods. At the same time shipbuilders found ways of designing and building ships which did not damage the market for shipping luxury goods. In fact they increased the profits from carrying such goods and simultaneously improved the potential for success in all shipping activities. More important than the increased profits to shippers was the progressive opening of new markets for waterborne transport. That in turn expanded the opportunities for experiment in ship design and for profit for shipbuilders. The development was by no means a simple one. The complexities of varying demand and production in different regions, political instability and a mass of other factors dictated varying responses from shipbuilders. Opportunities always existed in the movement of bulk goods. It was a question of being able to tap the potential within short-run constraints.

Yet the pattern over the years from 600 to 1600 is, in retrospect, unmistakable. The technical changes in ship design meant immediate and direct benefits for seamen, for shippers and for producers of almost all goods in Europe and throughout the world. The distribution of those benefits and the retention of them, however, depended on a number of factors external to shipping and shipbuilding. The changes in ship design did have, often through the medium of shipping, both short-term and long-term effects on European society. Some were certainly expected and were undoubtedly predicted at the time. Others were totally unexpected and in some cases took generations to become apparent.

Economic developments which dictated ship design choice and the social changes which grew from the improvements in ships must be discussed in rather general terms. Information on the development of medieval society is diffuse enough and diverse enough to guarantee an impression of complexity which in turn serves to obscure or leave in doubt the general pattern of social change. Knowledge of the medieval economy is limited by a lack of data on even the most essential of activities. Aggregate figures for economic activity must be built up from a few individual cases where data have survived. There is some consensus, however, on the long-term changes in population, on changes in gross output in agriculture and in manufacturing and, with even less reliability, on the ratios of factors used in the production of some goods. While the uncertainty closes the door to statements of a high degree of precision it allows a certain freedom from being mired in the detail of minor economic and social changes which were, in fact, swamped by long-run developments. The lack of precise information makes it necessary to see Europe as a collection of sizeable regions rather than as a group of separate and independent political and linguistic units. It was, after all, the regional differences in climate and history which served in part to create the spectrum of trading opportunities and the context in which shippers and shipbuilders had to function.

The history of ship design is on more solid ground than the history of the economy. Still there has never been complete agreement on the pattern of change. The traditional sources, contemporary illustrations of ships and the mention of ship types in documents, have formed a sound basis for describing the evolution of European vessels. Information from nautical archaeology has recently served to supplement and expand that body of knowledge.[12] Improvements in ships can be separated into changes in three broad categories: the systems used for propulsion, the systems used to control the ships, and the form and construction of the container, the hull of the ship. The shape of the superstructure offers an easy and convenient source for differentiating types. But it was not crucial to the economics of operation of the large majority of sailing ships. For seagoing ships the three major aspects of design had to be synchronised so development in one depended on and in many cases led to changes in the others. A crucial consideration in the design of the container was the potential carrying capacity of the vessel. There is no convenient measure. First efforts to establish a standard were made in the middle ages. But many different units were used and often they had different bases. The only practical solution, and that used here, is to try to convert all measures into tons burden — that is, the weight in tons of 2,240 English pounds or 1,018 kilograms which the ship could carry. The figures are then comparable to modern measures in deadweight tonnage.[13] Because of problems with conversion, inaccuracy of measurement and misunderstanding of what was being measured there is an error of as much as 25 per cent in either direction. The result is a statistical unreliability which makes it difficult to draw specific conclusions about developments in carrying capacity. At least the data are more reliable for seagoing vessels, for the larger ships in use in the middle ages, if only because of the quantity of surviving evidence. Information from smaller craft, rivergoing or coastal vessels, because of problems of measurement, can unfortunately only form a supplement to material on the evolution of hull design. On questions of changes in control and propulsion, however, information from smaller craft is an integral part of any basis of judgement.

To claim effects on society from some technological change long after it has occurred certainly makes such arguments suspect. On the other hand, to take a short space of time may well obscure results from innovation which take many years to work their way through various social relationships. The choice of periods of up to 250 years and periods defined largely by major changes in ship design is a compromise to avoid the errors of both extremes. The time span may appear too long but, given the pace of technical change and of economic growth in the middle ages compared to the nineteenth and twentieth centuries, the error is probably in the right direction. The division of the 1,000 years from 600 to 1600 into these units tends to mask both the long-term economic and social results of the development of improved waterborne transport and the pattern of change in ship design itself. The ties with past practice felt by all shipbuilders certainly gave the development of ship design an evolutionary character. Despite any externally imposed temporal division and despite varying paces of change and diversions into unfruitful experiments at different times and places, the long-term result was the development by shipbuilders of increasingly efficient and versatile ships with expanding capabilities. Concentration on the technical change in ships can too easily lead to ignoring the economic pressures on the technicians, the external technical improvements which created new possibilities for shipbuilders and the potential for social change which the improved instrument of communication generated. Ships, like all goods, were not produced in a vacuum but rather within the context of human needs. Ships, like all capital goods, could and did deeply affect the many individuals who benefited from their use.

NOTES

1. Carlo M. Cipolla, *Guns and Sails in the Early Phases of European Expansion 1400-1700* (Pantheon Books, New York, 1965). Lewis Mumford, *Technics and Civilization* (Harcourt, Brace and Co., New York, 1934), pp. 120-3. For a more negative and incorrect view of the importance of improvements in medieval transport technology, A. Joris, 'Transports et voies de communications au moyen âge', *Cahiers de Clio*, XXIII (1970), p. 40.

2. H. J. Habakkuk, *American and British Technology in the Nineteenth Century: the Search for Labour-Saving Innovations* (Cambridge University Press, Cambridge, 1962). Edwin Mansfield, *The Economics of Technological Change* (W. W. Norton Co., Inc., New York, 1968). Paul Samuelson, 'A Theory of Induced Innovation along Kennedy-Weisäcker Lines', *Review of Economics and Statistics*, XLVII (1965), pp. 343-56. Jacob Schmookler, *Invention and Economic Growth* (Harvard University Press, Cambridge, Mass., 1966). For a discussion of some significant detriments to adoption of innovations see Nathan Rosenberg, 'Factors Affecting the Diffusion of Technology', *Explorations in Economic History*, X (1972), pp. 3-34.

3. M. W. Prynne, 'Henry V's Gracedieu', *MM*, LIV (1968), p. 122.

4. Having a man on board who could make repairs was a necessity and dates from well before the middle ages. By the thirteenth century and probably earlier specialist ship carpenters on board were common. On Venetian vessels these men had a special area set aside for them. F. C. Lane, *Navires et Constructeurs à Venise pendant la Renaissance* (SEVPEN, Paris, 1965), p. 23. There was a similar area set aside on a seventh-century Byzantine ship. *HSUA*, p. 143. Sixteenth-century regulations suggest that younger men went on voyages to gain experience and then when older settled down to work in a port. Probably old practice by that date, the situation put young men most susceptible to new ideas in a position to be exposed to such ideas. Ernst Baasch, *Beiträge zur Geschichte des deutschen Seeschiffbaues und der Schiffbaupolitik* (Lucas Gräfe und Sillem, Hamburg, 1899), pp. 276-7.

5. On the widespread diffusion of fore-and-aft sails, diffusion which took place well before that alleged by previous scholars, see Joseph Needham, *Science and Civilization in China*, vol. IV, *Physics and Physical Technology*, part III, Civil Engineering and Nautics (Cambridge University Press, Cambridge, 1971), pp. 589-617. Richard Lebaron Bowen, Jr, 'The Origins of Fore-and-Aft Rigs', *AN*, XIX (1959), pp. 155-99, 274-306.

6. Nathan Rosenberg, 'The Direction of Technological Change: Inducement Mechanisms and Focusing Devices', *Economic Development and Cultural Change*, LVIII (1969), pp. 1-24. For a more theoretical treatment of the same principle see Hans P. Binswanger, 'A Microeconomic Approach to Induced Innovation', *The Economic Journal*, LXXXIV (1974), pp. 940-58.

7. Nathan Rosenberg, 'Science, Invention and Economic Growth', *The Economic Journal*, LXXXIV (1974), pp. 90-108. In Rosenberg's words the elasticity of supply of inventions to the industry remained nearly constant below infinity but above zero over the period. And there was no scientific development which served to flatten out the supply curve.

8. The extreme statement is from *HSUA*, p. 67, but the view is one which is widely held.

9. Michel Mollat, *Le Commerce Maritime Normand à la Fin du Moyen Age* (Librarie Plon, Paris, 1952), pp. 345-6. R. Munro-Smith, *Applied Naval Architecture* (Longmans Green and Co. Ltd, London, 1967), p. 43. The increase in scientific knowledge has by the twentieth century made ship design more a question of compromise. On the effects of science and the ability of increased knowledge

to define technique and economic success in the twentieth century see Almarin Phillips, *Technology and Market Structure: A Study of the Aircraft Industry* (D. C. Heath and Co., Lexington, Mass., 1971).

10. Ralph Davis, 'Merchant Shipping in the Economy of the Late Seventeenth Century', *Economic History Review*, second series, IX (1956), pp. 59-65.

11. Location of the production of minerals, for example, was fixed by geography but the level and price elasticity of demand determined whether the minerals were luxuries or not. Copper, iron, salt were always bulk goods and depended heavily on transport costs for the quantities sold. Gems, gold, silver were always luxuries.

12. For a survey of techniques and major discoveries see *Underwater Archaeology A Nascent Discipline* (UNESCO, Paris, 1972).

13. For a summary of the problems involved and of various measures used see F. C. Lane, 'Tonnages, Medieval and Modern', *Economic History Review*, second series, XVII (1964), pp. 213-33. Often medieval figures indicate not carrying capacity in weight but rather in terms of volume. Such figures are converted here to tons of 100 cubic feet, that is 2.83 cubic metres. This is about the same as modern gross registered tonnage and since sailing ships, depending on design, had the overwhelming majority of space below decks available for cargo such a figure is not too much greater than modern registered tonnage. Rules for calculating tonnage were developed by shipwrights in the fifteenth and sixteenth centuries and were then taken over by governments. Those rules can be used, though with care, to generate figures for deadweight tonnage. W. Salisbury, 'Early Tonnage Measurement in England', *MM*, LII (1966), pp. 41-51, 173-80, 329-40, LIII (1967), pp. 251-61. Paul Gille, 'Jauge et Tonnage des Navires', *TCHM*, I, pp. 85-93. R. De Bock, 'Tonnen, Tonnenmaat en Lasten', *MAB*, XII (1960), pp. 117-33. A. van Driel, *Tonnage Measurement: Historical and Critical Essay* (Government Printing Office, The Hague, 1925), pp. 6-34. Hélène Antoniadis-Bibicou, *Etudes d'histoire maritime de Byzance* (SEVPEN, Paris, 1966), pp. 129-33.

1 THE LOSS OF ROMAN WAYS: 600-750

The fall of the last Roman emperor in the West in 476 was an event of little political significance and even less importance for commerce and shipping. The centre of the Mediterranean economy had long before shifted eastward, a fact acknowledged by the transfer of part of the Roman government to the shores of the Bosporus by Emperor Constantine in 330. The Byzantine Empire with its capital at Constantinople emerged as the strong state of the Mediterranean in the fifth century. In the sixth century it was the base for an effort to re-establish the entire former Empire under Emperor Justinian. Success was not complete but the result by 600 was unification of much of the Mediterranean coast under one government and the protection of trade by that government. The stability created by Justinian's conquest was destroyed by the emergence of a new political force from Arabia. The adherents to the teachings of the prophet Mohammad in the years after 630 very quickly established themselves on the southern and eastern shores of the Mediterranean, taking some of the richest provinces of the Byzantine Empire and presenting a direct threat to the continued survival of the Empire itself. That made the Mediterranean a battleground between

Illustration above: A simple open coastal vessel of early medieval ancestry, Gravelines, oldest town seal, first half of the thirteenth century.

33

two competing powers. It remained so for some centuries.

The former western provinces of the Roman Empire were ruled by a series of Germanic kings, leaders of tribal groupings which had migrated into the Empire in the fifth and sixth centuries. The remnants of Roman administration in the West gave a certain stability to government but in the course of the seventh century that disappeared. By 711 and the loss of Spain to invading Muslims the surviving German successor states on the Continent were the Lombard kingdom in Italy and the kingdom of the Franks. The latter was passing through a constitutional crisis which was not resolved until the mid-eighth century. The confused political situation in western and northern Europe left little or no institutional support for commerce or for the development of shipping. The direction taken by technical change in ship design there was a reflection of the retrogression in politics, in learning and in the economy.

Just as Europe inherited Roman language, literature and political institutions so too did it inherit Roman practice in ship design and shipbuilding. The essential features of Roman ships formed the starting point for builders in the Mediterranean in the middle ages. In northern and central Europe Roman influence on existing Celtic practice was surprisingly limited. The first- and second-century Romans built essentially two types of ships: galley and merchantman. A number of sub-groups or variations on the basic designs can also be identified. The differentiation into these two types was established by the middle of the second millennium BC. The Romans simply pursued the possibilities created by their inheritance from the Egyptians, Phoenicians and Greeks. The better-known galley was powered by oars and was long relative to its width. Though the galley was usually equipped with sails and though merchantmen might sometimes also have oars, it was always easy to distinguish the two types by the shape of the hull. Merchantmen were short, almost tubby and nothing like the slender galleys.

The Romans, having swept the seas of all opposition, needed only a light vessel for patrol and coast-guard work. The light and fast Liburnian type was the answer.[a] One bank of oars was adequate. Later versions may have had two banks of oars. There was always just one man to each oar. Speed and manoeuvrability were the principal features of the Liburnian. There was a single ram, the principal offensive weapon of the galley, at the bow. At the stern was a cabin for the commander. A single square sail was rigged to a single mast stepped amidships. A small square sail, an artemon, was slung under the bow to act as a headsail. The yard, often made of two spars fished together, could be as long as the mast. The sail only got in the way in a fight so it was retractable and easily stowed between the lines of rowers. There was also a second and smaller rig which could be easily raised and may have been used to get out of difficulty. The sails were made of oblong blocks of cloth sewn together with boltropes on the edges and leather patches at the corners for reinforcement. Galley crews were free men. If there were any slaves on board they were the servants of the commander.[1] Galleys stayed close to shore not because of the frailty of the ship or lack of knowledge of navigation but because they needed to be close to supplies and had to stop at night since there was no place on board for the men to sleep. The vessel was controlled by using the oars and by side rudders, one on each side of the stern. The galley was originally designed for both trade and piracy. For short-distance trades and trades where speed was important, such as the shipment of animals, it was useful. It also made the ideal warship for the Mediterranean. Cargo vessels, on the other hand, were invariably slow and hard to handle relative to galleys. They were double-ended but on larger vessels the bow was low compared to the stern.[b] As a result they were anchored at the stern. Power came from a single large square sail on a mast stepped amidships or slightly forward. There was an artemon to aid in steering and by the third century there might also have been a small triangular sail above the mainsail, probably only used in fair weather, to aid in driving the ship.

On smaller merchantmen there was a handful of oars to be used in emergencies or as an auxiliary driving force. In some of the largest merchantmen there were three masts with a short mizzenmast added at the stern which also carried a square sail. This was probably to aid in handling as much as for propulsion. Merchantmen carried less canvas than was feasible and carried it low. This kept down speed, 4 to 6 knots with a favourable breeze, but it made the vessel much safer. The main-yard was very long and needed multiple lifts, ropes running from the deck to the top of the mast and then to blocks on the yard, to raise it. A massive forestay was needed to hold the mast in place. Shrouds, also for holding the mast, ran from the uppermost plank of the hull to the top of the mast and had tackles so that they could be adjusted. That meant it was not possible to use ratlines — that is, to make rope ladders out of the shrouds by adding small connecting pieces of rope. For getting to the top of the mast there was a rope ladder at the back of the mast. Sail was shortened by raising it up to the yard, not by lowering it. To do that Romans used brails, lines running up through the sail to the yard and then down to the deck. Thus sail could be shortened without going aloft. Also it was possible to shorten only a part of the sail and even to make a triangular sail out of the square one if the master wanted.

Added to the sails for control were two large steering rudders, one at either side of the stern. These were heavier than on galleys, better protected and more firmly fixed. They were manned by a single helmsman who held two tiller bars which ran to the centre of the ship from the rudders. On larger ships a slightly more complex arrangement was fitted. In any case the system was efficient.[2]

The shape of the hull was derived from Minoan practice of the second millennium BC. It was well rounded with curving stem and stern posts. The length-to-beam ratio was about 4:1 but could be as little as 3:1. It was kept low to add cargo space and also for safety. On freighters of any size there was a second deck. The deckhouse at the stern could be a fully enclosed cabin for the captain and perhaps a few select passengers. Most of the passengers, however, camped on deck. There was usually a galley fitted aft for heating meals.

Freighters could be built to massive proportions. The smallest ships used on the open sea in trade were of 70 or 80 tons. The average was undoubtedly higher. Even by the fifth century BC ships of 100 to 150 tons were not uncommon and there were vessels up to 500 tons. In the third century BC there was a move towards building bigger warships and this may have caused an increase in the size of merchantmen. At that time perhaps the biggest cargo vessel of the classical world was built under the supervision of Archimedes at Syracuse. It was a grain carrier of 1,700 to 1,900 tons. Vessels of that size were not built again until the sixteenth century. In the first, second and third centuries AD, however, the Romans had an ambitious programme for the transport of the annual grain tribute of 150,000 tons from Alexandria in Egypt to Rome. The ships used also provided excellent passenger service with, in one case, 600 people carried. A size of 1,300 tons was usual for such vessels, with measurements of 55 metres over-all length, 13.72 metres broad and 13.25 metres deep in the hold. There were of course smaller vessels, size and dimensions depending on the job of the ship. For heavy goods such as wine or building stone dimensions would be 19 to 33 metres long and 7 to 10 metres broad while larger cargo vessels would rise to 40 metres by 10 metres. The total number of ships in service and the total tonnage of the Roman merchant marine was probably not equalled again in Europe until the sixteenth century. Roman merchant vessels, unlike the galleys, were manned by slaves. In fact even the master was often a slave.[3]

Roman ships were built like fine pieces of furniture. For strength they relied on the outer shell of the hull.[4] The external planking was placed end to end and held together by mortise and tenon joints. Both the upper and lower plank were given alternating projections and grooves to fit into each other. Wooden nails, treenails, were then run through the planks and tenons. The treenails in turn were held in place by nails. The planks or strakes were .035 to .10 metres thick. The tenons were .05 metres thick and at times rising to nearly .10 metres. The tenons could reach halfway into the plank. Tenons were usually about .10 metres across and on seagoing ships mortises were never more than .25 metres apart and usually much less. The extreme and not uncommon case was that the tenons were next to each other forming an almost solid wall. This formed a strong and perfectly watertight compartment.[c] In construction the keel and posts at either end were laid down first. Then the hull planks were fitted in this careful manner. After the hull was finished the frames were added inside the hull for lateral strength. They were not regularly spaced but usually not over .25 metres apart and often closer together. They were secured to the completed hull with treenails which in turn were held in place by bronze spikes. After that heavy external planks were added running from stem to stern to give added strength at one or two points on the hull. These wales were held in place by spikes or bolts and were matched by similar planks, stringers, on the inside. Finally there were massive through-beams resting on the frames that extended through the sides of the ship to give some stiffening. The hull planking had to be a malleable wood — shipbuilders apparently preferred cypress — so that one strake could be practically fitted and formed to the one below. The keel, posts and tenons were of hardwood, usually oak.

This shell technique of construction may have been copied from practice in the Indian Ocean and Red Sea. No matter its origin, which is still very much open to question, the method can certainly be distinguished from skeleton construction. In the latter system, strength came primarily from an internal frame which was set up first. The external planking was added for watertightness. The vessel was a covered frame. In shell-building the internal frame was there only as a supplement to the external planking. Hull planks were joined together and whether it was edge to edge or overlapped did not matter to this essential principle. In shell construction the exoskeleton determines everything about the ship. In skeleton construction the strakes have to be bent to the endo-skeleton so it is the framing which determines the form of the vessel. The categories are extreme but do accurately describe the two major and quite different approaches of Europeans in the middle ages to the problem of building a boat. At the same time both approaches were subject to modification and rarely reached the limit of either method.

1: Northern European Clinker-building with Overlapping Planks (top)
and Roman Mortise and Tenon Construction (bottom)

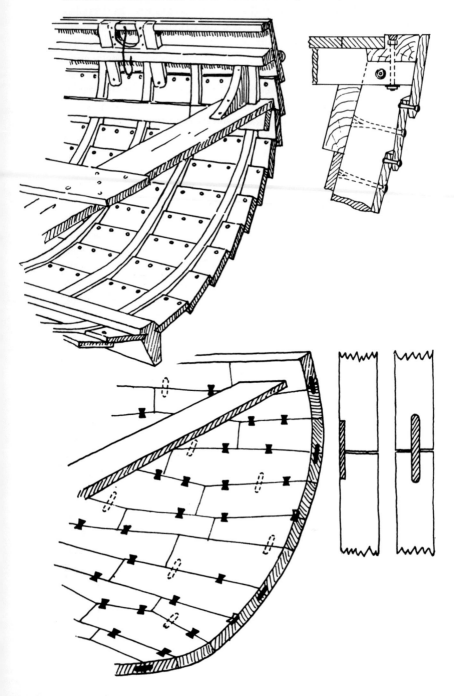

Of course there was interaction between the two methods yielding composites or hybrids of both. The two approaches to the building of a boat presented entirely different problems. With shell construction work could be checked at each step against what had already been done. A plank could be tried against the next one and altered if the fit was not perfect. Frames were shaped to fit into the already constructed hull.[d] It was time consuming but it was incremental. On the other hand, with skeleton construction hull shape could only be known after all the ribs were cut and set up. To cut all the ribs to get the desired hull shape drawings were a great advantage but drawings were first used only in the last years of the sixteenth century. So the usual practice was apparently to set up the keel, posts and one or three main ribs, then bend battens to them to give a mould or indication of the shape of the hull. Then the builder knew how to cut the rest of the ribs. Once that was done, he could proceed to cover the hull with strakes.[5]

Roman shipbuilders were not bothered with such problems since they used shell construction. All planking, even for the decks, was joined with mortises and tenons. The method gave a vessel that was excessively strong. The approach, dating from the time of Homer and probably before, seems to have been exclusive to classical Greece and Rome. Apparently it was used on all vessels from the smallest skiffs to the largest grain carriers.[6] The availability of low-cost labour, the size-able work force in shipbuilding and the tradition of building which was well established throughout the Roman world must have contributed to the continuation of that unique form of shell construction. The result was a vessel of the highest quality. The vessel was finished off with a protective covering. There was no need to caulk the seams – that is, to fill them with some pliable substance – since they were watertight. Instead a layer of wax was used on the hull, often with colouring, to protect the timbers. For smaller vessels, those that were beached, this was enough. For those with hulls that would never leave the water it was necessary to have some protection against the *teredo navalis*, the shipworm, which thrives in warm water and which slowly bores through a wooden hull. The Roman solution to the problem of marine borers was a layer of tarred fabric and then lead sheets over that, held in place by many copper tacks.[7] Though Roman cargo ships might not be all that manoeuvrable, though crews may have had troubles with them in storms, and though they could probably not sail closer than 80° to the direction of the wind, these vessels were still reliable, sturdy and capable of moving large quantities of goods.

The Byzantine Empire and the German successor states in the West, with the exceptions of the Anglo-Saxons and the Franks, inherited the traditions of ship design from the Romans. They did not, however, inherit the thriving economy and sizeable transport of bulk goods typical of commerce in the first and second centuries AD. The wars and internal political disturbances of the third to sixth centuries disrupted trade within the Empire. They also led to higher taxes on both land and commerce which undermined the basis of trade. More serious than any action of government, though, was the recurrence of plagues. An outbreak in the second half of the second century took a heavy toll and another outbreak in the second quarter of the sixth century was probably even more severe. The countryside, especially in the western part of the Empire, was depopulated. Land which had been cultivated was abandoned, some of it turning into malarial swamps which increased the spread of disease and prevented recovery. Deforestation during the Imperial period, in part to supply the needs of shipbuilders, also disturbed the run-off of water from the hills, increasing flooding and the growth of swamps. Land, then, was in relative abundance, especially in the West. Total production of agricultural goods fell. Byzantium responded to the new situation by becoming a more maritime empire with less concern for the holding of land than had been typical of the earlier Roman Imperial government. Byzantine emperors took more interest in the promotion and taxing of trade and industry. They set up or rather extended the system of controls over border trade, especially trade to the East through the Persian Empire. To divert trade away from the lands of that traditional enemy, they also attempted to expand use of an old route for exchange of goods with the Orient. Trade to the Indian Ocean was well established in the reign of Augustus Caesar and by the third century AD Romans were trading directly to Burma and Malaysia. They may even have sailed to China. The trade in spices and silks was not abandoned by the Byzantines. In fact it increased, thanks to government support. The road system, especially in the western part of the old Roman Empire, deteriorated.[8] The Byzantine Empire was increasingly tied together by transport on the sea and not by transport on land.

The novel economic situation forced changes in the relative number of different types of ships. Galleys became more practical for trade compared to large sailing ships. Their greater speed, bought at higher cost, was an advantage worth paying for in the transport of luxuries.[e] Sailing ships did not disappear. The largest of sailing ships, those of over 1,000 tons used for the Alexandria-Rome grain trade, were no longer built, however. When the capital was moved to Constantinople the population of Rome fell from its zenith of perhaps close to 1,000,000 and so could be fed by grain shipments from nearby North Africa and Sicily. The revival of trade under the guidance of Byzantine authority in the sixth and seventh centuries did not reach the earlier level of the Roman Empire. The government no longer sponsored the shipment of massive quantities of grain over long distances. Moving the grain tribute from Egypt to the Bosporus was nothing like the problem of moving it to Rome. Without a government guarantee of cargoes for such large ships they disappeared along with the ability to build them.

There was at the same time a general erosion of quality in the construction of ships. Roman methods were slowly abandoned. The decline in trade and rising costs of commerce associated with higher taxes and a decrease in security forced shippers and in turn shipbuilders to be more conscious of the high cost of Roman construction methods. At the same time the cost of skilled labour in all likelihood rose. The fall in population could hardly contribute to a fall in wages while a decrease in the number of shipbuilders gave those that continued to work in the trade a scarcity value. The sensible solution, and one which became apparent in the seventh century, was to turn to lighter construction and to adopt, to some degree, the skeleton technique. The result was a hybrid form where shell-building was partially abandoned. The pattern is suggested by two wrecks excavated at Yassi Ada, Turkey, one from the fourth century and the other from the seventh. Instead of building the entire hull and then adding internal frames, builders first pieced together the lowest strakes in a way similar to the old method. Then the frames were cut to fit and set up and the rest of the planks above the waterline pinned to the frames. This meant from the fourth century the gradual disappearance of the old system of tenoning. By 600 tenons were apparently used only as guides in setting the lower planks in place and they were no longer held in place by treenails. They had a good deal of freedom of movement within the mortises and were spaced irregularly and farther apart, more than .90 metres at the middle of the ship. Strength then came to a greater degree than in the past from the internal frames. Those were heavy and placed close together. Some of the frames were bolted directly to the keel. The planks of the hull were on the other hand relatively thin, some .035 to .040 metres thick. Above the waterline the hull was made up of alternating wales and planks. The wales were half-timbers, hardly finished, and they were bolted to the frames. They were still matched by stringers inside the frames. Deck beams were supported by hanging knees, triangular pieces of wood typically found underneath the timbers they are designed to support but in this case found above them. All fastenings were of iron.^{f} In general the method of construction was simpler and the materials more massive and not as well finished. The hull was not the finely built watertight case of the Roman period so the seams had to be caulked. Apparently anything at hand was used for that job.

The form of construction of sixth- and seventh-century ships suggests a partial change from the Roman shell technique to skeleton construction. It is not possible to say precisely how much the ship depended on frames and wales for strength, and conversion to the uniquely western technique of skeleton building was not yet complete. For example, planks were still formed after being put in place in the hull, unlike skeleton construction where all such work was done in advance. However, the major step towards the invention of skeleton technique had already occurred by 600. The reason was apparently economic. The new method meant that far fewer man-hours of labour were needed in shipbuilding.[9] It also meant fewer nails, bolts and other fasteners. There was undoubtedly an increase in risk but, since vessels were smaller than those in use in the Imperial period, the chances of making a mistake in construction were decreased. The increase in the number and relative size of frames meant that more wood was used per ton of carrying capacity. The wood had to come from larger thicker hardwoods for those frames. The type and form of wood needed for the skin of the ship changed little. In the early Byzantine Empire there was no shortage of shipbuilding timber, so no effective constraint existed to prevent the conversion to skeleton construction.

Shipbuilders also dropped the Roman practice of hull protection against the shipworm, at least for cargo ships. It was still used for warships in the tenth century.[10] Even in Roman times smaller cargo ships did not have lead sheathing and the change to smaller vessels by the seventh century certainly contributed to the decrease in the use of such protection. The new building method meant that the condition of the exterior hull was not as crucial to the structural integrity of the ship. In general shipowners relied more on repairs. They chose to use the labour of ship carpenters throughout the life of the ship rather than make the same very heavy investment in capital and labour that had been typical of their Roman predecessors. These trends to less expensive construction, smaller vessels and a general decrease in investment in shipping were the logical results of a fall in the total volume of commerce.

The Byzantine Empire inherited from Rome the responsibility of maintaining order at sea. Byzantium in fact enjoyed such naval dominance that fleets were only built for specific tasks, such as meeting the threat of Vandal pirates based at Carthage or Avro-slavs from the Balkans. The naval situation changed completely in 645 when Alexandria fell to the Arabs and Byzantium was faced with a threat to its control of the Mediterranean. The result over time was the emergence of a complex naval organisation in Byzantium and of certain ship types to deal with Arab attacks. Throughout the history of the Empire there was pressure on government to promote the development of the navy and merchant marine. Apparently the only check on a strong Byzantine fleet was the availability of money for its support. The two were connected. Much of the money for the fleet came from taxes on trade carried in merchant ships which in turn relied on the navy for protection.

Byzantine warships are known largely from written sources. Though most of the sources date from the tenth century, it appears that the essential design features had been established by 600. In general Byzantine warships were of middling size, larger than Roman ones and with some major modifications to make them higher and stronger warships with maximum firepower crowded into a fixed space. To get that they gave up speed and carrying capacity. There was still a differentiation between ships with a length-to-beam ratio of about 3:1 and long ships where the ratio was always greater than 6:1. The typical Byzantine longship was the dromon. It was presumably developed from the Roman Liburnian. Dromon appears to have been a generic term for all oared warships but was used also to distinguish the most common of Byzantine warships. It was two-banked, that is with two levels of 25 oars on each side. The 100 oars were accommodated in a length of from 40 to 50 metres. The beam was about 5 metres. There was always one man per oar on the lower banks. In bigger dromons a wider beam made it possible to have two or three men for each oar on the upper ranks. That gave greater speed. It also meant that many of the rowers on the upper banks could be released for fighting duties when the ship grappled with an enemy. It was in general a blunt ship and had little or no upperworks and a low waist. Draught was shallow, about 1.5 metres. Displacement was usually less than 120 tons. Shields were hung along the sides to protect the rowers as was later done in Viking ships. The oarsmen below were protected by the deck. The bottom was almost flat amidships while at the bow and stern the ribs were almost vertical above the keel. There were no internal stringers. Strength came from the strakes and external wales. The hull was narrow and trim. In general construction appears to have been lighter than that for merchant vessels. That was to be expected since the dromon, which meant 'runner', was built for speed.

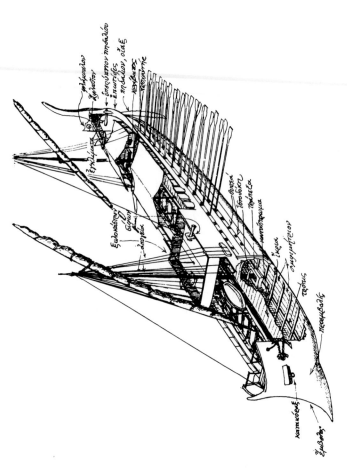

2: Byzantine Dromon from about 850 with Four Rows of 25 Oars

There were two other types with the same lines as the dromon. The *ousiakos* may have been the ancestor of the larger dromon. It carried a crew of some 108 men. Ramming was its major offensive action. A larger version, and indeed the largest of Byzantine warships of the seventh and eighth centuries, the *pamphylos*, carried a crew of at least 162. On that type there were two men at each of the upper oars. The difference among the three types did not depend on hull design or dimensions but rather on the size of the crew and the way the vessel was used in a fight. All had rams, but the dromon was expected to come alongside an enemy ship and use its large crew to take the ship in hand-to-hand combat. There were three gangways, one on each side for marines so they could repel boarders and another in the middle which also acted as a stiffener to prevent hogging. Sagging of the ends was a constant problem with longships and turned up even in second-millennium BC Egypt. On most Byzantine warships there was a platform at the bow to give marines a base for firing at the enemy and on the biggest dromons there was a similar platform amidships. Hull planking below these castles was strengthened to support them. The top of the castle amidships could be 6.5 metres above the keel. There were also a quarterdeck and poopdeck aft with a place for the commander to recline on the quarterdeck. Oars approached 10 metres long with about 30 per cent of the length inboard. They had hollow blades.[g] There were two rudders set in pegs on the gunwales aft and held fast there, like the oars, with leather. Propulsion came not only from the oars but also from two sails, one on each of the masts. Some of the larger dromons may have had three masts but the mainmast and mainsail were always much larger than any others. Apparently masts were not lowered in action and so may have been permanently stepped. Yards were in two pieces, fished together. When not in use the yards were kept on crutches on the central gangway.

This dromon was the major unit, in its various forms, of Byzantine naval forces throughout the tenth century. There were other types including the galley, a single-banked dispatch vessel, and the *dromonia* which was probably nothing more than a little dromon with two banks of oars but too light to do battle in the Mediterranean. Rather it was used in the ninth and tenth centuries against the small and lightly built vessels of the Russians on the Black Sea, vessels probably like those of the Vikings. Byzantines typically used cypress as the chief building material for all their warships, like their Roman predecessors. Western Mediterranean builders used a greater variety of wood if for no other reason than that they had more at hand.

Cargo vessels were also pressed into naval service. Indeed some ships passed back and forth from the navy to the merchant marine. In the expedition against the Vandals in 533 the Emperor Justinian sent a fleet of 92 war vessels – dromons – and 500 transports. The navy, and there may have been a standing force with naval bases and shipyards from the reign of Justinian, was expensive, relying heavily on the labour of rowers.[11] They were not slaves or convicts but rather paid sailors. The fact that they could double as fighting men once ships grappled made them even more valuable. If building technique changed for warships as it did for merchant vessels then capital expenditure at the outset was lower and that could be offset against the high labour cost involved in using rowers. Sailing ships were still too small and too unreliable to be used effectively in battle and their firepower was not any greater than that of warships.

The most effective defensive weapon of Byzantine warships was an incendiary solution known as Greek fire.[h] It was effective only at a short range and so one of the major functions of warships was to get close enough to the enemy to use it, something not possible with round ships. Greek fire, according to the traditional story, was invented by a Syrian who left his Arab-ruled homeland to bring it to Constantinople. Machines were built to fire the new invention and from 672 it was used against the Arabs. It was probably some combination of sulphur, saltpeter and petroleum. It was a liquid and so was fired from siphons with one large siphon fitted in the bow of each dromon. There might be additional flame throwers amidships and on the poop on the largest of dromons. There were defences against these and other incendiaries. Sides could be covered with hides and those in turn covered with smooth substances to protect against fire.[12] But it took some time to develop these defences and when the Byzantines first used Greek fire against the Arabs it proved an overwhelming advantage and was decisive in driving off the second Muslim siege of Constantinople in 717.

Not all cargo vessels were round ones. Trade was still carried on in long rowed vessels. These were used to carry passengers and cargo which needed rapid transport or, in wartime, to carry dispatches. In general such merchant galleys were beamier than dromons. Merchant galleys are mentioned more frequently than are the coasters and larger sail-powered cargo carriers because merchant galleys were pressed into service in wartime. Nevertheless, and despite the fact that they were similar to Greek and Roman merchant galleys, it is still not possible to know exactly what they were like. It is clear that different types of merchant galleys existed, that size varied, that each carried a mast and sail but that oars were the principal form of propulsion.

Byzantine cargo vessels, oared or not, were rarely larger than 300 tons. A writer in the early seventh century described a ship of that size as having unusually large proportions. He also mentioned a ship of 230 tons but the shipbuilder, apparently through lack of experience with vessels of that size, was not able to launch it. The best example of a Byzantine ship yet excavated is a coaster of 40 tons and such vessels were probably not uncommon. The smaller size and smaller crews gave less protection against attack by pirates or enemy forces. But for the sixth and much of the seventh century this was not a problem in most of the Mediterranean, thanks to the power of the Byzantine fleet.[13] The smaller coasters carried what bulk goods were traded. The volume of such trade fell while that in luxuries rose relative to the total volume of trade. The change was perhaps most obvious in the Black Sea. Byzantium imported a sizeable quantity of its oriental goods through Black Sea ports. Increasingly, merchant galleys must have been pressed into service to carry these luxury items.

The smaller size of all vessels and the increasing accent on speed, in the merchant marine, both results of the relative rise in importance of goods of high value per unit volume, contributed to the abandonment by Byzantine shipbuilders of Roman techniques. The square sail, the only sail used on large ships in the classical world, was dropped and replaced by the lateen sail. This change in the propulsion system generated different manpower requirements on cargo ships and increased the sailing capabilities of all vessels. The lateen sail is triangular or a quadrilateral which is almost triangular, the former version being the type used by the Byzantines. The leading edge of the sail is stretched to a dipped yard. This type of sail was known in Roman times as were forms of lug and fore-and-aft spritsails, sails with many of the same properties as the lateen. All were used on small craft. These may have developed from the way Romans trimmed their square sails in some circumstances.[i] In any case the earliest known illustration of a lateen sail is from the second century AD. Another illustration dates from the fourth century AD. An early fifth-century description and another of the sixth century show that lateens were not uncommon on larger ships. The first picture of a lateen sail being used by Byzantine sailors is from about 800. By that date, though, the lateen sail was the dominant one for all Mediterranean craft. The sprit-rig and the lateen sail may in fact have been introduced into the Roman Empire from the Far East, from Indonesia through Ceylon where triangular sails were in use well before the classical era. That form of rig, then, was available to Roman ship-

3: The Lateen Sail in the Mediterranean from a Greek Manuscript of c. 880

builders. They chose to use it for smaller craft, for coasters and fishing boats only. The Byzantines promoted it to use on all vessels. Since the size of vessels was falling the change was not as dramatic as it might at first appear. The earliest dromons may have had square sails but certainly by 533 the typical rig was two masts, one amidships and the other as close to the bow as possible, both carrying long yards and a lateen sail hanging from each. On the largest dromons the third mast set close to the stern also carried a lateen sail.[14]While in the sixth century this may have been new for warships, the use of lateens was well established on cargo ships.[j]

The lateen had certain distinct advantages. It was not a true fore-and-aft sail — that is, its leading edge did not pivot on the mast. For example, with the spritsail, a rectangular piece of canvas held up by a long sprit running from the base of the sail on the mast to the upper outer point and with the leading edge attached to the mast, changing direction just meant putting the helm over. The sail comes over by itself. With the lateen, on the other hand, if the yard is just brought around then the sail presses against the mast. Sailors tried to avoid coming about with a lateen sail since that meant that the yard had to be carried over the masthead in order to keep the longest edge of the triangle into the wind. The spritsail is much easier to handle. A much longer sprit is needed for each square metre of sail area, however, than with the yard of a lateen sail. A longer sprit also meant a taller and stronger mast and presented greater problems of stability, already a concern with dromons with length-to-beam ratios in excess of 6:1. By allowing the lateen to bag slightly it is possible to generate an eddy of wind inside the sail and get more force than with a sail kept perfectly flat. So, all in all, using the lateen sail instead of the spritsail or the square did not involve a great sacrifice in propulsion.

The principal advantage of the lateen sail over the square rig was that the former made it possible to sail closer to the wind, as close as 60°.[15] Sailors of large Roman vessels may not have been completely confined by the cut of the sail to going only before the wind but it is clear that they preferred that situation. Lateen rig expanded opportunities. Presumably not as much time had to be spent in port waiting for a fair breeze. Ships were more manoeuvrable, which certainly must have recommended the rig to warships as well as to coasters. There were disadvantages. The lateen sail required more skill and more men to handle it per unit of area than the simpler square sail. Carrying the yard over the masthead was difficult work, especially in a strong wind. Unlike a square sail a lateen cannot be shortened. The Roman system of brails disappeared. When winds freshened the only option was to change to a smaller sail and, if the wind was strong enough, a smaller yard. That meant that more rigging had to be kept on board and space had to be found to stow it. The increase in manpower probably did not mean an increase in crew size on small ships. For warships there was always more than enough labour at hand. So for the moment no new cost was implied by the different type of sail. Given the size of Byzantine vessels and the inherent advantages of the lateen sail, its adoption for almost all ships was a logical choice. By increasing the capabilities of vessels Byzantines may have been able to decrease the size of ships and perhaps their number for each ton of goods moved per year. All this implied a greater efficiency in shipping, which helped to counteract the general decline in markets. The Byzantine types — warships, round cargo ships and trading galleys — all showed their Roman ancestry but at the same time had certain marked advantages over their predecessors. The most notable changes, such as in the method of constructing the hull and in propulsion, lowered transport costs. The risks involved in moving goods and people by sea must have increased with the lower quality of ship-building practised by the Byzantines; but that was a necessary sacrifice. The general insecurity of life on land probably made greater insecurity at sea more easily acceptable.

In the western Mediterranean shipbuilders followed the pattern in the East. Many of the major seaports remained in Byzantine hands into the eighth century. Trade was carried on with the Byzantine Empire and presumably shipbuilders could and did move within the Empire. The result, especially with Byzantine towns in North Africa and in Italy, was the construction of ships following the Roman tradition but with modifications. In ports outside the Byzantine Empire there must, however, have been some loss of shipbuilding skill, because of a general decline in trade and therefore a loss of interest in maritime affairs. The Germanic tribes which established successor states in the western part of the Roman Empire had no reason to destroy commerce and ship-building. But in most cases their lack of knowledge of government, of business and of maritime affairs meant apathy. The exception was the Vandal kingdom established in North Africa. After seizing the old Roman province in 439 Gaiseric, the king of the Vandals, established a pirate fleet based at the port of Carthage. The skills were Roman, the personnel was Roman and the ships were in all likelihood Roman as well. The ships were used to transport Vandals to attack the islands of the western Mediterranean and to attack Rome itself in 455. On the death of Gaiseric in 477 organised attacks decreased. In 533 a Byzantine fleet took North Africa and put an end to Vandal naval activity.[16]

In the Latin West there was no government in a position to mobilise a naval force as Byzantium did in 533. As long as the Byzantine Empire kept the western Mediterranean under the defensive umbrella of its fleet, the absence of a strong government in the West did not create a problem for shipping. As the Byzantines came under ever greater pressure from Arab attacks and as what government there was in the West further deteriorated, piracy must have increased. By about 700 pressure from pirates and a general instability must have directed expenditure away from trade goods. Ships in the West became small and probably resembled the coasters of the eastern Mediterranean. The adoption of the lateen sail in the western Mediterranean may have been the result of it being brought there by Arab fleets. More likely the warships and merchant vessels of the Byzantine Empire, certainly lateen-rigged in the sixth century, were the source of the conversion to the different type of sail. The goods carried by ships in the western Mediterranean were probably even more likely to be luxuries than those carried by ships in the eastern Mediterranean and Black Sea. Discussion among historians continues on the nature of trade between the two parts of the Mediterranean basin in these years. There does seem to be general agreement, however, that the West bought goods such as silks and spices which could only be obtained from the Far East and in exchange westerners sent slaves and sylvan products. Except for timber and logs, all of these goods were of high enough value to make speed important in their delivery. This was especially true of slaves. At the same time large ships were not an advantage. It was probably not even an advantage in the shipment of lumber since logs were often simply towed behind the ship. With shipping in both directions handling goods with similar transport needs, there was little reason for western shipwrights to deviate from the pattern set in the eastern Mediterranean. There was a limited coastal trade in the West and of course some fishing. So shipbuilding did not by any means cease. At the same time there was internal trade in those typical bulk goods of the Mediterranean: grain, wine and olive oil. Rome still received grain in the early seventh century from Sicily. Distances were not great so again there was no pressure for larger ships. In fact distances covered by shippers in the western Mediterranean were probably less than in the eastern part of the sea.

For bulk goods most packaging had changed by the seventh century from the clay jars, the *amphorae* typical in the Roman Empire, to barrels. This was a major and even revolutionary change in shipping.

While the jars took up as much as 40 per cent of cargo space, the wooden barrels lowered that proportion to almost ten per cent.[17] The process of change was a slow one but may well have occurred sooner in the West than in the East. It meant another source of falling transport costs. It was yet another reason to build smaller vessels. Ship size could be reduced by up to 30 per cent with no noticeable difference in payload when the change was made to barrels.

Despite general economic and political confusion, despite commercial decline, there was a number of significant advances in the techniques of shipbuilding and shipping. The advances were in part generated by exactly that economic malaise. The Mediterranean cargo ship of 750, though smaller, was more efficient, and especially more efficient for its specific tasks, than the massive Roman cargo ship of the first and second centuries AD. The improvement in ships contributed to the survival of commerce in the face of shrinking markets. The ability of the Byzantine Empire to survive and to maintain some prosperity in part depended on the more efficient shipping sector.

The development of Arab naval forces remains something of a mystery. In general Arab policy was to leave the indigenous political and economic arrangements intact. In the short run that meant a continuation of the shipbuilding traditions of the Byzantine Empire along the conquered eastern and southern shores of the Mediterranean. The military struggle with the Byzantine Empire dictated conflict at sea, however. The Greeks used their naval superiority to threaten Arab conquests. The governor of Syria, Moawiyah, who was later to found the Ommayad caliphate, appreciated the importance of sea power and so in 648 organised the first Arab naval expedition, that against Cyprus. The success of the expedition led to expanded naval operations. The first actions were largely piratical and Byzantium did not see these Arab naval advances as a major threat, at least nothing like the threat on land. That changed with the defeat of a Byzantine fleet commanded by the emperor at the Battle of the Masts by a smaller and inferior Arab fleet in 655.[18]

Byzantine naval organisation did not change immediately but it was clear that a new type of navy was required. The Greeks added flotillas of coast-guard vessels to interdict Arab pirate raids. This was especially important along the south coast of Asia Minor. The fleet of dromons, heavy warships for the protection of Constantinople and major Aegean trade routes, remained intact. Byzantium then had a permanent fleet, a standing force requiring continuous support. The administrative system of themes, districts responsible for fitting out and maintaining ships and crews and with taxing power all integrated into a single command structure, gave the Empire the necessary defensive force. The system had been instituted by about 700. The direct threat to Constantinople by an Arab fleet from 672 to 678 was certainly an inspiration to action. The second siege by the Arabs in 717 led to a reorganisation of the system of themes. Theme fleets after that were to act as forward defences in the Aegean and along the coast of Asia Minor. A new command system developed at the same time. Provincial fleets were given a great deal of autonomy. Theme fleets were equipped with all types of vessels from the smallest galleys to the largest dromons. They also had Greek fire. It meant the diffusion to the provinces not only of power but also of knowledge of the construction of the largest of warships. It also meant more effective action against the Arab pirates and assurance of protection for commercial shippers along the major trade routes. The system was established in full and functioning effectively by the middle of the eighth century, giving a renewed tranquillity to the eastern Mediterranean. The reorganised navy could not, however, prevent Arab expansion in the West. The progressive fall of Byzantine naval bases and then the conquest of Spain in 711 gave the Arab fleets a free hand in that part of the Mediterranean.[19]

The Arabs used former Byzantine naval bases in Egypt and the Coptic Christian shipbuilders who worked there. Some of these artisans were imported to the Syrian coast by Moawiyah to build the first Arab war fleet. One thousand Copts and their families were sent to Tunis after it was established as an Arab naval base in 700. Crews were typically Egyptian in the eastern Mediterranean but the marines were Arabs. The largest Arab warship, the qarib, was a two-banked galley like the dromon and may have had the same design. Arabs also had lighter galleys for patrol work. Although the direct evidence on Arab warships is scarce, still the fact that they used the same personnel, the same ports and the same raw material supplies suggests that early Arab war fleets were just re-creations of Greek fleets. The Arabs, however, seem to have respected the superior experience of Greek sailors. Their loss of over four times as many warships due to storms from the seventh to the tenth century compared to the Greeks demonstrates how much Arab seamen had to learn. The Arabs preferred to do their fighting on land, to use ships as transports. When forced into a naval battle they tried to make it into a land battle as much as possible, grappling with enemy ships and then leaving the fighting to the Arab marines. As a result Arab warships were probably on average larger than Byzantine ships in order to carry extra troops. That meant they were slower as well. There was also a minor change in the shape of the lateen sail, Arabs using a sail of quadrilateral instead of perfectly triangular shape. It was a short-luff dipping lug sail rather than a true lateen. Differences in performance and in manning were marginal, however, and the rig was essentially the same as that on Greek ships. Though Muslims used lateen sails in the Mediterranean, they apparently did not in the Indian Ocean. It may have been Portuguese ships around 1500 that finally brought the rig to the Arabian Sea.[20] In the Mediterranean though, Muslim ships always carried lateen rig.

The Arab conquests gave them all the supplies of naval stores which they needed to carry on an effective naval campaign against the Greeks. They obtained the raw materials for the development of a commercial fleet the equal of the Byzantines'. Arabs also had the option to raid the coast of Asia Minor to get timber. At least in the early years of the contest between Arabs and Byzantines, neither side suffered a shortage of wood or any other stores such as iron for nails and palm fabric and papyrus for rope. The Arabs did have a problem moving wood from mountainous regions to the shipbuilding yards. The great rise in demand for timber in the seventh century and to the end of the ninth century to build the massive fleets of the two competing naval powers presented a second problem for the Arabs. The forests of the southern Mediterranean had already suffered from gradual deforestation from the early years of the Roman Empire and so by the fifth century some districts were left without trees. The expansion of waterborne commerce within the Arab empire also put new demands on the forests. The end result was a lively trade in wood throughout the Arab world and the emergence of a number of small ports specialising in handling wood. The trade was important economically but also strategically and the Byzantines tried to deny Arabs this necessary raw material by outlawing the export of shipbuilding timber. The prohibition included Byzantine ports in Italy where wood supplies were more abundant and more easily accessible and where Muslim markets were close by. The typical use of the lateen sail meant that long spars were required, long or longer than the masts themselves. Tall fir-trees, then, became especially valuable. Improvements in Byzantine coastal defences may have been in order to deny Arabs access to supplies of cypress for planking from Asia Minor. The government of Egypt even embarked in the seventh century on a programme of forest legislation to protect domestic supplies. A great deal of wood was also imported, from as far afield as India. Though the Arabs were not really free of problems with the supply of shipbuilding wood, their conquests and raids at least throughout the eighth century guaranteed that they could get enough wood for their needs.[21]

The Arabs could not match the superior Byzantine naval organisation. They always had difficulties when they challenged the Greek navy at sea. The Byzantines effectively used Greek fire to tip the balance in their favour if there was ever a question of superior strength, despite the fact that Arabs used the weapon from the first half of the ninth century. The total destruction of an Arab fleet said to number 1,000 dromons off the coast of Cyprus in 747 by a smaller Greek fleet drove the Arabs from the seas for the following 80 years. The Byzantines were then able to clear the seas, to enforce order and put an end to piratical raids. The peace which followed for the next 75 years was beneficial for Greek commerce. It must also have been an advantage to Muslim shippers. In their first challenge to Byzantine naval supremacy the Arabs did not produce anything novel in the design of warships. That was to be expected since they faced the same conditions as did their Greek adversaries. Indeed, the pattern of trade seems to have been changed little by the early Arab conquests, with the exception of the end of the shipping of the grain tribute from Egypt to Constantinople. If anything the Arab conquests brought an expansion of trade and increased prosperity for the regions captured. If the Arabs did cause decline in the extensive commerce, it was because of a changed political situation after about 700, internally and in relations with the Byzantine Empire. Both Arabs and Greeks moved towards the restriction of trade with each other. The Greeks developed a system of funnelling trade through certain specified border stations, directing commerce into a more fixed pattern.[22] The over-all decline in trade created adverse conditions for the development of ships. The shrinking of opportunities meant a stability in ship design from the sixth to the end of the eighth century. The sudden injection of a new religious and political force into the Mediterranean in the seventh century did generate, in reaction, new forms of naval administration. That, in turn, laid the basis for the development in government shipyards in the ninth century of a new type of heavier ship. But for commercial vessels the situation was hardly changed.

In northern Europe shipbuilders faced entirely different problems. The tides of the Atlantic Ocean and North Sea, the less reliable winds, the greater likelihood of storms, all created requirements for ships which never existed in the Mediterranean. Moreover, commerce and naval activity were not subject to any effective government direction. The economy itself could not match that of the Mediterranean basin in complexity, diversity, or prosperity. Byzantine influence in the North appears to have been nil. And, despite the long presence of Romans in the North, their shipbuilding traditions left no indelible mark. While Gaul and Britain were part of the Roman Empire the Romans concentrated their activities inland, leaving coastal and river transport and, along with it, shipbuilding to indigenous Celtic populations. The Romans did build some types of Mediterranean design in the North, adapted for the different conditions, and they did use galleys there but, with the decline in trade and the withdrawal of Romans from the North in the third to the fifth century, those Roman types and building techniques disappeared, thus allowing the domination of northern waters by types which had existed during Roman rule and were used by the numerous Celtic merchants of the Empire.

Celtic ship design included at least five different traditions. Julius Caesar commented on one of these, the seagoing cargo vessel powered by sail which was built by coastal peoples of northern Gaul. The type was relatively flat-bottomed, was built entirely of oak, had heavy ribs held in place by iron bolts and was planked, the planking probably being fitted end to end. Unlike in Roman ships, the planks did not have mortise and tenon joints. Stem and stern were relatively high. The mast was carried forward, about one third of the way back from the bow. On larger vessels there was a deck. There was no keel. The vessel had high freeboard.[k] The ship could be beached and was able to sail in the open sea, making long-distance voyages along the Atlantic coast from Britain or northern France to Spain.[23] A second Celtic type, also mentioned by Caesar as being in use in southwest Britain, was the curragh. It is usually associated with Ireland and apparently used extensively along that coast and out into the Atlantic. Curraghs were skin boats with wickerwork used to fill in the space between the ribs. Hides were then stretched over the hull to give watertightness. They could reach 12 metres in length and could carry a sail though they were more commonly rowed. The shape of the hull allowed them to bob like corks and so they were well suited to the open ocean and capable of regular voyages to the Faeroes and Iceland from Ireland.[24] The stern was drawn up more sharply than the bow.[l]

There were other Celtic types, perhaps partially influenced by Mediterranean design but still retaining their unique characters. The extensive riverborne commerce of the northern Roman Empire made for the wide diffusion of these types. Excavation at Zwammerdam in the Netherlands in the old bed of the Rhine River, a natural barrier which formed much of the northern border of the Roman Empire, has unearthed the variations made in the simple dugout design to carry goods on inland waterways. The four wrecks all date from around 200 AD. One of them was built using Roman techniques. The rest were of an entirely different type. In the simplest form a tree was hollowed out. The next step in the evolution was apparently the addition of planks, one on each side, to allow deeper draught without swamping. In its most sophisticated form the river boat had a floor made of planks placed edge to edge. At each side the last floor plank was L-shaped so it was at the same time the first plank of the side. A second side plank was placed above it overlapping the first, not inside but outside it. There were also right-angled frames nailed both to the floor and to the side planks. The final result was a box which could ride deep in the water. The biggest of the Zwammerdam wrecks was 36 metres long. Another, 22.75 metres long, was made of oak and could carry 30 tons of heavy cargo such as building stone. These boats were probably pulled along the rivers and not sailed. This punt or pram type reappears often throughout northern Europe, for example in a fishing boat from about 1300 found near Flasterbo in southern Sweden and in a vessel from about 1100 excavated near Egernsund, Denmark, which was probably a ferry.[25] Apparently many Celtic types were elaborations of the simple punt design.

The largest of Celtic types from the Roman period and before used sails. Most, however, were towed or relied on oars as a means of propulsion. Construction of Celtic vessels ranged from skeleton as with the curragh to skin as with the heavy planked sailing boat. In some cases the two were combined. Control was given by various forms of paddles and steering oars designed to handle specific problems. One strange feature was that nails for attaching planks to ribs were often bent over after being driven through. The points were bent even further to pass almost at a right angle into the rib.[m] Nailing planks to ribs in this form was a vestigial feature of Celtic shipbuilding and may constitute a measure of Celtic influence on the design of later types.[26] This collection of different designs left northern Europe, after the departure of the Romans, with a wide variety of ships for a whole range of purposes. The variety served as a source of numerous features and approaches which could be and were absorbed into other types.

Along with the various Celtic design traditions two general types were typically used by the Germanic peoples who migrated to the borders and into the Roman Empire. These were probably modified versions of Celtic types. They were for use along the coast and not inland. Broadly the vessels can be divided into those intended to transport men, devoted to maximising speed, and those primarily intended for cargo, designed to get more space in the hold. In solving the latter problem of moving goods, shipbuilders along the south coast of the North Sea found two successful approaches, each in turn fostering a long design tradition. All three types by the seventh century were built with shell technique. The ribs, the internal frames, in general were only there as an afterthought.

For moving men the German tribes used a vessel that was essentially a rowing barge. A ship built in the fourth century and excavated in the late nineteenth gives an excellent impression of the nature of these ships.[n] The Nydam ship, almost 24 metres long, had a length-to-breadth ratio of 6.3:1, a figure comparable to that of Mediterranean dromons. There was no mast or arrangement for a sail. Propulsion came from 15 pairs of oars rowed against oarlocks lashed to the top hull plank or gunwale. The hull was clinker-built, that is with overlapping planks. The ribs were inserted after the planking had been completed and were naturally curved to fit. The ribs were lashed to projecting clamps which had been left on the inside of the hull planks. There was no keel but just a centre-line plank which was wider and thicker than other planks. Since it was not a sailing ship, the lack of a keel was not a serious problem. Fragments of another boat found in the same place and of about the same date but built of fir did show that it was possible to build a keel. The Nydam ship was double-ended and the stem- and sternposts rose about 3 metres above the line of the centre plank. The side planks or strakes, five on each side, were single pieces of oak. Unlike on earlier vessels, the planks were fastened to each other with iron rivets. This new and superior method of holding planks became popular and typical during the fifth and sixth centuries. Control was given by a large side rudder. It is not clear exactly how this was fitted.[27] All in all it was a simple vessel designed to handle a simple problem – the rapid movement of a number of men. Though the Nydam boat itself showed a number of primitive features, by the seventh century builders had made enough improvements to make the type a durable seagoing vessel.

The two types of cargo vessels, the hulk and the cog, owed a great deal to Celtic designs. Knowledge of the hulk is based on an eighth-century ship found at Utrecht. The location of the find suggests that the vessel was a type of riverboat with the ability to travel in the open sea. The strongly built hull had the form of half an egg shell or a hollowed-out banana.[o] It had no keel but rather a very broad centre plank which made it easy to beach. There were no posts. The ends were rounded with the planks just coming together. The Utrecht ship had an

4: Hulks from the Utrecht Psalter of the Early Ninth Century (top) and the Utrecht Ship of c. 800 (bottom)

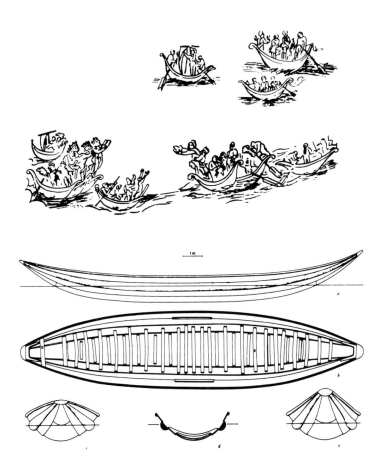

over-all length of almost 18 metres. As expected, it was beamier than the Nydam rowing barge. The centre plank was made from one log. The two strakes on each side overlapped. Wooden pegs held them in place. Over the seam between the two planks on each side a heavy, almost half-round plank was added. This gave watertightness as well as lateral strength. The 38 curved floor timbers found inside were small and offered little in the way of support. The vessel was probably decked. One estimate of carrying capacity is about 23 tons. Control was given by two side rudders, as can be seen in vessels in nearly contemporary illustrations. The ship had only two oars, inadequate for propulsion. There was a mast step, however, about one-third of the way back from the bow. There was a small rectangular hole in the eleventh floor timber and this was probably for a mast but no other strengthening was found. Without some other support for the mast it would have been extremely difficult to use the sail at sea. There may have been some strengthening at deck level or the mast may have been only for towing. Still, the size and shape of the hull suggest a fast sailing ship capable of travelling in the North Sea. The location of the mast step well forward is similar to practice on Celtic sailing ships.[28] By 750 the hulk had already passed through a number of changes and was established as an effective cargo carrier in the North Sea, used by Frisian traders for voyages to England. It was strong and therefore relatively reliable. The hulk could negotiate the tidal estuaries and rivers of the Low Countries and Britain and reach existing ports.

The cog or kaag was also used for carrying goods in the Low Countries. Knowledge of this quite different design is based on a find made at Bruges of a boat from the second or early third century.[P] There was no keel and the bottom was flat with the planks laid end to end. There were posts with a sharp angle to the bottom. The planks on the sides, of oak like the rest of the boat, were nailed to the heavy ribs. The angle between sides and bottom was also sharp, about 32°. The Bruges boat, about 14.5 metres long, and 1.4 metres at its greatest width, was even beamier than the Utrecht hulk. The planking on the sides was probably not overlapping but rather fitted edge to edge as in other Celtic sailing vessels. The type was double-ended. The ship could not be beached. Rather it was designed to ride with the tide into a sandbank and settle there for loading and unloading during low tide while it was lying dry. The vessel was refloated with high tide. Conditions in the Wadden Zee on the north coast of the Low Countries were ideal for the use of this cog and similar conditions were common along much of the south coast of the North Sea. While the hulk was a vessel for the high seas the cog was a special vessel for areas with sandbanks and tidal harbours. The cog was a sailing vessel. The mast was held in place by a widened rib as on other large Celtic sailing cargo ships. The sail was a square one. There was one or perhaps two side rudders for control. The design of the hull meant there was high freeboard.[29] That, along with the other features, guaranteed relatively large carrying capacity, and won the cog the dominant position as a coastal trading vessel from the Low Countries north into Scandinavia in the relatively peaceful eighth century.

The cog then was the ideal ship for the trading network of Frisian merchants. These merchants were responsible for much of the inter-regional seaborne commerce of northern Europe in the seventh and eighth centuries. They undoubtedly used both the cog and hulk types since they needed these two different vessels in the two large spheres of their activity, to Britain and to Scandinavia. The hulk could also be used effectively along the Rhine, and the Rhine Valley was a significant source of their trade goods. The volume of Frisian trade was small and, though the distance through which the merchants moved goods might be great, from the upper Rhine to the central Baltic coast of Sweden, voyages were accomplished in short stages. They avoided open waters, preferring to stay close to the coast. Even with voyages to England, sailing in the open sea was kept to a minimum. By the end of the sixth century northern Europe was generally sparsely settled. Therefore most areas had no trouble in supplying the needs of the Frisian merchants. The principal problem was cultivating enough land to generate needed grain. Timber, furs, honey and numerous other products could be taken from forests which were always nearby. Since essential goods were close at hand, traders were left to deal in luxuries and, more important, luxury manufactures. For example, the glass trade, started during the Roman Empire, continued and Frisians shipped drinking glasses made in the Rhineland to Sweden from the mid-seventh century. Frisians bought slaves in England, presumably for shipment to the Continent. They also got wool there for the Low Countries cloth industry. The high-quality product was an important export. The connection with the Rhineland gave Frisians access to some agricultural goods such as grain and wine but more important in value were goods brought over the Alpine passes from the Mediterranean, such as silks and spices. Frisians also exported Frankish swords which enjoyed a reputation for high quality in northern Germany and Scandinavia. They also carried less exotic wares of local origin. Certainly the principal function of the Frisians in the years before 750 was to distribute luxuries. They extended the trading network to new areas, especially to the Baltic. Indeed, in the early middle ages there was no lack of trade routes, only a lack of resources and of demand to exploit them.[30] Frisians played an important part in the development in the eighth century of the Scandinavian ports of Hedeby, near modern Schleswig, and Birka on Lake Mälar near modern Stockholm. Birka for example had a *kugghamn* or cog harbour, presumably suited to the design of that Frisian ship type. The port of Dorestad, which by 750 had exceeded the much older nearby Utrecht as the major port of Frisian trade, had close ties with the new port of Hedeby.[31] The high point of Frisian trade was probably reached in the 100 years after 750. The goods and methods of transport stayed the same as in earlier years. In the North the ships were needed to move luxury goods and people. The former are mentioned in written sources while bulk goods rarely appear, the principal exception being Rhine wine. The latter included not only missionaries but also migrants. Slaves fell into both categories. The requirements of transport then were for fast ships with crew size of little importance. Shipbuilders failed to fulfil those precise needs. Cargo vessels tended to be heavy like the Utrecht ship. They did not become large because of the lack of long-distance bulk cargoes. There was short-distance bulk carriage, especially on rivers and inland waterways. Ocean transport was largely an extension of that shipping. At least ship design did reflect that need. The lively trade along western Europe's rivers attests to the continued successful use of boats of Celtic design like those found at Zwammerdam.

Waterborne transport faced strong competition from overland carriage. For many of the luxuries value was so high relative to volume that transport, no matter the form, had only a small effect on price. Goods from the Mediterranean travelled part of the way overland, across the Alps, and so could easily continue by land rather than transfer to water. With goods of such high value merchants preferred to sell them as quickly as possible. It was not wise to tie up limited funds for too long. Land transport was always faster than water even with political instability and the poor condition of the roads. Travel by land was also less restricted. Given knowledge of navigation, skippers tended to adhere to one route while travellers on foot or horseback could move rather freely. It was a more flexible means of moving goods, if more expensive per kilometre, than moving goods by water. That competition may have kept shipbuilders from extensively exploring designs for the rapid movement of luxury goods.

For the movement of people fast ships were built and used. For the migration across the North Sea from Germany to Britain, Saxons used vessels which were the successors of the rowing barge found at Nydam.

The migrants themselves supplied the manpower needed to pull the oars so the expense of the crew was not a consideration. An impression of one vessel used in that traffic, from about 600, was found in the earth at the bottom of a burial mound at Sutton Hoo in England.[q] This was a great open rowing boat of an over-all length of 27 metres. There was no keel. Instead there was a heavy centre-line plank, rounded at the bottom. On each side were nine strakes clinkered to each other, held by iron rivets. Twenty-six ribs stiffened the hull. There is no question that they were added afterwards. The ship was of shell construction. There were 38 oarsmen altogether. The planks were not single pieces but made up of several lengths of timber riveted together at overlapping joints or scarfs. That and the use of more and thinner strakes formed a significant improvement over the construction of the Nydam boat. Not only was the hull made more flexible but also the need for finding trees of the right length and shape was eliminated. Control was given by a side rudder. There is no evidence that there was any type of mast or sail to supplement the oars.[32] The cargo was relatively light and so the barge rode high in the water, an advantage for oarsmen. The voyage from Saxony to England was not that long. Saxons first infiltrated into Frisia and from there they made their way along the coast and then turned west for the short trip to the coast of Kent or East Anglia. Free-board was low so that the oars could function. The vessel was not there-fore suited for the open sea. The Kvalsund ship of about 700, found in western Norway, was similar to the Sutton Hoo ship showing many of the same improvements. It was shorter but still had a length-to-beam ratio typical of a rowing barge. The centre-line plank was reinforced with a fillet on the underside which made it stronger, giving something closer to a true keel. As a result the vessel was more stable. It was possible to have a broader hull and there was more room on board. The rudder was also markedly improved. Again no sign of a sail was found.[33] Up to 750 this was still essentially a coastal vessel without the capabil-ity for long-distance open sea travel of the hulk or for that matter of the Celtic sailing cargo ship or the curragh. The rowing barge did, on the other hand, solve the problem of moving people in the seventh century. By the eighth the migration period had ended and as a result the design of this type could and did change.

In the years to 700 Scandinavia apparently had few sailing ships. Certainly examples of sailing ships existed. Northern Europeans prob-ably knew that ships in the Mediterranean typically carried a sail. Illustrations suggest, however, that it was not until 700 that sails were in general use, except on small craft, in Scandinavia. Sailing ships like the Celtic cargo ship were known in the Atlantic and to a lesser extent in the North Sea up to 750.[r] But further north sails were only added in the sixth and seventh centuries.[34] The influence from nearby regions certainly promoted the change. Important as that influence may have been, the need was to build vessels to handle the trade of the region, a trade which was increasingly connected with that of Frisia. The longer distances, the smaller crew on a cargo ship compared to a ship carrying men, and the heavier load on board, all recommended the conversion to a different form of propulsion.

The slow pace of change in design throughout the North must have been in part the result of a lack of over-all demand for ships. The quantities of goods handled could not compare with those moved in the Roman period, largely for demographic reasons. Since demand for ships was limited so too were opportunities for experiment and for the development of a stable industry where builders in company with other builders could devote their time exclusively to improving ships. The situation bred a wide variety of types and if anything an increasing variety as Celtic designs remained in use besides those developed to deal with specific conditions and circumstances.

The ships which were built did not apparently yield any great fall in the cost of transporting goods. The general decline in specialised production for a wide market, the basis of long-distance commerce, meant a decline in the carriage of goods. The demand for ships, and especially for ships of special type, declined in turn. Since shipbuilders had to produce vessels able to handle a variety of tasks, the scope for economising and design development was also limited. A feature added to make the ship handle better on rivers might detract from performance at sea, for example. In sum there was a loss of skills, a technical retrogression. Though this was more obvious in the Mediterranean it was true in the North as well. The disappearance of Roman political organisation in the North, for example, meant the disappearance of quays. Harbours turned into beaches and so builders had to construct vessels that could be run up on the shore for loading.[35] The need was for simpler ships as well as easier ways of building them. The poorer economy could not afford the relatively expensive capital goods that were Roman ships. By adjustments shipbuilders were at least able to ease this downward spiral. The losses in the durability of ships were partially compensated for by lower original cost. At some point that compensation was enough to offset the loss and halt the decline in shipping, but at a much lower level.

The presence of piracy, or more precisely the lack of governments strong enough to suppress piracy, was to blame for the sharp decline in travel. Shipbuilders, however, did not help. They failed to overcome the problems of moving people. Over all then, individuals could only move about with difficulty. The lack of contact not only contributed to the cultural poverty usually associated with the 'Dark Ages' but also meant a decrease in economic opportunities. The turn to smaller vessels throughout Europe meant decreased opportunities for people to move. Only in the North Sea did sizeable numbers travel by sea, and there it was only in one direction. Even there numbers declined to 750. The design of ships did nothing to prevent the decline in interregional contact. In fact the new types contributed to it.

The volume and the pattern of trade which emerged meant that the merchant community was smaller relative to the total population than had been the case before. The number of shipbuilders also fell. The industry was less important numerically, economically and socially. Backyard shipbuilding, with the exception of naval construction in the eastern Mediterranean, was the rule. This lack of specialisation among builders had an effect on technology. More important, the generally smaller commercial and shipping sector deprived the economy of workers relatively more productive than those in agriculture. Productivity in the shipping sector also declined. The conversion to smaller vessels meant that the number of sailors and especially masters did not fall by the same percentage as the fall in the total volume of commerce. The conversion to the use of the lateen sail in the Mediterranean meant crew size did not fall as rapidly as tonnage since it took more men to handle that sail than a simple square sail. Crewmen had to be more skilful to handle the lateen. The new sail did offer some productivity gain because of shorter over-all time for voyages, but that could not offset the losses associated with decreased size. The share of the population living in cities fell. This was especially noticeable along the coast since large ports and port facilities were no longer needed. Goods were not marshalled at a single location so it took vessels longer to gather a full cargo or forced them to travel with less than their maximum payload. This meant in turn higher costs and constituted another reason for moving to, on average, smaller ships. These types, it is true, put less strain on finance and for many duties they sufficed, as they had in the Roman Empire. But the result could only be a long-term rise in costs for the shipment of goods and so a fall in the volume of trade, a fall in average productivity for the society and a drift away from urbanisation. These were changes which shipbuilders through their designs did not effectively combat. The emergence of the Arab challenge to the Byzantine Empire led to a complete change in the organisation of naval forces and also in the level of violence in the Mediterranean. For the first time in centuries naval powers created a continuing struggle. Governments had to develop a system of administering these massive organisations. Unlike the administration of armies which could expand or collapse with the level of hostilities, naval organisation had to have a continuing existence to maintain the ships. That meant keeping up shipyards and employing skilled shipbuilders. The growth of navies in the eastern Mediterranean led to an expansion of government bureaucracy. In northern Europe political organisation was nothing like that in the South. There was not the same confrontation between two powerful states. Northern Europe did not have the infrastructure and established pattern of trade that existed in the Mediterranean. The large oared ship, most effective in fleet action in the Mediterranean, was not built in the North. Thus there was no pressing need for governments to develop a sizeable and continuing naval force. In the North, because of the size and scope of vessels in use, commerce and the whole business of shipping was in the hands of private traders with no connection with government. Both constraint and support from political authority were rare. This meant greater flexibility in water transport. Indeed, throughout Europe, the design of ships promoted such flexibility. The advantage gained was small, however.

The pattern of development in ship design was set in the seventh century at least for the years up to 1000. There was to be a concentration on relatively small vessels for cargo. The size was small in comparison to Roman predecessors and the types which would follow, and apparently small relative to the potential size of ships. It was impossible to support the large crew and the high capital cost associated with a larger ship given the small cargoes available, the lack of back cargoes, the poor organisation of commerce and the potential for instability. Defensibility was based on speed rather than on size. Shipbuilders concentrated, especially in the Mediterranean, on supplying ships with greater speed and manoeuvrability. Warships in a sense were already differentiated from cargo vessels. They certainly were in the Roman Empire. The addition of Greek fire to the Byzantine naval arsenal made the warship even more unique. In the North cargo ships were easily differentiated from the rowing barges used for naval purposes and also used to carry people. At least in the broadest sense there was specialisation in ship design. The principal change of the years to 750 was the choice made by shippers and shipbuilders to accept high unit costs for moving goods. The ship types of these years reflected the choice and over time made it the only choice. The direction was away from the large efficient bulk carrier. It took some centuries and a rather devious route for shipbuilders finally to arrive at the design for such a type.

NOTES

1. Lionel Casson, 'Sailing', in Carl Roebuck (ed.), *The Muses at Work, Arts, Crafts and Professions in Ancient Greece and Rome* (MIT Press, Cambridge, Mass., 1969), p. 174. Also L. Casson, *The Ancient Mariners, Seafarers and Sea Fighters of the Mediterranean in Ancient Times* (Victor Gollancz Ltd, London, 1959), p. 213, and *Ships and Seamanship in the Ancient World* (Princeton University Press, Princeton, 1971), pp. 141-7, 231-8, 322-6. To people of the middle ages the typical Roman ship was the galley, and it was that vessel which they drew to illustrate Roman ships: Lucien Basch, 'Ancient Wrecks and the Archaeology of Ships', *IJNA*, I (1972), p. 2.

2. Romola and R. C. Anderson, *The Sailing-Ship* (George G. Harrap and Co. Ltd, London, 1926), pp. 49-51. In *HSUA*, pp. 72, 76-7, Throckmorton rightly notes that no wrecks of Roman merchantmen of above 300 tons have yet been found. The number of big ships was small and so is the chance of excavating one. That means that knowledge of the largest ships comes from contemporary illustrations and descriptions only. Lionel Casson, *The Ancient Mariners*, pp. 174, 218-20, points out that the triangular topsail may date from the Hellenistic period. But there are no surviving illustrations of Hellenistic merchant ships so it is only possible to guess about the earliest date of that kind of sail. Also see L. Casson, *Ships and Seamanship in the Ancient World*, pp. 224-8, 239-43, 269, 275-85.

3. Lionel Casson, 'Sailing', pp. 189-90, *The Ancient Mariners*, pp. 216-17, 235-6, and *Ships and Seamanship in the Ancient World*, pp. 171-81, 185-90, 297, 329. J. S. Morrison in *AB*, pp. 155-66.

4. The understanding of Roman ship construction has changed over the last 25 years. Compare Romola and R. C. Anderson, *The Sailing-Ship*, p. 52, with Arne Emil Christensen, Jr, 'Lucien Basch: Ancient wrecks and the archaeology of ships A comment', *IJNA*, II (1973), p. 138. The change has come about largely because of new archaeological evidence.

5. Lucien Basch, 'Ancient wrecks and the archaeology of ships', pp. 15-18. *AB*, pp. 60-8.

6. Lionel Casson, *Ships and Seamanship in the Ancient World*, pp. 201-8, 211, and 'Sailing,' pp. 191-4. Lucien Basch, 'Ancient wrecks and the archaeology of ships', pp. 23-30. Arne Emil Christensen, Jr, 'Lucien Basch: Ancient wrecks', pp. 138-43. While mortise and tenon construction was not the only shipbuilding method in use within the political boundaries of the Roman Empire, it was certainly the dominant one in the centre of the Empire, that is in the Mediterranean basin.

7. D. J. Blackman, 'Further early evidence of hull sheathing', *IJNA*, I (1972), pp. 117-19. The earliest known example is from the fourth century BC. Lionel Casson, *The Ancient Mariners*, p. 217, *Ships and Seamanship in the Ancient World*, pp. 211-12, and 'More Evidence for Lead Sheathing on Roman Craft', *MM*, LXIV (1978), pp. 135-42 and also the reply by Honor Frost, pp. 142-4.

8. Archibald R. Lewis, *Naval Power and Trade in the Mediterranean A. D. 500-1100* (Princeton University Press, Princeton, 1951), pp. 15, 26-7, 33-7. The road system was built originally for the movement of troops and was not suited to commerce. The size of the Imperial merchant marine demonstrates that. But

merchants did use the roads and the lack of government interest in them was certainly no help to commerce. See also Lionel Casson, *The Ancient Mariners*, p. 232, and, George F. Hourani, *Arab Seafaring in the Indian Ocean in Ancient and Early Medieval Times* (Princeton University Press, Princeton, 1951), pp. 38-40.

9. The description of seventh-century shipbuilding is heavily based on the seventh-century Yassi Ada ship. Another ship found at Pantano Longarini in southern Italy shows some of the same features and gives support to the conclusions. Lionel Casson, *Ships and Seamanship in the Ancient World*, pp. 208-9. Frederick van Doorninck, 'The 4th century wreck at Yassi Ada an interim report on the hull', *IJNA*, V (1976), pp. 119-31.

10. R. H. Dolley, 'The Warships of the Later Roman Empire', *The Journal of Roman Studies*, XXXVIII (1948), p. 51. Aly Mohamed Fahmy, *Muslim Sea-Power in the Eastern Mediterranean from the Seventh to the Tenth Century A.D. (Studies in Naval Organization)* (Tipografia Don Bosco, London, 1950), p. 85.

11. Hélène Antoniadis-Bibicou, *Etudes d'histoire maritime de Byzance A propos du 'Theme des Caravisiens'*, pp. 21-2, and 'Problèmes de la marine byzantine', *Annales (ESC)*, XIII (1958), p. 376. G. La Roërie and J. Vivielle, *Navires et Marins de la rame à l'hélice* (Editions Duchartre et van Buggenhoudt, Paris, 1930), pp. 85-7. R. H. Dolley, 'The Warships of the Later Roman Empire', pp. 47-53. Archibald R. Lewis, *Naval Power and Trade in the Mediterranean*, pp. 22-30. Ekkehard Eickhoff, *Seekrieg und Seepolitik zwischen Islam und Abendland* (Walter De Gruyter and Co., Berlin, 1966), pp. 136-50.

12. Louis Bréhier, 'La Marine de Byzance du VIIIe au XIe Siècle', *Byzantion*, XIX (1949), p. 9. The Syrian was Callinicus from Baalbek (Heliopolis). F.W. Brooks, 'Naval Armament in the Thirteenth Century', *MM*, XIV (1928), pp. 115-19. R. H. Dolley, 'The Warships of the Later Roman Empire', p. 52. Lionel Casson, *The Ancient Mariners*, pp. 241-3, and *Ships and Seamanship in the Ancient World*, pp. 152-3. *HSUA*, p. 135. An incendiary compound similar to Greek fire was used by the Byzantines in 516.

13. *HSUA*, pp. 139-40.

14. H. H. Brindley, 'Early Pictures of Lateen Sails', *MM*, XII (1926), pp. 9-14. His discovery of the illustration of 880 in the Bibliothèque Nationale in Paris convinced scholars for a number of years that the lateen sail came into use by Greeks in the eighth and ninth centuries and that they had borrowed it from the Arabs. R. H. Dolley, 'The Rig of Early Medieval Warships', *MM*, XXXV (1949), pp. 51-5, doubts an Arab origin for the lateen since they were landsmen. The absence of any illustration of lateens on Greek ships may be explained by the suppression of artistic work during the period of the Iconoclastic emperors (723-843). Lionel Casson, *Ships and Seamanship in the Ancient World*, pp. 244-5, 277. Richard Lebaron Bowen, Jr, 'The origins of fore-and-aft rigs', pp. 155-60, 183-7, and 'Note: The Earliest Lateen Sail', *MM*, XLII (1966), pp. 239-42. In the light of Casson's evidence he felt compelled to change his opinion and claims that the Indonesians got the sail from the Romans and not the other way around. G. La Roerie, 'Note: Fore and Aft Sails in the Ancient World', *MM*, XLII (1966), pp. 238-9: Casson's claim for the presence of the lateen sail in the ancient world is not without opposition. Joseph Needham, *Science and Civilization in China*, vol. IV, part III, pp. 588-90, 606, 617.

15. Richard Lebaron Bowen, Jr, 'The origins of fore-and-aft rigs', p. 183. Lionel Dimmock, 'The Lateen Rig', *MM*, XXXII (1946), p. 35. Barbara Kreutz, 'Ships, Shipping and the Implications of Change in the Early Medieval Mediterranean', *Viator*, VII (1976), pp. 79-99. J.H. Parry, *Discovery of the Sea* (Weidenfeld and Nicolson, London, 1975), pp. 11-14, and *The Age of Reconnaisance* (New American Library, New York, 1963), pp. 74-5.

16. Louis Bréhier, 'La Marine de Byzance du VIIIe au XIe Siècle', p. 1. Archibald R. Lewis, *Naval Power and Trade in the Mediterranean*, pp. 13, 19-20. Walther Vogel, *Geschichte der deutschen Seeschiffahrt* (George Reimer, Berlin, 1915), pp. 51-2. The Romans apparently tried to deny barbarians knowledge of shipbuilding and to some degree were successful.

17. F. C. Lane, 'Progrès technologiques et productivité dans les transports maritimes de la fin du Moyen Age au début des Temps modernes', *Revue Historique*, 510 (April-June 1974), pp. 278-9.

18. Hélène Ahrweiler, *Byzance et la Mer La Marine de Guerre La Politique et les Institutions Maritime de Byzance au VIIe – XVe Siècles* (Presses Universitaires de France, Paris, 1966), pp. 17-18. Aly Mohamed Fahmy, *Muslim Sea-Power*, pp. 116-17. Archibald R. Lewis, *Naval Power and Trade in the Mediterranean*, pp. 54-7. Ekkehard Eickhoff, *Seekrieg und Seepolitik*, pp. 19-22. George F. Hourani, *Arab Seafaring*, pp. 55-9.

19. Hélène Ahrweiler, *Byzance et la Mer*, pp. 19-34. Louis Bréhier, 'La Marine de Byzance du VIIIe au XIe Siècle', pp. 2-7. Hélène Antoniadis-Bibicou, *Etudes d'histoire maritime de Byzance*, pp. 53-8, 115. Archibald R. Lewis, *Naval Power and Trade in the Mediterranean*, pp. 60-5, 73-5. Lynn T. White, 'The Diffusion of the Lateen Sail', *Medieval Religion and Technology* (University of California Press, Berkeley, 1978), pp. 256-60.

20. Lionel Casson, *The Ancient Mariners*, pp. 186, 244, and *Ships and Seamanship in the Ancient World*, p. 154. Aly Mohamed Fahmy, *Muslim Sea-Power*, pp. 80-1, 103-5, 120-7. Richard Lebaron Bowen, Jr, 'Note: The Earliest Lateen Sail', p. 241. The Arabs may have got this different type of sail from the Indian Ocean where it was introduced by the Romans. The Arabs then diffused the sail through the Mediterranean. Ekkehard Eickhoff, *Seekrieg und Seepolitik*, pp. 152-5.

21. Hélène Antoniadis-Bibicou, *Etudes d'histoire maritime de Byzance*, pp. 22-4. Aly Mohamed Fahmy, *Muslim Sea-Power*, pp. 76-84. Maurice Lombard, 'Arsenaux et bois de marine dans la Méditerranée musulmane (VIIe – XIe siècles)', *TCHM*, II, pp. 53-66, 81-96. Prohibitions of the export of wood by Byzantines did not begin until the early ninth century.

22. Archibald R. Lewis, *Naval Power and Trade in the Mediterranean*, pp. 69-72, 79-99. For a contrary view see Renée Doehard, 'Méditerranée et économie occidentale pendant le haut Moyen Age', *Cahiers d'histoire mondiale*, I (1954), pp. 579-81. Aly Mohamed Fahmy, *Muslim Sea Power*, pp. 127, 137. Ekkehard Eickhoff, *Seekrieg und Seepolitik*, pp. 48-50, 154-6.

23. E. G. R. Taylor, *The Haven-Finding Art. A History of Navigation from Odysseus to Captain Cook* (Abelard-Schuman Ltd, New York, 1957), p. 66. She translates the statement from Caesar's *Gallic Wars*, as does Lionel Casson, *Illustrated History of Ships and Boats* (Doubleday and Co., New York, 1964), p. 59. Romola and R. C. Anderson, *The Sailing-Ship*, pp. 59-62. James Hornell, 'The Sources of the Clinker and Carvel Systems in British Boat Construction', *MM*, XXXIV (1948), pp. 244-5. *HSUA*, pp. 118-22. The Blackfriars boat of the second century AD excavated in London by Marsden, about 16 metres long, almost 6.5 metres broad and just over two metres deep amidships, seems to have been of the type described by Caesar. The vessel was of about 30 tons. A vessel that Marsden also investigated at New Guy's House, London, appears to have been a smaller version of the same type. Detlev Ellmers, 'Keltischer Schiffbau', *Jahrbuch Römisch-Germanischen Zentralmuseums Mainz*, XVI (1969), pp. 73-82. The same type was apparently also used along the Rhine.

24. *FHMN*, p. 76. Detlev Ellmers, 'Keltischer Schiffbau', pp. 106-16. Archibald R. Lewis, *The Northern Seas, Shipping and Commerce in Northern Europe A.D. 300-1100* (Princeton University Press, Princeton, 1958), pp. 106-7, 168-9.

HSUA, p. 115. Caesar saw skin-boats like these in 55-54 BC and used them in 49 BC having his men build them along the Spanish coast.

25. M.D. DeWeerd, 'Schepen voor het Opscheppen', *Spiegel Historiael*, VIII, 7/8 (July-August 1973), pp. 390-7. Ole Crumlin-Pedersen, 'The Ships of the Vikings', in Thorsten Andersson and Karl Inge Sandred (eds), *The Vikings* (Uppsala University, Uppsala), pp. 39-40. Peter Marsden, 'A boat of the Roman period found at Bruges, Belgium, in 1899, and related types', *IJNA*, V (1976), pp. 44-7.

26. Detlev Ellmers, 'Keltischer Schiffbau', pp. 75, 81, 118-21. On other Celtic design traditions and the inventiveness of Celtic shipwrights in dealing with specific conditions, see pp. 84-106. Lucien Basch, 'Ancient wrecks and the archaeology of ships', pp. 41-3, differs, claiming that Blackfriars boat does not exhibit true shell technique but his argument is not convincing. *HSUA*, p. 122. *AB*, pp. 68-70.

27. Ph. Humbla, 'Björke-båten från Hille Socken', *Från Gästrikland* (1949), pp. 5-30. This vessel, built about 100 AD, was a smaller version but still essentially the same type and a forerunner of the Nydam boat. The preserved boat is now in the provincial museum in Gävle, Sweden. Romola and R. C. Anderson, *The Sailing-Ship*, pp. 66-8. Tacitus about 100 AD mentioned the use of double-ended craft by the Suiones, a tribe he placed in Scandinavia. He may have been referring to vessels similar to that found at Nydam. Harald Åkerlund, *Nydamskeppen En Studie I Tidig Skandinavisk Skeppsbyggnadskonst* (Sjöfartsmuseet, Gothenburg, 1963), pp. 155-7. The measurements, which he reported again in the English summary cited here, are based on a correction factor for the shrinking of the vessel. That is one of the few aspects of Åkerlund's radically revisionist and imaginative work which is convincing. *HSUA*, pp. 162-4. Archibald R. Lewis, *The Northern Seas*, pp. 46-8, is undoubtedly right in saying that the Nydam type was not like the ships used by Saxon pirates to attack Roman Britain in the third and fourth centuries AD. But exactly what type of vessel they used is not known. *AB*, pp. 178-83.

28. Siegfried Fliedner, ' "Kogge" and "Hulk" Ein Beitrag zur Schiffstypen-geschichte', *Die Bremer Hanse-Kogge Fund Konservierung Forschung* (Verlag Friedrich Röver, Bremen, 1969), pp. 54-62, gives a complete and exhaustive discussion of the derivation of the name of the hulk type. *HSUA*, pp. 186-7. *FHMN*, pp. 59-63. The identification of the Utrecht ship as a hulk is based on later coin evidence. He believes that planks were originally end to end in this type with the external plank over the seams to hold them together. This is likely. Paul Heinsius, *Das Schiff der Hansischen Frühzeit* (Verlag Hermann Böhlaus Nach-folger, Weimar, 1956), pp. 70-4. Johannes P. W. Philipsen, 'The Utrecht Ship', *MM*, LI (1965), pp. 35-46. The iron nails found with the ship were either used for minor structural features or added later in repairs. The ship may have been as much as 200 years old when buried. Edward P. von der Porten, 'Note: The Utrecht Boat', *MM*, XLIX (1963), pp. 50-1.

29. Siegfried Fliedner, ' "Kogge" and "Hulk" ', pp. 39-54. The name cog is connected to Frisian usage and apparently meant 'shell'. For other theories on the origin of the name see Paul Heinsius, *Das Schiff der Hansischen Frühzeit*, pp. 12, 70-6. M. A. Nagelmackers, 'Le bateau de Bruges', *MAB*, VIII (1954), pp. 193-201. Ole Crumlin-Pedersen, 'Cog-Kogge-Kaag Træk af en frisisk skibstypes historie', *Handels- og Søfartsmuseets På Kronborg, Årbog* (1965), pp. 96-102. *FHMN*, pp. 63-4, 69-70. Samuel Eliot Morison, *The European Discovery of America The Northern Voyages A.D. 500-1600* (Oxford University Press, New York, 1968), pp. 15-27. *HSUA*, pp. 122-3. From similarities to the Blackfriars boat he sugges-ted an earlier date for the Bruges boat and the possibility that it was a Celtic vessel predating German incursions into the Roman Empire. While his recent work

has confirmed a Celtic origin the critical point is the extensive use of this type by German-speaking traders. Peter Marsden, 'A boat of the Roman period found at Bruges', pp. 23-9, 37-44.

30. Herbert Jankuhn, 'Der fränkisch-friesische Handel zur Ostsee im frühen Mittelalter', *Vierteljahrschrift für Sozial- und Wirtschaftsgeschichte*, XL (1953), pp. 205-22, 228-30. All writers cite coin evidence, which is extensive, for the scope, pattern and dating of Frisian trade. More generally Herbert Jankuhn, *Haithabu: Ein Handelsplazt der Wikingerzeit*, fourth expanded edition (Karl Wachholtz Verlag, Neumünster, 1963). Dirk Jellema, 'Frisian Trade in the Dark Ages', *Speculum*, XXX (1955), pp. 15-23. Barbara Rohwer, *Der friesische Handel im frühen Mittelalter* (Robert Noske, Leipzig, 1937), pp. 7-9, 23-37. P. C. J. A. Boeles, *Friesland tot de Elfde Eeuw* (Martinus Nijhoff, The Hague, 1927), pp. 127-30, 152-5, 162-71.

31. Ole Crumlin-Pedersen, 'Cog-Kogge-Kaag', pp. 116-21. For a more sceptical view of Frisian activity in the Baltic see Aksel E. Christensen, 'Birka Uden Frisere', *Handels- og Søfartsmuseet På Kronborg, Årbog* (1966), pp. 17-38. For reports on renewed archaeological investigations at the site of Dorestad see *Spiegel Historiael*, XIII, 4 (April 1978), pp. 194-314.

32. R. L. S. Bruce-Mitford, *The Sutton Hoo Ship Burial A Handbook* (The Trustees of the British Museum, London, 1968), pp. 40-3, 48-51. The grave goods are important for, among other things, showing the close ties between England and Sweden in the seventh century. The wood of the ship has completely disappeared and only the impression is left. Many details are not known, such as the height of the stem and sternposts and the nature of the decoration. *HSUA*, p. 124; he, like most other writers, finds it hard to believe that a vessel the size of the Sutton Hoo ship would not have had a sail. If there was a sail it was obviously small and for propulsion of little significance compared to the oars. *AB*, pp. 178-88, on finds of this type. Angela Care Evans, 'The Sutton Hoo Ship', in Valerie Fenwick *et al.*, *Three Major Ancient Boat Finds in Britain*, National Maritime Museum, Monographs and Reports, no. 6 (1972), pp. 26-33.

33. *HSUA*, pp. 164-5. The importance of the Kvalsund boat lies in its transitional nature showing the change to the use of iron rivets in Norwegian boat construction. Haakon Shetelig and Fr. Johannessen, *Kvalsundfundet og Andre Norske Myrfund av Fartøier* (John Griegs Boktrykkeri, Bergen, 1929). Similarity to later Viking ships is not unexpected since reconstruction of the ship from the few pieces found is based on ninth-century finds.

34. Sibylla Haasum, *Vikingatidens Segling och Navigation* (Scandinavian University Books, Stockholm, 1974), p. 56. The evidence for the introduction of sails to Scandinavia in the seventh century comes from drawings on stones on the island of Gotland. That was one result of the work of Sune Lindqvist, *Gotlands Bildsteine* (Kungl. Vitterhets Historie och Antikvitets Akademien, Stockholm, 1942).

35. *FHMN*, p. 158. There is some question as to whether deterioration of quays led to a change in ship design or the generally smaller size of ships led to the abandoning of quays.

NOTES TO ILLUSTRATIONS

a. Lucien Basch, 'Ancient wrecks and the archaeology of ships', *IJNA*, I (1972), p. 2. *HSUA*, pp. 84-5. Björn Landström, *The Ship*, nos. 94-6. Lionel Casson, *Illustrated History of Ships and Boats*, nos. 49-50. Claude Farrère, *Histoire de la Marine Française*, pp. 6-7. G. La Roërie and J. Vivielle, *Navires et Marins de la rame à l'hélice*, vol. I, pp. 57-9.

   b. Lionel Casson, *Illustrated History of Ships and Boats*, nos. 60-2, 65, 66. *HSUA*, pp. 72, 80, 86. G. La Roërie and J. Vivielle, *Navires et Marins*, vol. I, pp. 63-9, 76. Björn Landström, *The Ship*, nos. 103-10. Romola and R. C. Anderson, *The Sailing-Ship*, pp. 49-51. G. S. Laird Clowes, *Sailing Ships, Their History and Development*, part I, plate V. Claude Farrère, *Histoire de la Marine Française*, p. 6. Richard Lebaron Bowen, Jr, 'The origins of fore-and-aft rigs', *AN*, XIX (1959), p. 278.

   c. Lionel Casson, *Ships and Seamanship in the Ancient World*, nos. 159-60, and *Illustrated History of Ships and Boats*, no. 56. *HSUA*, pp. 70-1.

   d. Lionel Casson, *Ships and Seamanship in the Ancient World*, no. 163, and *Illustrated History of Ships and Boats*, no. 56.

   e. Lionel Casson, *Ships and Seamanship in the Ancient World*, nos. 138, 141.

   f. *HSUA*, pp. 137-8, 140-2, 154, 157-8. Hélène Antoniadis-Bibicou, *Etudes d'histoire maritime de Byzance. A propos du 'Thèmes des Caravisiens'*, between pp. 24 and 25, no. 1. Frederick van Doorninck, 'The 4th century wreck at Yassi Ada. An interim report on the hull', *IJNA*, V (1976), pp. 122, 130.

   g. R. H. Dolley, 'The Warships of the Later Roman Empire', *The Journal of Roman Studies*, XXXVIII (1948), plate V. The pictures are of his model of a dromon which leaves something to be desired. Björn Landström, *The Ship*, nos. 221-4, for later dromons. *HSUA*, p. 132: this is a rare illustration of a late Roman warship from northern Europe. Its relationship if any to the dromon is an interesting and unanswered question.

   h. *HSUA*, p. 145. Lionel Casson, *Illustrated History of Ships and Boats*, no. 52, and *Ships and Seamanship in the Ancient World*, no. 134.

   i. Lionel Casson, *Illustrated History of Ships and Boats*, nos. 64, 70-4, *Ships and Seamanship in the Ancient World*, nos. 147, 175-9, 180-2, 188, and 'The Sprit-Rig in the Ancient World', *MM*, XXXXVI (1960), p. 241. Richard Lebaron Bowen, Jr, 'The origins of fore-and-aft rigs', pp. 156, 187, and 'Note: The Earliest Lateen Sail', *MM*, XLII (1966), p. 240. Björn Landström, *Sailing Ships*, nos. 70-6. *HSUA*, pp. 148-9.

   j. H. H. Brindley, 'Early Pictures of Lateen Sails', *MM*, XII (1926), opposite p. 12. Hélène Antoniadis-Bibicou, *Etudes d'histoire maritime de Byzance*, between pp. 24 and 25, nos. 2-3. Björn Landström, *The Ship*, nos. 209, 215, 218. Richard Lebaron Bowen, Jr, 'The origins of fore-and-aft rigs', p. 184. Romola and R. C. Anderson, *The Sailing-Ship*, pp. 102-3.

   k. Detlev Ellmers, 'Keltischer Schiffbau', *Jahrbuch Römisch-Germanischen Zentralmuseums Mainz*, XVI (1969), pp. 74, 78, 80. *HSUA*, pp. 117, 120-1, 126-9.

   l. *FHMN*, pp. 68, 153. Detlev Ellmers, 'Keltischer Schiffbau', pp. 107-9. *HSUA*, p. 125. Romola and R. C. Anderson, *The Sailing-Ship*, p. 60. *AB*, nos. 68, 69, 75.

   m. Detlev Ellmers, 'Keltischer Schiffbau', p. 75. Peter Marsden, 'A boat of the Roman period found at Bruges, Belgium in 1899, and related types', *IJNA*, V (1976), p. 37.

   n. Romola and R. C. Anderson, *The Sailing-Ship*, pp. 67-8. *FHMN*, pp. 26, 108. *HSUA*, pp. 163, 171. M. A. Nagelmackers, 'Le bateau de Bruges', *MAB*, VIII (1954), p. 207. Björn Landström, *The Ship*, nos. 136-7. A. W. Brøgger and Haakon Shetelig, *The Viking Ships, Their Ancestry and Evolution*, p. 36. Bernhard Hagedorn, *Die Entwicklung der wichtigsten Schiffstypen bis ins 19. Jahrhundert*, p. 4.

   o. J. P. W. Philipsen, 'The Utrecht Ship', *MM*, LI (1965), opposite p. 4: the model built as a reconstruction is not reliable. E. P. von der Porten, 'Note: The Utrecht Boat', *MM*, XLIX (1963), p. 51. *FHMN*, pp. 54-5, 285-6. *HSUA*, pp. 198-9. Ole Crumlin-Pedersen, 'Cog-Kogge-Kaag Træk af en frisisk skibstypes historie', *Handels- og Søfartsmuseets På Kronborg* (1965), pp. 95, 97. Siegfried Fliedner, ' "Kogge" und "Hulk" Ein Beitrag zur Schiffstypengeschichte', in *Die Bremer Hanse-Kogge Fund Konservierung Forschung*, no. 45. *AB*, nos. 124, 125.

    p. M. A. Nagelmackers, 'Le bateau de Bruges', p. 200. Ole Crumlin-Pedersen, 'Cog-Kogge-Kaag', pp. 98-9. *FHMN*, pp. 65, 290. Peter Marsden, 'A boat of the Roman period found at Bruges', pp. 26-7, 37, 39, 42.

    q. R. L. S. Bruce-Mitford, *The Sutton Hoo Ship Burial A Handbook*, *passim*. A. W. Brøgger and Haakon Shetelig, *The Viking Ships*, p. 39. *HSUA*, p. 131. *AB*, nos. 121, 122.

    r. *HSUA*, pp. 161, 169. Björn Landström, *The Ship*, nos. 138-45, 159. Ole Crumlin-Pedersen, 'Cog-Kogge-Kaag', p. 125. *FHMN*, p. 28. A. W. Brøgger and Haakon Shetelig, *The Viking Ships*, pp. 48-9, 95. *AB*, no. 123.

2   VIKINGS AND BYZANTINES: 750-1000

The rapid emergence of the Carolingian Empire, built on the Frankish kingdom of the Merovingians, created a unified state for western Europe. It also created a government with an economic and monetary policy. These creations, together with peace, could only help in the expansion of shipping. After 840 and the death of Charlemagne's son, Louis the Pious, political organisation became fragmented. The breakdown of the high levels of government led to chaos or at least insecurity through much of northern Europe as the stronger tried to improve their condition by force. Outside the Empire in lands to the north, Scandinavians embarked on a series of raids on the settled regions of the West which turned into two centuries of attacks by groups of these Vikings against Britain, Ireland and the Continent. The Viking attacks came in waves. They added another source of disruption, especially along the coasts and rivers, since the Vikings came by sea.

By the year 1000 a certain measure of stability had been re-established. In France the smaller political units which emerged brought some peace, as did the restored Roman Empire now in a central European

Illustration above: A Scandinavian sailing ship of the thirteenth century with the lines of earlier Viking cargo ships, Bergen, Norway, oldest town seal, second half of the thirteenth century.

form. The eastern frontier of the Empire was stabilised by the establishment of Christian kingdoms in Hungary and Poland. The same was true in Scandinavia where certain former tribal chieftains had been able to claim sovereignty as kings. This successful establishment of monarchical governments on the fringe of Europe meant, if nothing else, that violence was better organised, less sporadic.

In the Mediterranean, on the other hand, the naval contest between the Byzantine and Arab Empires continued, if anything, with greater intensity. The internal difficulties of the Caliphates made for changes in the level of Muslim naval activity and led by the end of the tenth century to a fragmented political structure with a number of Muslim states having varying ties among themselves. The Byzantines faced the threat of these states and also a challenge on the Black Sea from Russia. The Empire survived these assaults as well as a number of internal political crises and revolts. There were signs of a growing weakness in the Empire, however, and not on its northern border where there was some success against attacking Bulgars, but in the east in Asia Minor and in the west in south Italy. By 1000, in both southern and northern Italy, a number of port towns had increased their trade and their investment in shipping to the point where they could deploy some naval strength. They were not major naval powers but they were in a position to play an active part in Mediterranean commerce and to develop and expand their own shipbuilding.

The ships of northern Europe continued to include most of the types present before 750. Some were subjected to continuing development while others remained largely unchanged. Some types all but disappeared. In England at least in the eighth and ninth centuries wooden vessels replaced the large seagoing Celtic curragh. Building with wickerwork was not sturdy enough and perhaps required too much repair for carrying goods on the high seas. The smaller version using the same type of construction, the coracle, was still used but only for carrying small quantities of goods and people short distances. In general Celtic types were restricted to the coasts, to coastal fisheries and especially to the rivers. The form of the vessels remained consistent but they became, if anything, smaller. Many Celtic types were originally intended for river transport and had been thus used during the Roman period and before. Their efficiency in that capacity was recognised and their use was not challenged. The Celtic designs which enjoyed continued development were those that had by 750 already been found useful by Frisians. They were not pure Celtic types by that time, retaining only some features from their predecessors. In the hands of Frisian builders and shippers these types had passed into use for long-distance trade.

Builders in England in the ninth and tenth centuries developed a new type of oceangoing cargo ship. Its origins were Scandinavian rather than Celtic. It was called a keel because the addition of that heavy central piece set it apart from contemporary Frisian vessels, the cog and the hulk. The keel was a further development of the Scandinavian rowing barge like the one found at Kvalsund. It began as a warship for carrying men but by the tenth century was a cargo ship for carrying goods, especially across the North Sea and along the Atlantic coast. There was a single square sail on the single mast. The angle of the posts was sharper than on earlier rowing barges. There were oars but only at the ends because the centre of the vessel was an open hold for goods. The oars were used just to manoeuvre and to get in and out of harbours. The hull was clinker-built and similar in proportions to those of contemporary Scandinavian cargo ships. The length-to-breadth ratio was in the range of 3.5:1 to 4.5:1. A boat found in Kent from about 900 seems to fit into this category of ship. Though primarily for coastal trading the vessel was capable of crossing the Channel. Ribs were massive and set close together. The hull planks were nailed to the ribs. The posts were nearly vertical meeting the keel at something near right angles, a practice found on seventh-century Scandinavian vessels but later abandoned for most ships. The sides were not square with the bottom but instead met with horizontally overlapping planking. The keel itself was not straight but was lower amidships than at the ends. This was an advantage when trying to get the vessel off a beach so it was designed to use the simplest harbours. Strakes were pieced together and thin, the maximum thickness being only .03 metres.[a] The timbers amidships suggest a strong base for heavy cargo and toll records from the early eleventh century show that this type was used to carry wine in barrels from the Continent to London. Cargo was presumably carried around the mast.[1] The keel by 1000 was a common cargo vessel built in England and used along the coast of Britain, the Atlantic coast of France and the south shore of the North Sea. In a sense the keel was a substitute or alternative type to the hulk since they seem to have been used along many of the same routes. The keel sailed better in open waters and faster as well because it had a keel, but the hulk did better on rivers and in shallow waters. The keel could carry more goods for each metre of length. Since neither type was overwhelmingly superior in all trades they were used side by side. It is doubtful whether keels were built in the Low Countries, however, since designing for travel along rivers took precedence there.

Both the hulk and cog continued in much the same forms through the tenth century. Both types were popular with Frisians trading from the Low Countries and especially from the commercial capital of the area, Dorestad. Illustrations on coins confirm this fact.[b] Frisian trade apparently continued to expand until the mid-ninth century. Frisians, taking advantage of inclusion in the Carolingian Empire, extended their ties up the Rhine and to England and Scandinavia. They moved goods in cogs east along the coast to the town of Hollingstedt where the goods and perhaps the entire ship were carried overland to Hedeby on the Baltic coast. So the Frisians portaged their cogs into the Baltic. The need to move them overland kept them small as did the typically shallow harbours in the Baltic. Moreover, those harbours were often hard to reach, being on rivers. Still, the Frisian vessels had cabins, a great advantage in comfort over Scandinavian open boats. The goods handled continued to be the same, the Frisians acting as middlemen between the handicraft industries of the Rhine Valley and the land-intensive industries, such as hunting, of the North. Trade to the Mediterranean through the Rhine Valley and the Alps — trade which developed in the reign of Charlemagne — was badly affected by attacks of Hungarian raiders in the late ninth and in the first half of the tenth century. On the other hand there seems to have been a revival of trade along the west coast of France and to Spain. The Frisians took part in that as well, for example fetching olive oil from Aquitaine for customers in the Rhine Valley. The Frisians still carried wine to Scandinavia in jars, despite the expense compared to carriage in barrels. Shipping to Scandinavia continued into the tenth century despite attacks by Vikings on Frisia and on Dorestad itself.[2]

The Frisians established trading colonies in the major ports of their trading network, following the practice of late Roman and Byzantine merchants who still maintained colonies of merchants in the Frankish kingdom in the sixth century. Since their ships and navigational techniques fixed certain trade routes as optimal, the Frisians knew which ports would be most used. They established colonies in London and York, in Hedeby and Birka, in Worms and Mainz and as far away as Rome. In Rome from 779 they had their own quarter with a church. It continued to exist until about 1300. From the early ninth century there were resident Frisian merchants living in ports, owning land or holding it on long-term lease and, if not living there all the time, at least using it as their base of operations and maintaining a family life in their home ports.[3] Frisian trade was certainly not promoted by the

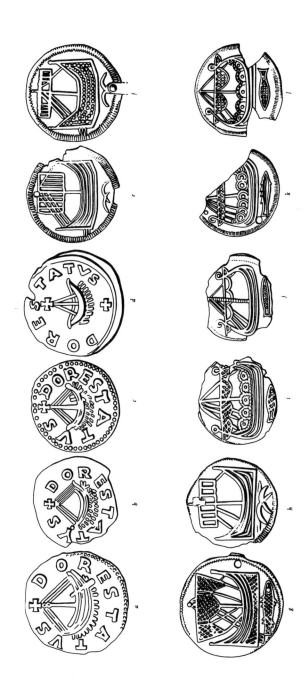

5: Ships on Carolingian Coins of Dorestad : a-d hulks, e-h cogs and i-l Scandinavian warships

hostile actions of Scandinavians. The interruption of production throughout coastal regions, the attacks on ports and the periodic establishment
of regions ruled by Vikings all made the task of the Frisian merchant
harder. He also had to face competition from the Vikings since they
acted as traders, sometimes bypassing established Frisian trading
connections or finding alternative sources for goods. The Northmen
first attacked Friesland in 810. The raids intensified and major assaults
were mounted from 834 to 885. Dorestad was sacked in 834 and again
in 835. The town was finally destroyed in 860. Merchants, and with
them trade, migrated to Utrecht and to Tiel, the former keeping the
Scandinavian connection and using cogs, the latter continuing trade
with England using hulks.[4]

The adverse conditions did not immediately yield a change in ship
types. Rather, advance in ship design seems to have been suspended like
trade. The English keel and the Netherlandish cog and hulk remained
much the same. The only major response to the Viking attacks was in
warships. King Alfred the Great of England concluded that he could
defend his realm only with a naval force able to meet and defeat the
Vikings before they landed. He had ships built at the end of the ninth
century for just that job. The design was probably similar to that of the
English keel but King Alfred's ships were much larger. They were rowing boats with 30 oars to a side, which meant they had to be more than
40 metres long, much longer than a contemporary Viking ship. These
vessels were reported to be bigger, faster and higher in the water than
contemporary Danish or Frisian ships. The total fleet by the mid-tenth
century was said to number 3,600 vessels but that is certainly an
exaggeration.[5] These were not ships for the high seas. They were for
coastal defence and designed to move a large number of men quickly
to a point of attack. Frisian sailors were used to man them since the job
was beyond the skill of Englishmen. The design of these ships appears to
have had no effect on other vessels in northern Europe, however. They
were special-purpose ships and were useful only for their single task.
As the Vikings changed from hit-and-run raids to attacks by large
armies these English warships lost their function. The long ship in the
North developed not from the ships of Alfred the Great but rather from
the highly effective Scandinavian sailing ship.

The development of the Viking ship in the eighth century was the
most important change in European ship design from 750 to 1000. It
combined many features of earlier types and incorporated major
advances over those designs. It is probably correct to downgrade some
of the extravagant claims made for these ships. The success of modern

full-size reconstructions, however, does indicate some of the remarkable capabilities of the type.[6] The Viking ship marked a significant improvement in the ability to move people. It demonstrated the advantages of certain major design features, features later borrowed by builders outside Scandinavia. The design of the Viking ship was by no means static. It too was improved as the potential of the type was explored.

There was in eighth- and ninth-century Scandinavia a need for a vessel to carry men. The poor farmland of the Norwegian and Swedish coasts made farmers into part-time fishermen so there were always boats and boat builders among the farms. The vessels were used to travel among the relatively isolated settlements in the fjords. There is evidence that the population of Scandinavia was rising through the eighth and ninth centuries, and this increased the need to move goods but, more important, to move people so that they could resettle elsewhere. Migrants covered ever-increasing distances, more regularly over open waters. This was in a sense a continuation of the migration of people from Scandinavia dating from the first century AD. By the eighth century the type of vessel for the migration had been markedly improved to deal with the high seas and longer voyages. The Viking ship was primarily a ship for moving men. The demand was formed by the social organisation in Scandinavia. These tribal societies were grouped into clans in which family connections were the qualification for status. The aristocrats of the society, the landowners and leaders of the clans, had boats built for their private use. The vessels had to serve to carry them and their relatives and retainers. The ships had to be good for fighting since authority depended on physical strength and the support of relatives. Settlements were never large nor were the kin groups themselves, so the boats themselves did not have to be of any great size. The owners of these ships had a great deal of say in the design of the ship, a fact that could certainly lead to whimsical requirements. But the leader of the clan group was himself constrained by fear of other groups, by the size of his band of followers, by the weather and by the waters of the fjords. All those problems were reflected in the final design of the Viking ship.

Scandinavian society was based on continuing conflict. Physical prowess in battle was praised. The continuation of family vendettas to adjudicate disputes guaranteed fighting. The economy was a confiscatory one, the seizure of goods or land being considered almost the same as the purchase or exchange of property. This was especially clear in commerce. The dividing line between trade and piracy was not clear cut. There is in fact some question as to whether such a categorical differentiation existed among Scandinavians. Buyers of ships then wanted a vessel primarily to carry people, but also usable in both trade and fighting. The only constraint on these voyages of raiding was the ability of the ship to make the trip. Equipped with their new ship from the mid-ninth century on, Vikings were able to attack Iberia at least six times and in one case they even went as far as the Dardanelles and perhaps even to Alexandria.[7] They pursued the established trade routes in search of any opportunity, living off what they could buy, barter or take. All Viking ships had to be light and fast and that kept unit carrying costs high. Typically the goods freighted were luxuries. Though there was a clear distinction between warships and ships intended for trade, even the latter had relatively small carrying capacities and many of the same design features since they were subject to similar constraints. No matter the goal, the Viking ship of the ninth and tenth centuries was a vessel with good manoeuvrability, with great potential range, with good stability and excellent handling characteristics. Properly sailed it was a safe ship. It was also easily beached and refloated and light enough to be moved across land for short distances.

This new type made possible all of the extensive voyages throughout northern European waters, through Russia to the Black and Caspian Seas and across the North Atlantic to Iceland, Greenland and Canada. The voyages of discovery and colonisation were a side effect of the development of a successful deep-sea sailing vessel. They were at the same time the product of better navigational techniques developed to deal with long-distance open-water sailing. The Vikings did make mistakes in navigation but in most cases these caused only mild inconvenience. They may also have benefited from, on average, better weather in the North Atlantic with steadier winds and longer summers than were to be typical of the late middle ages. Still, weather conditions in the North were always worse than those in the Mediterranean, making navigation more difficult. The improved navigational techniques of the Vikings may in fact have developed as part of a compulsive sequence in which the increased capabilities of their ships led them to investigate and experiment with long-distance sailing to try and exploit more fully the potential of the ship.[8]

The Viking ship built originally for Scandinavian aristocrats was not the longship which was built after 1000. It was smaller and if anything more versatile. Knowledge of Viking ships is based on finds of partially preserved ships among others from Oseberg, Tune and Gokstad in Norway, Ladby and Skuldelev near Roskilde in Denmark and of an early or even pre-Viking ship at Äskekärr in Sweden. The rare illustrations from the years up to 1000 and information about ships and sailing from the Norse sagas supplement the archaeological evidence. It is possible to distinguish two basic types of Viking ships. The better-known type is the warship, primarily a personnel carrier for coastal and short sea voyages, the finest example being the Gokstad ship. The other type is the cargo ship. Both shared the same characteristics of fine curving lines and double-ended pointed hull. They were both clinker-built. The warship, however, had a length-to-beam ratio of from 4.5:1 to over 7:1. For cargo ships that ratio was from 2.3:1 up to 5:1. The warship relied on oars for propulsion and on larger warships there was an auxiliary sail. For the cargo ship the sail was the source of power. The few oars at bow and stern, as with the English keel, were only used in special circumstances. The ship had higher freeboard to hold more cargo in the open space amidships. With warships freeboard had to be low to get an efficient angle of entry into the water for the oars.[9] For cargo ships the greater angle was no problem since the oars were rarely used.

Despite these and other distinguishing features which show up in the wrecks, the two types were just variations on the same design. This is obvious from the cross-section of the ship.[c] The keel had become a fully integrated part of the construction. It was heavy and full. Posts were scarfed to the keel at either end. From the keel clinkered strakes ran out in a smooth curve, almost flat amidships. Then the planks turned upward just at the top of the ribs. The angle is very sharp on warships and not so extreme on cargo ships. Running across the ship at that point and resting on the tops of the ribs are the *bites*. Above that was more planking reaching a heavier strake at the waterline called the *meginhufr*. Between these two heavy planks ran the cross-timbers separated from the *bites* by small posts. This combination of keel, ribs, planks and cross-timbers gave the ship its strength and stability and also its speed, since all the structural apparatus was very low. This also gave the vessel a shallow draught. It is the opposite of the Byzantine cargo ship which was a large box, an internal frame, covered with planking. The Byzantine ship as a result had a much greater carrying capacity than a Viking ship of the same length. To add some capacity the sides of Viking ships were built up with further planks, few for the warship and more for the cargo ship. These were clinkered and also attached to hanging knees which sat on the cross-timbers. The ship had a great deal of elasticity since strength came primarily from the external planking and compact internal frames. The ribs were there to keep the planking together but they were there also to maintain the shape of the vessel.

There is no question that Viking ships were of shell construction.

6: Midship Sections of Northern European Clinker-built Boats from the Hjortspring Boat (c. 300 BC) to the Ladby Boat (c. 1000)

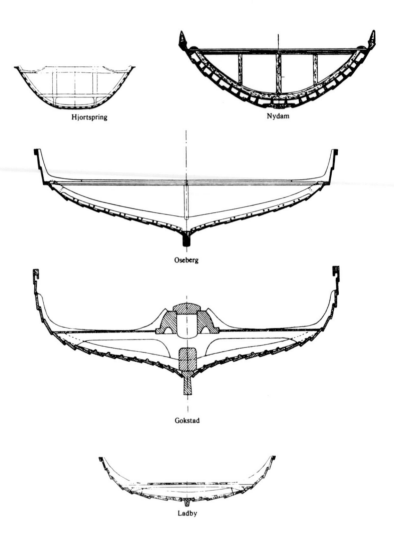

Hjortspring

Nydam

Oseberg

Gokstad

Ladby

The keel was laid down first, the posts attached, and then planking added up to the waterline. The heavy *meginhufr* was riveted on and then the ribs and cross-timbers were put in place. Builders selected wood shaped as much like the end product as possible, thus keeping the number of joints to a minimum. Then the hanging knees and upper planks were added. Narrower planks led to the posts in a rising curve and above them were decorative pieces. The next step was to add the large block to hold the side rudder. A withy was passed through the rudder to hold it to that block and to the heavy frame at the stern designed to take the strain. These were balance rudders and if the turning axis was right only the slightest effort was needed by the helmsman handling the tiller to overcome the friction of the suspension system. Since the ship was perfectly symmetrical the movement of the rudder turned the ship easily.[d] Experiments with full-scale models show that the helmsman with one finger on the tiller could overcome all the efforts of the rowers to get the ship to go in the opposite direction. Since the rudder extended as much as half a metre below the keel it was necessary to be able to raise it by rotating it on the large block of wood.[10]

Both types of Viking ship had the same form of rig but the arrangement for holding the mast was slightly different. In warships on top of the ribs amidships there was a large block of oak, a simple form of keelson, which was held in place by knees on its sides and by resting over the ribs. In this piece there was a socket for the base of the mast. It was rounded and open forward so that the mast could be slipped in. Above that and lying on the cross-timbers was the mast partner or mastfish, a name given it because of its distinctive shape. The mast partner was the largest single piece of wood in the ship. These timbers were put in the ship as the ribs and cross-timbers were being added. The mast partner was held to the cross-timbers by two mortise and tenon joints. The hole in the mast partner corresponded to that in the heavy piece below and was open at one end. The arrangement made it possible to slide the mast through the hole in the mast partner and then swing it up. Once raised the mast was kept in place by a wedge which fitted into the open end of the mast partner. The system was much simpler and less dangerous than trying to raise the mast vertically. It was also quicker. On cargo ships the mast was held permanently in place by similar heavy pieces of wood. The height of the mast was probably a little more than half the length of the ship, the length of the yard a little less. That gave a sail with a small area relative to the size of the ship. The mast was held in place by a single forestay running to the bow and two

7: The Gokstad Ship, Preserved in the Vikingskiphuset, Oslo

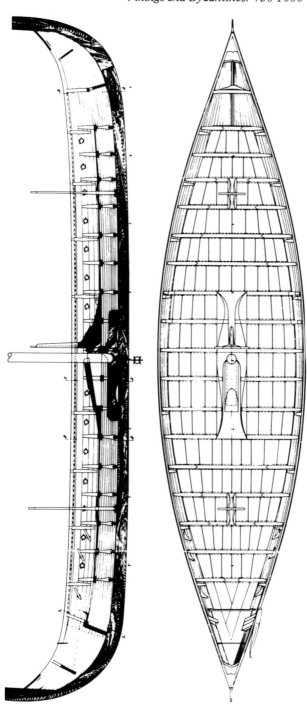

backstays. The sail was square. To hold the sail close-hauled and keep it from flapping there was a spar on each side fitted in a small wooden block on the gunwale abreast of the mast and running to the opposite edge of the sail.[e] This *beitiass* compensated for some of the limitations of the square rig. It was possible using the two spars to change course without having to wait for the wind to change, apparently common practice even in the ninth century. Though Viking ships could go to windward, it was still probably much faster to row. Running before the wind, speeds of 8 knots were easily attained and a maximum of 11 to 12 knots was possible. The average on long voyages, however, was probably more like 3 to 4 knots.[11]

The Gokstad ship, dated about 900, is the best example of the warship type. The Tune and Oseberg ships from the ninth century are smaller but show similar characteristics. All these belong to that class of ships with 12 to 32 oars, private vessels called *karven*. The Gokstad ship had 16 strakes to each side. The cross-timbers were at the tenth plank and then strakes 11 to 16 were held in place by the hanging knees. Plank 14 was stronger and was pierced with 16 holes on each side for the oars. A small shutter over each oarhole ensured that water would not enter when the oars were not in use. A small slit in the oarholes made it possible to pass the oars out from inside the ship. The distance between the ribs was about one metre, which gave space to pull the oars since there was one rower on each side above each rib. By having oarholes freeboard could be greater thus giving protection from the sea when sailing heeled over, all without sacrificing power since the angle at which the oars entered the water was still low.[f] The Gokstad ship was built entirely of oak. There was a slight but even curve to the keel so that it drew .30 metres more amidships than at the stem or stern. The scarf joints of the planks were always pointed aft so that water and ice would be shed when the ship was in motion. Planks were held to each other by iron nails. The ribs on the other hand were lashed to projections left on the planks for the purpose. The ribs were not fastened to the keel. There was a rack along the gunwale to carry shields, 32 for each side but these were only hung there while in harbour to show the rank and honour of the ship. The mast was about 13 metres high, the yard 10 to 11 metres long, giving a sail area of about 70 square metres. The oars were about 5.5 metres long and small and narrow for minimum weight. Since this was a coastal vessel it was equipped with beds and tent poles for the camp which was made every night.[12] Three small boats were found with the Gokstad ship, the longest being under 10 metres.[g] These showed all the same features of construction as the large ship, of course without the rig.[13]

The Tune ship, shorter than the Gokstad ship by some four metres, had about the same length-to-beam ratio. It also had the same thin planking to keep it as elastic as possible. The hull cross-section was different. The Tune ship rode lower in the water. The strakes were slanted more markedly outward so it would lie better in the water and also keep out spray when heeled over under sail. The Oseberg ship, on the other hand, showed in general a weaker build. This vessel was slightly beamier than the Gokstad ship. With only twelve strakes on each side, it had lower freeboard than the Gokstad ship.[h] There were 15 pairs of oars. It was probably more of a pleasure craft and not used in the hard conditions warships typically faced. The foundation for the mast was weaker than with either of the other two ships. In fact, it had broken under pressure and had been repaired with two large iron bands. In the Gokstad ship the floorboards were loose and only placed on top of the cross-timbers but those on the Oseberg ship were nailed in place. There was apparently not as great a need to get at the bilge where, on the Gokstad ship, equipment and food were stored. The Oseberg ship was also luxuriously decorated with fine carvings.[14] In all these vessels there was no place for the oarsmen to sit. Presumably they brought along sea chests with all their personal gear and moved those into place when it came time to row.

Warships found in Denmark at Ladby and Skuldelev show the same characteristics.[i] The Ladby ship dating from the mid-tenth century was more of a rowing barge than the Gokstad ship, since it had a higher length-to-breadth ratio. There were only seven planks to each side. Ribs were lashed to cleats on the planks in the typical fashion for warships. It did have a sail since there were four rings on the gunwales to hold shrouds. The Skuldelev warships date from about 1000. One warship was much like the Ladby ship and had a crew of only 24 oarsmen. The other, unfortunately not as well preserved, shows the tendency towards longer warships of the late tenth and eleventh centuries. At more than 29 metres long it had from at least 40 up to a possible 60 oars.[15] The structure remained the same but this longship marked a departure from the typical Viking warship of the ninth and tenth centuries.

Not as many cargo ships have been found. The earliest, the Äskekärr ship, dates from the end of the eighth century. Its length-to-breadth ratio was considerably less than that of the warships. It had the earliest maststep yet found on a Scandinavian ship.[j] There can be little question it was intended to be a sailing ship. It had a side rudder and 13 planks to each side. By 1000 cargo ships were longer than the approximately

9: The Oseberg Ship, Preserved in the Vikingskiphuset, Oslo

16-metre length of the Äskekärr ship, and they were able to carry up to 60 people. This *knarr* type was not like smaller cargo ships which could only survive in the Baltic and North Seas. The knarr could make long-distance voyages in the Atlantic and it was regularly used for trips to Iceland and Greenland. Knarrs were used from 870 to carry colonists to Iceland. The typical cargo was 20 or 30 family members, their cattle, goods, fodder and furniture. Typically the knarr was a better sailer than the warship, having a deeper draught. There was no mastfish since the mast was permanently set. There were short half-decks at the bow and stern. The keel was flat or rather hardly curved. The capacity of knarrs was probably at least 10 tons and often higher. The large Skuldelev cargo ship had a capacity of 30 tons and knarrs travelling to Iceland must have been able to carry 50 tons. These were only some 25 metres long, not much longer than the Gokstad ship. The smaller Skuldelev ship, a cargo carrier for the Baltic, could handle only some 9 tons and had a crew of ten to twelve men. The larger Skuldelev cargo ship, the knarr, had a crew of twelve while for the largest ones used in trading to Iceland 16 was a logical figure. This gave them manning ratios much lower than for a warship but the same as, or more than, for a cog. One distinctive feature of cargo ships was the fact that frames, instead of being lashed to the planking, were held with wooden nails, treenails. This was the case in the Äskekärr ship, so the practice already existed by 800. It meant sacrificing some elasticity and lightness but for the cargo carrier neither was as crucial as strength.[k] The Skuldelev finds also show that the ribs or frames were set closer together, about .90 metres, than was the case with the warship.[16] The Skuldelev knarr shows that all the variations on Viking cargo ships still owed much to the open rowing barge. Cargo ships never had any cabin or permanent protection for the crew. For coastal trade and travel that was no problem but on voyages to Iceland conditions for the crew must have been hard.

The Viking ship, because of the improvements made over its predecessors, required more labour for its construction. Moreover, the labour had to be more skilled. Selection of timber was less crucial. Since planks were scarfed and pieced, a wider variety of trees could be used. Careful selection was still needed in finding timber, though, since the frames had to have the right natural shape. Once the timber had been collected more work was needed to form it into this type of ship than to earlier northern types. There was, in fact, a division of labour in building these ships, with one man in charge of the entire project while certain workers with special skills were given the job of finishing

10: Two Viking Cargo Ships from Skuldelev: Baltic Ship (top)
and Seagoing Knarr (bottom)

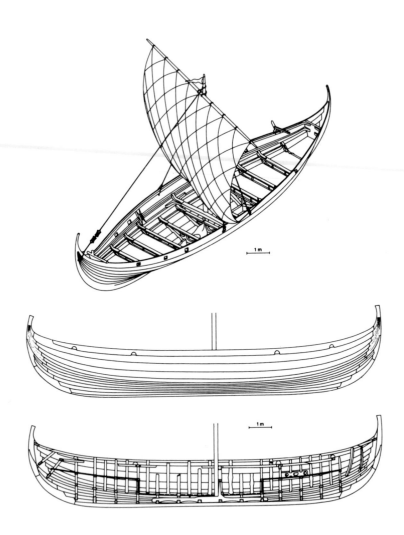

certain parts such as the keel, stem and stern. Specialists must also have been employed to do the carving. Despite what appears in written sources, these men had a wide variety of tools. Their kit was well developed including axes, adzes, augers and gouges. They also had saws but only small handsaws.[1] The timber was not cut from logs. Instead the logs were split and then dressed to shape. On the Skuldelev ships marks show the use of axes and planes and other tools but no sign of a saw. The frame saw was known and used in the Roman Empire and such saws were used during the middle ages. Scandinavian boat builders did not use this big saw for ripping timber into boards, perhaps out of ignorance or, just as likely, they may have found sawn planks too weak for the job.[17]

If population was rising then there should have been no problem in finding a larger number of workers. Finding skilled craftsmen was, of course, more difficult. But as these shipwrights turned out a better product, since the invention of the unique cross-section arrangement of frames and timbers made their ships more productive, the rewards to these men could rise, thus making boat building an attractive job. The employer, the landowner and leader of the family group, for his own reasons was obviously very interested in promoting shipbuilding thus also contributing to better rewards for skilled ship carpenters. The promotion of design improvement by shipowners, combined with borrowing from other designs and the apparently independent invention of the shaping and support of the clinkerbuilt hull, all combined to expand the capability of Scandinavian ships. The Viking warship was faster than its predecessors, like the Sutton Hoo ship, and had the added potential of using sail power to get it to the scene of fighting. It was the advantage in fighting that brought the new design into widespread use, Vikings using these ships on their first raids on the British Isles in the years before 800. With the success of those first attacks Vikings made more and more frequent voyages, which gave them a chance to improve their sailing techniques and gave builders more opportunities to experiment with the designs. If the Vikings were not quite convinced about the superior effectiveness of their warship, they had a removable dragon's head at the prow to scare the enemy.[m]

At the same time as the Viking warship gave Scandinavians a superiority in fighting, the increased reliability, speed and range of the cargo ship also gave them an advantage in commerce. The simultaneous development of a cargo ship which incorporated all those beneficial features of the fighting ship meant that the Vikings could move goods at lower costs than had previously been the case in Scandinavia. Crew requirements fell sharply with the adoption of sailing ships. The cargo ship did not imply a great loss in speed compared to the rowing barge. Luxury goods could then be moved marginally slower for a sizeable saving in costs. That made it possible to ship such goods greater distances out into the Atlantic, and still do so at a profit for the trader. The Vikings continued with the same trading pattern and goods as the Frisians. In fact some of their raiding voyages to the West may just have been voyages to get manufactures from the Rhineland. The Vikings added to the collection of luxury goods handled by the Frisians other luxury items from the East, from Persia and the Byzantine Empire, brought by river through Russia to the Baltic and then re-exported to western Europe. The Vikings sold furs and slaves from the North around the Black Sea for silver coins and the spices and silks of the Orient. They also traded in some bulkier goods. The capacity of 50 tons was enough to make economic the export of dried cod from Iceland by about 1000, thus saving the colony from disaster since to that time there was no export good and the balance-of-payments deficit with the Continent was impoverishing the settlers. The success of Scandinavian colonies in Russia depended less on improvements in ship design, that is once the basic *karv* had been developed, than on the internal political situation. Scandinavian trade routes stretched over such great distances were highly vulnerable to disruption.[18] The result of Viking voyages was to extend the realm of northern trade, to promote the full integration of Scandinavia into a northern trading network and to intensify trade within that network. The emergence of northern Europe about the year 1000 from the difficulties, political and economic, of the preceding 150 years was certainly a result of the end of raids by Vikings in their warships. But it was also a result of the ability of Scandinavians to turn their new type of vessel to commercial advantage.[19] Despite improvements in both the cargo ship and the warship and despite the advantage of the design, the Scandinavian type was still capable of only limited services. The warship had to be beached at night since there were no quarters for the crew. There was no protection for anyone on board on long voyages. The vessels could not sail in the winter. Skippers of cargo ships waited in port until they had a favourable breeze. Though cargo ships could carry up to 50 tons this was still not a very large payload. In the tenth century that did not present a problem but in the years after 1000 it became clearer that the essential design of the Viking ship was not capable of development into an effective carrier for the bulk goods of the northern trade.

At the end of the tenth century quays began to be built again in northern Europe, for the first time since the end of Roman rule. This too was an indication that the Viking ship was not able to solve all transport problems. Viking ships were beached and goods then unloaded along a gangplank. The same was true with hulks and keels. Thus ports were typically an open piece of beach or shore without obstructions. To supplement facilities there might also be sledges and a windlass to help haul the vessel on shore.[n] The method was simple and predated Roman times.[20] Viking ships were ideal for this type of port facility. But so long as only that simple type of loading place was used, there was a limit to the size and carrying capacity of ships. A large ship could not be beached without taking grave risks. The cog with its flat bottom and without a keel could not use a simple beach, so builders could not experiment with that type built for waters with sandbanks and tidal harbours outside a limited area. The simple form of loading place made it hard to handle cargo and still keep it from getting wet. Time available for shifting goods was limited by the tides, and it took a great deal of manpower to move cargoes on and off ships. Quays appear in written records in the early eleventh century so presumably they were first built not long before 1000. In the course of the eleventh century quays were built in the major ports of the North and Baltic Seas, thus providing opportunities for moving more goods more safely and for building larger ships. Using a simple see-saw device — cranes did not appear until the thirteenth century — goods could be shifted in the same amount of time using fewer men.[21] Stevedoring became a less important task for sailors. With the introduction of quays, ships of the Scandinavian type lost one advantage which had recommended them. Designers no longer had to incorporate the ability to be beached into their ships. With that constraint removed it was to their advantage to pursue quite different designs from the Scandinavian type.

For southern Europe in the ninth and tenth centuries comparison with the North is almost impossible. The differences in ship design were dramatic and obvious in almost every feature: the steering system, the method and form of propulsion and the design of the hull and its supports. It was not the climate alone which made for this distinction. Differences were also generated by a dissimilarity in the demand for transport of goods and men. Certainly luxuries formed the most valuable portion of goods transported in both regions. But in the North these tended to be manufactures from handicraft industries in the region. In the South where such industries were more widespread there was less need to distribute these goods. The luxuries shipped in the South were typically the products of the Orient, silks and the spices which could only be grown in south and southeast Asia. In general trade goods, even luxuries, were of higher value per unit volume in the Mediterranean than in the North. The conversion to using barrels for moving bulk goods, however, came earlier and more fully in the North than in the South. All these factors and the different political situation, along with the stronger influence of Roman designs, combined to make ships of the Mediterranean a collection quite distinct from those of the North.

The Byzantine navy continued to face the challenge of Muslim seapower. The challenge might wax and wane but the Byzantine warships remained consistent in design. The naval and commercial situation changed much for the worse in 827 when the Arabs conquered the island of Crete, thus gaining control of the major sailing route from Egypt and the eastern shore of the Mediterranean to the West. This placed them in a position to challenge Greek commercial vessels in the Aegean, and increased the pressure on the fleets of the themes set up to defend the coasts. The loss of trade, much of it transferred to Arab shippers, meant less money available in the Byzantine Empire for the theme fleets and the Imperial fleet at Constantinople. This, in turn, led to a decrease in the ability of Byzantium to deploy adequate protection along the trade routes and along the coast. The cost and the size of the navy grew but the expansion was not enough to overcome the Arab strategic advantages. The Mediterranean became a no man's land between Christian and Muslim naval forces with Crete as a base for pirates. Greek shippers were forced to rely on local trade and the use of coasters. The smaller vessels which had become typical cargo carriers in the Empire in the years to 750 remained throughout much of the ninth and tenth centuries the standard cargo carriers. The loss of Crete led to the loss of Sicily by the Byzantines. It was impossible for the navy to command the waters around that important outpost. The slow conquest by Arabs from North Africa was completed by their capture of the naval base at Syracuse in 878. Losses in the West also meant loss to the Byzantines of trade in the Tyrrhenian and later even the Adriatic Sea. The longest trading voyages of the eighth century were no longer feasible. For Greek shippers the average distance of a voyage must have fallen sharply.

After 870 the Byzantines, realising the importance of the loss of Crete, embarked on a vigorous naval counter-attack. Their goal was to re-establish the old borders, to pacify the Aegean, assure communications by sea there and above all to retake Crete. The last was accomplished in 961. It was followed by the recapture of Cyprus and re-establishment of Byzantium as the arbiter of affairs in the eastern Mediterranean.[22] The naval expansion also led Byzantine builders to increase the size of their warships. The larger size of oar-powered vessels in the tenth century made an important contribution to change in cargo ships. The recapture of Crete required enormous effort from Byzantium. The 960 expedition against the island included the largest Byzantine fleet ever fitted out. According to contemporaries there were 100 dromons, 200 other ships of all types armed with Greek fire and 307 transports. Some of the warships had as many as 250 rowers. Some of the supply ships were equipped with ramps to disembark horses quickly. This massive fleet could be assembled and fitted out in part because of improvements in Byzantine naval administration in the second half of the ninth century. A new command structure was combined with a reinforcement of the fleets of themes and granting the themes more autonomy.[23] All these developments completed the system of naval administration which was founded in the seventh century. The stability in the administration and organisation of the navy was reflected in the tenth century in a consistency of design and in the greater maximum size of Greek warships.

Despite the reopening of the sea lane from the Black Sea to the West and despite the return to Byzantine dominance of the eastern Mediterranean, Greek merchants and shippers were not able to seize the opportunities which the navy had created. Native merchants certainly did not suffer from the recapture of Crete but the situation of the eighth century was not restored. Byzantium proved unable by force of arms to reestablish a dominant position in south Italy; thus one end of the trade route was not within the scope of the Byzantine restrictive trading system. More important, though, was the government policy or perhaps lack of it which allowed more and more of the trade of the Empire to fall into the hands of foreigners and especially those just at the periphery. The government concern with restoring borders and the need to fight border wars led to a policy in the late tenth and early eleventh centuries of ignoring the fleet and the protection of commerce. Byzantium fitted out a strong navy only sporadically, at times when good administration was combined with enough money in the treasury. The decline in commerce also meant a shortage of skilled personnel for the navy. As early as 910 the navy recruited Russians in sizeable numbers. Those Varangians supplied manpower throughout the tenth and eleventh centuries. All in all, the Byzantine Empire was relatively passive in long-distance trade and Greek merchants did not trade outside the Empire.[24] So the Byzantine success in retaking Crete created as many, or more, possibilities for Italian as for Greek shippers and merchants.

In those circumstances as little improvement was to be expected in cargo ship design as in design of the ships of the Byzantine navy. The slow pace of development was another sign of the erosion of Byzantine maritime strength. There were instances of larger ships having an extra pair of steering oars at the bow to give a total of four.º The expansion in the control system was not matched by any change in the sails. One or two lateen sails, with three on the largest warships, was typical. The dromon retained its basic design. The variations were in size rather than in form. The *pamphyle* was the smallest combat galley with only some 40 men on board. The *chelandia* was a transport but descended from the fighting galley. It was a massive slow vessel, having four rows of oars with one row of benches above the other as in classical times and two men to each bench. The newest member of the family was the largest of the fighting galleys, the *pamphylon* or big dromon. The measurements were much the same as with earlier dromons, with length and draught only slightly increased. It carried more than 200 and as many as 300 men, was well armed and despite that was still faster than other galleys. The hull was more built up, thus improving sea-worthiness and reliability. The higher sides were to accommodate the extra row of benches for rowers. Thus there were 56 to 60 benches on each side. There were only a few of the two large types in the fleet but vessels on this scale were needed in the campaigns mounted against Crete for a half-century before it finally fell. The sheer size of these ships was impressive and Byzantines used that fact to gain diplomatic advantages.[25] By 1000 the naval forces of the Fatimids of Egypt had at least been able to check Byzantine naval power. The result was a stability of relationships, a stability in the navy and naval administration and a stability in ship design.

The Byzantines had to face another threat at sea, this one from the Russians in the Black Sea. Because of the volume of trade and the size and character of the population of the Black Sea littoral this challenge did not generate anything like the problems of that from the Arabs. The Russians probably used vessels of Scandinavian design, specifically the *karv*. Russian armadas attacked Constantinople four times between 860 and 1043 but they were able to mount such an assault only when the Byzantine navy had been weakened in action elsewhere. Still, the threat from the north further complicated Byzantine naval defence and required the maintenance of a flotilla of small, highly mobile galleys to patrol the Black Sea. The Russians, like the Vikings in northwestern Europe, were divided on whether they were interested in plunder or in trade. Typically, attacks against Byzantium were followed by the renewal of trading arrangements. Russian naval strength was, after all, based on exactly those ships used to carry goods along the rivers north to the Baltic. In any case, it appears that Byzantine shipbuilders had ample opportunity to see the building style of northern Europeans. Scandinavians trading and fighting in the Black and Mediterranean Seas, both for and against Byzantium, had ample opportunity to observe the design of southern ships. Despite that, the two approaches to ship design remained distinct.

By the end of the tenth century the shortage of timber had become an acute problem for the Arabs. The loss of Crete and, soon after, Cyprus to the Byzantine Empire was a major factor in denying them supplies of shipbuilding timber. The attempt by the Fatimids to dominate the Mediterranean, their attacks on Byzantium, on Italy and on Spain in the ninth and tenth centuries, all increased the demand for ship timber. The contest over Crete in the middle of the tenth century, leading to the use of larger ships, placed an even greater strain on already stretched supplies throughout the Muslim world from Mesopotamia to Spain. The control of the principal east-west trade route in the Mediterranean had given them access to stores from Sicily and North Africa, including iron and timber; it meant expansion of the merchant marine, a source of skilled manpower for the navy and a prosperity which was a source of finance for the navy, and it also meant a greater demand for wood. Even during the period of their naval dominance in the ninth century Arabs were forced to import wood from Italy, Dalmatia and Anatolia. Crete itself was a major source of timber, supplying cypress for building galleys on the island and in Egypt, and it was also the centre of the wood trade. When it fell to Byzantium the Muslim position became critical. Recognising this, Byzantine emperors tried to prevent the export of timber and other naval stores from the Empire and from Italy through Venice. Though the embargo was only partially effective it certainly served to aggravate Muslim difficulties. Areas which had been sources of timber in the seventh and eighth centuries increasingly showed signs of deforestation. Transhumance, introduced in some cases by nomads, contributed to deforestation in many areas. Government efforts to control the cutting and use of the limited timber supplies in areas of greatest shortage, for example in Egypt, did not solve the problem of precariousness of supply. The reconquest of Crete and of Cyprus and of northern Syria by the Byzantines meant that Egypt, the naval centre of the Fatimid Empire, was reduced to importing wood all the way from India and smuggling contraband wood from Venice.[26] High prices were the result of those difficulties and led to the decline of Fatimid naval power in the late tenth and eleventh centuries. Presumably at the same time, there was a decrease in the number and size of commercial vessels. Muslim builders had generally built ships larger than those of the Greeks. They probably had little trouble in scaling down those designs to comply with the change in demand since the vessels used by Muslims in the Indian Ocean, while similar to those of the Mediterranean, had always been smaller.

Shipwrights in the Arab states, however, failed to overcome, through design change or through invention, the shortage of wood supplies. Losing a source of a major raw material has often proved to be a force for directing technical change into efforts to save or replace that good. It did not happen with the Muslims or for that matter with any other builders in the middle ages. Technology in related fields had not reached the point of presenting a viable alternative to wood for hulls and masts. At the same time there were always builders − in the case of the Muslims it was Italians − who had abundant sources of wood and who could use that advantage to offer vessels at lower prices, thus creating a fall in orders for builders already short of timber and so decreasing their chances for developing designs which would save wood. Marginal savings could be made, of course, but those would lead to increased risk and at some point the probability of loss would outweigh any saving. The easiest way to save wood was to build larger ships, thus decreasing the amount of wood required for each ton shipped. There were two problems with that solution. First, the conditions which accompanied a wood shortage were exactly opposite to those which promoted construction of larger ships. A decline in the volume of commerce, the loss of major long-distance trade routes and the presence of many shipbuilders looking for work for their yards, all decreased profitability and the likelihood of the construction of large ships. Second, larger ships typically had to be built from larger trees to get strong enough frames. Generally a wood shortage meant a shortage especially of just those bigger, taller and thicker trees. Moreover, in the middle ages the loss of a supply of a raw material did not, as in the last two centuries, occur in a short period of time. Governments could not close off supplies instantly and wars were not so general as completely to stop the movement of goods. Egypt, after all, was still able to import wood from Dalmatia through Venice and from India and that mitigated against the pressure to change designs. Slow deterioration does not apparently have the same effect on technicians as a sudden shock. Throughout the middle ages the loss of wood supplies or the long-term increase in the cost of such supplies formed the one problem which builders and designers never overcame. Invention never allowed shipbuilding to escape from reliance on abundant supplies of wood. The deterioration of supplies led, with the rarest of exceptions, to the deterioration of shipbuilding. It was a recurrent pattern in medieval Europe and the Renaissance.

The re-establishment of Byzantine naval strength and the decline of the Fatimid navy were in part the cause of a change in the character of piracy in the eastern Mediterranean. The western part of the sea did not completely escape the shift. Throughout the tenth century piracy usually meant coastal raids. Ships were used to carry men to the district selected, the men disembarked, carried out their raid and returned to the ships. The practice of descending on the coast not only damaged shipping and commerce but also led to the impoverishment of many areas along the shores. The fleets of the Byzantine themes were originally set up to meet precisely that threat. The original Arab fleets, especially in the western Mediterranean, were pirate flotillas. The effectiveness of the Byzantine navy in dislodging pirates and in protecting the coasts, combined with a declining interest among Arabs in what was, at best, a dangerous profession, turned piracy after the tenth century from coastal raiding into the more familiar method of attacking ships at sea. The Muslims were apparently the first to make the change. It made piracy easier and, if commerce was lively, more profitable. The process was a slow one but change did present entirely new problems to governments, shipbuilders and shipowners.[27] Defence against piracy became more complex. The coast-guard fleets of the Byzantines lost much of their value. Pirates became by definition involved in sporadic activity. Their ability to strike at almost any point at almost any time left governments without effective methods to deal with them. Coastal raiders had often stayed for some time sweeping the countryside so it was possible to reinforce local defences or bring up reserves to trap the pirates. Such options were no longer open. For shipbuilders defensibility of ships became a more pressing requirement. The two simple solutions, increased size and increased speed, were seemingly contradictory for sailing ships, but this was not necessarily the case. Large crews which could fight off attacks became more of an advantage, and contributed to the trend towards larger galleys. Longships were kept in use for carrying goods which could not be called luxuries. A galley was, after all, much more manoeuvrable and defensible than a sailing ship with the same capacity. For shipowners there was a significant addition to costs, as they had to use ships which were larger than needed for the job or retain a crew larger than needed to handle the vessel or simply pay bribes to pirates when they came alongside the ship threatening to take it. The response of using larger galleys was apparently typical also in the western Mediterranean.

The design of ships there continued to follow Roman and earlier Byzantine traditions. Venice, for example, the most successful port in the western Mediterranean in the ninth and tenth centuries, was still legally a part of the Byzantine Empire. Though political ties loosened over time, the commercial ones increased. In the years from 900 there were signs of a general expansion in the commerce of towns in the western Mediterranean, and, more than that, of a counter-attack by seamen from certain Italian towns against the naval power of the Muslims. The economic and naval difficulties of Byzantium while Crete was in Arab hands gave Italian merchants and pirates an opportunity to make inroads into traditionally Greek trading areas. The Italians, and especially the Venetians, did not hesitate to trade with Muslims and over time they were able to establish themselves as the intermediaries of trade between the eastern and western Mediterranean. After 961, despite the capture of Crete, the Byzantines found themselves relying on Italian merchants and Italian towns to handle their trade with the West and to maintain contact with the Muslim markets.

The towns of the Campanian coast of Italy were from the early ninth century involved in fighting and trading with Muslims in Sicily, and were forced into a policy of destroying Muslim pirate nests when they were established on the Italian mainland. The next step was to attack Muslims on the islands of the western Mediterranean and along the African coast. Towns further north, especially Pisa and Genoa, became most active in that fighting in the tenth century. They acted like traditional pirates descending on coastal districts. All this contributed to the development of indigenous naval and commercial strength, something which Byzantium found it could not control.[28] Even though the Greeks lost the carrying trade to Italian shippers, Byzantine industry, agriculture and trade were as prosperous as ever in the past, thus giving shippers more goods to carry.

Since towns like Pisa and Genoa were committed to piratical attacks against the Muslims they used warships — warships like those of the Byzantines. Venice too, because of problems with pirates in the Adriatic, found it had to maintain a navy. The ships used by Venice were of the larger type like the *pamphylon* and the *chelandia* developed in the East in the tenth century. These bigger galleys had a more extensive superstructure, something like castles built up above the decks, which allowed marines to fire down on the enemy. Greek fire and heavy catapults were apparently not used as naval weapons. Simpler spears, rocks and arrows were the standard missiles. Rig remained the same: two masts each carrying one lateen sail. There were two banks of rowers and the arrangement of rowers was the same as in the earlier dromons. The ports on the west coast of Italy, at least in the eighth century, did not deploy dromons like the Byzantines, so they were probably still using galleys of the Roman Liburnian type. By the tenth century, however, they had adopted something more like the typical dromon design but lower, wider and faster. The development and extensive use of these larger types gave Italian towns, and especially Venice, a naval advantage over Muslims. It allowed her, over time, to pursue a policy increasingly independent of that of Byzantium. The larger warships also offered examples of a type with greater carrying capacity which could be turned effectively to commercial use with a minimum danger of piratical attack. Though the inspiration for these larger galleys may have originally been naval, generated by the contest between Byzantium and the Fatimids, it was turned to the greatest advantage by Italian traders to carry their increasing share of the east-west trade through the Mediterranean. Such vessels are mentioned as carrying 1,000 men and more and, therefore, when they were not fitted out as warships, there was certainly space for a sizeable cargo.[29]

As commercial vessels these ships served to bring back luxuries from Byzantium and especially from Constantinople itself. Along with the spices of the Orient the Italians brought back manufactures from Byzantine shops and agricultural products not easily acquired in the West. The West sent timber, iron and slaves in exchange but that was probably not enough to cover the cost of goods imported from the East. Given the relative value of the goods, most ships probably left the West filled and returned with a good deal of empty cargo space. There was another trade added to these, that in pilgrims. The idea of religious pilgrimages was already established in Latin Christendom in the sixth century. But it expanded in the tenth century, in part thanks to a general religious revival and the emphasis placed on pilgrimages by the monastic reform movement of the Cluniacs. Pilgrimages were no longer limited just to Compostella in northwestern Spain or to Rome, both usually reached by land, but were expanded to include the ultimate in pilgrimages, that to the Holy Land. The Muslims who held the Holy Land did not object to such pilgrimages and in no way tried to prevent them. The groups of pilgrims were large and the total number of trips grew over time. The new larger galley was well suited to carrying these people. Its speed was an asset since the health of everyone was at risk at sea. The longer one spent on the voyage the greater was the likelihood of disease. The vessels still stayed close to the coast, moving only cautiously into open water. The masters needed landmarks to guide them and with such large numbers of people on board the ships had to stop at night.

The pilgrim trade added the final element to the basis for Italian commercial expansion, expansion which would continue throughout the thirteenth century. The growth began in the context of maritime disorder, of piracy and war at sea by rival powers seeking the support and aid of the Italian towns. Faced with this atmosphere of disorder the Italian port towns and more specifically the shipbuilders in those ports borrowed designs which were best suited to deal with naval action. They had the basis of known designs and they could borrow design features from other parts of the Mediterranean. But the need for effective fighting ships set stringent limits on their ability to borrow and to develop ship types.

Mediterranean shipbuilders converted to carvel-building. The carvel-built ships retained the edge-to-edge planking typical of Roman ships. But first tentative steps taken in the sixth century towards greater reliance on internal structure for support of the hull by 1000 had changed to almost complete use of the frames to give the ship strength and form. The planking was then just a covering to keep the water out. The change was exclusive to the Mediterranean Sea. Some ships were only partially carvel-built, where the shell had some vestigial function in protecting the vessel and holding its shape. Undoubtedly Mediterranean builders gradually, through experiment, moved towards complete skeleton construction. A ship excavated at Serçe Liman off the coast of Turkey and dated 1024/1025 shows no sign of the old Roman technique of mortise and tenon joints to create a stiff hull. Rather it had heavy frames and light planking attached to them with nails or small treenails. The vessel was a sailing ship of moderate size, about 17 metres long over all. In 1000 not all ships built in the Mediterranean were of pure skeleton build but by that date it was clear that carvel-building would be the typical construction method for all vessels beyond the smallest in that part of Europe. The skeleton system was unique to southern Europe, developed there and diffused from there. At least Mediterranean carvel-building had moved to the stage where after the keel and posts were fixed many, if not all, of the frames were set up. They were then connected to each other and to the posts by one or two heavy side planks, wales, running the length of the ship.[P] Then the hull planking was added.[30]

Skeleton construction started at least by the early years of the Byzantine Empire. It was impossible to support the many highly skilled workers needed to build the fine piece of furniture that was a Roman ship, so the Roman construction method was gradually abandoned. It was not necessary to give up shell construction completely because the demand for shipping tonnage fell. The loss of skilled ship carpenters did not press the adoption of extreme design changes to save labour. In the second half of the tenth century the volume of trade, at least in Italy and to some degree in Byzantium, did rise. Shipbuilders then faced a demand for a larger number of ships. That alone might have put pressure on the available supply of skilled ship carpenters. Added to it, however, was the need to build the ships more quickly to meet the needs of sporadic naval campaigns and, equally important, there was a demand for bigger ships. The greater size in tonnage and also in height out of the water meant that designers had to find a way to support the bigger unit. The solution was to move fully to the use of the skeleton to supply strength. For skeleton-building the shaping of the keel, posts and frames required skill of the highest level. The addition of the planking, on the other hand, could be done by carpenters with less knowledge and experience. The latter work was relatively simple since the frames gave the form. The planks, after being cut to shape, were nailed to the frames. Strakes were scarfed so mistakes could be corrected without great difficulty. This led, in the course of the eleventh and twelfth centuries, to a division among ship carpenters, with some retaining the status of designers of ships and others being relegated to more repetitive tasks. This latter group must have been relatively easy to generate since population was rising and the training period for such men did not have to be long. With edge-to-edge hull planking and with no connection between the planks, the ship had to be caulked, caulked well and caulked again at regular intervals. This maintenance work could also be handled by men with lesser training. The same was true of the replacement of planks which had been attacked by the shipworm. The change in construction from the Roman method meant a big saving in the labour costs of building a ship. Weighed against that were rises in the cost of maintenance and probably an increase in risk. This change to skeleton-building was a sign of greater technical skill, of an ability to develop an alternative type of construction suited to the immediate demands of shippers. It did not show a technical superiority to Roman shipbuilding, however. After all, the Italians of the tenth century were not called on to build cargo ships anything like as large as those of the Romans.

Skeleton construction was used for sailing ships as well as for galleys.

The round ships used in the Roman and early Byzantine Empire had their descendants which were used primarily for the carriage of bulk goods. The much lower length-to-beam ratio compared to the galley gave the type its distinctive shape. There was a pair of steering oars and one mast with a lateen sail. In general these vessels were used over short distances; they also stayed small. That is not to say that the total volume of bulk carriage was insignificant. Rather, these types relied on frequent trips rather than a large hold to keep up the volume of goods moved annually. Expansion in total output, an increase in demand for tonnage and the example of the larger size of naval vessels contributed to a probable increase in the average size of these round ships. But they still remained far below their maximum potential size, a potential which was increased by the adoption of skeleton construction.

The form and character of demand for ships was different in northern and southern Europe. Shipbuilders faced different requirements in the two parts of Europe and so the ships they built evolved along distinct paths. There were similarities in some of the results. Since all shipbuilders sought to increase the capability or efficiency of the vessels they built, the outcome of better designs was to expand the economic possibilities. The rise in the value of trade, usually accompanied by an increase in volume, led directly to an improvement in total welfare. But the character of design changes had some effect on how that improvement was distributed.

The Viking ship was the product of the demand of aristocrats, of Scandinavian landowners, for a vessel which could do everything that contemporary coasters and fishing boats could do plus have the capacity to carry their kinship groups. The vessel produced for them satisfied those needs and more. The Viking ship was effective for trading and for raiding. The success of the first raids increased the tempo of such operations against western Europe. In the East the success of the first trading expeditions into Russia had the same effect of promoting the use of this type. The Vikings started out as amorphous groups of pirates or traders but after their first successes they began to have some cohesion. More important than that, the unit of operation of these men became the group in the sailing ship; this was the effective fighting or trading unit. It was the mutual reliance of these men in each vessel which gradually took precedence over the mutual reliance of the kinship group. A naval or military unit replaced the family unit, and meant a deterioration in the power of the aristocrats over their relatives and especially over dependants who worked on or near their lands. The naval power which came with the improved ship brought about the establishment of some naval organisation. That organisation was not based on the independent action of aristocrats, however, but on the action of ships, of units of a naval force in the service of some monarch. The embryonic Scandinavian kingdoms which had emerged by 900 did not owe their existence to the design of the Viking ship. But the ability of the kings to mobilise forces to defeat powerful aristocrats and to contest for the loyalty of their followers did depend on the way fighting and trading were carried on with that vessel. By the end of the tenth century Viking attacks were not the piracy of independent freebooters but rather raids organised and directed by a monarch as part of an over-all political strategy. This change derived in part from the unique development of Scandinavian ship design in the eighth and ninth centuries.

The construction of ships became more complex. This was most noticeable in western and northern Europe where the entire business of shipbuilding and also of shipping took on some of the attributes which had long been familiar in the Byzantine Empire. The larger number and larger average size of ships and the longer distance of the voyages contributed to changing what had been a simple matter into an operation involving many people in different capacities. Trade at sea and, more important, the maintenance of a naval force now required more personnel, more skilled personnel and an administrative apparatus far beyond the capabilities of western European governments of the seventh and eighth centuries. Governments of states with a coast or governments of politically independent towns had a new task to perform, to protect and defend their shores and their merchants' ships. Many of the new governments, for example the increasingly localised governments of France, failed to take on the task. But governments such as the English monarchy, the monarchies of Scandinavia and especially a number of Italian port cities found that maritime operations and naval power were an integral part of their existence, their welfare and their prosperity. Albeit tentatively, they developed some kind of naval policy. They emerged with governments noticeably different from those of states tied just to the land. The political units with maritime connections had different sources of income, different types of expenditure and a different perception of their function as governments, all of which made them more than just givers and enforcers of laws.

The increase in the percentage of the population living in towns, a trend which became clear by the end of the tenth century in western and northern Europe, was a logical result of the improvements made in

ships through the eighth, ninth and tenth centuries. The Viking *karv*
and the knarr made possible profitable trade from Scandinavia to the
Near East and into the North Atlantic, to Iceland, Greenland and North
America. These trading connections were highly fragile. The volume of
trade was small. The goods, be they silver coins from Persia or white
falcons and polar bears from Baffin Island, were of high value and could
rarely form the basis for a continuing trade in bulk. The nature of the
trade and the long distances involved meant these routes were highly
susceptible to changes in weather and the more expected changes in the
political climate. Despite that, they did expand the scope of trade and
of European trade goods. That extension at the geographic margin led
to the intensification of trade at the centre. The ships built in the ninth
and tenth centuries were as efficient or more efficient in terms of annual
costs to move a ton of goods than were their predecessors; this led to an
increase in the volume of trade in the North. There is every indication
that the volume of goods which changed hands in the Mediterranean
also increased, even if some of those goods were originally seized by
force by Italian or Muslim pirates.

The extension and expansion of trade allowed for greater specialisation in production or at least created the possibility for farmers or
manufacturers to find a market for any surplus they might produce.
Shipping was not inexpensive enough for consumers to rely on long-
distance transport of essential supplies. Those were still produced within small regions. On the other hand, there was an opportunity to
expand any specialist local production, such as the manufacture of glass
or of woollen or silk textiles. Those industries then found it to their
advantage to be located in a port or in a town easily accessible to waterborne transport. In the tenth century there is some evidence that industry inland which relied on local markets and transport overland declined
relative to industry near the coast.[31] While, in the Mediterranean, industry had never become as localised as that in northern Europe, there is
still some suggestion in the growth of ports like Venice, Amalfi, Pisa
and a number of others that the process there was similar.

Towns along the shore could not grow when they were under constant threat of attack from pirates. A city the size of Constantinople,
which was sure to be defended by the government, was not in danger.
But for most towns, and especially smaller port towns, there was a good
chance of being raided. The situation was the same along shorelines
held by Christians or by Muslims since both sides indulged in piracy. It
was impossible to defend most ports since they lay in the open and
were often surrounded by hills. The only way to protect the population

was to hold that high ground. The simple solution, and one followed through much of Italy, the Balkans and Asia Minor, was for people to move to the hills and protect themselves behind fortress walls. The change in the methods of piracy after the tenth century decreased the direct threat to the stability and safety of life in smaller ports. The change in political circumstances, along with the development of ships which contributed to that change in piracy, created an opportunity to return to a secure life for many urban dwellers. Such towns could expand since town sites did not have to be periodically abandoned. It was the same kind of movement back to the shoreline which was simultaneously promoted by the economics of shipping. In northern Europe the depredations of the Vikings were similar to those of Arab pirates. Certainly these attacks did not help urbanisation at ports such as Dorestad, which Vikings raided and burned until it was no longer worth bothering with. Still, the Vikings, because of their interest in trade, did generate urban centres within Scandinavia. The Vikings did bring towns to Ireland where they had not existed before. Moreover, the general economic recovery in the North in the second half of the tenth century and, more important, the change in the character of Viking attacks from hit-and-run raids to the organised deployment of forces for political gain gave something like the same result as that in the Mediterranean, that is after the tenth century.

Port facilities improved throughout Europe. Not only were quays built again for the first time in the North since the Roman withdrawal but also harbours were restored or improved in the South. Town governments such as those in Italy, realising the importance of trade to their prosperity, devoted more effort to keeping up docks. Private individuals could and did do the same. Throughout western Europe by 1000 there was a turnaround in the quality of ports. The process of deterioration and simplification was checked and a start was made on improving facilities. Mediterranean ship types were well suited to quays but they could also be beached and then unloaded and loaded. This had all the same problems of inefficiency as in the North. The lack of tides in the Mediterranean meant that the ship had to be hauled out of the water — effort which could be saved by using quays. The improvement of port facilities was a logical concomitant of larger towns, of the tendency towards urbanisation. At the same time those facilities could act to draw ships and trade to a port. The greater concentration of population in port towns, the concentration of trade goods and merchants in those towns and the better facilities for the exchange and shipment of goods, all meant that shippers could find a cargo more easily. The time spent in port could fall and so the total quantity of goods moved annually by a ship could rise. That implied a saving to the shipowner and a saving to society in total resources needed for a given quantity of transport. The trend of the years before 750 had then been reversed. The trend became clearer after 1000.

The choice of carvel-building for ships by Mediterranean builders and shipowners did not decrease the number of shipbuilders. Rather, over time, it increased the need for men to carry out the more frequent repairs. The absolute and relative rise in the number of shipbuilding workers in port towns made the industry more important to the economy of ports. Moreover, shippers had to use ports where they could be sure of finding men to do repair work. Certainly, a skipper along with his crew could do much of the periodic caulking and the irregular repairs to a ship. He could still use small ports or the beaches for docking. But there was clear pressure on skippers to use ports with repair facilities, ports with a body of men able and available to do caulking and repair work. There was, then, a long-term trend towards the concentration of trade in larger ports, a tendency which was by its nature cumulative and self-reinforcing. The improvements in design, the extension of trade routes, increased specialisation in production, the changing character of piracy, the move to carvel-building in the Mediterranean, all contributed to an increased urbanisation. The development of towns and the concentration of population was not so much because of the increase in total production and total population but because of the rise in the total quantity of goods carried by water. Agriculture could never generate urbanisation on a sizeable scale. Commerce on land was too flexible to force the concentration of people into specific locations with specific geographical features the way seaborne commerce did.

The larger galleys of the western Mediterranean in the hands of Italian merchants and skippers proved to be profitable carriers of goods. The expansion of the total volume of trade and the effective naval action which drove Muslim naval forces and pirates back from the major sea lanes contributed to the greater possibilities for successful, that is profitable, shipping operations. Investment in shipping, which meant principally an investment in the ship itself, therefore rose both absolutely and relatively. In northern and southern Europe, but especially in the South, there was an alternative to investment in land. That is not to say that there was no investment in ships before the tenth century. But in previous centuries the money was usually raised by the skipper himself and possibly with the help and co-operation of a merchant. The new-found profitability of trade in Italy drew in a new group of investors, men who otherwise had nothing to do with trade or ships. Traditionally their investment had been entirely in land. Land remained for them and for the economy in general the overwhelming stock of productive capital. The alternative of investing in commerce was, in part, because of improvements in ship design. It was an attractive alternative in terms of immediate return and potential return since possibilities in shipping were certainly expanding more rapidly than in agriculture. The development of the Viking ship had a similar effect but with the added result that the landowners became not only owners of ships but also active in their operation.

The development of improved ships allowed for the diversification of investment by the rich, especially noticeable in Italy. This served to lessen the division between merchants and landowners. In northern Europe professional merchants had been attached to a single nobleman or monastery and acted as the supplier of goods for that specific consumer. The consumers had little part in the operations of trade. The distinction decreased through the ninth and tenth centuries. It was never as extreme in southern Europe but any indication of such a separation economically and socially was further eroded by the introduction of landowners as passive investors in ships and in trading ventures. Landowners then became involved in the same activities as merchants. Merchants presumably seized their earliest opportunity to join in the same activities as landowners by diversifying their own investments into land. In northern Europe there emerged a body of professional merchants, men who devoted their full energies to shipping and trade. They were not tied to or supported by one specific customer. They were not part-time farmers who did some sailing and trading in the summer to supplement their incomes. Their operations took on a new permanence. That professionalisation of traders undoubtedly existed in the South, indeed it may never have disappeared through the early middle ages. But the improvements in ships, the growth of trade and the participation of other investors all served to intensify the professionalisation of merchants, to make their function more important and to improve their own position both socially and politically. That pattern became more obvious in the following 250 years.

The increased capital requirements and the participation of landowners generated group ownership of vessels, and thus distributed the risk. Part ownership, the division of ownership among a number of shares, 8, 16, 32, was known in the Roman Empire so it was not a novelty in the middle ages.[32] It was little used in the early middle ages, however, because of the small scale of investment. The rise in risk

relative to Roman ships increased the need for such a division of ownership. Even stronger pressure came from the need to raise greater quantities of capital. Ships were never cheap but the increasing size of cargo
galleys in the tenth century made the need to find new sources of financial support crucial to successful shipping operations. The general result
was a broadening of investment to include more people and people with
more different types of income and wealth. This was more and more
the case as ships became more expensive and the number of ships
increased. It is perhaps easy to overemphasize the importance of investment in ships relative to land or to armament on board or to cargoes.
The point, however, is that investment in ships rose over time and an
increasing share of all European investment went into ships. The presence of the necessary capital and its mobilisation made possible the use
of novel ship designs.

Many Italian towns began their expansion by piratical activities, by
attacking Muslim traders and towns to seize goods. This was certainly
less true of Venice than, for example, Pisa but the Venetian government did not hesitate to raise a fleet and become involved in fighting
when it was thought that there was a threat to the trading position of
Venetian merchants. The governments of Italian towns typically became
committed to a policy of violence, to the protection and support of
those men whose function was violence at sea. Indeed it was those very
men, enriched by their acts of piracy and settled down to a life of
trading or of owning land, who came to be the administrators of the
towns. The ships which these men used, the increasingly large galleys
modelled on the Byzantine dromon, were easily used for war. They
were fully interchangeable and could be converted from the carriage of
goods or pilgrims to warships in a matter of minutes. With such vessels
in use, the result was that violence became an integral part of maritime
policy. The Vikings in the North had ships which enjoyed, to some
degree, the same dual capabilities of warship and cargo ship, or at least
troop transport. The Vikings found it difficult to comprehend a difference between trading and raiding. In the Mediterranean, while that
distinction might be perceived, the character of the ships in use was
even less constraining in the ability to shift from one to the other. The
political instability around the Mediterranean, the failure of Byzantium
to maintain protection for shipping throughout the ninth and first half
of the tenth century, and the religious undertones of the contest helped
to make fighting at sea a fully accepted part of life. By 1000 a level of
peace had been restored in the Mediterranean. Trading could and did
become the typical function of merchants and of shippers. But the

design of the ships did not change with the increase in stability. The potential for violent action remained. Nor did town government policy change. Violence was always a part of the thought and action of the governments of Italian port towns. Since they had the equipment they could and they did use their naval potential to gain trade advantages. That was a typical feature of Mediterranean commerce in the following centuries. It placed a new demand on shipbuilders to produce ships which could bring a return to investors and still be used against pirates, against Muslims and, increasingly important, against commercial competitors.

NOTES

1. Ole Crumlin-Pedersen, 'The Viking Ships of Roskilde', *Aspects of the History of Wooden Shipbuilding*, The National Maritime Museum, Greenwich, Maritime Monographs and Reports, no. 1 (1970), p. 11. He thinks there was no difference between the English keel and the Scandinavian cargo vessel but, given the dates of development and later illustrations, a strict correlation is doubtful. *FHMN*, pp. 47-58, 89; his claim for independent and parallel development in England and Scandinavia seems more likely. Valerie H. Fenwick, 'The Graveney boat. A pre-conquest discovery in Kent', *IJNA*, I (1972), pp. 119-29. The stempost has been lost so it can only be assumed that it was fixed at a right angle like the sternpost. The keel did extend for the full length of the vessel, 6.5 metres. It was only .08 metres thick, however, and .445 metres across. See also Valerie H. Fenwick *et al.*, *Three Major Ancient Boat Finds in Britain*, pp. 9-25. Basil Greenhill, 'The Graveney Boat', *Sjøfartshistorisk Årbok* (1970), pp. 33-40; no maststep was found but there is every indication that there was a sizeable one resting on the floor timbers. *AB*, pp. 221-6.

2. Dorestad was the largest and most important town in Frisia. It had the chief toll station of the Carolingian Empire, the mint for the area of the lower Rhine, and itself covered twelve hectares, which incidentally made it less than half the size of Hedeby. *FHMN*, pp. 237-8. Herbert Jankuhn, 'Der frankish-friesische Handel zur Ostsee im frühen Mittelalter', pp. 228-32, 237, and *Haithabu . . .*, pp. 148-9, 240-2. Dirk Jellema, 'Frisian Trade in the Dark Ages', pp. 30-4. Barbara Rohwer, *Der friesische Handel im frühen Mittelalter*, pp. 14-15, 32. Archibald R. Lewis, *The Northern Seas*, pp. 184-6, 190-200, 220-6, 296-7.

3. *FHMN*, pp. 17-23, 179-84. Dirk Jellema, 'Frisian Trade in the Dark Ages', pp. 25-6, 35; the colony system continued after 1000 with a Frisian trading guild at Sigtuna, the successor of Birka, and colonies in ports such as Bremen and Riga. J. F. Niermeyer, 'Het Midden-Nederlands rivierengebied in de Frankische tijd', *Tijdschrift voor Geschiedenis*, LXVI (1953), p. 168. There were four *scholae* of merchants at Rome and the Frisians were the last, following the Anglo-Saxons.

4. Barbara Rohwer, *Der friesische Handel im frühen Mittelalter*, pp. 75-87. Dirk Jellema, 'Frisian Trade in the Dark Ages', pp. 34-5. J. H. Holwerda, *Dorestad en Onze Vroegst Middeleeuwen* (A. W. Sijthoff's Uitgeversmij. N.V., Leiden, 1929), pp. 16-22, 135. He blames the shift of trade from Dorestad on a flood of 864 which changed the mouths of the Rhine. Such a change would have been more final than the attacks of Vikings. In any event the increasing competition from ports like Hamburg and Bremen in the North Sea and Dordrecht in Holland

after 1018 relegated Frisian trade to a position of lesser importance.

5. G. Asaert, *Westeuropese scheepvaart in de middeleeuwen* (Unieboek, Bussum, 1974), p. 19. His claim that this was the greatest breakthrough in shipbuilding of the period is not valid. A. W. Brøgger and Haakon Shetelig, *The Viking Ships, Their Ancestry and Evolution* (Dreyers Forlag, Oslo, 1971), p. 135. Archibald R. Lewis, *The Northern Seas*, pp. 262-3, 315. His suggestion that this type may have been inspired by Byzantine dromons must remain pure conjecture without any substantiating evidence. P. H. Sawyer, 'Wics, Kings and Vikings', in Thorsten Anderson and Karl Inge Sandred (eds), *The Vikings* (Uppsala University, Uppsala, 1978), p. 28. His suggestion that competition between merchants and pirates led to advances in ship design in this period is thrown into question by the failure of the merchants, the Frisians, to innovate despite the tremendous advances of the pirates, the Vikings.

6. Sibylla Haasum, *Vikingatidens Segling och Navigation*, pp. 57-8. Her complaint that scholars too easily accept claims for excellent sailing qualities for these ships is sound. The basis for her statement is questionable: Ole Crumlin-Pedersen, 'Viking Seamanship Questioned', *MM*, LXI (1975), pp. 130-1. A. W. Brøgger and Haakon Shetelig, *The Viking Ships*, pp. 91-2; in 1893, for example, a full-size replica of the Gokstad ship sailed from Norway to Chicago crossing the Atlantic in less than four weeks. Ole Crumlin-Pedersen, 'Two Danish Side Rudders', *MM*, LII (1966), p. 257.

7. Archibald R. Lewis, *Naval Power and Trade in the Mediterranean*, pp. 147-8, 197. The Viking ability to attack Iberia depended on the weakness of the navy of Ommayid Spain. See also Archibald R. Lewis, *The Northern Seas*, pp. 245-52, 285. Bailey W. Diffie, *Prelude to Empire* (University of Nebraska Press, Lincoln, 1960), pp. 6-8.

8. G. J. Marcus, 'The Navigation of the Norsemen , *MM*, XXXIX (1953), pp. 112, 117-31. Navigation was done by dead reckoning, probably aided by some simple method of measuring the height of the sun. If '*i* ings did have a compass it was a primitive affair giving only an indication of die tion and not consistently used for navigation. Roald Morcken, 'Europas eldste sjø..ierker', *Sjøfartshistorisk Årbok* (1969), pp. 7-48; the Scandinavians had marks on shore for navigation well before they appeared in the Mediterranean. Roald Morcken, 'Norse Nautical Units and Distance Measurements', *MM*, LIV (1968), pp. 393-401. His claims for the extensive use of celestial navigation by the Vikings are based on thirteenth-century sources. Sibylla Haasum, *Vikingatidens Segling och Navigation*, pp. 87-110; a number of other aids to navigation were used. E. G. R. Taylor, *The Haven-Finding Art*, pp. 65, 72-84. N. Rosenberg, 'The Direction of Technological Change: Inducement mechanisms and focusing devices', pp. 4-5, 10.

9. Olaf Olsen and Ole Crumlin-Pedersen, 'The Skuldelev Ships (II)', *Acta Archaeologica*, XXXVIII (1967), p. 118. Ole Crumlin-Pedersen, 'The Viking Ships of Roskilde', p. 11. *FHMN*, pp. 33-5, 118-19.

10. A. W. Brøgger and Haakon Shetelig, *The Viking Ships*, pp. 77-8, 85-6, 90-2. Olaf Olsen and Ole Crumlin-Pedersen, 'The Skuldelev Ships (II)', pp. 108, 155. Ole Crumlin-Pedersen, 'Two Danish Side Rudders', pp. 251-7. This type of rudder was superior to the later sternpost rudder in that it required less energy to turn it.

11. Ole Crumlin-Pedersen, 'Kaellingen og Kløften . . .', *Handels- og Søfarts-museets På Kronborg, Årbog* (1972), pp. 63-80. G.J. Marcus, 'The Navigation of the Norsemen', pp. 114-15. A. W. Brøgger and Haakon Shetelig, *The Viking Ships*, pp. 48, 86-94; on smaller Viking ships shrouds and stays may not have been used at all – the low aspect ratio rig could be held in place by the base alone. Sibylla Haasum, *Vikingatidens Segling och Navigation*, pp. 20-1, 59-83. For a more positive and at the same time more cautious view about the sailing qualities

of Viking ships, Erik Anderson, 'Hals og skaut mast og segl, Både og råsejilrigninger på Norskekysten', *Norsk Sjøfartsmuseum, Årsberetning* (1975), pp. 47-100.
   12. Romola and R. C. Anderson, *The Sailing-Ship*, pp. 70-6. A. W. Brøgger and Haakon Shetelig, *The Viking Ships*, pp. 79-99, 129; the word *karve*, Old Norse *karfi*, comes from the Greek *karabos*, Russian form *korabi*, and is mentioned for a number of expeditions by Scandinavians to the Black Sea. The type was well equipped to handle the river routes and portages of Russia. *AB*, pp. 211-14.
   13. On an experiment in reconstructing an exact replica of one of these boats, interesting especially for the method used, see Sean McGrail and Eric McKee, *The Building and Trials of the Replica of an Ancient Boat: The Gokstad Faering*, The National Maritime Museum, Greenwich, Maritime Monographs and Reports, no. 11 (1974), 2 parts.
   14. *HSUA*, pp. 166-8. A. W. Brøgger and Haakon Shetelig, *The Viking Ships*, pp. 104-15. *AB*, pp. 208-11.
   15. Knud Thorvildsen, *The Viking Ship of Ladby* (The National Museum, Copenhagen, 1967), pp. 5-6, 20-2. Olaf Olsen and Ole Crumlin-Pedersen, 'The Skuldelev Ships (II)', pp. 140-5. The measures reported in this survey have since been revised for the larger warship. It proved longer than expected. Ole Crumlin-Pedersen, 'The Viking Ships of Roskilde', pp. 8-9. *HSUA*, p. 184. The top three strakes of these warships were of ash which may explain why the English called the Vikings *aescmen*, *aesc* meaning ash.
   16. G. J. Marcus, 'The Evolution of the Knörr', *MM*, XLI (1955), pp. 116-17, 119-20. The knarr was also called the *hafskip*. See also G. J. Marcus, 'The Navigation of the Norsemen', pp. 112-15. *FHMN*, pp. 45-6, 257-62. Olaf Olsen and Ole Crumlin-Pedersen, 'The Skuldelev Ships, A preliminary report . . .', pp. 171-4, and 'The Skuldelev Ships (II)', pp. 108-9, 127-32.
   17. A. W. Brøgger and Haakon Shetelig, *The Viking Ships*, p. 76. The evidence for division of labour comes from a thirteenth-century writer describing events which occurred about the year 1000. Olaf Olsen and Ole Crumlin-Pedersen, 'The Skuldelev Ships (II)', pp. 160-1. W. L. Goodman, *The History of Woodworking Tools* (G. Bell and Sons Ltd, London, 1964), pp. 125-6, 131-2. Henry C. Mercer, *Ancient Carpenters' Tools*, third edn (The Bucks County Historical Society, Doyletown, Pennsylvania, 1960), pp. 14-17, 92-3; Norwegian boat builders continued to split their wood rather than saw it into the seventeenth century. Sean McGrail in *AB*, pp. 234-8.
   18. Herbert Jankuhn, 'Der fränkisch-friesische Handel zur Ostsee im frühen Mittelalter', pp. 231-6. Archibald R. Lewis, *The Northern Seas*, pp. 271-5, 349-82. Else Ebel, 'Kaufman und Handel auf Island zur Sagazeit', *Hansisches Geschichtsblätter* XCV (1977), pp. 1-21.
   19. *HSUA*, p. 183; Baltic commerce especially along the south coast was also increased by development both in design and number of Slavic vessels; the Scandinavians appear to have traded to Russia through Finland and avoided the south coast. *FHMN*, p. 89.
   20. The holes in the forepost of, for example, the Graveney boat may have been to take the rope from a windlass to haul it out of the water. Valerie H. Fenwick, 'The Graveney boat', p. 125. *FHMN*, pp. 138-46.
   21. *FHMN*, pp. 150-1, 158-69.
   22. Archibald R. Lewis, *Naval Power and Trade in the Mediterranean*, pp. 103-9, 132-42, 186-9. Hélène Ahrweiler, *Byzance et la mer*, pp. 35-9, 92-115; the loss of Crete was largely a result of internal political difficulties in the Byzantine Empire and not any long-term decline in Byzantine sea power. It was almost an accident, the island being taken by some freeboaters from Spain. Ekkehard Eickhoff, *Seekrieg und Seepolitik*, pp. 1-3, 65-70.

23. Hélène Antoniadis-Bibicou, *Etudes d'histoire maritime de Byzance*, pp. 98, 115-16. Hélène Ahrweiler, *Byzance et la mer*, pp. 97-9. Archibald R. Lewis, *Naval Power and Trade in the Mediterranean*, pp. 185-6. He gives a total figure for the fleet of 3,360 vessels, which seems too high. It comes from contemporary chronicles. Ekkehard Eickhoff, *Seekrieg und Seepolitik*, pp. 81-2. His total of 40,000 men for all Byzantine fleets is probably accurate.

24. Hélène Antoniadis-Bibicou, *Etudes d'histoire maritime de Byzance*, pp. 35-6, and 'Problèmes de la marine byzantine', p. 335. Hélène Ahrweiler, *Byzance et la mer*, pp. 102-3, 117. She is perhaps too positive about the revival of Byzantine shipping in the second half of the tenth century.

25. Louis Bréhier, 'La Marine de Byzance du VIIIe au XIe Siècle', pp. 12-15; a fleet including eleven *chelandia* carrying 1,450 soldiers was sent to south Italy to escort a mission to the Lombards – the show of strength was of course a bargaining ploy. G. La Roërie and J. Vivielle, *Navires et Marins*, p. 88. For figures on the size of the Byzantine navy see Hélène Ahrweiler, *Byzance et la mer*, pp. 91-2, and Hélène Antoniadis-Bibicou, *Etudes d'histoire maritime de Byzance*, pp. 92-4. Hélène Antoniadis-Bibicou, 'Problèmes de la marine byzantine', pp. 330-2, 336. Ekkehard Eickhoff, *Seekrieg und Seepolitik*, pp. 135-7, 147-8, 316, 342.

26. Archibald R. Lewis, *Naval Power and Trade in the Mediterranean*, pp. 150-63, 189. Maurice Lombard, 'Arsenaux et bois de marine dans la Méditerranée musulmane', *TCHM*, II, pp. 58-60, 64-7, 72-3, 81-97. Embargoes on the export of wood from Byzantium date from the start of the ninth century. Ekkehard Eickhoff, *Seekrieg und Seepolitik*, pp. 124-34.

27. Hélène Ahrweiler, *Byzance et la mer*, p. 269. She dates the change in piracy to the twelfth and thirteenth centuries but her own evidence suggests that this is much too late a date. On piracy in general, Regina Goutalier, 'Privateering and Piracy', *The Journal of European Economic History*, VI (1977), pp. 199-213. This is a summary report of the International Commission on Maritime History meeting held in San Francisco in 1975 on exactly that topic.

28. Hélène Antoniadis-Bibicou, 'Problèmes de la marine byzantine', pp. 198-202. The Carolingian Empire tried to stabilise the naval situation in the western Mediterranean in the early ninth century but that gave way to a return to piracy as the Empire collapsed, leaving the coastal towns to fend for themselves. They did not revive until the tenth century.

29. Archibald R. Lewis, *Naval Power and Trade in the Mediterranean*, pp. 205-6. Maurice Lombard, 'Arsenaux et bois de marine dans la Méditerranée musulmane', p. 59. Ekkehard Eickhoff, *Seekrieg und Seepolitik*, pp. 4, 151. *HSUA*, p. 207. Jules Scottas, *Messageries Maritimes de Venise XIVe et XVe siècles* (Société d'Editions Géographiques, Maritime et Coloniales, Paris, 1938), p. 52.

30. Lucien Basch, 'Ancient wrecks and the archaeology of ships', pp. 17, 34, 39-40. His illustration of Mediterranean skeleton construction is dated 1290 but archaeological evidence suggests that the change had occurred earlier. George F. Bass and Frederick van Doorninck, 'An eleventh century shipwreck at Serçe Liman, Turkey', *IJNA*, VII (1978), pp. 119-32.

31. Archibald R. Lewis, *The Northern Seas*, pp. 292-5, 388-98.

32. L. A. Boiteux, *La Fortune de Mer, le Besoin de Securité et les Débuts de l'Assurance Maritime* (SEVPEN, Paris, 1968), p. 45. *FHMN*, pp. 267-9. Herbert Jankuhn, 'Der frankisch-friesische Handel zur Ostsee im frühen Mittelalter', p. 235. Jelle C. Riemersma, 'Trading and shipping associations in 16th century Holland', *Tijdschrift voor Geschiedenis*, LXV (1952), pp. 330-1.

NOTES TO ILLUSTRATIONS

a. Valerie H. Fenwick, 'The Graveney boat. A pre-conquest discovery in Kent', *IJNA*, I (1972), pp. 120, 122. *FHMN*, pp. 27, 43, 56, 128. A. W. Brøgger and Haakon Shetelig, *The Viking Ships*, p. 163. Ole Crumlin-Pedersen, 'Cog-Kogge-Kaag', p. 123. *AB*, nos. 36, 150-5.

b. Siegfried Fliedner, ' "Kogge" und "Hulk" ', nos. 2-3, 58-9, 70. *FHMN*, p. 56. *AB*, no. 133.

c. Romola and R. C. Anderson, *The Sailing-Ship*, p. 75. *HSUA*, p. 167. Olaf Olsen and Ole Crumlin-Pedersen, 'The Skuldelev Ships, A preliminary report on an underwater excavation in Roskilde Fjord, Zealand', *Acta Archaeologica*, XXIX (1958), pp. 164-5, and 'The Skuldelev Ships (II)', pp. 95, 117, 150. *AB*, p. 149.

d. A. W. Brøgger and Haakon Shetelig, *The Viking Ships*, p. 114. Ole Crumlin-Pedersen, 'Two Danish Side Rudders', *MM*, LII (1966), pp. 253, 259.

e. A. W. Brøgger and Haakon Shetelig, *The Viking Ships*, pp. 84, 87. *FHMN*, pp. 37, 97. Björn Landström, *The Ship*, nos. 152, 155.

f. A. W. Brøgger and Haakon Shetelig, *The Viking Ships*, pp. 55, 71, 83, 88. *HSUA*, pp. 176-8. Bernhard Hagedorn, *Die Entwicklung der wichtigsten Schiffstypen*, plate I. Björn Landström, *The Ship*, nos. 151-3. G. La Roërie and J. Vivielle, *Navires et Marins*, vol. I, p. 177; *AB*, nos. 35, 139, 140.

g. A. W. Brøgger and Haakon Shetelig, *The Viking Ships*, pp. 41, 98. *HSUA*, p. 179. *AB*, nos. 28-30.

h. A. W. Brøgger and Haakon Shetelig, *The Viking Ships*, pp. 57, 59, 61, 66-9, 96, 104-7, 110-12, 161. Romola and R. C. Anderson, *The Sailing-Ship*, pp. 71, 73. Lionel Casson, *Illustrated History of Ships and Boats*, nos. 76-76A. *HSUA*, pp. 172-5, 177. Björn Landström, *The Ship*, nos. 148, 150. G. La Roërie and J. Vivielle, *Navires et Marins*, vol. I, pp. 172, 174, 181. *AB*, nos. 136-8.

i. *HSUA*, pp. 194, 200-1. Olaf Olsen and Ole Crumlin-Pedersen, 'The Skuldelev Ships (II)', pp. 132-3, 143. Knud Thorvildsen, *The Viking Ship of Ladby*, pp. 21, 23. *AB*, nos. 141, 142, 144.

j. *HSUA*, p. 194. *FHMN*, p. 315.

k. *HSUA*, pp. 184-5. *FHMN*, p. 39. Björn Landström, *Sailing Ships*, nos. 152-4. Olaf Olsen and Ole Crumlin-Pedersen, 'The Skuldelev Ships (II)', pp. 75, 85, 97, 109, 121, 123, 131. *AB*, nos. 37, 146-8.

l. A. W. Brøgger and Haakon Shetelig, *The Viking Ships*, p. 80. *HSUA*, pp. 196-7. W. L. Goodman, *The History of Woodworking Tools*, p. 123. *AB*, nos. 161-3.

m. *FHMN*, p. 289. Björn Landström, *The Ship*, nos. 146, 158.

n. *FHMN*, pp. 125-31, 155, 186-96.

o. G. La Roërie and J. Vivielle, *Navires et Marins*, vol. I, p. 88.

p. Lucien Basch, 'Ancient wrecks and the archaeology of ships', p. 40. George F. Bass and Frederick van Doorninck, 'An 11th century shipwreck at Serçe Liman, Turkey', opposite p. 120.

3   CRUSADERS' SHIPS AND COGS: 1000-1250

After the Viking attacks and the breakdown of government in the ninth and tenth centuries, political authority in western Europe tended to devolve on more local authorities. Though the evolution was different in France, in England, in Scandinavia and in the Empire the result in the years after 1000 was towards more effective if still largely localised government. The consolidation of authority, be it by kings, regional heads or local nobles, and the institutionalisation of conflict led to a decline in violence or at least channelled the violence so that it became more regularised, more predictable and less severe. The Church combined with royal governments to promote some stability, a stability based on the at least tacit agreement of landowners. To achieve that stability kings needed and got troops and money from the towns. Those products of the rising volume of commerce were for the most part directly subject to the kings and became a major source of royal power. The result of political evolution by the thirteenth century was the monarchy of the high middle ages, probably best represented by France under King Louis IX, St Louis.

In the Mediterranean politics followed a different course. The Iberian

Illustration above: English warship with castles of keel type, Pevensey, oldest town seal, thirteenth century.

kingdoms formed in the reconquest of the peninsula from the Moors closely followed the northern pattern of consolidation. In Italy, on the other hand, towns enjoyed virtual independence. Efforts by the Holy Roman Emperors, especially Frederic I Barbarossa and Frederic II, to bring these towns under Imperial control led to long wars but to no change in their political status. The economic expansion of the period and the rising total income of townspeople added to feelings of self-confidence and commitment to independence growing out of the wars. The crusades constituted another reason for the political strength of Italian city-states. Pilgrimages to the Holy Land as well as attacks on Muslim ports and shipping were already popular before Pope Urban II called in 1096 for an expedition to wrest control of the Holy Land from the Arab government. The difference was in the unprecedented scale of response to Urban's call. Soldiers and pilgrims filled the available ships of the Italian ports. The successful conquest of the Holy Land by 1100 and the establishment of Latin Christian principalities there created a continuing demand for transport for support of those states. The Muslim efforts to drive out the Christians led to a protracted if sporadic war placing irregular demands on Italian shipping. The Italian towns were the necessary intermediaries for the crusader states. It took only two or three years after Urban II's call for the towns to realise they might gain from giving the crusaders naval support. For their invaluable help Italians got trade concessions in the Levant. This was another reason for a rise in the volume of shipping. One of the great expeditions to reinforce the Christian states, the Fourth Crusade, was diverted and ended with the conquest of Constantinople in 1204, which further weakened an already struggling Byzantine Empire. The crusades were important to the Mediterranean for both economic and political reasons. The major crusades meant a large and sudden demand for shipping services, over long distances. The involvement of Italian city-states in the fighting drew them both politically and commercially further east. In the end the contest between Christian and Muslim, between the Byzantine and Fatimid Empires, was replaced by competition among the new naval and economic powers in the Mediterranean, Venice, Pisa and Genoa.

Italian towns enjoyed unquestionable commercial success from the tenth to the thirteenth centuries. That success coincided with the ever more general adoption of skeleton-building. By no means was the new approach to shipbuilding the sole reason for commercial growth in the Mediterranean during the high middle ages. Skeleton-building was known in all parts of the Mediterranean from the eleventh century on yet not all regions and ports enjoyed the same pace or scope of commercial success. Some Italian towns, especially those with the greatest degree of political independence, were better able to exploit the new possibilities. The towns of southern Italy, united under Norman rule, while still prosperous and playing a significant role in Mediterranean shipping, did not fare as well as their counterparts in the northern part of the peninsula. There was a shift in the commercial balance from the eastern to the central Mediterranean in the period and yet there is no evidence of Italian ships being superior, more advanced in design than those of the Greeks or the Muslims. The surviving written evidence refers largely to ships used by crusaders, however. Those ships constituted a special case. They give an impression rather than a precise picture of vessels used in regular cargo and passenger services. Moreover, the information is concentrated in the towns of Venice and Genoa, the two primary ports of debarkation for crusaders, so it leaves out the trading towns in central and southern Italy and in Catalonia in Spain. Despite the problems with the evidence, it is clear that the major breakthrough to the use of skeletal building of frames and hulls on ships can only be part of the explanation for the rise of Latin Christian traders to a position of dominance in the Mediterranean. It is possible that, over the long term, access to stands of tall hardwoods, especially oak, may have offered a comparative advantage to northern Italians and Catalans because such trees were needed to make the heavier ribs typical of the new system of building. Throughout the Mediterranean, after the adoption of skeleton-building, there was typically just elaboration and extension of existing designs rather than significant breaks with past practice.

From 1000 to 1250 galleys were built as before. There was little or no improvement over the tenth-century larger version with castles. These vessels still showed their ancestry in the Roman light galley. By the thirteenth century there was a standard galley rig with two masts, the forward mast raked forward. The second mast was stepped just astern of the middle of the ship. On some galleys there was a third mast. Each had a single lateen sail. A second set of smaller yards and sails was carried for strong winds. With a good breeze dead aft the galley would rig a square sail; it was the awning for protecting the rowers hung from the longest yard. So Mediterranean sailors knew about the square sail. They preferred the lateen because of its versatility. On galleys there was plenty of manpower to handle it, so the labour requirement was no constraint. The abundance of manpower was expensive. The oars, each manned by one rower, were still the principal form of propulsion. Hulls were long relative to the beam, setting such galleys apart from the round ships which relied exclusively on sails for power. Lengths of such ships ran from about 12 to 25 metres. They carried 20 to 30 oars but longer galleys had as many as 60 or even 80. No matter the length, they were never more than 2 metres high. Control of the galley came from two side rudders at the stern. The hull was carvel-built and rode low in the water.[a] The cargo space was, of necessity, small by almost any standard. Galleys were fast, cost less to build and were more easily defended than cargo ships. They were the carriers for short haul of relatively light goods and long haul of highly valuable goods. They served for the distribution within the western Mediterranean and the Adriatic of goods brought from the East. They also carried the wealthiest crusaders and pilgrims to the Holy Land, people who could afford to pay a premium for speed. Over-all they were more comfortable and safer and there was less chance of sickness than with sailing ships.[1] The galleys were also warships. They were ideal for attacking pirates or competitors at sea. All the Italian towns had their collection of galleys for trading and for defending their interests. They found, as did the Byzantines and the Arabs before them, that the galley had to be used for naval activity in the Mediterranean with its relatively calm waters and light and variable summer winds.

Pressure for design change was clearer in the case of round cargo ships. All together the changes in demand led to an increase in the number and size of sailing ships. Crusaders needed large ships since they went to the Holy Land with retainers, equipment and horses. They also generated highly concentrated demand for transport. Though some crusaders made the voyage to Syria each year, expeditions were typically great events mobilising large numbers of soldiers who all had to be moved in one season. Along with the sudden demands of soldiers there was the sustained and growing demand for the carriage of bulk goods. Oriental goods came across the Indian Ocean along the route used by Romans in the third century AD. They also came by caravan through Mesopotamia and by land across Central Asia to ports on the Black Sea. There were also many goods called spices, goods requiring some care in shipment, relatively rare and of high price for their bulk, which could be and were produced along the shores of the Mediterranean. Used principally for seasoning food and for medicinal purposes, they were the logical items to be added to the budgets of people with rising incomes. Such goods could be moved in larger quantities as demand rose and that too raised the number of ships in commerce. Those ships still had to face pirates. There was no single dominant naval power to stop piratical attacks and, though Venice deployed the most powerful naval force in the eastern Mediterranean, she did not use that force to defend peaceful trade. She, like other contending states in attacks on their enemies, acted much like pirates. The Venetians particularly took the opportunity to plunder the Byzantine Empire. Pirate fleets were made up of professionals of any nationality willing to sell their collective services to anyone offering them personal gain.[2] The belligerence which was the normal condition between Christian and Muslim, despite government truces and thriving trade across religious lines, increased the possibility for loss due to hostile action. The pirates did benefit from having more to steal. There were more ships sailing, carrying larger and more valuable cargoes.

Round ships, the carriers of bulk cargoes, were not defenceless. They still carried soldiers, often men specifically hired to protect the ship, who, of course, imposed an extra charge on the cargo. With sailing ships this could make the difference whether or not it would pay to ship a certain cargo. These ships moved along the coasts, rarely venturing into open waters. A through cargo which would fill the ship for a long-distance voyage was exceptional: one of the few through cargoes was the carriage of pilgrims and crusaders going to the Holy Land. In general round ships called at ports along the coast looking for a market for goods they had and for other cargoes to move to the next port. As time passed, these routes and trading relationships became more settled. Transportation became more regularised.[3] A commercial network or rather a series of such networks developed for the maritime republics. The Levant, Byzantium, all of Muslim Africa were integrated into Italian trading relations. These ships were slow because they stopped at each port and would wait for a favourable breeze before leaving. At sea they were slower than galleys because of the shape of the hull.

Design of Mediterranean cargo ships had changed from that of the seventh-century Byzantine coaster, but the similarities outweighed the differences. The use of lateen sails and the extreme reliance on internal frames for support of the hull were the two most obvious changes. Some data have survived for the exceptional cargo ships supplied to crusaders, and especially for those intended for the Ninth Crusade led by King Louis IX of France. He planned to attack Tunis and ordered ships from Genoa and Venice. The most impressive thing about the ships was their size. One of the vessels built at Genoa had four ship's boats, one of them equipped with 52 oars. The largest ship carried 100 horses, crusaders and their attendants. Vessels of that size could carry up to 1,000 pilgrims on a regular voyage. A capacity of 600 tons with a

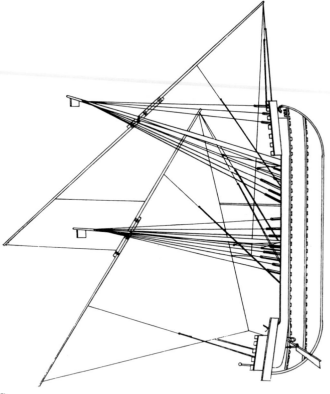

11: Two-masted Genoese Sailing Ship Built for the Crusade of
King Louis IX of France

crew of up to 100 men seems to have been the upper limit of mid-thirteenth-century Italian round ships. One Venetian ship was 36 metres long, without the overhanging castles. The keel was only 23 metres, the maximum breadth was 13.3 metres and the height 12.85 metres. It was among the 120 special ships for carrying horses ordered by Louis IX but, other than the addition of ports below the water-line to make loading and unloading easy, the vessel was designed like other big cargo ships. The waterline was probably at about the level of the first deck. Two decks were common on such ships but not necessary for lesser cargo ships carrying up to 50 horses. Vessels built at Genoa for the same purpose were similar and, if anything, slightly less beamy.[b] The length-to-breadth ratio was between 3:1 and 4:1 for all these ships.[4] These were special vessels but their rigging and sails seem to have been the same as for all round ships, no matter the size. The length-to-breadth ratio was higher, however.

On the largest ships there were three masts, but this was rare; the usual number was two. The mainmast was raked forward as with the galley rig. The masts were stepped in the keelson, the heavy timber on top of the keel. The mainmast would be about the same length as the ship itself, impressive in a vessel the typical 20 to 30 metres long. The yard for the mast, made of two spars fished together, was longer than the ship by as much as 30 per cent. The after- or mizzenmast and its spar were smaller but the spar was still longer than the ship. An extra spar was carried on board for each yard in case one broke. The ship also carried from four to seven sails, the surplus as reserve or for changing with a change in the weather.[5] While the orders of crusaders did lead to the construction of large lateen-rigged cargo ships, they appear to have been nothing more than imitations of earlier designs done to a larger scale. Certainly some adjustments had to be made to construct such large vessels but they were apparently minor, and Mediterranean shipwrights had no problem with the larger size. The crusaders' ships proved seaworthy. In fact the construction of the largest of crusaders' ships coincided precisely with the period when lateen-rigged cargo ships in the Mediterranean reached their maximum size, that is in the second half of the thirteenth century.

A smaller version of the round ship, the *tarida* as it was called in Genoa, had oars as well as sails which were, incidentally, large for the size of the vessel. It was obviously a compromise design, an effort to gain the best from the galley as well as the round-ship design. Such vessels owed more to the design of the cargo ship, the oars acting to supplement power — crucial for moving quickly in or out of port. The *tarida* was used for the same types of jobs as other round ships. The larger the ship the greater the danger of loss each time it made port. For the frequent coastal trade the *tarida* was better suited. The use, and therefore the construction, of very large sailing ships depended on ports with relatively easy access existing at the ends of a route along which large cargoes could be carried at a profit. The use of larger ships also depended on the rise in bulk cargoes handled by Mediterranean shippers in the eleventh, twelfth and thirteenth centuries. The distances might not be great but a larger total volume of necessities such as salt, grain and olive oil was moved in the thirteenth century, and in larger ships. By that time the Venetian government expected sailing cargo ships to be of about 95-470 tons.[6]

Control on all round ships came from two side rudders at the stern which could be raised when in port. A second pair of steering oars might also be fitted, presumably larger and designed to be used in strong winds in the open sea. The hull was built with edge-to-edge planking. The posts were curved and the entire hull was rounded. Cargo was typically loaded and unloaded through the large openings, hatches, in the main deck. By the thirteenth century a third deck was sometimes added on larger vessels. At either end there were superstructures, castles, to accommodate passengers. For crusaders the number and size of these enclosed spaces were increased to house noble travellers. For merchants and crew a cabin or covered space at each end of the ship was usually enough. The addition of decks increased the volume of carrying capacity but the weight of capacity did not rise proportionally. Heavy cargoes could only be carried below. The main deck was kept clear when the ship was at sea for reasons of safety, thus placing a limitation on merchants, since to get the maximum out of the multiple-deck ships they had to get a mix of heavy cargoes for the hold and lighter cargoes for the space between the decks.

The frames and beams of these Mediterranean cargo ships were lighter and more numerous than on contemporary northern vessels, implying a need for more external protection. Heavy planks running the length of the ship, wales, were common. They were not to be found just at the load waterline, but were spaced evenly from the keel all the way to the gunwale. Stringers ran along inside the wales. In one thirteenth-century Italian ship the stringers were the only part of the vessel not of oak. At the bow the ends of one of the beams projected through the hull, apparently to hold the anchor and not to act as a bumper like the projecting beam-ends of northern ships. On larger ships, however, rows of projecting beam-ends ran along the sides. The beams may have been secured to the tops of the ribs and served to keep them in place, thus reinforcing the skeleton. The beams also supported decks.[c] Travel on such a vessel could not have been comfortable with so many people on board. Yet there were surprisingly few complaints from pilgrims or from the knights going on the crusades, people who were not used to sea travel.

The greater volume of trade handled by cargo ships meant that they could expand their activities and increasingly replace galleys in the movement of all goods including luxuries. Galleys were thus left to function as warships. Certainly galleys were not completely displaced in the carriage of goods but the largest proportion of goods in volume and probably also in value went in round ships. That shift was aided more by the increase in the number and the frequency of sailings of round ships than by the increase in maximum size. By the thirteenth century the size of a ship was being measured in terms of the number of wine casks it could carry. There was a variety of different measures adopted, each port with its own variation, but the approach was usually the same. The reported figures can often create more confusion than clarification. Barrels had completely replaced jars for carrying bulk goods. The regular use of such a measure shows that round ships were carriers worthy of consideration. The measure was meaningless for galleys.[7]

The establishment of Fatimid power in North Africa and Egypt in the late tenth century contributed to the commercial expansion in Muslim lands which preceded that in Christian Europe. Tunisia was originally the centre of Fatimid power but the region declined when the capital was moved to Cairo and when the size of ships grew to the point where they could make continuous through voyages from prosperous Spain to the Levant without having to stop on the way. Attacks by Berbers from the interior from the 1050s on guaranteed the economic decline of Tunisia and a shift in the interests of both Muslim and Christian traders to possibilities further east. The Ayyubids replaced the Fatimids in the 1170s and ruled Egypt and Syria until the mid-thirteenth century. While they continued their predecessors' interest in naval affairs, they had as little success against Christian naval forces. By the end of the twelfth century those forces dominated the Mediterranean in the East as well as in the West. Even so the sea was still the main avenue for moving goods. Going overland was expensive, especially since it took so long compared to travelling by sea and river. While, throughout much of the middle ages, there was no strict distinction between vessels capable of sailing the high seas and those which could be used on rivers, Muslim builders did produce types with some degree of specialisation. Seagoing ships could go from the Mediterranean to Cairo but typical practice was to take off goods and passengers in, for example, Alexandria and travel up the Nile by some riverboat such as *jurum* which were barges each equipped with one sail. There were seagoing barges, *qarib*, which carried heavy loads over long distances and were propelled by oars. The typical vessel for the Mediterranean, though, was the *qunbar* which appears to have been much the same as Byzantine and Italian cargo ships. In the largest version they carried three masts and as many as 800 men. Muslims operated galleys as well, though, as with Christian shipping, they seem to have been only infrequently used for carrying cargo. Indeed, distinction was made between merchant ships and warships at least in written records. By the mid-eleventh century the cargo ships could already carry up to 400 passengers. Even though these must have been large ships, it was still the practice to take them out of the water for repairs during the winter, a season when they never sailed.[8]

Political instability in North Africa, the establishment of first the Almoravid and then the Almohad states, acted to deter trade because of the intolerance shown by both religious sects to non-members and also the wars and piracy which were part of their growth and decline. There was only sporadic success in their establishment of naval forces. By the mid-thirteenth century almost all of Spain and the Balearic islands had been conquered by Christians and all aspects of North African commercial life had been gradually infiltrated by Italians and Catalans. Muslim ships became a rarity in the western Mediterranean. At the same time the new Christian kingdoms of Iberia expanded their naval forces and merchant marines, often with the help of Italian experts.

Shipwrights had more chances than before to change the design of Mediterranean ships but the changes they made were limited, which is even more surprising since they were exposed to a number of options in the form of designs from other parts of the Continent. Shipbuilders in the western Mediterranean throughout the eleventh and twelfth centuries may have borrowed some features of Greek ships but the changes, which had begun in the tenth century, were few. Despite the ties of the Vikings with the Black Sea, despite the activity of Scandinavians in the Mediterranean, and despite the presence of ships from northwest Europe bringing crusaders to the Holy Land, southern shipbuilders did not adopt any of those northern types nor seemingly any features from them. There can be no question but that shipbuilders in the South saw

northern vessels. The Norman state established in southern Italy and
Sicily in the eleventh century relied to some degree on naval power.
The Normans started using typical northern types but abandoned them,
after a defeat in 1081, for dromons like those of the Byzantine navy. In
the First Crusade a fleet from Norway sailed to the Holy Land. The
ships then went to southern Greece and ran to Constantinople under
full sail, probably to show off the decoration and colour of the sails.[9]
Other northern types appeared in the Mediterranean. Pirates from the
Low Countries were already in the South at the start of the First
Crusade. The increase in the number of pilgrims going to the Holy Land
after that campaign brought more northern ships. Successive crusades
meant the formation of fleets in the North, 190 ships in all for the
Second Crusade in 1147, which then sailed to Syria. These fleets
followed the coasts of Spain and Portugal to get to the Mediterranean
and often stopped to help fellow Christians in the fight against Iberian
Muslims. By the thirteenth century the ships used included cogs, but
now significantly changed from the coastal trader of the tenth century.
Northern ships proved that they were better in rough seas than Mediterranean galleys with low freeboard. There must have been other advantages which southerners noticed. If nothing else, northerners learned
how to sail to Iberia and in the Mediterranean.[10] They moved from port
to port as did all sailors in the Mediterranean, thus giving maximum
exposure for the designs. It is not known if Mediterranean shipwrights
ever tried to build ships like the northern ones. Some Scandinavian
designs were taken over on the north coast of Spain but influence
stopped there. It is certainly true that the presence of those types did
not lead to any immediate or great change in the design of southern
European ships. One explanation may be that northern ships could get
into, but not out of, the Mediterranean. The prevailing winds and
strong current in the Strait of Gibraltar make it hard for any sailing
ship to go from east to west. For ships of northern European design
before the fourteenth century it was apparently impossible.[11] The
traffic then was entirely one way and the advantages of designs with
such a serious limitation led Mediterranean builders to take an interest
in improving the capabilities of oared vessels for voyages to the Atlantic
rather than adopting northern types.

All in all, modification and extension of designs dating from Roman
times were sufficient to meet rising demand in the Mediterranean. The
methods familiar to builders there proved adequate. It took some time
to develop facility with skeleton construction and even by 1250 the full
implications of that approach had not been explored. Shipbuilding yards

did not have trouble with finding labour. Population was growing and urban populations were growing even faster. Shippers faced the same conditions so they could get the sizeable crews needed to defend their ships and handle the lateen sails. Since the yards were long and heavy, the job took a good deal of muscle power; this was true not only for bringing the sail around to the other tack but also for the lowering and changing of yards and sails which were done with changes in the weather. Supplies of timber and other raw materials were plentiful for Italian and Iberian shipbuilders. The reforestation of those areas and of the south of France and Dalmatia from the fourth to the tenth century – a result of the shrinking of arable – gave builders more than enough wood for their needs. Only by the twelfth century was deforestation evident and then only on the island of Sicily. Byzantium enjoyed plentiful supplies of raw materials, especially in southern Greece.[12] There was, then, no single pressing problem for shipbuilders. Labour, raw materials, equipment were all available and earlier success with their ships made it reasonable to continue to pursue the same or slightly modified designs. The unique talents of Italian shipbuilders were widely recognised. They were brought to Iberia, for example, to help establish a navy for the kingdom of Castile and also for the kingdom of Portugal. It was obvious that in Italy men could and did produce vessels well suited to contemporary demands. On the other hand, it was not a simple matter to adopt northern designs. Northern ships had not been developed to their full potential. They required modification to fit the weather and tidal conditions in the Mediterranean. So there was an initial sizeable effort needed before northern types could be produced in the South. This threshold was high enough to keep southern builders from crossing it in the thirteenth century. At that point there was no pressing need to change. They were already passing on savings to ship-pers in the form of larger round ships.

There had been some improvements in navigation by 1250. Some progress had been made with the compass. Vikings may have used a magnetised needle. Such a needle floating freely in a bowl was apparently widely used by European mariners by the twelfth century. The needle was no compass, however. Sailors used it only to indicate direction. Only when it was calibrated, that is combined with a card, and fixed on a dry pivot and used along with a chart did the compass become an effective navigational tool. Up to about 1250 the compass was used in place of stars or the sun to determine direction when the sky was overcast.[13] With a floating needle skippers were still limited to following the coast and to staying in port in the winter to avoid storms and cloudy skies. The limited sailing season disappeared in the century after 1250 with the improvement of navigational tools but up to that date there was, as yet, no imbalance between ship design and navigation which might force builders to change their vessels.

The commercial and naval power of the Byzantine Empire continued to decline. The process which began with the abandonment of Mediterranean trade to non-Greek merchants and shippers was accelerated as the Empire was forced to make further concessions to foreigners. The Byzantine navy and merchant marine did not collapse overnight. The decline of the merchant marine ensured the decline in naval strength, however, no matter the acts of successive governments. Meanwhile the Italian towns, the competitors of Byzantium, pressed their commercial advantage, using it in support of their navies and using their naval strength to improve their trading position. In part the Byzantine decline came from success. The naval victories over the Russians in the first half of the eleventh century along with the capture of Muslim pirate nests in south Italy ensured a measure of security. Then the Constantinople government allowed the navy to decline, especially the coastal defence forces. It was also a logical concomitant of the changing character of piracy. By the 1060s with the Turks advancing in Asia Minor and the Normans threatening the western provinces of the Empire, there was no effective Byzantine fleet to hold back the two enemies. A combination of commercial decline, short-sighted reform of the navy and attack from two strong adversaries at the two ends of the Empire put Byzantium in an impossible position. The only solution was to find allies and the Italian towns were the logical choice, especially the old Byzantine port at the head of the Adriatic, Venice.

Venice, in exchange for naval support against the Normans, insisted on further trade concessions which allowed Venetians to increase their share not only of the external trade of Byzantium but of the internal trade as well. This sequence was repeated each time the Normans of south Italy and Sicily posed a threat to Byzantine interests in the West. The Empire committed itself to the defence of Asia Minor and to Crete and Cyprus and so had to leave the West to allies. The concessions meant a lowering of tax income destined for the navy and heavier charges on Byzantines living along the coast, a combination which could lead only to disaster in the long run. The Byzantine naval revival of the twelfth century was temporary. The Empire was too dependent on foreign merchants and foreign naval strength to pursue the old policy of dominance at sea. Byzantine naval troubles were matched by a contraction of fleets in Muslim states in Africa and Spain. The vacuum of the eleventh century gave western naval forces an opportunity which they seized. They did not have everything their own way. Byzantium still deployed some naval forces as did the Fatimid Caliphate. But certainly after the First Crusade, with Norman states at either end of the Byzantine Empire and with Italian merchants and shippers enjoying new privileges in the Levant, the balance of strength had been irretrievably tipped in favour of Italian shipping.[14] The final result of the expansion of Italian shipping, the decline of the Byzantine merchant marine, and the breakdown of government in Byzantium was the conquest of Constantinople in 1204 by western knights in the Fourth Crusade. The Latin Empire which they established relied on Venetian support just as did the original conquest. At that point fighting was reduced to a contest between Venice and Genoa over which town was to have the greater trading advantages in the lands of the Empire.

By the middle of the thirteenth century the Byzantine Empire, long a source of new developments in ship design, especially in the design of warships, had a much diminished shipbuilding industry. There was no sign of improvement in the technology of shipbuilding. Byzantines throughout the eleventh and twelfth centuries used the same types of merchant ships as did the Italians except that those of the Byzantines were on average smaller since demand for shipping services had not risen as much in the eastern as in the western Mediterranean.[d] The Greeks did not even make marginal design improvements as did the Italians. Governments only sporadically devoted themselves to the construction of war fleets, let alone the improvement of them. Greek shippers and merchants were less effective in using commercial vessels than were their Italian competitors because they were burdened with higher duties. They also had to suffer from piratical attacks which the government could not prevent. Many of those attacks, not incidentally, were by Italians. To relieve domestic shipping of piracy the Byzantine government had to make further trade concessions to Italian towns, thus leading to even less efficient use of ships by Greek traders. Under the general circumstances of a self-reinforcing downturn in commerce and political instability, the stagnation and, if anything, retrogression in Byzantine ship design was not unexpected.

The pattern in northern Europe from 1000 to 1250 was the opposite of that in the South. Rather than marginal improvement in established designs there were major changes in certain types, extension in the capabilities of existing types and, through borrowing of features, an increase in the variety of ship types available. Indeed, the pace of change in the North had long been faster than that in the Mediterranean and the disparity grew after 1000. By Mediterranean standards northern ships in 600 had been primitive. But by 1250 the gap had been all but obliterated. The northern economy remained far behind that of the South, however. In the volume and in the value of goods traded, in the total production of the region, in population, in every indicator of economic prosperity the regions along the Atlantic, North Sea and Baltic coasts could not compare with those in the Mediterranean basin. Certainly the volume of trade in the North increased to 1250, perhaps even more rapidly than in the South, though starting from a smaller base. Lengths of trading voyages remained typically short. The exception was the carriage of crusaders to the Holy Land. Only in the thirteenth century did northern merchants find goods and routes to give them the same kind of trade that Italian merchants enjoyed in the long haul of luxury goods from the Levant to the Adriatic and Tyrrhenian Seas. The volume of bulk goods shipped rose in the North, as in the South. But in the North it was not a deviation from past practice. The proportion of bulk goods in trade may actually have fallen and not risen. Builders in the North, to meet the consistent demand for bulk carriage, produced vessels suited to the task. In fact they appear to have overshot the mark. They developed ships which could do more than was necessary, a common problem with technical change since it is always difficult to predict the final result of any innovation. In the process shipbuilders created entirely new trading opportunities.

Scandinavian ship types continued a pattern of improvement based on the breakthrough with Viking ships. The leading figures in the Scandinavian kingdoms insisted that builders construct the largest possible warships. In the process they became longships. Size was reported by the number of rooms, the space between two ribs for two oarsmen, one on each side. *Karvs* of some 6 to 16 pairs of oars were too small to be measured by rooms. Longships were of 15 rooms or more. Above 30 rooms they were called dragonships. Even with .70 metres for each room, .30 metres less than on the Gokstad ship, the typical longship was 24 metres long and the largest more than 30 metres long. These ships were, like the larger Skuldelev warship, a longer version of the Gokstad ship. The length-to-beam ratio was extremely high. They were still fast rowed vessels. Rig was the same with a single square sail. The method of fighting did not change. The function of the ship was to get the men to the scene using the sail, and then with oars and careful steering to bring the vessels into position and then to grapple with the enemy. The advantage with longships was their high freeboard, 5.6 metres in one thirteenth-century dragonship. The freeboard on the

Gokstad ship was only about 1 metre. The use of oarholes made it possible to build up the sides without changing the angle at which oars entered the water. The longship, then, was a high platform for shooting down on the enemy. The majority of battle fleets still consisted of smaller vessels, few of which were of over 25 rooms, so in battle the giant dragonships were a class apart. The first of the dragonships was built about 1000. Their number was never large. For Norway only 16 are reported from 995 to 1263. Longships had another advantage in battle. They could carry a large number of men, about eight per room. The greatest longships were not highly seaworthy but they were very expensive. So vessels of over 30 rooms were generally built just for kings trying to assert their dominant position. The optimal size of a longship was 20 to 25 rooms with some ten men per room. These longships retained some of the manoeuvrability of the smaller *karvs*. The last of the big longships was built in the mid-thirteenth century.[15] For most operations the smaller vessel had already proved itself superior. The ships built for the expedition of William the Conqueror against England in 1066 were little bigger than *karvs*. These ships showed improvements in the rig with ropes stretched to give better control of the sail.[e] They probably eliminated the need for the *beitiass*. In general, though, the Norman ships were just Scandinavian warships.

With the dragonship Scandinavian builders had reached the design limits of the Viking warship. It was technically impossible to extend the length. Longer vessels tended to hog, the bow and stern being lower than the keel amidships. In heavy weather the ship could break in two. Building the ship broader to counteract the problem and in general to increase seaworthiness meant changing the character of the design. The technical limit of length was also one of manpower since rowers could only sit so close together. Having tested the limit builders and their customers agreed, except in rare cases, on the optimal size and design. The result was an efficient fighting ship and one which dominated northern European waters through the eleventh and into the twelfth century. These warships apparently borrowed the nailing of frames to the planking from cargo ships, a practice which gave them the added strength necessary if they were being made longer. Warships were significantly different from cargo ships and the difference, already clear in the ninth century, was accentuated. That is not to say that warships were never used to carry goods or that cargo ships were never used in battle. Warships could not be and never were used in any regular trade. When they were not on expeditions or guarding the coast warships were laid up in protected dugouts along the beach.

Scandinavian governments, to supply defence, to exploit the warship design and to establish control over the rather independent landowners along the coasts, set up a system of recruiting such ships for royal fleets. By the thirteenth century there was an extensive system for the construction, maintenance and manning of a navy which could be called out by the king. Local fleets, based on districts, were combined with a central fleet built by and for the monarchy. The *ledung* ships supplied locally were typically of 20 to 25 rooms and under 30 metres in length. The full muster for Norway was 310 ships but it was never called out. A fleet of 200 ships was the maximum until the thirteenth century when the total rose to over 350. For Denmark the fleet in theory was 1,100 ships. Sweden had a similar system. The fleets were to be not only offensive weapons in the hand of the king, but also a type of police force to stop piracy and protect trade.[16] Though they did not eradicate piracy completely, these fleets did introduce a stability which further channelled interest away from the freebooting of the Viking period towards peaceful trade. The type of ship, the style of naval warfare and the geography of a large number of ports contributed to the development of this form of naval organisation. It was the most extensive system for generating forces at sea in northern Europe in the middle ages.

The increase in trade along established routes in the Baltic and North Seas generated pressure on shipbuilders also to improve cargo ships. The impetus was more diffuse than with warships where demand was concentrated among an ever smaller number of buyers. The process was similar, however, with the builders refining the design of the Viking ship. The principal change, beginning even before 1000, was in the cross-section of the cargo ship. The cross-pieces resting on the frames, the *bites*, were moved down. Indeed the whole system of cross-timbers seemed to move downward on to the frames and the frames themselves became flatter. More cross-beams had to be added above. These ran between heavy planks on the sides. Hanging knees were added above them to hold higher planking. By the twelfth century the *bites* were so far down that they had all but disappeared, not even reaching the ends of the frames. By the mid-thirteenth century there was nothing left of the *bites* and the frames were floor timbers. But there could be as many as three levels of cross-beams above the floor timbers.[f] Strength came from having the floor timbers close together, about .5 metres apart. The change simplified construction and increased the quantity of heavy timber needed. It made the ship sturdier and not incidentally increased cargo space in the centre of the ship. It is almost possible to date finds of cargo ships by the degree to which the *bites* were moved down. The same may be said for the distance between the ribs or floor timbers which decreased throughout the middle ages.[17] Apparently cargo ships followed the trend towards greater size. They never reached the dimensions of dragonships but lengths of 25 metres must have been common. Breadth would be about 9 metres giving a ratio to the length well below that for warships. The rig was the same, with sails broader than on warships. The side rudder remained throughout the twelfth century. The result was a vessel capable of handling bulk cargoes. It was used to move grain from England to Norway in the thirteenth century and to carry dried fish back in exchange. Whale oil and luxuries from the North like falcons, hawks and furs filled out the cargoes.

While cargo ships always had a lower length-to-breadth ratio than warships, another noticeable feature, especially after 1000, was a lower length-to-depth ratio for cargo ships. It was not so much through being broader that cargo ships increased capacity, though there was a fall in length-to-breadth ratios, as by becoming deeper − a characteristic which was well suited to bulk carriage and made beaching the ship more difficult, though harbour improvements were making the latter point less relevant. The shift to relatively straight and in general more upright posts at the bow and stern was made for the same reasons.[18]

The knarr was mentioned less often after 1000 though it was certainly still in use in voyages to Greenland. Other names for cargo ships, such as *buza* and *byrding*, became more common. The written evidence is not complete enough to be able to identify the distinguishing features of these types. The buss was used throughout the North and Baltic Seas. Such vessels were even mentioned as part of crusader and pilgrim fleets, so they were known in the Mediterranean. They were also mentioned as fishing boats as early as the tenth century. Though it may have begun as a type of warship, by the eleventh century the buss was a cargo ship. By the end of the thirteenth century the name was a generic term for Scandinavian cargo ships. The *byrding* seems to have been more suited to coastal trade than the buss although it too was used on ocean voyages to Iceland and to England.[19] By the thirteenth century the buss had presumably dropped the auxiliary oars at either end of the ship, though they may have been retained on smaller vessels.[g] Relying exclusively on sail, the crew size could be reduced, another advantage for the buss in bulk trades.

Despite the clear improvements in the Scandinavian cargo ship, it still was not able to compete as a bulk carrier with the improved cog. A buss might be as long as a contemporary cog but there is no evidence

12: Cross-sections of Northern European Ship Finds: (a) Viking Baltic Cargo Ship, 1000; (b) Seagoing Knarr, 1000; (c) Galtabäck Boat, 1100; (d) Buss from Bergen, 1300; (e) Bremen Cog, 1380

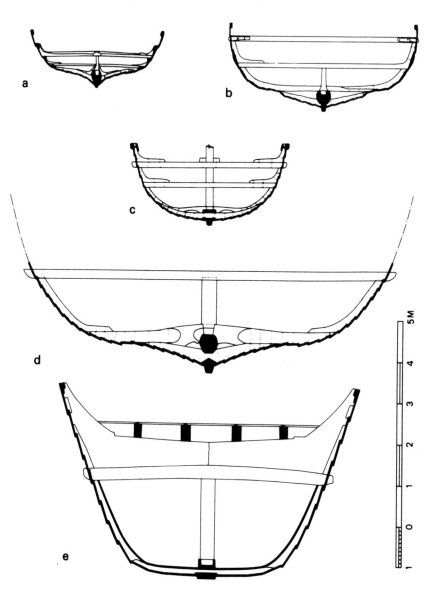

that it could match that cog in total carrying capacity. Moreover, the Scandinavian merchants and shippers who used busses worked at a disadvantage relative to the Germans who used cogs. The latter were closer to sources of cargo and to larger populations. They also appear to have enjoyed a more effective organisation of their trade. If the cog was not overwhelmingly superior in design to the buss, it was at least enough of an improvement to lead Scandinavians to acquire the new type of vessel, as early as the second half of the twelfth century.[20] The keel, the English type derived from the Scandinavian warship, was also superseded. Whether the improved buss or the cog was the reason for its gradual disappearance is impossible to say. By the mid-thirteenth century bulk cargo, especially over longer distances, was typically carried in northern Europe by cogs. The change in the cog which made this possible was the most important improvement in the design of northern European ships in the years from 1000 to 1250.

The new cog was no longer a coastal trader for use among sandbanks but a true deep-sea trader. The change was so great as to create an almost entirely new ship type and one with a much greater range of possibilities. Essentially the change was to add a keel to the simple long narrow cog. This was probably tried for the first time in the early eleventh century, perhaps because of the example of Viking ships. Otherwise the cog retained most of the features of the earlier version. The bottom was almost flat with planks placed edge to edge. There was a sharp angle at the sides where the vessel turned up. There was also the characteristic sharp angle of the posts to the keel. Over time the flat bottom became smaller and the turn of the sides became less sharp. The heavy keelson added amidships served in part, as on Viking ships, to hold the mast in place. On cogs the mast was stepped a bit forward, more efficient in running before the wind. The posts rose higher than the planks and the stempost was typically higher than the sternpost. The reverse clinkering, with the bottom plank overlapping the next one higher, continued and appears in the oldest town seal which is certainly an illustration of a cog, that of Lübeck of 1226.[h] High freeboard was kept as well. The rib framework was presumably attached directly to the planking.[21] The sharp straight stempost of the cog and its deeper draught made it go through the water better than the smoothly curved knarr or the keel. The cog was stronger, a better sailer, as versatile and with larger carrying capacity for each metre of length than the contemporary keel, knarr or older keelless cog.

The cog, by the end of the twelfth century, could be and was used in long-distance trade both along the coasts and across the open sea. By the second decade of the eleventh century traders from Saxony were sailing to England and to Iceland. Frisian sailors apparently made such trips as soon as they had the improved cog, since the older version was not capable of such voyages on the high seas. Frisians also increased their voyages to Norway, not possible before the improvement in ship design.[22] The new design had another advantage: the type could be built bigger. Small cogs remained in use but throughout the eleventh and twelfth centuries shipbuilders progressively tried to build larger cogs. The hull shape of the original cog with a flat or nearly flat bottom and sharp angle to the sides gave a spacious container. Increasing shipments of grain in northern Europe, along with a rise in transport to the Holy Land, gave shipbuilders a ready market for larger bulk carriers. Pilgrims and crusaders making the trip entirely by sea had to carry extensive provisions, not to mention equipment, so space was important. By the thirteenth century the use of the word 'cog' meant, if nothing else, that a ship was large. It is impossible to estimate an average size for cogs up to 1250. Cogs would have been as much as 30 metres long. Breadth did not exceed 9.5 metres and draught would have been between 3 and 4 metres. This certainly was not the technical maximum. The length-to-breadth ratio of about 3:1 made it a tubby vessel. Port charges from the eleventh century suggest that the buss and cog were not much different in size. By 1250, however, the cog had grown so much that, compared to typical Viking ships of 1000, there had been at least a fivefold increase in potential carrying capacity. In fact thirteenth-century ships were not much smaller than those of the sixteenth. The cog was not as fast as a Viking ship but the sacrifice in speed was small. The number of trading voyages per year, especially within the North Sea, was probably about the same with both types. What was affected was the return on investment. The volume of goods shipped rose sharply. The original outlay for each ton of capacity declined since one ship could be built where four or five were needed before. The size of the crew did not grow proportionally with the increase in size. A knarr of 50 tons had a crew of 12 or 14 while the crew of a 200-ton cog was 18 to 20.[23] There can be no question, then, but that the adoption of the new cog and the increase in its size represented significant savings, especially in the movement of bulk goods.

The high freeboard of the cog increased with over-all size, making it more defensible. If that was not enough, superstructures were added fore and aft. These castles, perhaps borrowed from the Mediterranean where small decks were often fitted above the main deck at the bow and stern, were unquestionably for defence. From these platforms archers and other soldiers were well above water level and would usually have a height advantage over any attacker. A small platform or fighting top was added for the same purpose at the top of the mast on larger ships. Cogs were unlikely to fall prey to pirates. With castles added, the cog was superior to any Scandinavian warship. Even the longest of dragonships with castles were still no match for the high cogs. Scandinavian monarchs abandoned their muster fleets and in Denmark the requirement was changed from the supply of longships to the supply of cogs.[24] Cogs in case of war could carry large numbers of men. On the other hand, they were not fast enough or manoeuvrable enough to make them strong offensive weapons, and here may lie the reason for the survival of warships similar to earlier Scandinavian vessels in thirteenth-century England. The Cinque Ports along the Channel coast were required to supply the crown with a specific number of ships for a fixed period. Contemporary seals show long, low clinker-built boats with a single square sail, a single side rudder, no oars and small castles added at the bow and stern.[i] In wartime they were equipped with a wide variety of devices to hurl projectiles at the enemy. For patrol work in the Channel, for amphibious operations in the British Isles and for attacks on the French coast, this type was clearly superior to the cog. Calls on the Cinque Ports decreased as time went on and English kings came to rely more and more on rented cogs for their naval forces.[25]

The tubby design with a low length-to-beam ratio made the cog slow by contemporary standards. For bulk carriage, of course, this was of little importance. The proportions seem to have been much the same no matter the size of the cog. The clinkering of the hull was also the same. Construction even for the largest of cogs was still of shell type. The ends of some of the cross-beams projected out through the hull. Ribs were heavy and they were close together, sitting on and attached to the flat and still relatively broad keel. There were at least two small decks at either end of the cog and on the larger ones there was at least one through deck.[26] The result was strong, massive and solid construction, which made for a heavy ship but also a sturdy one.

Moving the cog presented problems but builders retained the simple rig of a single square sail on a single mast. The mast was held in place by one large forestay running from the stempost and two backstays. There was one addition to the rigging – a bowsprit.[j] This small yard at the bow was probably to stretch lines from the lower edges of the sail. They would keep the leading edge taut when going to windward. The extension gave better leverage than was obtained just by attaching the lines to the stempost. The bowsprit appeared in the thirteenth century and was added also to other types of ship. The collection of mast, spar and bowsprit made up the total rigging for the cog. There were lines to control the sail but these by 1250 were certainly no improvement on Scandinavian practice. Sail area was probably between 82 and 175 square metres depending on the size of the vessel. Though compared to earlier vessels the cog sail was large, the sail area per ton was much lower, one-tenth or less of ninth-century Viking ships. The sail could not get much larger since it was already hard to handle the heavy yard. At the stern there was typically a windlass used to raise the sail and also to haul the anchor. Sail could be increased by the addition of bonnets, strips of cloth which were sewn to the bottom of the main sail. If wind freshened they could be easily removed. That simple arrangement, clearly in use by the thirteenth century, meant that a much larger sail could be rigged, up to a total of 335 square metres, but without the problem of hoisting all the heavy cloth. Sail could also be shortened by using reef-points.[k] These short pieces of rope going through the sail in rows were for tying up the rolled sail.[27] Reef-points could not compare in efficiency with the brails used by Romans but they served a similar purpose. With bonnets or reef-points the cog sail had a wide range of variation. Still, the vessel was probably no better going to windward than was the Viking ship. The sail was heavy and less plastic than its predecessor, so it was not easy to handle.

The system of control changed much more dramatically. The balanced side rudder was adequate for the cog until the late twelfth century. Then builders began to fix rudders on the sternposts of cogs — an easy operation thanks to the straightness of the sternpost. The tiller was usually passed over the top of the post.[l] That, combined with the deeper hull with a keel and the bowsprit and bowlines for the sail, made it possible at least to handle the now much larger cog. The size of the sternpost rudder, as long as the post, made it heavy and hard to move. It may have been first used on riverboats in the Low Countries where the advantages clearly outweighed the disadvantages. It was then transferred to the bigger seagoing cog. Side rudders were abandoned not because they were inefficient but rather because on such a tall ship with such high freeboard they had to be made extremely long. With the ship heeled over to port a rudder on the starboard side had to extend a long way to reach the water. The bigger the side rudder the harder it was to build in one piece and the harder it was to fix properly to keep it attached and still minimise friction in turning. For a large ship with a keel, like the cog, the sternpost rudder, then, was a positive improve-

13: Sternpost Rudders: Elbing Seal, 1242 (top) and Ship on the Font in Winchester Cathedral, from the Low Countries, 1180 (bottom)

ment, especially in going to windward. It was particularly valuable in long reaches, for example going around Cape Skagen, the northern tip of Jutland, getting in and out of the Baltic. The voyage was a difficult one and involved going through the Great Belt or the Sound. The Danish coast was not marked or charted so, until the thirteenth century, routes through Lymfjord in north Jutland or the overland route to Hedeby or later to Lübeck were preferred. By the mid-thirteenth century, in part as a result of the building of the new bigger cog with its sternpost rudder, merchants from western Europe were appearing in markets in southern Sweden, presumably sailing directly through the Kattegat.[28] So the combination of improvements embodied in the cog not only expanded the volume of transport but also opened new trade routes and forced adjustment in old ones.

Building the new type of cog probably required less labour, especially skilled labour. The nature of the improved design decreased labour requirements while the increase in the size of the vessel lowered labour costs for each ton built. Moving the now larger main pieces of the ship, posts, ribs and so on, meant that more muscle power had to be deployed on the shipbuilding wharf, but skilled workers were not affected. The tendency was to concentrate the orders for new cogs in the hands of a smaller number of yards. The total number of ships built grew more slowly than the total tonnage, so certain builders, highly skilled men able to deal with the new design, found themselves with an increasing proportion of the orders. The same process led to the concentration of orders in a smaller number of places, locations with the skilled and unskilled manpower for building these ships and with a market for them.

Builders apparently moved to the use of the frame saw to cut wood. By 1250 the typical method of preparing planks in the Low Countries and in Germany was by sawing and not by splitting logs. More and heavier ribs and the increased piecing of the hull with scarfed planks meant that hull planks did not have to be as strong or as pliable as with Viking ships. The frame saw, a blade in the middle of an open rectangular frame, was used in the Mediterranean basin throughout the middle ages.[m] In the North, however, even by the mid-thirteenth century the coversion to saws from axes and adzes for preparing ships' timbers was not complete. It took less time to saw a log than to split it and the saw was more accurate than the axe and adze. The greater precision compensated in part for the loss in strength of the wood. The final consideration was the sharp decrease in waste when the saw was used. Much less wood had to be thrown away. Wood was always expensive in terms of time and effort needed to gather in the right types and shapes, so the economic reason sealed the decision. In addition to the saw, the ship carpenter by 1250 had an improved auger for drilling holes in planks and ribs. Builders always had a wide variety of augers but from the eleventh century they added the specialised breast auger to that collection. With a pad on the top the carpenter could put his full weight behind the force of the biting edge.[n] Turning power was separated from direct pressure on the wood, thus making it a more powerful tool, which was also easier to use in cramped spaces, of which there were many in the hull of a ship.[29] These augers were added to the broad range of axes, adzes, planes and handsaws already used by ship carpenters. They contributed to the productivity of the shipbuilder and also increased the difference between the skilled ship carpenter and the unskilled worker on the shipbuilding wharf.

The cog took over an ever-increasing portion of seagoing carriage but the hulk was not driven from northern European waters. It was still better than the cog at riding in estuaries or in moving along rivers. Hulks grew in size but not as dramatically as cogs. The hulk retained its crescent shape. The strong curved boards came together at the ends but there was still no actual stempost or sternpost. The hulk kept the side rudder longer than the cog, perhaps because it was typically smaller. The rig was the same with a single square sail on a single mast, and there was a bowsprit. There were castles at the bow and stern. The distinctive feature was the construction of the bow. Without a post the bow was held together, among other methods, by ropes wrapped around the stem. With that type of bow the hull must have been smoothly rounded and without a keel.[o] The planks, though originally placed edge to edge and then held in place by heavy external pieces, were by the thirteenth century clinkered, as was the practice with the cog. The older method placed an intolerable limit on size.[30] Though it could carry bulk goods such as wine from the western Low Countries and presumably from France to England, the hulk was still relegated to a position of lesser importance than the cog. In a sense the earlier situation was reversed and the hulk was the more specialised vessel suited to specific conditions while the cog was a general-purpose vessel.

Documents from the twelfth and thirteenth centuries show that cogs and hulks were not the only sizeable sailing ships in northern waters. The English keel, for example, still appeared in contemporary records.[p] So did the buss, the bark, the ewer and many more.[31] The problem is that illustrations and archaeological finds are not sufficient to fix design features to all those names. It is always possible that two names were

14: A Ship of the Cinque Ports, the Seal of Winchelsea, Thirteenth Century (left), and a Hulk, the Seal of New Shoreham, Second Half of the Thirteenth Century (right)

used for the same type. It is also possible that the increase in surviving names of northern ships is a result of the increasing volume of surviving documents rather than any profusion of designs. Nevertheless, the unavoidable impression is that there was a greater variety in the design of northern European sailing ships in the thirteenth century than ever before. The expansion in the volume of trade was one reason. More important, though, was the growth of trade in certain specific items along fixed routes which made it possible to build ships suited for a specific task. Moreover, competition for the carriage of goods increased. Merchants and skippers from throughout the Low Countries and not just from Frisia were involved in moving goods by sea. Shippers appeared from England, Scandinavia, German towns, and Slavic settlements along the south coast of the Baltic. For the movement of luxuries specialised design was of little importance; the only need was speed to move the goods as quickly as possible without allowing shipping costs to become extremely high. The form of the container and indeed its size beyond a low threshold were of little significance. For bulk goods, however, the situation was different. Those goods came in various forms and degrees of lumpiness. Most could be broken down into smaller units but there was a gain to be made from keeping the units as large as possible. Larger wine barrels, for example, meant savings in space on board and in handling. So for bulk goods shipwrights found themselves increasingly working on building vessels which would better serve a specific need. By the mid-thirteenth century they had only begun since the opportunity and the demand for such development was relatively new. The trend towards specialised designs became clearer over time.

To handle these goods more ports were equipped with quays. By 1250 most significant ports had at least one. The older form of landing was not abandoned. A beach or shore was usually kept open at major ports so that Scandinavian warships and related cargo ships like the keel could be beached. Inland and coastal vessels were the primary users of such shores while the seagoing ships turned to the quays. The change was not a result of the increasing use of the cog; it was rather the result of the rise in the quantity of goods handled by ports, the greater efficiency to be had from quays, and the increasing size of ships which made working at the beach more difficult. It was simpler to roll wine casks off the deck onto a quay along a short gangplank than up or down a gangplank at a steep angle. The quays were simple and rarely of stone; wood was the usual material. The economies derived from these quays led shippers to seek out ports equipped with them, thus contributing to the centralisation of trade in certain towns. The deeper draught of the cog also gave an advantage to ports closer to the sea, especially those at the mouths of rivers. These ports enjoyed a position as a transshipment point. All these factors contributed to the centralisation of shipbuilding in certain towns. Especially in Germany, shipbuilders were no longer just living along the shore, operating from a farmstead. That kind of building did continue but more typical as time passed was the professional shipwright who lived in a port town and worked on a specified piece of ground set aside for shipbuilding by the town government. The shipbuilding yard in town was still little more than a stretch of shoreline sloped so that ships could be let down or hauled out. The rise in output from such yards made them more permanent. In the growing port towns all the necessary materials and equipment and the market for the ships were easily accessible.

The quays also dictated a feature of design. Northern European ships, with the exception of eighth- and ninth-century hulks, did not have wales. The sides of ships did not have or need protection. Builders were much more worried about the bottom, which suffered abrasion when the ship was landed. With the widespread use of quays the ships needed some protection against the buffeting which the planks would take as vessels rode by the quay. The problem was not as acute as in the Mediterranean since northern clinker-built hulls could take more punishment. One solution was simply lightering the cargo, off-loading it into small vessels to move it to the market in the port or upstream to other towns. But, in case the cog had to lie at a quay, builders equipped it with bumpers in the form of projecting beam-ends.[32] Certainly, this method was not as good as the Mediterranean solution of using wales. There may have been some gain in strength, the beams serving to keep the sides of the vessels from losing shape. In the Mediterranean it was the ribs which were held by the beams but in the North the beam-ends held the hull planking itself. On the other hand, there was a sacrifice in the strength of the hull, as it was pierced along its length so the beams could pass through.[q] The sacrifice was necessary, however, if quays were to be exploited.

The changes in ship design in northern and southern Europe from 1000 to 1250 promoted social and economic developments already under way in the tenth century. Turnaround time for cargo ships continued to fall. Specialisation in production and production for export, for sale beyond individual regions, increased. There was a true international commerce in, for example, textiles stretching from the Baltic to the eastern Mediterranean, involving farmers producing the raw materials, artisans making the cloth and merchants and shippers distributing it.

The tendency towards urbanisation was even more marked. The changes were more noticeable in northern than in southern Europe. The northern region started from a lower level; but also there the technical changes in ships were greater. The widespread use of quays was combined with more economical ships, especially the cog. The process of specialisation of production by region may in fact have gone further in the North than in the South. The similarity in climate in the Mediterranean basin mitigated against specialisation in agriculture but the lack of a bulk carrier with the potential of the cog contributed to the failure there to concentrate production to the same degree. The faster pace of specialisation in the North made for a clearer division between industry and agriculture, a division which was, of course, by no means complete by 1250. With the migration of handicraft industry to towns there was a sharper as well as greater distinction between town and country. The lower costs of transport, especially between towns, fed that trend towards the separation of both personal and geographic functions.

The increased productivity of ships meant that shipbuilders were more productive. It gave them a social status not usually accorded men who worked with their hands. For example, shipbuilders were now and again mentioned by name in Norse sagas. Fewer shipbuilders spent their summers as farmers. They specialised in their trade rather than working part-time, another indication of their increasing economic value. These men, the master builders, became responsible for the entire operation of building the ship. They were directors of a complex operation employing workers of various levels of skill and buying a wide range of materials. Buyers deferred to shipbuilders' expertise in planning, expenditures and the execution of the job.[33]

Oddly enough, the augmented importance of shipbuilders was not shared by seamen. Certainly skippers, with their knowledge of navigation and handling larger ships, could expect to see their increased responsibility reflected in a higher relative income. But ordinary seamen, the workers on board, seem to have experienced a decrease in their value, especially in the North. At least in southern Europe, crewmen on round ships were called on to handle the sail, to raise and take down the yards with changes of weather. Their large numbers on each ship — that is, the high number of seamen per ton — may have kept the average wage of seamen low. In the North, men working a cog had to supply little more than muscle power for raising the yard and for loading and unloading cargo. Handling the simple sail was an easy matter. Adding bonnets or taking in sail with reef-points could not compare in complexity or skill with handling a lateen-sail. In the North, according to the law, a ship had only two types of men, the skipper and seamen. On Mediterranean vessels, on the other hand, there was a number of grades of skilled workers. In any case, seamen were still consulted on what action was to be taken, especially when the question was whether or not to sail out of port. The risk was still great enough, despite design improvements, to make voyages dangerous, and the stake of the seamen was recognised in their shared authority on major decisions. Their stake included not only their lives but also the small quantity of cargo, usually carried on deck, which each sailor was allowed to bring along and trade on his own. In northern Europe, even in the thirteenth century, the costs of ships were still low enough for some seamen to own part of the vessel they worked. This was not the case in southern Europe. Though families might still own and operate smaller coasters, the typical organisation of shipping there was for the ship to be owned by a group of investors, with wealthy merchants as the principal shareholders. Not all of those merchants would take an active part in the operation of the vessel. In fact, there was an increasing tendency towards passive investment where any individual with some money, even a relatively small amount, would buy a share in a ship without any intention of using it for trade. The only interest of the investor was a return from the successful operation of the ship.

Ships in both northern and southern Europe were made more defensible and also more reliable in the two-and-a-half centuries to 1250. The decreased risk of total loss promoted that kind of passive investment even more. The potential for high returns had a similar result.[34] The rise in the total investment in ships over those years, along with the rise in the volume of commerce, meant more employment at sea as well as in shipbuilding yards. The growth and increased investment presumably affected fishing and coastal and local shipping as well. By 1250, then, more people, absolutely and relatively, were directly or indirectly involved in waterborne commerce than at any time since the later Roman Empire. Undoubtedly, the numbers of people involved in land transport grew too, but the pace and sustained nature of growth in employment probably did not match that in shipping. There were improvements in wagons and carriages and in harness which certainly meant significant savings in moving goods by road. The technical changes were sporadic, however, and did not demonstrate the continuing and general development which was common with ships throughout Europe. Even though workers in shipping still formed only a small percentage of the total population, their numbers probably grew faster than the numbers of workers in any other sector.

Technical change in Mediterranean ships was not as great from 1000 to 1250 as in the years before or after those dates. The growth of commerce, the commercial revolution beginning in the tenth century and going on to the thirteenth, though it had its basis in better ships, was rather a product of other forces. Long-term growth in total output in agriculture and in handicraft industries, technical change in agriculture and in trades other than shipbuilding, improvement in climate, population increase, all contributed more effectively to the dynamic growth.[35] Technical change was most rapid not in ship design but in methods of doing business. Invention came from Italy and further development of methods and diffusion of established Italian practice fed commercial growth. By 1250 technical advance in business methods had moved well ahead of that dealing with the physical problems of moving goods. There was an expanding potential in commerce, more fully recognised as the talents of Italian merchants were diffused throughout the Mediterranean basin. To exploit those possibilities, however, more efficient methods of shipping were needed. That imbalance created, from the thirteenth century, a new pressure on shipbuilders to improve their product.

Changes in warships, like those in cargo ships, were limited from 1000 to 1250 but the social and political effects of the changes were more obvious and more dramatic. Throughout the eleventh century warships were built to move men to the sight of battle, as quickly as possible; they served merely to mobilise manpower. Divisibility of units was desirable. The muster system, evolved in Scandinavia in the tenth and eleventh centuries, was the most extensive example of that approach to warships. In 1066, when William the Conqueror wanted to attack England, he gathered shipwrights together, had his transports built in a short time and then used them to move his men to a landing across the English Channel. The cog changed naval operations. These vessels could serve as warships, and could dominate fighting because they were so high out of the water and because they could carry many more men for each metre of length than could any other type. Governments could not ignore the naval superiority of the cog. They were still transports for getting infantrymen to the scene of battle, be it on land or on the decks of the cogs. The use of cogs presented problems, however. Governments could not just order a fleet of cogs at short notice. The amount of wood involved, the larger shipyards needed, the larger number of workers, all meant that it took some time to construct a war fleet. Governments realised that they had such fleets already available in the hands of native and foreign merchants. Few, if any, changes were needed in these ships in order to use them for naval purposes. Cogs owned by foreigners could be seized in case of war, but, as such an action might lead to retaliation, a safer course was to get cogs from domestic merchants. The logical choice was to rent the ships, crew and all, for the period of the fighting. The government meanwhile could and did build cogs for naval action and then in peacetime rented them to merchants for trade.[36] This made for a different type of naval organisation. A general levy of ships and men along the coast was less important than having cash and men to distribute it in time of war. Naval strength was more a product of the number and availability of merchants' vessels in a country or region. The change in navies began by the thirteenth century and was more noticeable over the following 200 years. The new situation pressured northern governments and those in Iberia to take a greater interest in shipping and shipbuilding – an interest in those operations not just as a potential source of tax income but for strategic purposes as well. The connection between strength and prosperity and the prosperity of shipping and shipbuilding had already been noted in Italian towns.

In Italy the residual knowledge of Byzantine policy and understanding of sea power had made an impression. The point was also made by the Italian pirates of the tenth and eleventh centuries who used their skills to gain capital and trading connections. The need for an active government interest in shipping was made more dramatic by the crusades. Transport for the large numbers of soldiers was arranged between kings and noblemen on one side and the town governments on the other. Private individuals, shippers and shipbuilders, were not in a position, either socially or in terms of resources at their disposal, to deal with orders of that scale from those men. The demand, its size and form led municipal governments in the western Mediterranean into direct involvement in shipping and in turn in shipbuilding. Their involvement increased as resident merchants urged their governments to try to expand their share of the crusader markets. There was also a large market to capture in the pilgrim trade. Once governments were committed to efforts to control shipping, the degree of involvement and their concomitant interest in shipbuilding depended on ship design. Town governments established regulations on the numbers of people who could travel aboard ships. They fixed load limits. They had to develop rules for measuring the capacity of ships first for pilgrims and then for general cargo. They required certain practices be followed. For example, scribes had to be carried on board to record all transactions.[37] The rules, originally to improve safety and reliability, forced governments into increased involvement in shipping and, over time, it led them to define demand, in fact to direct technical change.

The galley became less important in the carriage of goods in the Mediterranean. The rise in bulk shipment, including the crusaders and their horses and armament, made galleys relatively less valuable in moving goods. The value of the galley as a warship did not decrease, however. As warships, galleys were the responsibility of the state, built, maintained, fitted out largely by the town governments. It was becoming more difficult simply to enlist merchant galleys. To guarantee a force the state had to take an interest in the construction and maintenance of its own ships. Commercial galleys were subject to increasingly stiff competition from land transport. While improvements in wagons might be sporadic, they did still serve to lower costs and, together with better roadways, made moving luxuries by land a viable alternative. Galley traffic was the most likely victim of the success of road carriers. People tended to prefer travelling by road to going by river or along the coast, so the increasing movement of people, with the exception of pilgrims for the Holy Land, did little to help galleys maintain their position as cargo ships.[38] The naval contests between Italian towns for control of trading areas, on the other hand, made galleys as crucial as ever to those towns. The strength of a city-state depended on the ability to deploy galleys and the ability to man them. The rowers were citizens paid to do the job. So the number of men available at short notice to work in a battle fleet was an indication of the strength of a city-state. Since men were recruited from the general public, then, sheer population became a measure of power. The interest in numbers, the tendency towards numerisation in public as well as private affairs which was clear in Italian towns, was promoted by the type of fighting ship.

The ability to move goods economically over greater distances affected the relative economic importance, the share of total income and of total wealth, of regions and of groups of people. In the Mediterranean the Italian towns which served as trans-shipment points between central and western Europe and the Orient, towns like Venice and Genoa, fared better than other ports. The relative reliance on trade in luxuries in the South made the change less extreme than in the North. Moreover, in the Mediterranean, political and naval power was used without compunction to direct those economic forces. In the North, the economies of the various districts and regions were still different enough in character for the introduction of more efficient bulk carriers to bring more producers into the exchange of goods. The cog, but also the hulk and

Table 3.1: Principal Dimensions of Early Medieval Ship Finds

AD	Ship	L	B	L/B	D	F	R	T
200	'*Bruges	14.5	3.5	4.1	1.35	–	–	–
400	Nydam	23.7	3.75	6.3	1.2	0.5	1-1.1	–
600	Sutton Hoo	27	4.2	6.4	1.4	0.6	1.02	–
700	Kvalsund	18	3.2	5.6	0.9	0.35	1.05	–
800	*Utrecht	17.8	4.0	4.4	1.3	0.8	–	(23)
800	*Äskekärr	c. 14	3.7	1.8	–	–	–	–
800	Oseberg	21.4	5.1	4.2	1.4	0.75	1-1.1	–
875	Tune	c. 20	4.3	4.6	–	–	–	–
900	Gokstad	23.4	5.2	4.5	1.9	0.85	0.9-1.05	32
950	Ladby	20.6	2.9	7.2	0.7	0.25	0.91	–
1000	Skuldelev 5	c. 18	2.6	7.0	1.1	0.5-0.6	–	–
1000	Skuldelev 2	c. 32	4.2	7.6	–	–	–	–
1000	*Skuldelev 3	13.3	3.3	4	1.4	1	0.94	(9)
1000	*Skuldelev 1	16.5	4.6	3.6	2	1.5	0.9	(30)
1100(?)	*Eltang	17.5	3.9	4.4	1.9	–	0.9	(20)
1100	*Galtabäck	14	4.0	3.5	1.9	–	0.48-0.63	(15)
1100	*Falsterbo	13.5	4.5	3	2.7	–	–	(40)

*Ships designed principally to carry cargo.

AD, approximate date; L, length over-all; B, breadth; F, draught; D depth in hold; R, distance between frames; T, carrying capacity in tons. All other measures in metres except L/B. ( ) indicates estimated tonnage where there is not enough precise information.

Sources: *FHMN*, pp. 256-7; Sibylla Haasum, *Vikingatidens Segling och Navigation*, pp. 23-4, and others.

buss, increased the potential market for these producers. In the majority of cases this meant an increase in the value of their output. The ships might bring in goods which would effectively compete with some locally produced item. But there would be a net gain in lower costs of imported items and in improved markets for goods most efficiently produced in the region. By the mid-thirteenth century, agricultural producers, thanks to the lower cost of bulk carriage, had become more efficient. Not only farmers and landowners were affected. Fishing and forestry also increased output and revenue as a result of the wider market and lower transport costs for their products. The extension of trading connections in the years from 750 to 1000 was certainly more impressive and based on more obvious technical change than that in the following 250 years. But in the latter period the ship-design improvement generated greater total savings because more people were affected by it. The mundane improvement of the tubby and slow-moving cog led to a greater integration of the economies of the regions of northern Europe. At the same time, the lower costs of transport contributed to the integration of the whole European economy. In the following 150 years the pace of integration increased as did the pace of technical change in ship design.

NOTES

1. Eugene H. Byrne, *Genoese Shipping in the Twelfth and Thirteenth Centuries* (The Mediaeval Academy of America, Cambridge, 1930), pp. 5-6. Lionel Casson, *Illustrated History of Ships and Boats*, pp. 70, 76. Charles-Emmanuel Dufourcq, *La Vie Quotidienne dans les Ports Méditerranéens au Moyen Age* (Hachette, Paris, 1975), pp. 59-60.

2. Hélène Ahrweiler, *Byzance et la Mer*, pp. 192, 269-70. Jean Aubin, 'Y a-t-il eu interruption du commerce par mer entre le Golfe Persique et l'Inde du XIe siècle?', *TCHM*, VI, pp. 169-71. F. C. Lane, *Venice* (Johns Hopkins University Press, Baltimore, 1973), pp. 33-5. Charles-Emmanuel Dufourcq, *La Vie Quotidienne*, pp. 125-7, and *L'Espagne Catalane et Le Maghrib aux XIIIe et XIVe Siècles* (Presses Universitaires du France, Paris, 1966), pp. 428-30.

3. For example, Hilmar C. Krueger, 'The Routine of Commerce between Genoa and North-West Africa during the late Twelfth Century', *MM*, XIX (1973), pp. 419-20, 425-30, 438.

4. Romola and R. C. Anderson, *The Sailing-Ship*, pp. 108-9. Eugene H. Byrne, *Genoese Shipping in the Twelfth and Thirteenth Centuries*, pp. 9-11, 26. John E. Dotson, 'Jal's *Nef X* and Genoese Naval Architecture in the Thirteenth Century', *MM*, LIX (1973), pp. 162-5. He offers a valuable correction to the figures given by earlier writers which are inaccurate for Genoese vessels because of conversion errors.

5. Marco Bonino, 'Lateen-rigged medieval ships', *IJNA*, VII (1978), pp. 9-15. Romola and R. C. Anderson, *The Sailing-Ship*, pp. 104-6. Eugene H. Byrne, *Genoese Shipping in the Twelfth and Thirteenth Centuries*, pp. 5-8. John E. Dotson, 'Jal's *Nef X* and Genoese Naval Architecture in the Thirteenth Century', pp. 167-8. Bernhard Hagedorn, *Die Entwicklung der wichtigsten Schiffstypen bis ins 19. Jahrhundert* (Verlag von Karl Curtis, Berlin, 1914), pp. 38-9.

6. Anthony Bryer, 'Shipping in the Empire of Trebizond', *MM*, LII (1966), pp. 6-7. Antonia de Capmany, *Memorias Historicas sobre la marina commercio y artes de la antigua ciudad de Barcelona* (D. Antonio de Sancha, Madrid, 1779-92), vol. I, pp. 32-3. Gino Luzzatto, *An Economic History of Italy* (Routledge and Kegan Paul, London, 1961), pp. 87-9, 113-14.

7. F. C. Lane, 'Note: Stowage Factors in the Maritime Statutes of Venice', *MM*, LXIII (1977), pp. 293-4. R. H. Dolley, 'The "Nef" Ships of the Ravenna Mosaics', *MM*, XXXVIII (1952), pp. 317-18. John E. Dotson, 'Jal's *Nef X* and Genoese Naval Architecture in the Thirteenth Century', p. 166. F. C. Lane, 'Tonnages, Medieval and Modern', pp. 218-20, 229-30. G. B. Rubin de Cervin, ' "Nefs" or "Corbitae" ', *MM*, XL (1954), p. 184.

8. S. D. Goitein, *A Mediterranean Society*, vol. I, *Economic Foundations* (University of California Press, Berkeley, 1967), pp. 30-9, 278-80, 295-307,

477 n13, and *Studies in Islamic History and Institutions* (E. J. Brill, Leiden, 1966), pp. 301-10. F.W. Brooks, *The English Naval Forces 1199-1272* University of Manchester Press, Manchester, 1932), p. 2.

9. G. La Roërie and J. Vivielle, *Navires et Marins*, p. 91. Archibald R. Lewis, *Naval Power and Trade in the Mediterranean*, pp. 234-6. A. W. Brøgger and Haakon Shetelig, *The Viking Ships*, p. 169. Legend has it that King Sigurd, the Jerusalem traveller as he was known, gave up his ships in Constantinople as a gift. By that time they had probably been so infested with shipworm that they were of little use except as firewood.

10. G. Asaert, *Westeuropese scheepvaart in de middeleeuwen*, pp. 25, 33-5. W. A. Engelbrecht, *Schets der Historische Betrekkingen Portugal-Nederland* (Martinus Nijhoff, The Hague, 1940), pp. 1-5. Bernhard Hagedorn, *Die Entwicklung der wichtigsten Schiffstypen*, pp. 25, 36-7. Walther Vogel, *Geschichte der Deutschen Seeschiffahrt*, pp. 124-32, 138-45. Bailey W. Diffie, *Prelude to Empire*, pp. 12-27.

11. José L. Casado Soto, 'Arquitectura naval en el Cantabrico durante el siglo XIII', *Altamira* (Santander, 1975), pp. 23-56. I am indebted to P.T. van der Merwe of the National Maritime Museum, Greenwich, UK, for supplying me with a translation of this article. Archibald R. Lewis, 'Northern European Sea Power and the Straits of Gibraltar, 1031-1350 A.D.', in William C. Jordan *et al.* (eds), *Order and Innovation in the Middle Ages: Essays in Honor of Joseph R. Strayer* (Princeton University Press, Princeton, 1976), pp. 140-54.

12. Maurice Lombard, 'Arsenaux et bois de marine dans la Méditerranée musulmane', pp. 74-80. Hélène Antoniadis-Bibicou, *Etudes d'histoire maritime de Byzance*, p. 23.

13. F. C. Lane, 'The Economic Meaning of the Invention of the Compass', *American Historical Review*, LXVIII (1963), pp. 607-8. E. G. R. Taylor, *The Haven-Finding Art*, pp. 94-8. Heinrich Winter, 'Who Invented the Compass?', *MM*, XXIII (1937), pp. 95-102. Barbara M. Kreutz, 'Mediterranean Contributions to the Medieval Mariner's Compass', *Technology and Culture*, XIV (1973), pp. 367-72. W. E. May, *A History of Marine Navigation* (G. T. Foulis and Co. Ltd, Henley-on-Thames, 1973), pp. 45-6.

14. Hélène Ahrweiler, *Byzance et la Mer*, pp. 185-97, 229-30. Hélène Antoniadis-Bibicou, *Etudes d'histoire maritime de Byzance*, pp. 116-17. She sees the decline of the navy in the eleventh century as a symptom of the general breakdown of the Byzantine polity. That is true but begs the question. Archibald R. Lewis, *Naval Power and Trade in the Mediterranean*, pp. 194-201, 217, 225-46.

15. R. C. Anderson, 'The Oars of Northern Long-Ships', *MM*, XXIX (1943), pp. 191-5. Romola and R. C. Anderson, *The Sailing-Ship*, pp. 77-80. The claim of 90 metres' length for the largest of King Canute's ships is impossible as R. C. Anderson argued elsewhere. A. W. Brøgger and Haakon Shetelig, *The Viking Ships*, pp. 126-9, 136-59, 172-3. The measures come from an Icelandic source and may exaggerate the lengths. There appears to have been some experimenting in the thirteenth century with two decks of oars but that was highly abnormal. Ole Crumlin-Pedersen, *Traeskibet. Fra Langskib til Fregat* (Traebranchens Oplysiningsrad, Copenhagen, 1968), pp. 4, 24. There are reports of longships of 40 pairs, 45 pairs and 60 pairs of oars but these seem exaggerated. The largest was probably of 37 rooms.

16. A. W. Brøgger and Haakon Shetelig, *The Viking Ships*, pp. 162, 175-6. Archibald R. Lewis, *The Northern Seas*, pp. 448-9. Tradition dates the beginning of the Norwegian system of mustership at about 950. He suggests it may have been copied from the methods of Alfred the Great in England. Adolf Schück, 'Ledung och Konunghamn', *Sjöhistorisk Årsbok* (1950), pp. 97-128. G. P. Harbitz

156   Crusaders' Ships and Cogs: 1000-1250

et al., Den Norske Leidangen (Sjøforsvarets Overkommando, Oslo, 1951), pp. 11-160. Edvard Bull, *Leding* (Steenske Forlag, Oslo, 1920).

17. Ole Crumlin-Pedersen, *Das Haithabusschiff Berichte über die Ausgrabungen in Haithabu*, Schleswig-Holsteinisches Landesmuseum für Vor- und Frühgeschichte, Bericht 3 (Karl Wachholtz Verlag, Neumünster, 1969), pp. 29-32. *HSUA*, p. 186. *FHMN*, p. 47. Olaf Olsen and Ole Crumlin-Pedersen, 'The Skuldelev Ships', pp. 170-2.

18. *AB*, pp. 250-2. Harald Åkerlund, 'Skeppsfyndet vid Falsterbo 1932', *Sjöhistorisk Årsbok* (1950), pp. 93-100. The vessel is dated about 1300 with an over-all length of 13.5 metres and a capacity of about 40 tons. The Galtabäck boat from Sweden, dated about 1100, was about 13.1 metres long and with similar proportions. It showed the same change in internal frames as did the Eltang ship of about 20 tons from the twelfth century found in Denmark. Sigvard Skov, 'Et Middelalderligt Skibsfund fra Eltang vig', *Sœtryk af Kuml, Årbog for Arkaeologisk Selskab* (1952), pp. 71, 82-3. Knut Helle, 'Trade and Shipping between Norway and England in the Reign of Håkon Håkonsson (1217-63)', *Sjøfartshistorisk Årbok* (1967), pp. 24-6. Archibald R. Lewis, *The Northern Seas*, pp. 483-4. Carl V. Sølver, 'The Rebaek Rudder', *MM*, XXXII (1946), p. 117. Gerhard Timmerman, 'Schiffbauprobleme zur Hansezeit', *Handels- og Søfartsmuseet På Kronborg, Årbog* (1966), pp. 288-92.

19. Harald Åkerlund, *Fartygsfynden i den Forna Hamnen i Kalmar* (Almquist and Wiksells Boktryckeri AB, Uppsala, 1951), p. 157. He believes that Kalmar Find I may have been a *buza*. Narve Bjørgo, 'Skipstyper i norrøne sam tidssoger', *Sjøfartshistorisk Årbok* (1965), pp. 9-14, 20. A. W. Brøgger and Haakon Shetelig, *The Viking Ships*, pp. 154, 179-80. Paul Heinsius, *Das Schiff der Hansischen Frühzeit*, pp. 207-8. G. J. Marcus, 'The Evolution of the Knörr', p. 122.

20. A. W. Brøgger and Haakon Shetelig, *The Viking Ships*, pp. 181-2. *HSUA*, p. 190. Knut Helle, 'Trade and Shipping between Norway and England', pp. 8-14, 18-29. *AB*, pp. 259-69.

21. Harald Åkerlund, *Fartygsfynden i den Forna Hamnen i Kalmar*, pp. 151-2. Ole Crumlin-Pedersen, 'Cog-Kogge-Kaag', pp. 129-34. *HSUA*, p. 187. Wreck Q75, found in the polder land of the former Zuider Zee, dated from the twelfth century, shows all the features of the earlier cog and has a keel. The Eltang ship (see note 20) was a cog as well. *FHMN*, pp. 64, 69-71, 74-6, 120. Paul Heinsius, *Das Schiff der Hansischen Frühzeit*, pp. 104-12.

22. *FHMN*, pp. 238-47. Paul Heinsius, *Das Schiff der Hansischen Frühzeit*, pp. 73-6. The word cog to describe a large deep-sea trading vessel was not used until about 1200 in either the Baltic or North Sea. The delay of over a century is not unexpected given the nature of written records, the fact that they were in Latin and the kinds of people who kept them.

23. Roger Degryse, 'De maritieme aspecten van de keure van Nieuwpoort van 1163', *MAB*, XX (1968), p. 68. Paul Heinsius, 'Dimensions et Caractéristiques des "Koggen" Hanséatiques dans le Commerce Baltique', *TCHM*, III, pp. 9-11, and *Das Schiff der Hansischen Frühzeit*, pp. 89-102. Walther Vogel, *Geschichte der Deutschen Seeschiffahrt*, vol. I, pp. 126-8. F. W. Brooks, *The English Naval Forces*, p. 17. *FHMN*, p. 259.

24. Romola and R. C. Anderson, *The Sailing-Ship*, pp. 82-3. F. W. Brooks, 'Naval Armament in the Thirteenth Century', pp. 121-30. *HSUA*, pp. 190-1. The change to cogs from longships came in Denmark in 1304. The island of Sealand was required to supply 120 longships but after the change the requirement was five to ten cogs, reflecting the greater size and expense of the bigger ships. Adolf Schück, 'Ledung och Konunghamn', p. 128. The change from supplying longships led to a change in taxation. Governments were more interested in cash payments to build, equip and maintain cogs than in the labour of local farmers and

fishermen to build, maintain and man longships.

25. F.W. Brooks, *The English Naval Forces*, pp. 8-16, 54-68, 79-110, 168-94, and 'William de Wrotham and the Office of Keeper of the King's Ports and Galleys', *English Historical Review*, XL (1925), pp. 570-9.

26. Harald Åkerlund, *Fartygsfynden i den Forna Hamnen i Kalmar*, p. 152. Paul Heinsius, *Das Schiff der Hansischen Frühzeit*, pp. 109-14, 128-9. His argument that cogs were of skeleton construction based on the inverse clinkering and the methods of house building in Germany in the twelfth century is not convincing. J. H. Parry, *Discovery of the Sea*, pp. 20-2.

27. G. Asaert, *Westeuropese scheepvaart in de middeleeuwen*, pp. 93-5. H. H. Brindley, 'Mediaeval Ships', VII, *MM*, III (1913), pp. 14-16, and VIII, *MM*, IV (1914), pp. 110-11. A. W. Brøgger and Haakon Shetelig, *The Viking Ships*, p. 182. Paul Heinsius, *Das Schiff der Hansischen Frühzeit*, pp. 134-9, 145.

28. Romola and R. C. Anderson, *The Sailing-Ship*, pp. 85-90. *HSUA*, pp. 189-90. Paul Heinsius, *Das Schiff der Hansischen Frühzeit*, pp. 119-26. H. S. Vaughan, 'The Whipstaff', I, *MM*, III (1913), pp. 231-2, and II, *MM*, IV (1914), pp. 135-7.

29. A. W. Brøgger and Haakon Shetelig, *The Viking Ships*, pp. 164-5. W. L. Goodman, *The History of Woodworking Tools*, pp. 116-19, 125-32, 165-72. Henry C. Mercer, *Ancient Carpenters' Tools*, pp. 17-21, 179-80. Paul Heinsius, *Das Schiff der Hansischen Frühzeit*, pp. 127-8. The breast auger improved the efficiency of the youngest and least skilled carpenters since they were the ones given the job of boring holes for the treenails: J. T. Tinniswood, 'English Galleys, 1272-1377', *MM*, XXXV (1949), p. 280.

30. H.H. Brindley, 'Mediaeval Ships', V, *MM*, II (1912), pp. 44-52, VII, *MM*, III (1913), pp. 337-40, and VIII, *MM*, IV (1914), pp. 112, 130-3. *FHMN*, pp. 60, 120. Bernhard Hagedorn, *Die Entwicklung der wichtigsten Schiffstypen*, pp. 214-18, 222-4.

31. *FHMN*, pp. 57-9. Paul Heinsius, *Das Schiff der Hansischen Frühzeit*, pp. 201-10.

32. G. Asaert, *Westeuropese scheepvaart in de middeleeuwen*, pp. 133-5. Nantes, not an insignificant port, did not have a stone quay until 1492 so the process of adopting quays was a slow one. *FHMN*, pp. 159-64, 170-4. Bernhard Hagedorn, *Die Entwicklung der wichtigsten Schiffstypen*, pp. 22-3.

33. A. W. Brøgger and Haakon Shetelig, *The Viking Ships*, p. 162. Eugene H. Byrne, *Genoese Shipping in the Twelfth and Thirteenth Centuries*, pp. 25-6. Paul Heinsius, *Das Schiff der Hansischen Frühzeit*, pp. 150-1. Arne Emil Christensen, *Scheepveart van de Vikingen* (DeBoer Maritiem, Bussum, 1977), pp. 53-7.

34. G. Asaert, *Westeuropese scheepvaart in de middeleeuwen*, pp. 125-8. Eugene H. Byrne, *Genoese Shipping in the Twelfth and Thirteenth Centuries*, pp. 12-15, 22-4. Karl-Friedrich Krieger, *Ursprung und Wurzeln der Rôles D'Oléron* (Böhlau Verlag, Cologne, 1970), pp. 17-23, 71-6.

35. F. C. Lane, 'Progrès technologiques et productivité dans les transports maritimes de la fin du Moyen Age au début des Temps modernes', p. 277. He is right to say that no precise measure is possible of the contribution of technical change in shipbuilding to European growth. The necessary quantitative data do not exist. Data do not exist for any other possible explanatory factors, population being only a partial exception, so each must be weighed and estimates made based on non-numerical information.

36. M. Oppenheim, *A History of the Administration of the Royal Navy and of Merchant Shipping in Relation to the Navy* (John Lane the Bodley Head, London, 1896), pp. 4-6. Michael Lewis, *The History of the British Navy* (Penguin Books, Harmondsworth, 1957), pp. 13-18.

37. B. W. Bathe, *Seven Centuries of Sea Travel from the Crusaders to the*

Cruises (Barrie and Jenkins, London, 1972), p. 18. Eugene H. Byrne, *Genoese Shipping in the Twelfth and Thirteenth Centuries*, pp. 59-61. Paul Gille, 'Jauge et Tonnage des Navires', *TCHM*, I, pp. 92-3. F. C. Lane, 'Tonnages, Medieval and Modern', p. 221.
  38. Land transport also benefited from low charges in taxes and fees for road use. Over all, road transport continued to be highly flexible. R. S. Lopez, 'The Evolution of Land Transport in the Middle Ages', *Past and Present*, 9 (1956), pp. 17-29. F. M. Stenton, 'The Road System of Medieval England', *Economic History Review*, VII (1936), pp. 19-20.

NOTES TO ILLUSTRATIONS

  a. Anthony Bryer, 'Shipping in the Empire of Trebizond', *MM*, LII (1966), p. 10, figure 7. Lionel Casson, *Illustrated History of Ships and Boats*, no. 51.
  b. John E. Dotson, 'Jal's *Nef X* and Genoese Naval Architecture in the Thirteenth Century', *MM*, LIX (1973), p. 164. *HSUA*, p. 213. Marco Bonino, 'Lateen-rigged medieval ships', *IJNA*, VII (1978), p. 11. Björn Landström, *The Ship*, nos. 211, 214, 219, 230.
  c. Romola and R. C. Anderson, *The Sailing-Ship*, p. 105. Lionel Casson, *Illustrated History of Ships and Boats*, nos. 96-7. R. H. Dolley, 'The "Nef" Ships of the Ravenna Mosaics', *MM*, XXXVIII (1952), opposite p. 318. Bernhard Hagedorn, *Die Entwicklung der wichtigsten Schiffstypen*, p. 38. Paul Heinsius, *Das Schiff der Hansischen Frühzeit*, p. 36. G.B. Rubin de Cervin, ' "Nefs" or "Corbitae" ', *MM*, XL (1954), p. 184. Björn Landström, *The Ship*, nos. 225-9, 231.
  d. Hélène Antoniadis-Bibicou, *Etudes d'histoire maritime de Byzance*, between p. 24 and 25, plate IV.
  e. G. Asaert, *Westeuropese scheepvaart in de middeleeuwen* (Unieboek, Bussum, 1974), p. 48. Romola and R. C. Anderson, *The Sailing-Ship*, pp. 79-80. A. W. Brøgger and Haakon Shetelig, *The Viking Ships*, pp. 164-5. Lionel Casson, *Illustrated History of Ships and Boats*, nos. 77-8. Bernhard Hagedorn, *Die Entwicklung der wichtigsten Schiffstypen*, plate II. Claude Farrère, *Histoire de la Marine Française*, pp. 8-11. G. S. Laird Clowes, *Sailing Ships*, part I, p. 45. Björn Landström, *The Ship*, nos. 160, 161, 163. G. La Roërie and J. Vivielle, *Navires et Marins*, vol. I, pp. 177, 184-5, 187-8.
  f. Harald Åkerlund, 'Galtabäcksbatens, ålder och härstamning. II', *Sjöhistorisk Årsbok* (1948), p. 80, and 'Skeppsfyndet vid Falsterbo 1932), *Sjöhistorisk Årsbok* (1950), pp. 96, 99, 103. Paul Heinsius, *Das Schiff der Hansischen Frühzeit*, p. 52. *FHMN*, pp. 37-8, 40-2. Björn Landström, *The Ship*, nos. 189-91. Olaf Olsen and Ole Crumlin-Pedersen, 'The Skuldelev Ships (II)', p. 173. Gerhard Timmermann, 'Schiffbauprobleme zur Hansezeit', *Handels- og Søfartsmuseet på Kronborg, Årbog* (1966), p. 291.
  g. *AB*, no. 164. Siegfried Fliedner, ' "Kogge" und "Hulk" ', nos. 56, 63. Paul Heinsius, *Das Schiff der Hansischen Frühzeit*, p. 51.
  h. G. Asaert, *Westeuropese scheepvaart in de middeleeuwen*, p. 25. A. W. Brøgger and Haakon Shetelig, *The Viking Ships*, p. 181. *FHMN*, p. 65. Siegfried Fliedner, ' "Kogge" und "Hulk" ', nos. 43-6, 49-55, 76-7. Bernhard Hagedorn, *Die Entwicklung der wichtigsten Schiffstypen*, plates V, VI. Paul Heinsius, *Das Schiff der Hansischen Frühzeit*, p. 65, plate IX, nos. 19-20. Björn Landström, *The Ship*, no. 169.
  i. G. Asaert, *Westeuropese scheepvaart in de middeleeuwen*, pp. 40, 91-2.

FHMN, p. 44. Siegfried Fliedner, ' "Kogge" und "Hulk" ', nos. 78, 80, 81. Björn Landström, *The Ship*, nos. 164, 165, 167, 168. *AB*, no. 165. *HSUA*, p. 196.
    j. G. Asaert, *Westeuropese scheepvaart in de middeleeuwen*, p. 94. H. H. Brindley, 'Early Reefs', *MM*, VI (1920), opposite p. 65. Siegfried Fliedner, ' "Kogge" und "Hulk" ', nos. 81, 85. Paul Heinsius, *Das Schiff der Hansischen Frühzeit*, pp. 4, 41, plate II, no. 3. Björn Landström, *Sailing Ships*, nos. 162, 166. *HSUA*, p. 196.
    k. G. Asaert, *Westeuropese scheepvaart in de middeleeuwen*, opposite p. 32, p. 92. H. H. Brindley, 'Early Reefs', p. 79, opposite p. 80, and 'Mediaeval Ships', *MM*, II (1912), p. 131, opposite pp. 132, 133 and 166, p. 167, opposite p. 239, p. 241, III (1913), opposite p. 14. A. W. Brøgger and Haakon Shetelig, *The Viking Ships*, p. 181. Björn Landström, *Sailing Ships*, no. 163, and *The Ship*, no. 170. Paul Heinsius, *Das Schiff der Hansischen Frühzeit*, plate VI, no. 13. G. La Roërie and J. Vivielle, *Navires et Marins*, vol. I, pp. 196-7.
    l. *AB*, no. 40. G. Asaert, *Westeuropese scheepvaart in de middeleeuwen*, pp. 94, 105-6. A. W. Brøgger and Haakon Shetelig, *The Viking Ships*, p. 183. Romola and R. C. Anderson, *The Sailing-Ship*, plate III. Siegfried Fliedner, ' "Kogge" und "Hulk" ', nos. 6-7, 98. Bernhard Hagedorn, *Die Entwicklung der wichtigsten Schiffstypen*, plate V. Paul Heinsius, *Das Schiff der Hansischen Frühzeit*, p. 48, plate X, no. 21. G. La Roërie and J. Vivielle, *Navires et Marins*, vol. I, p. 193. Björn Landström, *The Ship*, nos. 174-7.
    m. Henry C. Mercer, *Ancient Carpenters' Tools*, p. 24.
    n. A. W. Brøgger and Haakon Shetelig, *The Viking Ships*, pp. 168-9. *HSUA*, pp. 196-7. Claude Farrère, *Histoire de la Marine Française*, pp. 7, 25. Henry C. Mercer, *Ancient Carpenters' Tools*, p. 179. Paul Heinsius, *Das Schiff der Hansischen Frühzeit*, p. 110. Olaf Olsen and Ole Crumlin-Pedersen, 'The Skuldelev Ships (II)', pp. 154-5.
    o. G. Asaert, *Westeuropese scheepvaart in de middeleeuwen*, opposite pp. 16, 107. H. H. Brindley, 'Mediaeval Ships', *MM*, I (1911), p. 44, II (1912), pp. 3, 47, IV (1914), p. 132. *HSUA*, p. 199. *FHMN*, p. 55. Siegfried Fliedner, ' "Kogge" und "Hulk" ', nos. 1, 8-9. Paul Heinsius, *Das Schiff der Hansischen Frühzeit*, p. 215. *AB*, nos. 39, 201, 202.
    p. Romola and R. C. Anderson, *The Sailing-Ship*, p. 81. Lionel Casson, *Illustrated History of Ships and Boats*, nos. 79-83. G. S. Laird Clowes, *Sailing Ships*, part I, p. 47. G. Asaert, *Westeuropese scheepvaart in de middeleeuwen*, opposite p. 17, p. 90. *FHMN*, p. 44. Paul Heinsius, *Das Schiff der Hansischen Frühzeit*, pp. 40, 44-5, 47-8, plate III, nos. 7-8, plate VII, no. 15. Siegfried Fliedner, ' "Kogge" und "Hulk" ', nos. 42, 82-4. G. La Roërie and J. Vivielle, *Navires et Marins*, vol. I, p. 191, plate VIII, nos. 1, 3, p. 202. Bernhard Hagedorn, *Die Entwicklung der wichtigsten Schiffstypen*, p. 31. Björn Landström, *The Ship*, no. 166.
    q. G. Asaert, *Westeuropese scheepvaart in de middeleeuwen*, p. 90. Richard Lebaron Bowen, Jr, 'The origins of fore-and-aft rigs', p. 281. Siegfried Fliedner, ' "Kogge" und "Hulk" ', nos. 79, 89. Bernhard Hagedorn, *Die Entwicklung der wichtigsten Schiffstypen*, plate IV, XIV. Björn Landström, *The Ship*, no. 179. G. La Roërie and J. Vivielle, *Navires et Marins*, vol. I, plate IX, no. 1, p. 203.

4   COGS, HULKS AND GREAT GALLEYS: 1250-1400

In Italy the city-states became involved in protracted wars among themselves. Some few states expanded and consolidated their positions. The fighting was not only at sea but for the maritime republics it was there that the decisive battles took place. One town eclipsed another, Venice finally defeating Genoa, though that did not destroy the trade or the authority of the loser. By 1400 Italy had an emerging system of sizeable political units which formed alliances among themselves. The Latin Empire, set up by crusaders at Constantinople in 1204, fell in 1261 to the remnants of the old Greek Empire. The Byzantine Empire was re-established only with the help of Genoese ships and Genoese troops, who were there to topple Venice from its privileged position in the Empire. Genoa, of course, received trade concessions for its efforts. The Greek Empire expended its limited resources in trying to retake provinces in Greece. Much of the equipment and manpower had to come from allies in Italy. By the end of the fourteenth century the Turks had unquestionably replaced Byzantium as the pre-eminent power in the eastern Mediterranean. After overrunning the Crusader States they moved into Asia Minor and the Balkans where they slowly expanded their empire at the expense of Byzantium. The Turks found that they
Illustration above: The great cog seal, Stralsund, 1329.

161

had to take to the sea and so introduced a new source of potential naval conflict for the Italian maritime states.

In Iberia the kingdoms which started in the Pyrenees in the ninth century had taken all but a small portion of the peninsula from the Moors. By 1400 the kingdoms were constitutionally and politically much like those in northern Europe. In their attitude and policy towards shipping, though, the kingdoms were much more like the Italian city-states. Catalan merchants and sailors, especially those from Barcelona, followed their Italian counterparts in shipping and trading throughout the Mediterranean and beyond — under the watchful eye of the governments which were increasingly looking for ways to improve domestic merchant marines and navies. Monarchs in northern Europe expanded their activities across a broader range within their own lands. They also tried to expand those lands, thus bringing themselves into dynastic conflict with other rulers. The extensive fighting, most notably the Hundred Years' War between England and France, disrupted trade and, moreover opened the field for pirates who were guaranteed support and safe harbour from at least one combatant. The failure of the Holy Roman Empire by 1250 made it possible for many princes and lesser nobles in Germany to pursue their own dynastic goals. The results for trade were similar to those in western Europe. The Free Imperial cities, the towns inside the Empire which had been able to keep from falling under the authority of a regional lord, banned together in leagues to promote their mutual interests. The best-known of the leagues, the Hanse, was made up of trading towns in northern Germany and along the North and Baltic Seas. Led by Lübeck, the Hanseatic League organised trading relationships outside the Empire, gained trading concessions for member towns and, when necessary, mobilised forces to protect mutual interests. By the late fourteenth century the League was strong enough to impose a crushing defeat on the king of Denmark and forced him to accept a peace which gave German merchants virtual control of trade inside his kingdom.

The greatest disturbance to the European economy came not from political but from demographic change. The Black Death, a pandemic of massive proportions, spread across Europe from 1346 to 1350. Population growth had already slowed and perhaps even stopped by about 1300. Europe was apparently facing a crisis where food production, given contemporary techniques, was only just able to sustain the population. Because of poor weather there was a major famine in the second decade of the fourteenth century. The general deterioration of the climate cut into food output and increased the likelihood of disease.

The bubonic plague in the middle of the century took the lives of about one-third of Europeans. After 1350 outbreaks recurred, preventing recovery. Population continued to fall, reaching the lowest point at some time in the first two decades of the fifteenth century. There can be no question but that this fall in population meant a fall in total output since labour was a large component of input in all productive processes. Whether output per person fell as well is a moot point. There is evidence that the volume of trade fell by more than the population. The demographic disaster was so great that it had a pervasive effect on the economy. The effects continued throughout the fifteenth century. The changes in the economy generated pressures on shipbuilders. They responded with new designs in the fourteenth century and established the basis for the major inventions of the fifteenth.

Builders continued to explore the possibilities of the cog design. The type became even bigger. The castles grew and became more a part of the fabric of the ship rather than simple additions. While in the mid-thirteenth century cogs of 100 tons were rare, by the first decade of the fourteenth century in the Anglo-Gascon wine trade 81 per cent of ships were of less than 150 tons but 16 per cent were from 150 to 200 tons and 3 per cent were over 200 tons, the largest reaching 300 tons. By 1400 average size was probably still around 100 tons but it was technically possible to build much larger long-distance carriers. The sheer volume of the wine trade between Bordeaux and England drew vessels which tested the technically feasible limits of size. At the height of the trade, in 1308 to 1309, more than 102,000 tons of wine, about 850,000 hectolitres, left the Gironde for northern points in one twelve-month period. The English market from the late twelfth century was dominated by these Gascon wines since they could be delivered in a volume and at a price to satisfy that market. Though the total volume of exports fell after 1350, concentration on the English market meant that the largest sailing ships were still used.[1] For protection, these larger ships had fenders, relatively short perpendicular pieces of wood running down from the gunwale. They were especially important to parts of the ship which were built up higher, that is at the ends where castles were sitting on top of the planking. Shrouds on the sides helped to support the heavier mast and they had ratlines. The shrouds often ran from fenders so the latter served a double purpose. The aftercastle became longer and lower to accommodate the cabin for the captain and important passengers. One cog had an oven for baking bread.[2] An example of a late fourteenth-century cog was recently discovered at Bremen.[a] In general the form of the ship confirms the accuracy of contemporary illustrations of cogs on town seals. As toll records indicate, the Bremen find had a through deck – and a deck in the aftercastle. There was a sternpost rudder. The ship was 23.5 metres long, the maximum width was 7 metres and the capacity has been estimated at 130 tons. There were two windlasses on board. The smaller one with a horizontal axis was used for hauling the anchor. The function of the larger one set on the aftercastle is unclear. The first three hull planks, those closest to the keel, were placed edge to edge. The remaining planks overlapped. There were only twelve planks on each side, consistent with the small number shown on seals. The keel was in three parts and not one. The pieces were scarfed together and those at the ends were at a slight angle to the central piece.[3] That form of construction appears on coins from ninth-century Dorestad. It made getting off sandbars easier and with larger ships it also saved having to find a piece of wood big enough for a full keel. Obviously, shipbuilders did not easily abandon the design features of earlier vessels. Still, enough changes had been made that, by the fourteenth century, cogs for long-distance bulk carriage like that found at Bremen were testing the ability of contemporary harbours to accommodate them.

The control system on the cog was improved by the addition of the whipstaff. The rudder, instead of just passing over the sternpost, went through an opening in the stern. There was a bar attached to the tiller at a 90° angle. The helmsman handling the bar could stand higher and see the action of the ship. For larger ships a fulcrum had to be added above the point where the tiller met the bar so that the helmsman could move the heavy rudder. The bar or whipstaff was in the same plane as the rudder. Moving it in one direction made the rudder move in the other. The helmsman could stay in much the same place while moving the rudder. He was usually under the aftercastle so there was the added advantage that he and the steering gear were protected in battle. Through a window he could keep an eye on the sails while steering. Builders added the fulcrum which made the mechanism effective some time in the fourteenth century.[4] The problem with the whipstaff was that it could only move the rudder through a small angle. In bad weather or when a major change in direction was needed, the heavy tiller itself had to be moved. Manpower, perhaps with the aid of ropes and tackles, did that job.

The propulsion system of the cog saw little change. The yard was held to the mast now by a parrel, a rope going around the mast through small wooden spheres, which turned as the yard was hoisted so that friction was sharply decreased. The rope, meanwhile, held the yard fast

15: The Bremen Hanse Cog, 1380, Reconstruction of 1979

to the mast. There were no lifts, no ropes with tackles running from the top of the mast to points along the yard. Roman builders had used lifts and they were common on southern ships throughout the middle ages.[5] Perhaps because the northern yard was always one piece and not two spars as in the South, lifts were not needed.[b]

The cog had early proved itself an effective warship and by the late fourteenth century it was the only warship of consequence in northern Europe. Governments built and used other types but they were generally to supplement cog fleets. Kings requisitioned cogs from their ports when they embarked on a naval campaign. They also kept small fleets of their own cogs at strategic ports. During the earlier part of the Hundred Years' War massive fleets of cogs were sent out by the kings of England and France, meeting in battles involving thousands of men.[c] But use as a warship was secondary to the principal use of the cog as a deep-sea commercial vessel.

The cog was the major carrier in the great trades of the towns of the German Hanse. Their continued prosperity, even in the face of the economic problems of the fourteenth century, depended on the relatively low cost of transport by cog. German merchants handled the export of surplus grain from Poland through ports on the Baltic. The wheat, and even more important the rye, were destined for the urban centres of western Europe, especially in Flanders. The cogs also carried timber and other sylvan products from Poland and Russia. Hanse merchants, most notably from Lübeck, exported the herring caught and packed along the coast of the province of Scania in modern southern Sweden. The cogs going west required a back cargo. The most important good carried back to northeastern Europe in terms of value was Flemish cloth but it did little to fill the holds. Hanse shippers found a solution to the imbalance in the volume of trade when, in the course of the thirteenth century, their cogs began to load salt produced along the shores of the Bay of Bourgneuf in southern Brittany. Grain was the primary good shipped from the Baltic ports and Hansards measured the capacity of ships in terms of the quantity of rye they could carry. The trading network of the Hanse merchants, based on these bulk goods, by 1400 stretched from Novgorod in Russia to Lisbon in Portugal.[6] The growth in the herring fishery increased demand for salt to treat the fish and so the two complementary trades combined further to increase the use of the cog.

The growth of the Scania fishery after the Hanseatic League defeated the king of Denmark in 1370 brought competitors for the German merchants from England and from Holland. German efforts to exclude these other shippers led the competitors to sail their own cogs directly to the Baltic and to compete in the lucrative grain trade. Towns in the Baltic, members of the Hanse such as Gdansk, Riga and Revel, had the largest cogs since they carried the bulk goods over the longest distances. There was a number of smaller ships carrying salt from Brittany to England and to the Low Countries. But Hansards found that they could compete on those routes with their large ships as well — that is, if they could find another cargo to take back to the Baltic after off-loading the salt. In the Scania herring fishery as many as 40,000 small boats with a crew of seven or eight men in each were used to catch the fish. As many as 500 big and medium-size ships carried the casks packed with herring to ports throughout northern Europe. Annual production at the end of the fourteenth century was about 100,000 casks. An average cargo was 200 casks, small for a deep-sea cog but large for the many coastal traders that carried the product to Lübeck and other nearby ports.[7] The growth of these interdependent trades meant more employment for German cogs and created a demand for ever more economic bulk carriers.

Other types competed with the cog for a share of the northern carrying trade. In general the success of these other designs was greater the shorter the haul. The keel appears in fourteenth-century illustrations. As always, builders were reluctant to abandon a design, especially when some use could still be found for it. Keels typically still carried a side rudder. The Scandinavian buss continued to hold some of the bulk trade of the North throughout the thirteenth and fourteenth centuries. It was modified by the addition of sharp posts and a stern-post rudder, presumably in imitation of the cog. The buss in the older form survived as well.[d] The modified type was much like a cog except for some difference in the arrangement of the ribs and the lowest planking and except for a higher length-to-beam ratio.[8]

Slavic types were still widely used. Presumably these were first developed in the seventh and eighth centuries when Slavs reached the shores of the Baltic, found Germans there using boats of originally Celtic design and probably modelled their own craft after them. Planks on Slavic boats were clinkered but, instead of being riveted, the overlapping planks were attached to each other with treenails. These boats existed side by side with typical German and Scandinavian designs. The eastward migration of German merchants and shippers and the establishment of German commercial settlements along the south coast of the Baltic led to the widespread use of cogs. The Slavic design, the pram, remained popular, however, for coasters and lighters and apparently for catching herring off Scania. They did not have strong steps for the masts but did have a large number of heavy ribs. The bottom was typically flat. One distinguishing feature of some Slavic types was an L-shaped plank to join the bottom and sides. The angle there was a sharp one and Slavic builders formed a single piece to serve as the last plank of the bottom and the first of one side.[e] This was exactly the same as the method used on one of the riverboats of the Roman period found at Zwammerdam. For warships Slavs used Scandinavian types.[9] For inland vessels, however, they, like German shippers, relied on the simple pram with its Celtic origins for lightering in harbours and for transport on rivers throughout the remainder of the middle ages.

In addition to the pram there was a wide variety of types built in northern Europe for the fishery and coastal trade. Most are not identifiable. The vessels were often of earlier design, modified to handle certain waters, harbours and cargoes. For example, Frisian trade not only continued but experienced some growth in relative volume and scope. Traders from Stavoren and other towns along the Frisian coast carried beer from Hamburg to the Low Countries, local agricultural products to England, and fish and grain from the eastern shores of the Baltic to the West. They carried goods for other producers, often acting as intermediaries. Many of the trips were short, such as that from Friesland to Hoorn across the Zuider Zee carrying beef cattle. The coasters and small seagoing ships of the Frisian traders were not the kind to appear in contemporary illustrations or records. Frisians probably used small cogs for most of their trade but they were not limited to that design. Records from the Low Countries and Germany mention many types, sometimes associated with special duties, and often the names are repetitions of names that appeared earlier.[10] None of these types posed a threat to the cog in deep-sea carriage but they did offer an ever greater variety of options to shippers. The growth of long-distance carriage made possible a growth in intraregional short-distance trade for the distribution of bulk goods from the deep-water ports. Builders thus had more chances to experiment with specialised designs, and more features to choose from in designing all ships.

The cog did face competition in long-distance bulk carriage from one type: the hulk, the carrying capacity of which always compared favourably with the cog because of the shape of the hull. While the cog had grown much faster than the hulk in the twelfth and early thirteenth centuries, the gap was gradually closed during the fourteenth, and the hulk became more of a threat to the cog. With a clinker-built hull and wood instead of ropes to hold the bow, the hulk went from about half the carrying capacity of the cog in 1250 to the size of the largest cog by the 1380s.[f] Shipbuilders then merged the cog and the hulk into one composite design. After 1400 the same ship might alternately be called a cog or a hulk; this was not illogical since the new type had features of both.[11] The merger was a logical result of the presence in each type of certain advantageous features. Though they had existed side by side for some centuries, builders had not combined them. The economic situation of the late fourteenth century gave shipwrights more reason to examine the possibilities. Relative to other prices, grain prices fell in western Europe after the Black Death. The growth in grain exports from the Baltic had been based on the pressure on land in the West, the demand for more food and the resulting high grain prices there. Because of the fall in population in 1346 to 1350 farmers in western Europe could concentrate their efforts on the most productive ground and thus output for each agricultural worker rose. Moreover, the plague had a massive deflationary effect on demand.

Around 1400 the cost of transport was almost half the price of Baltic grain delivered in Bruges. For other bulk goods the percentage could be even higher, for example 85 per cent for Portugese salt carried to Bruges. With more expensive goods moved over shorter distances the cost of shipment was inconsequential. Shipping wool from London to Calais added only two per cent to the price. For the trades of the Hanse, bulk goods going through often dangerous waters, the share of transport costs in the delivered price was crucial.[12] With grain prices falling, German merchants had to find a way to lower their costs just to retain their share of the shrunken market. The half of the price attributable to transport costs was a logical place to look for savings. Shipbuilders were thus under pressure to lower shipping costs, and did so by producing the new merged type. There was a time lag from the Black Death to the development of the combined design, on account of the replacement rate of ships. They were expensive capital goods and represented a sizeable investment, so they were rarely scrapped. It took some time to introduce a new type and even longer for it to show up in the surviving documents. Moreover, the decline in the total volume of trade after 1350 meant surplus capacity, so that the replacement rate was even lower than normal.

The new type was still clinker-built and of shell construction. The rounded form of the hulk was retained but added to it were a broad flat bottom, a strong keel and stem and sternposts like the cog. The flat section of the bottom was, if anything, increased relative to fourteenth-century cogs. For better manoeuvrability a second external stempost

16: A Two-masted Venetian Cog with Square Mainsail
and Lateen Mizzen, 1366 (top) and a Hulk with
Features of the Cog, Seal of Gdansk, 1400 (bottom)

was added as deadwood, though that had already been used on cogs. The ship presumably also had a heavy internal framework of ribs. The bow was still brought up something like earlier hulks while the stern looked much like that of earlier cogs. Forecastles continued to be triangular. The castles were built into the hull as integral parts, a trend already clear on all cogs.[g] There was no change in the rig nor in the length-to-beam ratio. No more wood was needed to build the modified type. Crew size was proportionally the same. With the changed hull shape and the flat bottom the new type could carry as much or more for each metre of length than the earlier cog. The retention of a gentle curve to the hull made the new type better at riding in tides and estuaries than the older cog. Draught was the same or less than a cog of the same carrying capacity. The keel and posts made the new type a better open-sea sailer than the earlier hulk. It was faster too.[13] The new hulk required no increase in investment, produced the same or greater carrying capacity for that investment, had the same or lower unit labour costs and had the potential for greater size without giving up the ability to visit all the harbours used by cogs. Throughout the fifteenth century builders took advantage of the shallower draught of the new type and built much bigger ships. The final result was lower unit shipping costs, exactly what Hanse merchants wanted.

Northern Europeans also built galleys in the fourteenth century. These galleys had a typically high length-to-beam ratio. Oars were the major source of power. There was a supplementary sail. Some of these galleys were based on older northern designs, derived probably from the Scandinavian dragonships. Others were modelled on Mediterranean galleys. In either case the decision to build them did not depend on economic but on political circumstances. Kings or their advisers decided that they needed galleys or other oared ships to supplement fighting fleets. The French royal government, having the example of successful naval powers bordering its Mediterranean coast, decided to create a navy based on that southern model. The French imported Genoese ships and then Genoese shipwrights north to the Channel. Based on Spanish examples, the Italian shipwrights built and maintained galleys at royal shipyards in Normandy. Presumably these galleys were just like those of the Mediterranean. Crews had to be imported. The special shipyard at Rouen was also the site for the construction of local types of rowed barges.[14]

In England barges and balingers were a common part of war fleets in the fourteenth century. While English galleys, presumably of Mediterranean design, could have up to 140 oars, no barge ever approached that figure. The maximum was 80 and for balingers the range was from 40 to 50 oars. Barges were apparently similar to balingers in design but heavier, usually in the range of 100 to 150 tons. These vessels were great consumers of manpower with one man per oar and a crew of sailors and marines perhaps greater than the number of rowers. Still, they were found effective doing convoy duty, privateering or carrying important individuals.[h] Barges could also be used for commercial voyages but presumably they then relied only on sail power and not on oars at all. While the Cinque Ports had supplied galleys to the English crown throughout the thirteenth century, the threat from Castilian galleys, built on the Genoese model, and then of French-built galleys at the end of that century, redoubled English interest in oared ships. Edward I ordered a galley fleet to be built in 1294. Some of the vessels were finished and the records are clear on the dimensions of the ships. If the design was consistent with that of earlier rowed vessels built in the North, it is hard to conceive how they could have sailed. But they did and in some cases proved effective fighting ships. Despite the interest in galleys, though, most ships used for naval purposes were large cargo ships needed to carry troops, horses and supplies to Continental battlegrounds. The largest of these English transport fleets, that of 1347, numbered 738 ships with 15,000 sailors needed to move about 32,000 troops to the siege of Calais.[15] The English government was less devoted to building and maintaining a war fleet of its own than to conscripting sailing ships and their crews when needed. The number of oared warships, compared to sailing ships in naval forces, was always very small. This fact, together with the serious limitations of the type, prevented edge-to-edge planked Mediterranean galleys from having much effect on shipbuilding in the North. Construction of cargo ships was largely separated from the building of the Mediterranean-style galleys. Since the latter could not operate in the strong winds, high waves, tides and currents of the open sea in the North, it is not surprising that shipwrights found no reason to adopt features of the southern types.

In the South itself the pace of design change quickened in the late thirteenth century and throughout the fourteenth, so much so that it exceeded that in the North. Up to about 1340 the possibilities for design development continued to increase. Trade remained buoyant. Moreover, the changing political situation, the loss of privileges in the Levant with the fall of the last bastion of the crusader states, and the re-establishment of the Byzantine Empire at Constantinople, created pressure on shipbuilders to meet changing needs. The penalties for failure were softened for shipbuilders by the introduction of marine insurance. Methods of mutual protection had long been practised by shippers at sea. Sailing in convoy better to fend off pirates was common in both northern and southern Europe. The fleets of salt ships going to the Bay of Bourgneuf from Hanse towns typically sailed in large convoys.[16] More common, though, were smaller groups of four or five ships which joined together at a port. In some cases the captains agreed to share all losses with others in the group. On an informal basis, this was highly inefficient since all ships had to wait until the last had filled out its cargo. In the fourteenth century, Italian municipal governments institutionalised convoys, setting times of departure and levying charges to support convoying warships.

Meanwhile, businessmen themselves independently developed a way to spread expected losses. They introduced a third party who, for a fee, would accept the risk. The development of marine insurance, by which the shipper could pay a premium and be guaranteed payment for loss of goods and ship, took a very complex path. By no means did all shippers use marine insurance in 1400. The process of adoption was a slow one. By the late fourteenth century, however, formulas for such contracts had been worked out in a number of Italian towns so that shippers could get insurance more easily. There was an experiment in fourteenth-century Portugal in which the king established two insurance funds which accepted all losses of goods and ships. All ships in the two major Portugese ports had to pay a two per cent duty on the value of their cargoes in order to fund the insurance programme. It was a case of the government forcing the distribution of risk and establishing insurance by law. The fund required vigorous government support and when that waned so did the fund.[17] At the same time, however, the appearance of effective commercial insurance removed the pressing need for enforced sharing of risk. No matter how it was institutionalised, the result was that risk could be quantified and easily and clearly subsumed in costs. Insurance did not eradicate risk. Shipbuilders were still constrained by the potential loss. The difference was that risk was an objective fact which could be measured and weighed by buyers and builders. They could then trade off risk against other components of cost such as manpower requirements and speed. The accuracy of insurers was of no consequence. The point was that they set the cost of risk and that was the cost that shipbuilders had to consider. At the least, the development of insurance must have made more simple the choice among different types of ships for different types of voyages and cargoes.

While insurance spread risk, the improvements in navigation after

1250 decreased it. A series of improvements in tools and methods gave navigators greater ability to know where they were and how long it would take to reach their destination. By 1300 the compass had made the transition from a primitive pointer to a needle swinging freely on a dry pivot. There was a card calibrated by the principal winds in the form of a wind-rose, or even in some cases by degrees, set under the moving needle. By the end of the thirteenth century and certainly by the early fourteenth, sailors were using this improved compass in combination with the new portolan chart. Portolan really meant a set of sailing directions, just like those dating from the Roman period. In the thirteenth century, as a supplement to the text, a chart was drawn to scale describing the coast and giving the locations of ports. Writers described the use of these charts and the compass, along with dividers and an hourglass, to estimate the ship's position by plotting a course and calculating her speed. Charts are first mentioned in use on board ship in 1270. Over the following century they became more numerous, even if they may all have been derived from the same source.[i] Loxodromes emanating from the wind-rose on the chart gave a set of courses. The navigator had to decide which of the loxodromes was parallel to the course he needed to take from his point of departure to his goal; this gave him the heading he needed to steer. The newest sailing directions laid this all out for him. If he was driven off course or had to tack he had, by 1400, a set of tables which allowed him to resolve his course — that is, to break his sailing down into two perpendicular directions and then calculate his position. With such a traverse table the navigator could reduce a zigzag course to a straight line and thus he knew how to steer to get to his goal.[18]

Italian and Catalan navigators could depend on their chart and compass. Celestial observations became a valuable but not indispensable supplement. In northern Europe the height of the sun and the position of the stars remained a principal source of information for navigators. But pilots along the shores of the North and Baltic Seas depended more on soundings taken with lead and line than on what they saw in the skies. In the Mediterranean, waters were clear and the bottom usually fell off sharply away from the shore. In northern Europe neither was true, and, as ships there typically stayed closer to shore depth soundings and knowing about the nature of the bottom were critical for safe navigation. Sailing instructions did not describe the use of the compass in those waters until the fifteenth century. The slowness of northern Europeans to take advantage of the new equipment was in part because they could get so much information by sounding and by watching the shore. Hermits and the church combined over time to increase the number of lights along dangerous coasts. Tall lighthouses were still a rarity, however, even in the Mediterranean. Northern navigators also had to worry about tides. By the late fourteenth century, tides were certainly well understood and mariners were receiving tide tables to help them make their way along coasts and into harbours. The navigational methods of Mediterranean sailors increased predictability. They always had a good idea of where they were. One late fourteenth-century writer claimed that the use of Italian navigational methods explained the lower number of shipwrecks in the Mediterranean, one for every 20 in northern Europe.

Better navigation not only made ships safer but also made them more productive. It was possible to sail in the winter. Of course, pilots still had to be careful of winter storms but they were in a much better position to deal with them. They always knew how far it was to the nearest safe harbour. Sailing across open seas presented no problem at all and long reaches out of sight of land, even in the cloudiest of winter weather, were practical. The sailing season was extended. There were more voyages per year. The effects were first felt in the last years of the thirteenth century. In the fourteenth, winter sailing in the Mediterranean and regular services from there to northern Europe became common.[19] Annual production of shipping services by a vessel, and especially of large ships making long-distance voyages, rose by as much as 50 per cent. Instead of one voyage each year they now made two. Certainly, there was an over-all gain in the productivity of capital. But there was also a fall in orders for shipbuilders; the total number of ships needed for a given volume of commerce fell. Then, in the second half of the fourteenth century, the volume of commerce fell as well. There were mitigating factors which kept shipbuilders from bearing the total effect of the improved productivity of ships from better navigation. With a greater frequency of voyages the size of ships did not grow as rapidly. It was not necessary to concentrate all shipment into a single voyage. Moreover, the fall in risk which meant lower capital costs to shippers, reflected in lower insurance premiums too, would be passed on in lower shipping charges. The lower prices kept the volume of trade from falling as much as it would have done with unchanged costs. The decrease of risk and the distribution of risk opened possibilities for experiment by shipbuilders in the Mediterranean; they were under pressure to improve ships just to retain their level of activity in the face of declining total demand after 1350 and the Black Death, and declining relative demand after about 1300 and the introduction of winter sailing.

One response was the development of the great galley, which was originally designed as a warship but was soon pressed into service as a cargo ship to compete with round ships in trades where speed was an important consideration. There were, by 1300, clear opportunities for trade between northern Europe and the Mediterranean. Exchange between Italian and Flemish merchants had for some years taken place at the fairs in the county of Champagne in east central France. All the merchants travelled then, but in the course of the thirteenth century Flemish traders more and more stayed at home and Italian merchants did their business in the Low Countries. With an active commerce in Flanders the next step was for the Italians to supply transport for the goods. The exchange was in luxury items and not the bulk goods which could be efficiently carried by northern cogs. The light galleys could not handle the goods economically. The solution was to build a bigger galley with enough capacity for a sizeable cargo, the ability to survive in northern waters and the speed to make an annual round trip to the North avoiding the worst weather. The new type was first built in the last decade of the thirteenth century not long after the first voyage of Genoese ships to Bruges and Southampton in 1277-78. To Flanders and England the great galleys carried high-quality wines, alum used as a mordant in the Flemish cloth industry, spices first shipped from the Levant to Italy and sub-tropical fruits collected along the coast of Spain. They brought back finished cloth or high-quality wool for the Italian cloth industry. Shipment added only 15 per cent to the cost of Flemish cloth delivered in Italy, a reflection of both the high value of the cloth and the efficiency of the great galley compared to its smaller counterpart. Small galleys carried 50 tons with a crew of 180 men, or .28 tons for each man. The great galley of 1320 could handle about 150 tons with an average crew of 150. At one ton for each man that meant a fall of more than 70 per cent in labour costs alone. Flemish cloth solved the problem of the North's lack of a good of high enough value per unit volume to match the spices, silks and other luxuries that came from the Mediterranean.[20] The cloth could fill the holds of these great galleys, give them a back cargo and make a critical contribution to the cost of the operation which was still high compared to the cost of transporting goods by round ship. With southern weaving shops making their own cloth, wool could be sent in place of the Flemish cloth. The cargo from the South was always more valuable than the back cargo, even more so after the change to the shipment of wool.

The great galley was also built for use in the Mediterranean. Venetians, being the first to exploit the design, were able to gain an advantage

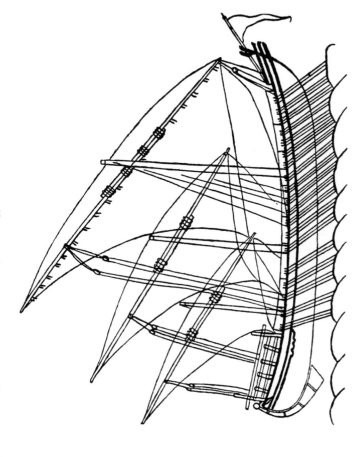

17: Venetian Great Galley from a Treatise on Shipbuilding, 1445

in trade to the Levant, carrying spices, Eastern goods and, of course, pilgrims. Galleys were well suited to the carriage of pilgrims, with lower insurance charges and fewer delays than round ships which relied exclusively on sails. The Venetian government increased the reliability of such galleys by subjecting them to strict regulation, thus making them even more popular with pilgrims. Since the ships stopped along the way, the traveller had a chance to see more things. Comfort was at a minimum at sea, however, since the pilgrims were packed between decks while some 150 sailors worked the ship from the deck above them. Ventilation was confined to four small hatches, so the smell must have been strong. The cost of operating the cargo galley was, of course, higher than that of operating a round ship but many commodities, including pilgrims, could sustain the relatively higher freight charges. The cargo galley was thus able to regain some of the trade lost to sailing ships by galleys from the eleventh to the thirteenth century. The change to the use of the great galley was aided by a change in consumption patterns and a relative increase in the volume of luxury goods shipped. Especially in northern Europe, but also in Italy, the income gains made by survivors of the Black Death went into buying spices to diversify diets and clothes with a bit more colour and style. These goods came from the Levant and the Far East and Italian merchants willingly acted as the intermediaries for moving the goods. The logical vehicle was the great galley.

The new type was still a galley with all the attributes of that design. The aim was to gain some of the advantages of the round ship but few features were borrowed from that type. Rather, builders merely increased the size of the galley. The length-to-beam ratio was still high, about 6:1 compared to 8:1 for a light galley. The larger size meant deeper draught, markedly deeper on Venetian craft. Galleys had traditionally depended on shallow draught to give them speed but this had to be sacrificed to obtain the larger carrying capcity. The hull was more rounded, giving something of the appearance of a full sailing ship. To move the larger hull there were three masts, each with a lateen sail. The masts were progressively shorter towards the stern. The type, in fact, moved better under sail than with the oars, an exceptional characteristic for a galley. The great galley continued to grow in size throughout the fourteenth and into the fifteenth century but builders were able to maintain the quality and advantages of the design as they explored its limits. The larger galleys could carry two tons for each man, still much less than the five to eight tons per man for round ships. The galley compensated for the difference by higher speed and also greater defensibility.

With such a large crew, pirates were reluctant to attack a great galley. The absence of castles did not affect the ability of the crew to handle trouble or to escape from it. Moreover, great galleys could act together in squadrons, making them even more formidable.[21] The oars were used only in special circumstances. The size of the ship made it hard work to handle the oars and the crew preferred to avoid that unpleasant task, but the ability to use the oars to get in and out of port, to manoeuvre or to avoid a lee shore gave the great galley its advantage in speed and reliability over the round ship.

For the lighter galleys, ship designers changed the arrangement for rowing by the thirteenth century. On Byzantine dromons and their successors there were two rowers to each bench, each rower handling a single oar. In the tenth century, when designers wanted to build bigger dromons, they simply added another layer of benches, each with two men, above the first. In the thirteenth century, Italian builders chose instead to increase the number of men on each bench to three. The use of oars of different lengths and the placing of the bench at an angle ensured that rowers would not interfere with one another. The arrangement may ultimately have been the optimal one for rowing a ship. The number of rowers was increased without placing any of them higher above the water which would have raised the angle at which the oar entered the water and thus decreased efficiency. Oars did not have to be very long and so their weight was kept down, thus limiting the amount of unproductive work the oarsman had to do on the return stroke. Outriggers on each side, part of a frame which went around the entire ship, offered a fulcrum beyond the hull to give rowers more leverage. The system of rowing changed in part to obtain more total force to propel the ship without increasing the complexity of construction. The greater carrying capacities which resulted made the great galley a commercial success. These big rowed vessels could navigate more effectively against a current — a critical advantage in getting out of the Mediterranean to make the voyage to northern Europe.[22] The new type of galley was also a naval success, superseding the old Byzantine dromon. Galleys always needed large crews, even larger after the change in the number of oars per bench. At least, with great galleys, buoyant demand for the luxuries they carried kept revenue up so the wage bill could be met.

The great galley was developed in the Arsenal at Venice, the government naval shipbuilding yard and depot for armaments. Builders there continued to build great galleys to the order of the Venetian state. Government policy affected and directed demand for ships, and the

18: Reconstruction of a
Mediterranean Galley with
Three Rowers to Each Bench
and Armed with Guns

first experiments with larger galleys began as part of the naval building programme during the second Genoese war which ended in 1299. Throughout the first half of the fourteenth century the Venetian government protected its own fleets of great galleys against all competition, thus gradually driving all galley building into the hands of the government and therefore into the Arsenal. The expansion of the communal shipyards there in 1303 and 1325 gave builders the space to handle the increase in work. The government had set out to centralise the building of warships, or at least to centralise it enough to guarantee a minimal fleet, and in time this led to expansion into, and then a monopoly of, the building of great galleys. However, Arsenal workers still only built a relatively small portion of Venetian tonnage, about ten per cent. They built vessels which were on average smaller than the large round ships produced by private yards. Throughout the fourteenth century the Venetian government increased the regulation of galley fleets and then turned to owning them, operating more and more of the ships itself or chartering them to merchants. The government wanted to keep some control over great galleys since they still could and did serve as valuable warships.

The largest proportion of Arsenal output was in light galleys, which typically had 25-30 benches to a side with three men for each bench. There was a single mast with a lateen sail. Control was supplied by three rudders. The two side rudders were joined by a sternpost rudder like that typical in northern Europe. By extending this design to its limits builders produced a poor sailing craft but one that was fast and highly manoeuvrable. The government in fact set limits on the size of galleys. Builders were apparently over-enthusiastic, their experiments were not highly successful and they were making the galleys into ineffective fighting ships. Galleys throughout the Mediterranean tended to become longer and lower during the thirteenth and fourteenth centuries. Over all lengths of 40 metres were not uncommon. The beam would then be under 5 metres. At the bow there was a covered platform for archers and for a manogel for firing projectiles.[j] Some defence against Greek fire was common, such as stretching hides over the hull. The ram at the bow was still a major offensive weapon.[23] The government of Venice brought the building of warships together in the Arsenal for political as well as for technical and financial reasons. The government, made up of the greater merchants, did not want to see any individual through the ownership of galleys achieve too powerful a position in the Republic. Having stumbled into a policy of a state-owned and -operated shipbuilding yard the government expanded that yard and expanded its work to include cargo galleys. The process had certain unforeseen results. The depot developed interchangeable parts to make easier the job of fitting out warships. To do that builders also had a tendency to standardise their designs. The builders in the Arsenal were not subject to the standard economic constraints which their private counterparts faced. Or, at least, they were buffered against them by a government which had its own needs. The government created novel demands for the designers in the Arsenal, demands which could only arise under those circumstances, thus making more likely the development of different designs. At the same time, the government released Arsenal designers from other constraints, giving them greater latitude in dealing with the ships they built. The cost of building was still important but producing what the government wanted counted for more.

The Mediterranean round ship continued in use in many trades despite the appearance of the great galley. The round ship was quite logically most popular for carrying bulk goods over short distances. The type retained its position as an effective tramp, moving from port to port carrying relatively bulky cargoes. The design was little changed from that of the twelfth century except that on average the ships were larger. The rudders had tackles fitted to them so they could be adjusted at sea and lifted up when in port. On some ships the upper portion of the rudder was protected by a small gallery. In the course of the fourteenth century the sternpost rudder replaced the older method of control on some round ships. As with galleys, in some cases there were three rudders, two on the sides and one on the sternpost. Projecting beam-ends were common, as were full decks, two and sometimes three on medium-size and larger craft. Wales ran the length of the ship above the beam-ends for added protection. The hull planks were placed edge to edge but strength came from the skeleton of ribs. There was a small forecastle around the stempost and one or two raised decks in the aftercastle at the stern. There were as many as three masts with the tallest forward and raked forward. Shrouds held the masts and they were set up in tackles to give better control. They could not take ratlines so there was a ladder to the top. Since the yard had to be carried over the masthead with the lateen sail, any platform at the top of the mast had to be at the side and had to be movable. A parrel held the two-piece yards to the masts. Lifts were probably used to hoist and to control the long yards.[k] The increase in the average size of these ships over those of the thirteenth and fourteenth centuries can be attributed to the rise in the number of very large ships.[24] Shippers typically found lateen-rigged round ships useful for a specific type of service and so these vessels remained much the same to retain that part of the carrying trade. Growth in bulk carriage tended to go to another and new type, or at least new for Mediterranean shipbuilders.

The traditional date for the introduction of the cog into the Mediterranean is 1304 but this is certainly too late. Builders in the South knew about the cog long before then. The story that it was brought into the Mediterranean then by Basque pirates suggests that it was not until the years around 1300 that Mediterranean builders became impressed with the potential of the type. The Iberians may have shown that the cog could be used on a regular basis and that it could be acclimatised to Mediterranean conditions, a possibility which sporadic visits by crusaders from the shores of the North Sea could not demonstrate.[25] The result was a major change in shipbuilding in the Mediterranean. The rapid adoption of the cog by Italian shippers can be explained by its relatively low operating costs. Costs were low because of the design of the cog, because of the changes in the technology of navigation and because of the nature of the market for shipping services in the early fourteenth century. The use of compass and chart made possible direct regular service across open water. Sailors had travelled out of sight of land for centuries but now they could do so with much greater security, and they could predict their movements. Something more like liner service, the regular movement between two distant ports, could be instituted in place of tramping along the coasts. There had been a service like that for pilgrims going to the Holy Land from Italy for some time and by 1300 certain bulk goods had become susceptible to similar treatment. Since with bulk goods, as opposed to people, it was unnecessary to stop at night, the galley did not enjoy the same advantage in carrying such goods. Agricultural goods such as grain and wine had to be moved greater distances than before as population had increased, prices had risen and marginal producing areas had found it possible to compete in distant markets. Wine from Crete found a ready market in Genoa. Grain too was shipped to Italian towns from further away, from the Crimea for example, and in larger quantities. As important was the transport of mining products and especially alum. Genoese merchants gained the right to carry alum from the islands of Phocea and Chios in the Aegean to the western Mediterranean. It was the ideal good for a bulk carrier. Alum went directly to Genoa, where it was distributed to buyers along the coast of the western Mediterranean and in northern Europe, in other types of vessels. All of these trades began before the introduction of the cog. However, for the direct shipment of such goods the cog was the ideal vehicle. Genoese shippers by the mid-fourteenth century found the cog could be used for moving alum to northern Europe as well, and for this trade they established themselves at Southampton in England, thus putting themselves close to the centres of the English cloth industry, and giving themselves a harbour deep enough to accommodate their cogs. The vessel was slow and turnaround time was high. In some cases Genoese cogs went straight from Chios to the North to avoid the delay of unloading and loading again at their home port. Lower labour requirements on board — the square rig was easier to handle than the lateen — kept costs down. Shipment by cog added only 16 per cent to the price of alum and 10-25 per cent to the price of grain, depending on the length of the voyage. Genoese merchants, by specialising in the transport of heavy goods and in the use of the cog, gained a strong commercial position, not to mention sizeable personal profits. Because of specialisation the Genoese measured the size of their ships in units of weight rather than in units of volume which was common practice almost everywhere else. Catalan merchants, like the Genoese, concentrated their efforts on building and operating cogs. They may, in fact, have preceded their Italian competitors. But Genoese cogs were the largest, normally 600 tons by about 1400, for shipping from the eastern Mediterranean to the English Channel. They were three times the size of large Hanse bulk carriers and as large or larger than the biggest lateen-rigged round ships ever used in the Mediterranean.[26]

The climatic change and the Black Death both promoted the use of the cog in the Mediterranean and in all intra-European trades. Specialisation in agricultural production tended to promote the movement of goods, more obvious in the North where a small change in average temperature could make it possible or impossible to grow certain crops. There was a rise in the relative demand for industrial goods after the mid-fourteenth-century plague. The industries required raw materials which had to be brought over greater distances since their production was usually dictated by geography. The use of the cog allowed industry to settle near markets rather than migrate to sources of raw material supply. The cog had a much smaller crew than a Mediterranean round ship of the same size. Cogs could also be built larger than round ships and with much less than a proportional increase in the size of the crew. Since, with fewer workers, there was pressure to raise wages after the Black Death, the use of the cog made it possible to pay seamen more. The simple single mast and single square sail were much easier to handle than two or three lateen sails, and required less manpower and less skill, thus keeping labour costs under control. There was a loss of manoeuvrability. The improved navigation techniques helped keep cogs out of situations where those poor handling qualities might be a liability. The saving in manpower could be in excess of 50 per cent and wages did not double, so there was a lower wage bill for each ton shipped by cog.

The cog was tubbier than the contemporary Mediterranean cargo ship, thus creating a saving in wood needed to build the hull. In general, an increase in length relative to breadth increased the surface area of the hull, and thus the quantity of wood needed 2.3 times as much as it increased hold space. The calculation is a rough one but the co-efficient was near that for most designs. The saving in hull planking on shorter vessels had already been discovered in the twelfth century in northern Europe when shipwrights changed from building keels and knarrs to building cogs. For shipbuilders in the Mediterranean in the fourteenth century the saving may have been more important. There were already some signs of problems with supplies of shipbuilding timber. Not incidentally, Genoa, which specialised in the building and use of cogs, had much more trouble in keeping local shipyards supplied with wood than had its great competitor, Venice.[27]

Ribs had to be larger, heavier but less numerous for cogs than for round ships so, though there was a saving in the total amount of wood needed, a premium, much greater than before, was placed on big tall oak-trees. Despite savings in wood, the cog still represented a massive capital investment. As the ships got bigger, the investment rose as well. With winter sailing possible, the capital was productive throughout the year and the outlay for the new type made more sense. Apparently, shipowners expected to cover all capital costs as well as operating costs quickly. For example, Catalan shipowners with prevailing freight rates under good conditions could expect to get their investment back within five to six months, the equivalent of four or five round-trip voyages to North Africa from Barcelona. If the cog was big enough then piracy was no longer a problem. The legally required crew size fell with the introduction of the cog since the type was more defensible. It was possible to use bowmen effectively from cogs with their high sides which offered the men protection and allowed them time to aim and fire their improved crossbows. Indeed, in the fourteenth century, while the number of sailors on average went down, the number of bowmen went up. The change in ship design led to a change in the weapons used on board, which in the long run led to an increase in the importance of men with technical skills, crossbowmen, and a decline in the importance of sailors.[28] Riding high in the water equipped with castles, few pirates or even hostile states could deploy the kind of force needed to overcome vessels of the size of the Genoese cogs of the late fourteenth century.

Shipbuilders in the Mediterranean changed the design of the cog to suit local conditions and local building skills. The hull was of skeleton construction common to Mediterranean ships. Two or three full decks were added. The keel became curved, as was common practice with Mediterranean ships. There were no tides to lift the ship off if it ran aground. With a curved keel goods were shifted, the vessel tilted and it it rode free. Whether this ever occurred with a large cog is doubtful, but the cog still got a curved keel. Skeleton-building was more effective for a large ship, and its execution also required less skilled labour — a particularly advantageous characteristic after 1350 when skilled workers became especially scarce, not because they were more susceptible to the plague but because it took some time to train craftsmen to replace those who had died. There was little question, then, of trying to build clinker-built cogs in the Mediterranean. Control was with a sternport rudder. With a curved keel, the space between rudder and keel was filled with deadwood. The other major change that came with the cog was the reintroduction of the square sail to the Mediterranean. It may well have been used there in special circumstances through the middle ages but the success of the cog made it the typical sail for large cargo ships. Southern builders improved the simple northern square rig. Reef-points were abandoned in favour of bonnets which were used exclusively. Lifts were added, as was a more complex parrel;[1] both made hoisting the sail easier. A more complex system of ropes allowed better control of the sail. Captains could then let the sail bag and billow, which was thought at the time to be more effective. All these additions still left the cog relatively difficult to handle. Compared to lateen-rigged round ships these cogs were poor sailers. In the second half of the fourteenth century, shipwrights attacked precisely this problem by adding a second or mizzenmast steeped near the stern and rising above the now low-slung aftercastle. It carried a lateen sail.[29] Since Mediterranean builders were accustomed to multiple masts, the addition did not mark a major invention.[m] The goal clearly was to increase the manoeuvrability of the tubby vessel and perhaps to decrease turnaround time, since the lateen sail would help in getting in and out of harbours. The lateen was rarely handled at the same time as the mainsail, so there was no increase in the crew. The innovation was an effort to meet the greatest disadvantages of the cog, and with it southern shipbuilders took the first step towards the invention of the full-rigged sailing ship.

By 1400 the variety of ship types in the Mediterranean had sharply increased compared to those that existed in 1250. In sailing ships the different sizes of lateen-rigged round ships had been joined by the northern cog, modified and improved to suit the needs of the South. Among longships there were two types of galleys. The change to three rowers per bench made the light galley a more effective warship. The great galley brought a new form of transport and gave galleys a much broader function in the movement of goods. The great galley could still be an effective warship. There was an over-all tendency to increase specialisation of design. Ships became suited more for certain tasks. The great galley took over some of the luxury traffic from galleys but also some of the traffic in less valuable items per unit volume from round ships. For most bulky goods there was the cog, while the round ship served a market half-way between that of the cog and the great galley. The greater diversification in design continued throughout the period of declining demand for shipping from the mid-fourteenth century. The variety of designs was perhaps a response on the part of shipbuilders to the shrinking of their market.

Information about ships increases sharply for the thirteenth and fourteenth centuries compared to earlier years. The material comes not only from illustrations but also from government records and from the private records of businessmen. The increased documentary evidence generates an impression of a faster pace of change and improvement in ship design, of major and distinct developments compared to, for example, the 250 years before 1250. The impression, however, is not simply or entirely the product of the greater quantity of data. In the Mediterranean, after the development of the larger galley in the tenth century, there was little change throughout the thirteenth century, while in the North, after the improvement in the cog early in the eleventh century, the same was true up to the mid-thirteenth century. From that point the pattern changed, however. Pressures from the economy, perhaps mounting for some time, became more direct and immediate. Pressures from governments became more commonplace and more overt. The precise demands of governments might not be the same as in the past but they increasingly turned to shipbuilders to solve problems and they increasingly placed constraints on builders in one form or another, often institutionalising those constraints. Government purchases were still a small portion of total shipbuilding sales but the character and form of government demand could and did have an effect on the design of ships.

By 1400 European shipbuilders had developed a bulk carrier capable of moving many goods economically and through all European waters. Continuing improvement in the type expanded the scope of its use and also the volume of goods carried. The process of lowering the cost of bulk carriage by innovation in ship design was, however, by no means complete. The unique economic circumstances created by the Black Death increased the pace of development and the use of bulk carriers. The success of builders in supplying profitable cogs and hulks to shippers affected the organisation of business and income distribution within Europe. The rise in the volume of bulk carriage, absolute at least to 1350 and relative both before and after that date, implied the concentration or potential concentration of transportation in the hands of a few people. The larger amounts of capital needed and the limited number of voyages along any given route in a year meant that few merchants could operate successfully. Trading in wine or alum was not like trading in spices, silks or specie. In luxury trades capital was certainly an important prerequisite but the higher unit profits made entry much easier. The ships and the organisation of luxury trades created opportunities for a number of traders. The limited points of supply and the limited trade routes for bulk goods acted to close the door on men wanting to make a start in that kind of trade. The greater capital requirements of bulk trades and lower returns per ton exchanged, inherent in the nature of the goods, made it a business for rich merchants. As those men gathered more capital into their hands, the merchant community changed. Though the total income of merchants went up, not all merchant incomes went up proportionally. In the North, where bulk trades were well established, so too was the tendency towards the concentration of business. The economy there was, in general, poorer than that in the Mediterranean so, instead of a shift in favour of a few traders, rather the long-term trend dating from the tenth century continued. The larger ships of the bulk trades also led to a concentration of investment in shipping. The pattern was the same throughout Europe. A larger proportion of the total investment of the commercial sector was tied up in a relatively small number of vessels. Rather than spreading the investment in those seagoing cogs across a larger number of passive investors, the sheer size of the amount involved and the changing character of business combined to lead to a decrease in the distribution of capital among owners and a decrease in the number of owners.[30] Passive investment still went on in smaller ships. But in the fourteenth century the long-term trend towards the spreading of the base of financial involvement in shipping was reversed. Those merchants successful in bulk trades were able to take an increasing share of the total investment in shipping. As the owners of a larger share of the profitable bulk carriers, those men were able to enjoy higher returns and so the process became self-reinforcing.

The rising relative portion of trade in bulk carriage meant that the effect of commerce on agriculture was more direct and more pervasive. Trade always had an indirect effect on agriculture. Trade and exchange always implied an increase in potential total output for agriculture. From the tenth to the thirteenth century, trade also made possible the sale of surplus production from farms and estates large enough and well enough organised to have a surplus ready for sale. Commercial agriculture, growing exclusively for sale and specialising in production for the market, existed by the eleventh century and was certainly common in twelfth-century Italy, where urbanisation had created a dependent population that had to import food from the countryside. Owners of land close to the towns organised their production to suit urban consumption; but that was entirely on a local basis. By the fourteenth century, agriculture of the same type – that is, where more effort was devoted to growing crops for a cash market – could expand among farms distant from concentrations of population; this was possible because of the falling cost of shipping the crops. The obvious example was the production of grain in Poland for markets in Flanders, but over time the examples increased and so too did the land turned over to production for the market. English wool could be exported to Italy and Spanish wool to that market and to the North. The growing of grapes for making wine forced producers to sell their output to get other foods. Wine had been exported from the Rhine Valley in the eighth century. In the thirteenth and fourteenth centuries the market for that and other wines expanded. Growers in southern France established a firm market in England and producers in Crete and the eastern Mediterranean were able to market some of their output in northern Europe. Consumers benefited from the greater selection of goods. Producers benefited from the wider market which created the potential for greater returns. The lower delivered cost of bulk goods promoted regional specialisation in agriculture and by no means just within small areas.

The Black Death left only a few pockets of Europe unaffected. With so much empty space there seems to have been surprisingly little migration, with the exception of migration from the countryside to nearby cities. The lack of interregional migration was in part due to the increased use of economic bulk carriers. As the total population of Europe grew throughout the twelfth and thirteenth centuries, there had been a major migration out of the region from the Alps to the North Sea and between the valleys of the Loire and Rhine. The Low Countries, especially, showed a surplus of births over deaths and people from that region joined people from throughout Germany in a trek eastward in search of agricultural land. As land was cleared of forests or reclaimed in the centre of Europe, opportunities there for farmers declined. The increasing number of agricultural workers had to go further afield to find land to work. The pandemic in the mid-fourteenth century led to a sharp drop in population in the central region of northern Europe, a larger absolute drop since the density was higher there; but there was no rush of population back into that area to fill the vacuum. Such a rush would not necessarily be expected. But weighing the factors which acted to push and pull migrants, the push to drive people out of newer settlements in eastern Europe had to be below a certain threshold to keep survivors there. The ability of farmers in Poland to continue to sell their surplus production in western Europe meant that it was not necessary for them to move back closer to the market. The lower cost of moving grain made it possible for them to stay in the East without giving up the ability to acquire goods like those available in the West and South. As population recovered in the fifteenth century, the distribution of population across Europe remained much the same.

The use of bulk carriers acted to block the diffusion of the superior business methods of Italian merchants. Those techniques were not as efficient when the problem was the movement of bulk goods. Italian businessmen had, over the tenth, eleventh and twelfth centuries, developed methods of generating capital, distributing risks and handling a diverse mass of cargoes going through a number of ports. That kind of multilateral trade, which at the simplest level was tramping from port to port, was common in the Mediterranean. It was not unknown in northern Europe but there trade typically meant moving a certain known cargo, a bulky cargo, from one port to another, the ports fixed by geography, and always at the same time of the year every year. These trades survived and prospered because of their very predictability. Back cargoes were established. Shipping dates were fixed. For example, in the North, ships wintered in certain ports and not just because of the difficulties of navigating but also because they were required to do so by laws which recognised the fixed nature of the seasonal bulk trades.[31] With such bulk trades, the existence of correspondents or agents at foreign ports was of little help in doing business. Merchants on board ship, who travelled with the cargo to look after the interests of merchants, needed only limited powers. In general, the methods of the Italians offered little saving. Since ships were best suited to bulk trade and since bulk trade dominated commerce in northern Europe, the adoption of the new business methods was a slow process.

The trend towards government involvement in shipping and ship-building continued, especially in southern Europe. By the fourteenth century, governments had added much more to the scope of their activities. In Portugal, for example, not only was there a project for mutual insurance of all shippers but the king also granted privileges to shipbuilders to promote construction. The efforts were especially direc-ted at building ships of over 100 tons, presumably so that Portuguese shippers could compete in bulk trades. The French government imported the building of Mediterranean-style light galleys to the North. The failure to go beyond that isolated government-sponsored imposition showed that it was impossible to declare a body of knowledge and techniques viable, except within a narrow framework and with contin-ued support from the state. The introduction of the new technology seems to have had no noticeable effect in the North, with the possible exception of forcing the English government to follow the same prac-tice in the short run. In Venice, by 1400, the government was not only building but also operating great galleys. The Venetian government in its shipbuilding policy was able to generate a demonstration effect on private builders, both in Venice and in the long run throughout much of Europe. The Arsenal at Venice was only the most famous of such institutions. It was the model for other government-operated wharves for building warships in Iberia and in France. The Arsenal at Venice offered an example of how to organise the business of shipbuilding not just for governments but also for private builders. Since men who worked in private shipbuilding also worked at the Arsenal and since the Arsenal performed a number of services for private shipbuilding yards, supplying them with cables and other parts when needed, local ship-wrights had full access to knowledge of how to operate a big shipbuild-ing business. For such a complex operation methods of accountability were required. Book-keeping practice had to be borrowed from merch-ants. The Arsenal had to develop ways of recruiting necessary labour, at the right times. It was able to function with a kind of informality despite the great claims made on the institution in times of war; this continued into the sixteenth century despite major expansion in output and personnel.[32]

The Arsenal also brought together men with a high degree of techni-cal skill. The task set by the government invited these men to exploit those skills, with a minimum of government interference in the execution of the technical side of their work. Since the institution, like its task, was a continuing one, shipbuilders at the Arsenal also had the problem of transmitting their knowledge and skill to each other and to their successors. Under such conditions, the first efforts were made to communicate about shipbuilding methods in something other than a verbal or personal way. Shipbuilders were forced to reconsider their approach to building and try to explain it both by word of mouth and in writing, at least in terms of the major proportions of the ships they built. Over the years the Arsenal increased the pressure on builders to organise their approach, resulting in the fifteenth century in written treatises on the art of shipbuilding. Over all, the example of the organisation and operation of the Venetian Arsenal and, to a lesser degree, similar institutions in other parts of Europe offered a guide for all shipbuilders and also for all departments of governments.

The change in the number of oarsmen in galleys presented new problems for the governments of Italian maritime republics and their competitors in the Mediterranean. The shift to three men to each bench meant an immediate 50 per cent increase in the manning requirement. The change in ship design dictated a change in the character of demand for seamen. Both the great galley and the cog needed fewer skilled seamen. The galley, though, needed more unskilled men, rowers. The status of oarsmen declined in the fourteenth century as their work became more specialised and menial. They were no longer expected to fight and trade and handle the sails or tiller. In fact, being an oarsman was taken more and more as a sign of inferiority. At the same time as the job was losing status, governments were faced with the task of finding more men for the navy. While in the thirteenth century the finding of crews to handle the oars was not a problem, after the Black Death and the fall in population labour was harder to find, especially for what was becoming a demeaning task. The rowers rowed less and crews were not kept up to the full complement. These could be only temporary stop gaps, however. By 1400 governments were still struggling with the problem of manning the galleys. It was well established that the manning of galleys, the fitting out and deploying of a fighting fleet, was inextricably interwoven with state power and with the general prosperity of the people in the Italian maritime states. That idea had been adopted in Iberia and to a certain degree in France as well, thus making it unquestionably the task of the government to find the men for the galleys.

The economic results of the Black Death, and especially the effects of the sharp drop in population on income per person and the distribution of income, continue to be the subject of debate. The development of ship design in the fourteenth century appears to have contributed to the greater concentration of wealth, with certain merchants better off because of their ability to trade successfully in bulk goods. Improvements in bulk carriers, by promoting production for distant markets, concentrated incomes in the hands of those in the best position to produce goods for those markets. Those economic results are at best difficult to measure but they were probably insignificant compared to the direct demographic effect of the plague and the loss of one-third or more of the population. Ship-design improvements, on the other hand, did allow for the repopulation of towns. Given the nature of the pandemic, the death rate in towns was probably higher than that in the countryside. Towns did shrink as a result but by no means did urban life cease. Rather there was, as before, migration from the countryside into towns. Shipping contributed to that trend towards urbanisation in exactly the same way as it had from the ninth century. If anything, the process was accelerated in the fourteenth and fifteenth centuries, giving Europe a more urban character. Improvements in ship design also contributed to the changing relative income of the regions of Europe. Northwestern Europe ran a trade deficit with southern Europe, that is with Italy, and with the Baltic. In both cases England, northern France and the Low Countries bought more by value from those regions than they sold there. They did not have enough goods to cover the cost of furs and grains imported from the Baltic nor did they have goods to pay for the luxuries brought north by the great galleys. Cogs from Gdansk and galleys from Venice found back cargoes so that their operation was economically viable. Trade was possible and the goods had access to markets in northwest Europe. But since the ships were not suited to handle the type and bulk of goods which that region had to offer, the deficit had to be covered by an outflow of gold and silver.

The Black Death, both through its primary effect on population and its secondary effects on the economy, enhanced the position of monarchs. The kings and princes of western Europe found themselves able to consolidate their position and, from the mid-fourteenth century, economic circumstances worked to their advantage.[33] In order to carry out their programmes kings needed money, and ready cash was the best asset. Merchants and shippers had just the ready cash which governments needed. Italian city-states had long relied on the easily taxable income of such men for their own political strength. Rulers in western Europe in the fourteenth century increasingly copied Italian procedures, exploiting the possibilities created by trade. The most convenient situation was to have resident merchants, preferably prosperous and preferably native, who could be persuaded to support the crown through tax payments on their business and through loans. Native merchants were in a weaker position when it came to granting loans and the king could often simply force them to concede. If he repudiated the loans there was little the merchants could do. The easiest way to get the money, however, was to levy regular charges on a continuing flow of trade. If it went through a fixed point and was in fixed goods, supervision was simple and taxation could go ahead with a minimum of administrative cost and a minimum of loss from corruption. Moreover, the promotion and manipulation of such trade was easier for the clumsy governments of northern Europe which were only beginning to generate reliable systems of administration. The best situation for a king, then, was to be able to tax and control trade in some bulk good or goods. Indeed, something of a colonial economy based on the export, in large quantities, of a domestically produced good was the simplest, and therefore preferred, form of trade. It had the disadvantage of being less lucrative both for merchants and for tax collectors than trade in luxuries where the value was likely to be higher, but then luxury trade increased the possibility of avoidance. The changes in ship design worked to decrease that avoidance and at the same time to promote just the kind of trade that was easiest for governments to tax. By the end of the fourteenth century, trade in established commodities between certain ports was commonplace. Even in the Mediterranean that type of commerce increased. Certain ports there fared well under these circumstances. Monarchs who could and did tap the income from those trades were in general the ones most successful in the political contests, both internal and external, of the fourteenth and following centuries. These monarchs realised that the next step was, through legislation, to make sure that they got within their borders and preferably in the hands of domestic merchants as much of the available trade as possible. They achieved this through direct subsidy or more commonly through limitation on or exclusion of foreigners. Moreover, if kings could assert their legal authority over those merchants and the ships that carried the goods, then royal courts would enjoy an increase in power and income, both critical for European monarchs.[34] All this had the effect of generating greater government involvement in shipping and trade and therefore, directly and indirectly, in ship design. Further, the changes in ship design fed the economic strength of the monarchs and allowed them to devote themselves even more to that involvement. If nothing else, merchants, shippers and shipbuilders became more important to the political authorities. Thus the concern with the regulation of trade, which had appeared in Italian port towns in the eleventh and twelfth centuries, became typical of all Europe.

NOTES

1. Margery K. James, 'The Fluctuations of the Anglo-Gascon Wine Trade during the Fourteenth Century', in E. M. Carus-Wilson (ed), *Essays in Economic History*, vol. II (St. Martin's Press, New York, 1962), pp. 125-50. E. M. Carus-Wilson, 'The effects of the acquisition and of the loss of Gascony on the English wine trade', *Bulletin of the Institute of Historical Research*, XXI (1947), pp. 146-9. Yves Renouard, 'L'exportation des vins gascons', *Histoire de Bordeaux*, vol. III (Fédération historique du Sud-Ouest, Bordeaux, 1965), pp. 254-7.

2. Bernhard Hagedorn, *Die Entwicklung der wichtigsten Schiffstypen*, pp. 17-21, 41-2. L. G. C. Laughton, 'The Cog', *MM*, XLVI (1960), pp. 69-70. Colin Platt, *Medieval Southampton: the port and trading community A.D. 1000-1600* (Routledge, London, 1973), p. 71. Walther Vogel, *Geschichte der deutschen Seeschiffahrt*, pp. 493-4.

3. The reconstruction of the Bremen cog continues at the Deutsches Schiffahrtsmuseum in Bremerhaven and more features of its construction will become clear as work progresses. *HSUA*, pp. 191-2. *FHMN*, p. 295. Siegfried Fliedner, 'Der Fund einer Kogge bei Bremen im Oktober 1962', *Mededelingen van de Nederlandse Vereniging voor Zeegeschiedenis*, VII (1963), pp. 8-16. Also see Siegfried Fliedner *et al.*, *Die Bremer Hanse-Kogge Fund Konservierung Forschung* (Verlag Friedrich Röver, Bremen, 1969).

4. H. S. Vaughan, 'The Whipstaff', *MM*, III (1913), pp. 232-6, IV (1914), p. 137. The Bremen find gives no indication of this improvement in steering gear, throwing into question the scope of the use of the innovation and the speed of its adoption.

5. Paul Heinsius, *Das Schiff der Hansischen Frühzeit*, pp. 134-5. Alan Moore, 'A Barge of Edward III', *MM*, VI (1920), p. 231; this long oared ship had a parrel for the yard. R. Morton Nance, 'The Ship of the Renaissance', *MM*, XLI (1955), p. 187.

6. A. H. De Oliveira Marques, 'Navigation entre la Prusse et le Portugal au début du XVe siècle', *Vierteljahrschrift für Sozial- und Wirtschaftsgeschichte*, XLVI (1959), pp. 477-90. Arthur Agats, *Der Hansische Baienhandel* (Carl Winter's Universitätsbuchhandlung, Heidelberg, 1904), pp. 16-53. A. R. Bridbury, *England and the Salt Trade in the Later Middle Ages* (The Clarendon Press, Oxford, 1955), pp. 25, 31-3, 38-58, 84-91; in the second half of the fourteenth century the political situation was especially advantageous for Bay salt producers and the Hansards were the first to capitalise on it. Walther Vogel, *Geschichte der deutschen Seeschiffahrt*, pp. 280-95.

7. Aksel E. Christensen, 'La Foire de Scanie', *Société Jean Bodin, Recueils*, V (1953), pp. 244-55; estimates of herring production and of the number of ships involved are not consistent. G. W. Coopland, 'A Glimpse of Late Fourteenth-Century Ships and Seamen from Le Songe du Vieil Pélerin of Philippe de Mézières (1327-1405)', *MM*, XLVIII (1962), p. 190.

8. Ole Crumlin-Pedersen, 'Cog-Kogge-Kaag', p. 132. *HSUA*, p. 190. Atle Thowsen, 'En studie i nord-norsk trebåtbygging', *Sjøhistorisk Årbok* (1966), pp. 38-57. This is a report of a find of a cargo ship of Norway, about 22 metres long, which shows all the features of modification.

9. The punt, still in use on some rivers, is of essentially the same design as the

pram. Ole Crumlin-Pedersen, *Das Haithabuschiff*, pp. 24-7. *HSUA*, p. 189. *FHMN*, pp. 95-6, 109-11.

10. F. C. Berkenvelder, 'Frieslands handel in de late Middeleeuwen', *Economisch-Historisch Jaarboek*, XXIX (1963), pp. 140-67. Walther Vogel, *Geschichte der deutschen Seeschiffahrt*, pp. 498-507.

11. Siegfried Fliedner, ' "Kogge" und "Hulk" ', pp. 67-9. Bernhard Hagedorn, *Die Entwicklung der wichtigsten Schiffstypen*, pp. 43-51. Paul Heinsius, 'Dimensions et Caractéristiques des "Koggen" Hanseatiques dans le Commerce Baltique', p. 19, and *Das Schiff der Hansischen Frühzeit*, pp. 210-18. Another type, the ewer, also grew in the thirteenth and fourteenth centuries so that it could be used on the high seas. It lacked many of the features of the hulk which allowed the latter type to compete effectively with large cogs. Dagmar Waskönig, 'Bildliche Darstellung des Holks im 15. und 16. Jahrhundert', *Altonaer Museum Jahrbuch*, VII (1969), pp. 140-1.

12. G. Asaert, *Westeuropese scheepvaart in de middeleeuwen*, p. 139. Philippe Dollinger, *La Hanse* (Editions Montaigne Aubier, Paris, 1964), p. 195.

13. Paul Heinsius, *Das Schiff der Hansischen Frühzeit*, pp. 218-25. He is mistaken in claiming a novelty in the flat bottom of the merged type since this was a distinguishing feature of cogs. Dagmar Waskönig, 'Bildliche Darstellung des Holks im 15. und 16. Jahrhundert', pp. 141-5.

14. Claude Farrère, *Histoire de la Marine Française* (Flammarion, Paris, 1962), pp. 14-23. Charles De La Roncière, *Histoire de la Marine Française* (Librairie Plon, Paris, 1909-20), vol. I, pp. 403-7. Armand Le Hénaff, *Etude sur L'Organisation Administrative de la Marine sous L'Ancien Régime et la Révolution* (Librairie de la Société du Recueil Sirey, Paris, 1913), pp. 18-27. G. La Roërie and J. Vivielle, *Navires et Marins*, pp. 91-3; galley fleets were especially large and numerous at the end of the thirteenth century when the French chose to establish a naval force to contest control of the Channel; obviously, the Mediterranean galleys made an impression on the French king, Philip IV. Louis Nicolas, *Histoire de la Marine Française* (Presses Universitaires de France, Paris, 1961), pp. 7-10.

15. J. T. Tinniswood, 'English Galleys, 1272-1377', pp. 276-315. R. C. Anderson, 'English Galleys in 1295', *MM*, XIV (1928), pp. 220-41. These galleys were clinker-built and had typical northern rig. They resembled Mediterranean galleys in little more than relative length. See also R. C. Anderson, 'The Oars of Northern Long-Ships', pp. 191-5. H. J. Hewitt, *The Organization of War under Edward III, 1338-62* (Manchester University Press, Manchester, 1966), pp. 87-92, 182-6, and *The Black Prince's Expedition of 1355-1357* (Manchester University Press, Manchester, 1958), pp. 33-42. Michael Prestwich, *War, Politics and Finance under Edward I* (Faber and Faber Ltd, London, 1972), pp. 137-48. J. W. Sherborne, 'English Barges and Balingers of the Late Fourteenth Century', *MM*, LXIII (1977), pp. 109-14. The largest fourteenth-century barge he found was of 300 tons, which was greater than many contemporary round ships.

16. Arthur Agats, *Der Hansische Baienhandel*, pp. 25-6. A. R. Bridbury, *England and the Salt Trade in the Later Middle Ages*, pp. 76-7. Charles-Emmanuel Dufourcq, *La Vie Quotidienne*, p. 80. The frequency of convoys depended on the level of danger. He compares the eastern and western Mediterranean.

17. L. A. Boiteux, *La Fortune de Mer*, pp. 34-8, 40-2, 65-89. F. E. DeRoover, 'Early Examples of Marine Insurance', *Journal of Economic History*, V (1945), pp. 172-87.

18. Barbara M. Kreutz, 'Mediterranean Contributions to the Medieval Mariner's Compass', pp. 371-5. L. Denoix, 'Les Problèmes de Navigation au Début des Grandes Découvertes', *TCHM*, III, pp. 132-5. F. C. Lane, *Venice*, pp. 119-20. D. W. Waters, *The Rutters of the Sea* (Yale University Press, New Haven, 1967),

pp. 8-12. E. G. R. Taylor, *The Haven-Finding Art*, pp. 98-138.
    19. G. W. Coopland, 'A Glimpse of Late Fourteenth-Century Ships and Seamen', p. 191. Patrick A. Beaver, *A History of Lighthouses* (The Citadel Press, Seacaucus, New Jersey, 1973), pp. 12-18. F.C. Lane, 'The Economic Meaning of the Invention of the Compass', pp. 607-14. W. E. May, *A History of Marine Navigation*, pp. 50-1, 176-81, 203-4, 213-15. Uwe Schnell, 'Bemerkungen Zur Navigation auf Koggen', *Jahrbuch der Wittheit zu Bremen*, XXI (1977), pp. 137-48.
    20. G. Asaert, *Westeuropese scheepvaart in de middeleeuwen*, pp. 56-60, 137. F. C. Lane, *Navires et Constructeurs à Venise*, pp. 6-7, and 'Tonnages, Medieval and Modern', pp. 230-2. Archibald R. Lewis, 'Northern European Sea Power and the Straits of Gibraltar', pp. 158-60. E. B. Fryde, 'Anglo-Italian Commerce in the Fifteenth Century: some evidence about profits and the balance of trade', *Revue Belge de Philologie et d'Histoire*, L (1972), pp. 345-51.
    21. Romola and R. C. Anderson, *The Sailing-Ship*, pp. 113-14. F. C. Lane, *Navires et Constructeurs à Venise*, pp. 14, 19-22, 222, 'Progrès technologiques et productivité dans les transports maritimes', pp. 293-4, and 'Venetian Naval Architecture about 1550', *MM*, XX (1934), pp. 181, 189. Michael E. Mallett, *The Florentine Galleys in the Fifteenth Century with the Diary of Luca di Maso degli Albizzi Captain of the Galleys 1429-1430* (The Clarendon Press, Oxford, 1967), pp. 24-9.
    22. John Francis Guilmartin, *Gunpowder and Galleys* (Cambridge University Press, Cambridge, 1974), pp. 69-70. F. C. Lane, 'Tonnages, Medieval and Modern', pp. 230-1. The word arsenal is of Arabic origin and was used throughout the Christian Mediterranean to describe a government yard for building warships.
    23. F. C. Lane, *Navires et Constructeurs à Venise*, pp. 93-7, 125-9. Up to the mid-fourteenth century the largest great galleys were built in private yards. See also F. C. Lane, 'Venetian Merchant Galleys, 1300-1334: Private and Communal Operation', *Speculum*, XXXVIII (1963), pp. 191-4, 200-3. Jacques Heers, *Gênes au XVᵉ Siècle* (SEVPEN, Paris, 1961), pp. 270-1. The Genoese did not use great galleys but rather built eight or twelve light galleys for the navy when war broke out. The light galleys were much the same as their Venetian counterparts.
    24. G. W. Coopland, 'A Glimpse of Late Fourteenth-Century Ships and Seamen', p. 188. R. Morton Nance, 'An Italian Ship of 1339', *MM*, I (1911), pp. 334-9, and 'The Ship of the Renaissance', pp. 180-4. Marco Bonino, 'Lateen-rigged Medieval Ships', pp. 15-17, 22-5.
    25. Siegfried Fliedner, ' "Kogge" und "Hulk" ', pp. 89-90. Bernhard Hagedorn, *Die Entwicklung der wichtigsten Schiffstypen*, pp. 39-40. Paul Heinsius, *Das Schiff der Hansischen Frühzeit*, pp. 78-9. Charles-Emmanuel Dufourcq, *L'Espagne Catalane et Le Maghrib*, pp. 40-5.
    26. G. Asaert, *Westeuropese scheepvaart in de middeleeuwen*, p. 60. Michel Balard, 'Notes sur l'Activité Maritime des Génois de Cagga à la Fin du XIIIᵉ Siècle', *TCHM*, VIII, pp. 379-80; in the 1290s Genoese merchants were using large and medium-size round ships for long-distance bulk carriage from the Crimea to Syria, Tunis and Genoa. Jacques Heers, *Gênes au XVᵉ Siècle*, pp. 274-8, 316-20, and 'Types de Navires et Spécialisation des Trafics en Méditerranée à la Fin du Moyen Age', *TCHM*, II, pp. 110-15. F. C. Lane, *Navires et Constructeurs à Venise*, pp. 43-5. Henri Bresc, 'Una flotte mercantile periferica: la marina siciliana medievale', in Henri Bresc *et al.*, *Studi di storia navale*, Centro per la storia tecnica in Italia, Pubblicazioni, IV, 7 (1975), p. 9; in 1367 a Genoese shipwright had to be brought to Messina to oversee construction of a *cocka*. F. C. Lane, *Venice*, pp. 122-4. By 1400 Genoese cogs even reached 1,000 tons. Venetians were held back from building such giants by the shallowness of their harbours. Still, by the mid-fourteenth century *cocka* was the usual term for a large

round ship in Venice.

27. Antonio de Capmany, *Memorias Historicas sobre la marina commercio y artes de la antigua ciudad de Barcelona*, vol. III, pp. 81-90. Jacques Heers, *Gênes au XVᵉ Siècle*, pp. 245-6, and *L'Occident aux XIVᵉ et XVᵉ Siècles* (Presses Universitaires de France, Paris, 1963), pp. 103-4. F. C. Lane, *Navires et Constructeurs à Venise*, pp. 35-7, and 'Progrès technologiques et productivité dans les transports maritimes', pp. 290-2. He suspects that crew size did not fall as much as possible because of the need to protect against pirates and that much of the saving in operating costs was lost because of longer turnaround time. Both features certainly reduced the social saving that could be gained from using the cog. This did not alter the fact that labour saving was great enough over many routes to make it worth while for shippers to change to cogs. Charles-Emmanuel Dufourcq, *L'Espagne Catalane et Le Maghrib*, pp. 531-40.

28. F. C. Lane, 'The Crossbow in the Nautical Revolution of the Middle Ages', in D. Herlihy *et al.* (eds), *Economy, Society and Government in Medieval Italy, Essays in Honor of Robert L. Reynolds* (Kent State University Press, Kent, 1969), pp. 161-72.

29. Romola and R. C. Anderson, *The Sailing-Ship*, pp. 110-12. Siegfried Fliedner, ' "Kogge" und "Hulk" ', pp. 91-2. F. C. Lane, *Navires et Constructeurs à Venise*, pp. 39-40. R. Morton Nance, 'The Ship of the Renaissance', pp. 180, 187-9.

30. Eugene H. Byrne, *Genoese Shipping in the Twelfth and Thirteenth Centuries*, pp. 12-14, 65-6. The major examples for the trend come from Genoa. Venice, by government policy, purposely prevented extreme concentration of ownership. It is hard to believe that the pattern was not similar outside Genoa. Jacques Heers, *Gênes au XVᵉ Siècle*, pp. 279-82, 288. F. C. Lane, 'Venetian Merchant Galleys, 1300-1334', p. 203.

31. G. Asaert, *Westeuropese scheepvaart in de middeleeuwen*, p. 120. Arthur Agats, *Der Hansische Baienhandel*, p. 25. In the fifteenth century, the Hanseatic League slowly abandoned legal prohibitions on winter sailing, largely because their competitors enjoyed greater flexibility in providing shipping services.

32. L. A. Boiteux, *La Fortune de Mer*, p. 40. W. A. Englebrecht, *Schets der Historische Betrekkingen Portugal-Nederland*, pp. 5-6. Gervasio de Artiñano Y de Galdácano, *La Arquitectura Naval Española (en Madera)* (for the author, Madrid, 1920), p. 18. F. C. Lane, *Navires et Constructeurs à Venise*, pp. 141-66. Bailey W. Diffie, *Prelude to Empire*, pp. 67-9.

33. Jacques Heers, *L'Occident aux XIVᵉ et XVᵉ Siècles*, pp. 191-5. Harry A. Miskimin, *The Economy of Early Renaissance Europe, 1300-1460* (Prentice-Hall, Inc., Englewood Cliffs, NJ, 1969).

34. Edwin M. Bacon, *Manual of Navigation Laws* (A. C. McClurg and Co., Chicago, 1912), pp. 9-14. Fredric L. Cheyette, 'The Sovereign and the Pirates, 1332', *Speculum* XLV (1970), pp. 40-68.

NOTES TO ILLUSTRATIONS

a. *AB*, no. 177. G. Asaert, *Westeuropese scheepvaart in de middeleeuwen*, pp. 89, 109. *HSUA*, pp. 202-3. *FHMN*, p. 66. Siegfried Fliedner, ' "Kogge" und "Hulk" ', nos. 107-10.

b. Romola and R. C. Anderson, *The Sailing-Ship*, pp. 87-8, 91. G. Asaert, *Westeuropese scheepvaart in de middeleeuwen*, pp. 31, 38, 94. *FHMN*, p. 65. Bernhard Hagedorn, *Die Entwicklung der wichtigsten Schiffstypen*, plates III, VI-XII. Paul Heinsius, *Das Schiff der Hansischen Frühzeit*, pp. 23, 55-7, 59-62,

77-8, plate VII, no. 16, VIII, nos. 17-18, XI, no. 23, XV, no. 31. Siegfried Fliedner, ' "Kogge" und "Hulk" ', nos. 47, 74, 88, 90-7, 99-102. *HSUA*, pp. 202-4. Björn Landström, *The Ship*, nos. 178, 180-5, 187, 309. G. La Roërie and J. Vivielle, *Navires et Marins*, vol. I, p. 201, plate VIII, no. 4, IX, no. 4. H. S. Vaughan, 'The Whipstaff', *MM*, IV (1914), pp. 142-3.

     c. G. Asaert, *Westeuropese scheepvaart in de middeleeuwen*, pp. 32, 52. Lionel Casson, *Illustrated History of Ships and Boats*, nos. 84-5. H. H. Brindley, 'Early Reefs', opposite p. 81. *HSUA*, p. 204. Claude Farrère, *Histoire de la Marine Française*, pp. 12-13, 20, 28, 30-2. Siegfried Fliedner, ' "Kogge" und "Hulk" ', no. 75. Bernhard Hagedorn, *Die Entwicklung der wichtigsten Schiffstypen*, plate XVI. Paul Heinsius, *Das Schiff der Hansischen Frühzeit*, plate V, no. 12, X, no. 22. Björn Landström, *The Ship*, no. 186. G. La Roërie and J. Vivielle, *Navires et Marins*, vol. I, pp. 195, 200, 211, 272.

     d. Romola and R. C. Anderson, *The Sailing-Ship*, pp. 82-3. G. Asaert, *Westeuropese scheepvaart in de middeleeuwen*, opposite p. 65. A. W. Brøgger and Haakon Shetelig, *The Viking Ships*, p. 185. *HSUA*, p. 197. *FHMN*, pp. 98-104. Paul Heinsius, *Das Schiff der Hansischen Frühzeit*, plate I, no.2, IV, no. 9, no. 12. Björn Landström, *The Ship*, nos. 192, 195, and *Sailing Ships*, nos. 170, 186, 188. G. La Roërie and J. Vivielle, *Navires et Marins*, vol. I, p. 206, plate VII, no.2, IX, no.2. Atle Thowsen, 'Foldrøyskipet Et middelaldersk skipsfunn fra Vest-Norge', *Sjøfartshistorisk Årbok* (1965), pp. 39-41, 47, 54.

     e. *HSUA*, pp. 189, 195. *FHMN*, pp. 98-104.

     f. Romola and R. C. Anderson, *The Sailing-Ship*, p. 87, no. 50. G. Asaert, *Westeuropese scheepvaart in de middeleeuwen*, pp. 90, 131. H. H. Brindley, 'Mediaeval Ships', *MM*, II (1912), opposite p. 5. G. S. Laird Clowes, *Sailing Ships*, part I, p. 49. Siegfried Fliedner, ' "Kogge" und "Hulk" ', nos. 10-13, 15. Paul Heinsius, *Das Schiff der Hansischen Frühzeit*, plate XII, nos. 25-6, XIII, nos. 27-9, IV, no. 10. Björn Landström, *The Ship*, no. 193. G. La Roërie and J. Vivielle, *Navires et Marins*, vol. I, p. 208.

     g. Romola and R. C. Anderson, *The Sailing-Ship*, pp. 96, 119, no. 74. G. Asaert, *Westeuropese scheepvaart in de middeleeuwen*, p. 92. H. H. Brindley, 'Mediaeval Ships', *MM*, II (1912), opposite p. 44. Siegfried Fliedner, ' "Kogge" und "Hulk" ', nos. 11, 14, 18, 20-1, 23-7. Bernhard Hagedorn, *Die Entwicklung der wichtigsten Schiffstypen*, plate XIII, XV. Paul Heinsius, *Das Schiff der Hansischen Frühzeit*, pp. 216-17, 221. Björn Landström, *Sailing Ships*, nos. 189-91, and *The Ship*, nos. 194, 197. G. La Roërie and J. Vivielle, *Navires et Marins*, vol. I, p. 207, plate IX, no. 3.

     h. Claude Farrère, *Histoire de la Marine Française*, p. 24. Alan Moore, 'A Barge of Edward III', *MM*, VI (1920), p. 242.

     i. G. Asaert, *Westeuropese scheepvaart in de middeleeuwen*, pp. 44, 116. Claude Farrère, *Histoire de la Marine Française*, pp. 60-1. E. G. R. Taylor, *The Haven-Finding Art*, figures X, XII, XV.

     j. Romola and R. C. Anderson, *The Sailing-Ship*, p. 113. Lionel Casson, *Illustrated History of Ships and Boats*, no. 86. Claude Farrère, *Histoire de la Marine Française*, p. 48. Björn Landström, *The Ship*, nos. 243, 244, 318. G. La Roërie and J. Vivielle, *Navires et Marins*, vol. I, pp. 83, 97.

     k. H. H. Brindley, Mediaeval Ships', *MM*, II (1912), opposite p. 44. Marco Bonino, 'Lateen-rigged medieval ships', pp. 16-17, 23. Lionel Casson, *Illustrated History of Ships and Boats*, nos. 93, 98-9. Romola and R. C. Anderson, *The Sailing-Ship*, p. 109, plate I. G. S. Laird Clowes, *Sailing Ships*, part II, plate II. Siegfried Fliedner, ' "Kogge" und "Hulk" ', no. 103. R. Morton Nance, 'An Italian Ship of 1339', *MM*, I (1911), p. 335. Björn Landström, *The Ship*, nos. 232-8.

     l. Lionel Casson, *Illustrated History of Ships and Boats*, nos. 89, 100-1.

Siegfried Fliedner, ' "Kogge" und "Hulk" ', nos. 104-5. José Maria Martinez-Hidalgo, *Columbus' Ships* (Barre Publishers, Barre, 1966), pp. 28, 38. G. La Roërie and J. Vivielle, *Navires et Marins*, vol. I, pp. 198-9. Marco Bonino, 'Lateen-rigged medieval ships', p. 21. Björn Landström, *The Ship*, nos. 239-42.
m.   Romola and R. C. Anderson, *The Sailing-Ship*, p. 111. Siegfried Fliedner, ' "Kogge" und "Hulk" ', no. 106. F. C. Lane, *Navires et Constructeurs à Venise*, p. 40, figure XI. José Maria Martinez-Hidalgo, *Columbus' Ships*, p. 26. Björn Landström, *The Ship*, no. 245.

5   THE GREAT INVENTION: 1400-1550

In 1453 Constantinople and the Byzantine Empire fell to the Ottoman Turks. By that late date the event was a minor one, both politically and economically. Turkish naval forces already presented a threat to Italian and especially Venetian commercial shipping. To hold and to improve their political position the Turks had found that they needed a powerful navy. By 1500 their holding of all the continental naval bases in the eastern Mediterranean had revolutionised sea power. In the sixteenth century the Turks challenged the power of Italian trading towns and of Spain in a series of naval battles. The Mediterranean was effectively divided into two spheres, with the eastern half patrolled by Turkish warships and the western half, along with the Adriatic, reserved largely for the warships of Christian states. In Italy itself the consolidation of certain states had led to the emergence by the mid-fifteenth century of a balance of strength among them, which changed, however, in 1494 with an invasion by French troops. After this invasion the Italian states were dragged into another general conflict but, instead of Christians and Turks, the contestants were the Habsburg and Valois dynasties.

By a series of marriages and convenient successions the house of

Illustration above: A three-masted ship but with square sails on each of the masts, seal of Louis de Bourbon, Admiral of France, 1463-86.

Habsburg had gathered together enough titles and states to make it the most powerful in Europe. In the person of the Holy Roman Emperor, Charles V, all the different states were united. Charles saw his job as the unification of Christendom. The kings of the House of Valois in France contested this bid for European hegemony, at the same time advancing their own dynastic interests, thus leading to almost continuous wars between France, on the one hand, and Spain, the Low Countries and the other states under Hapsburg rulers, on the other. England was a makeweight in these contests, as were the smaller states in Germany. The diminished position of the English crown was in part the result of the defeat suffered in the Hundred Years' War with France. By 1453 and the end of the war, the king of England had to surrender almost all his continental possessions. Despite a more aggressive naval and commercial policy from the late fifteenth century, England remained a state of secondary importance to the balance of political and naval power.

The Hanseatic League, meanwhile, because of internal strife and external pressure, faced the slow erosion of both political and economic power from the early fifteenth century. The counties of Holland and Zeeland were added to the lands of the Dukes of Burgundy in the fifteenth century, uniting them, among others, with the wealthy county of Flanders. Merchants throughout the Low Countries, then, could expect greater and more effective political support. That possibility was enhanced when the region became part of the massive holdings of the House of Hapsburg at the end of the century. Dutch traders, from Holland and Zeeland, were able to supply similar shipping services for less than their Hanse competitors. Dutch merchants also enjoyed close connections with monarchs in Scandinavia, who were able slowly to reassert their political power, supplanting the aristocracy and at the same time challenging the dominant position of German merchants by inviting Dutch traders to compete against them. The internal troubles of, and the fighting among, the principalities of the North, however, were peripheral to the struggle in central and western Europe.

The Protestant Reformation complicated the politics of Europe. Starting in Germany as a theological debate on questions basic to Christianity, it soon brought into question the entire character of relations between church and state. Pressures increased on all parties to take a side in the controversy. The Papacy, having declared the opinions of Protestants anathema, urged secular authorities to suppress the heresy. In doing so the church created a new network of allegiances which in some cases did and in other cases did not overcome other bases for political and military affiliation among states. Merchants were not totally immune from the pressures of the new religious controversy. At times states prohibited certain merchants from trading because of their religion. The importance of religion to both politics and commerce increased in the course of the sixteenth century, as both Catholics and Protestants mobilised forces for what both sides saw as a necessary struggle. These battles were far enough removed from the daily operation of most trade, and especially small-scale trade, however, that shipbuilders continued to function as they had for centuries, subject to the pressures of the economics of shipping and the sporadic and unique demands of government.

By the end of the fifteenth century, the pattern of design development had become general throughout Europe. Not only did contact among the various regions increase but also shipbuilders turned themselves to the construction of similar types in most of the major ports of the Continent. The fact that shipping had taken on a general European dimension was already evident in the late fourteenth century. The structure of demand for ships thus became increasingly similar for all builders. At the same time the invention and technical innovations of the fifteenth century made certain designs significantly superior to earlier ones and made the new forms acceptable for many jobs in many different places. This is not to say that regional and local variations were eradicated: quite the opposite. There was still a difference between types built in northern and those built in southern Europe. The climate, the nature of the winds and tides and the generally different sailing conditions in the Baltic, in the North Sea, along the Atlantic coast and in the Mediterranean still guaranteed variation in the way local builders executed designs. But shipbuilders, by borrowing and copying design features, did create a range of highly versatile vessels, vessels which, with minor adjustments, could be used anywhere in the world.

One of the major features of fifteenth- and sixteenth-century shipbuilding was the greater differentiation and specialisation in the design of smaller vessels — that is, ships and boats under about 50 tons. The introduction of certain new types of rig, including the transfer of lateen rig to northern Europe, made possible that greater differentiation. The smaller ships and boats were solid and reliable. They usually had higher manning ratios than had larger vessels, but the implied higher cost was often fully offset by faster turnaround time. Skippers used these vessels as coasters, tramping from port to port. In the tenth and eleventh centuries tramping had been a job reserved for the largest cargo ships, those of 200 tons and often more. By 1450, small vessels heavily outnumbered large ships; this was true when comparing all seagoing ships of over and under 100 tons. The large number of small ships gave shipwrights many more chances to experiment with improvements to those vessels, though typically the improvements were minor ones. Moreover, in the second half of the fifteenth and in the sixteenth century, the absolute and relative number of these smaller vessels rose. The general growth in the economy and the relatively faster expansion of commerce created more opportunities for using smaller vessels than for using the largest of seagoing ships. The coasters could carry anything. In periods of growth they could supplement large carriers on major routes, while opening and serving new and shorter routes.[1] Shipbuilders responded to the trade revival by building more ships and by building vessels better suited to the opportunites at hand.

The names given to these smaller craft are in many cases hard to match with a design. Still, there is an unmistakable impression that the variety of ship types grew in the fifteenth and sixteenth centuries. The variety is unfortunately bewildering but the repetition of certain names in many of the records suggests that certain types of smaller craft did enjoy a widespread popularity among shipbuilders. Crayers and balingers appeared alongside various barks, barges and snikkers in German and English records. There were also other local types. The balinger, for example, was a popular type. It may have started as a whaling boat used along the coast of Brittany and the Bay of Biscay. In the fifteenth century it changed from a small oared fishing boat to a sailing vessel with two square sails on two masts. A sailing balinger carried from 20 to 50 tons but there were larger balingers of up to 100 tons and in one case of 500 tons. A balinger was capable of sailing from the Low Countries to the eastern Mediterranean. The change to a sailing ship lowered the manning ratio and made the type economic for trade along the coast and for use between France and England and between Spain and England. The development of the barge in the fifteenth and sixteenth centuries is not as clear. Certainly, barges were used for ceremonial transport on rivers but they also acted as troop transports and cargo ships, going from 25 tons up to 240 tons. They too may have combined oars and sails for propulsion. The use of the name for northern European seagoing cargo carriers decreased in the fifteenth century, probably because of improvements in other ships which became more efficient and could replace the barge. Spinaces, later pinnaces, of around 20 tons appeared in English customs records, along with picards and many other types, including keels. How much the last owed to the Scandinavian cargo ship of the eighth century is not known but, by the fifteenth century, there were at least three different forms of keel, each with a single mast and single square sail.[2] Many of these types were used as lighters in harbours or for short-distance coastal voyages. That meant that they rarely exceeded 20 tons. Of course, they enjoyed the advantage shared by all these small types of being able to get in and out of almost any port.

In Normandy shipbuilders constructed all kinds of ships, from galleys of Mediterranean design to the biggest sailing vessels, but the large majority of their ships were small ones able to visit the ports among the coastal cliffs and travel up the Seine to Rouen. There were clinker-built barges similar to those in England. Balingers also came from Norman yards, as did crayers, galiots, brigantines, frigates and many others. There was also a number of fishing boats. These, like many of the other types, grew in size throughout the fifteenth and sixteenth centuries, so they could be used efficiently on the high seas. The opening of the Newfoundland cod fishery in the sixteenth century contributed to the growth of those ships. Vessels of 50 tons could make the trip to the New World and back but the average ship was closer to 80 tons and ships of 200 tons were not uncommon. As much of the work of preparing the fish was done on board, the manning ratios were high.[3] Growth in size did not change the basic and simple design of these different types. The pattern was apparently similar along the Atlantic coast of France.

In the Mediterranean the successors of lateen-rigged round ships carried the goods of local and regional commerce going by sea. The felucca was a small boat with two masts, each with a lateen sail. It was built in Portugal as well as in the Mediterranean. There were barks of various types, along with small galleys, presumably made broader and more like sailing ships in order to be economic cargo carriers.[a] Certain designs were imported from Iberia. Shallops, which started as whaleboats in the Bay of Biscay, and Portuguese barks with two square sails, one on each mast, easily found a place in the Mediterranean coasting ports.[4] But even the largest ports had their share of various smaller types to maintain contact with nearby coastal villages and towns.

If the variety of small types is confusing for fifteenth-century Germany, England, France and the Mediterranean, it is staggering for the Low Countries. Dutch shipbuilders, even more than their counterparts in the rest of Europe, were able to generate specialised designs. One reason was the poor and constantly changing conditions of the many harbours and inland waterways used by most ships in the Low Countries. Another reason was the increase in a broad range of maritime activities by Netherlanders. The fishery expanded rapidly as North Sea herring replaced Scania herring in European markets. Low Countries fishermen used a larger net and improved curing methods, with salting and packing of the fish done on board — thus necessitating a bigger fishing boat designed specifically to exploit the new techniques. Dutch builders supplied the herring buss. By 1500 it carried three masts, all detachable so that they could be taken down when fishing. There was a square sail on each and sometimes a square topsail above the main on the mainmast. The posts were sharply curved, giving bluff bows. The stern was flat. There was often a bowsprit, usually pointing down to give better control over the net when it was cast over the bow. Larger busses had a full deck with a large hatch to take the casks filled with fish. There was little resemblance to the thirteenth-century Scandinavian cargo carrier but presumably the two types with the same name at least had a common ancestor in the Viking cargo ship. Other deep-sea fishing vessels came from Dutch yards, such as the dogger and the hoeker, both for the cod fishery. The hoeker, like the buss, offered a specialised type for certain fishermen. Hoekers had flat sterns and two and sometimes three masts, each with a square sail. The hull was often pierced with many small holes to create a bath of sea water in the middle of the ship for the catch. Fish could be stored there and delivered fresh. Doggers, on the other hand, were typically used for producing salted cod though salting was also done on board hoekers.[b] Added to these types were the pinks, *schuiten* and *slabberts* of the coast fishery. The *schuit* was a small flat-bottomed boat with a sail. It could be and was used on inland waterways and indeed throughout the Low Countries. The design may have been typically the same as the second-century riverboats excavated at Zwammerdam. Another inland cargo and passenger carrier was the poon. It, like the pink, was short with a rounded bow and sharp sternpost. The bottom was flat, at least for part of the hull, and it could be beached anywhere. There were corvers, smacks and plats, which turned up in the fishery and also in the rapidly expanding cargo trade to ports in eastern England.[5] All these vessels were sturdy and designed to take the rough waters of the great rivers of the Low Countries and of the North Sea.

The fishing boats were unemployed for a sizeable part of the year because of the limited fishing season. Since they could weather North Sea storms they were well suited for cargo carriage. Skippers in the off-season went in search of cargoes for their busses and hoekers. Voyages as far as the Mediterranean were possible. The buss began as a small vessel of 30 or 40 tons but by 1550 was usually well over 100 tons and

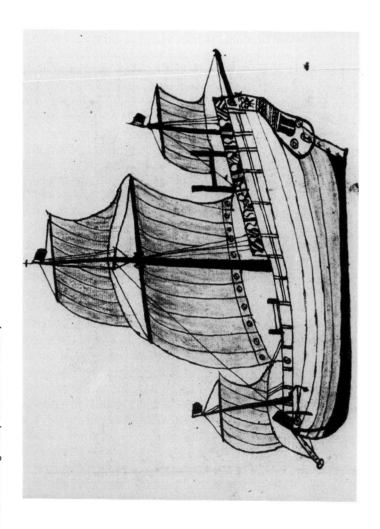

19: Dutch Herring Buss, Sixteenth Century

20 metres or more long. Crew size fell, by as much as 50 per cent, making it more efficient in fishing and an even better candidate for carrying cargo. By the mid-sixteenth century, Dutch yards produced vessels of buss design but destined exclusively for taking cargoes. There were other cargo ships, exclusively designed for short-distance carriage, such as the *heude*.[6] These were vessels, like the buss, of about 100 tons or less, and able to negotiate the estuaries, rivers and shoals of the south coast of the North Sea and the Channel. A small version of the cog was also popular on Dutch inland waters. The design still served, as it had in the seventh century, on the sandbanks and shoals of the Low Countries. The cog, like most of the other smaller cargo and fishing boats of the Netherlands, was derived from earlier designs. Dutch ship carpenters were familiar with these types and continued to build them, constantly adjusting them to changing demand. It was a matter of exploiting what was known.

Dutch builders did make a major change in many of the designs. The typical square rig of northern Europe was dropped and replaced by a sprit-rig. This form of fore-and-aft sail, known in the Roman Empire, had apparently fallen out of use, replaced by the lateen sail in the fifth and sixth centuries. Sprit-rig may have been used throughout the middle ages and just not have appeared in records or in illustrations. More likely it was simply forgotten. It is apparently one of the few cases where knowledge of a design feature was lost. In the fourteenth century, sprit-rig came back into Europe, first in the form of a sail on two poles with a common base — an arrangement common in southeast Asia. In any event, by the early sixteenth century, Dutch small craft carried fore-and-aft sails, either spritsails or gaffsails. The gaffsail was, like the spritsail, rectangular or trapezoidal but it was hung down from a yard, extending back from the mast and pivoting on it. The gaffsail in general could not be made as large as the spritsail. Both, however, had the advantage of having the leading edge of the sail stretched to the mast; as a result, they were better for going against the wind and especially good in a crosswind, something that Dutch small craft typically had to face. The spritsail could also carry a bonnet at the bottom so that size could be increased in fair weather.[7] A second sail was often added, hanging from the forestay. A triangular staysail had many of the same properties and thus further improved handling qualities. Dutch small boats typically carried this rig but it was also used on larger ships of up to 100 tons.[c] The rig increased manoeuvrability, cut down time wasted waiting for a fair breeze, and also required less manpower to operate than any competing rig. The result was a highly versatile craft well suited to short-distance carriage across the open sea and along the coast. For single-masted vessels it was markedly superior to lateen rig. It gave Dutch shippers an advantage in regional and local transport, and thus in the distribution of goods, which in turn drew more long-distance trade to ports in the Low Countries. The improved rig was adopted about 1400, and may have been taken on in response to the troubled state of the Holland economy in the late fourteenth century. While escaping the worst immediate economic effects of the Black Death, the Dutch economy suffered in the years just before and after 1400. The revival and expansion after the middle of the century served to increase opportunities for experiment and the adaptation of fore-and-aft rig to Dutch ships.

As to the improvements in fishing boats, the changes in productivity wrought by the Black Death led to greater consumption per person of protein foods, of meat, cheese and also fish. The pressure on producers to increase output, combined with the improvements in related technology, in the catching and preserving of fish, created an imbalance which brought ship carpenters to concentrate their efforts on finding the right combination of design features to make fishing vessels more productive. Since the size of the market had grown relatively and there was upward pressure on prices, it was possible to build a ship of specialised design. If it could be used to carry cargo in the off-season, that was a lucrative but not a necessary benefit. As the absolute size of the market for fish grew throughout the fifteenth and sixteenth centuries, shipbuilders took the opportunity to improve the design and to make it even more specialised. In the process they also made the ship more efficient. The Dutch example is only the most extreme and the most impressive in the development of specialised smaller craft. The greater variety of these vessels and their greater efficiency constituted a valuable addition to total shipping services in Europe. Since Dutch shipbuilders went to the greatest extremes of specialisation, it was Dutch shippers who reaped the greatest advantages.

Galleys were still used. They survived as warships until the nineteenth century but by 1400 they were already different from their twelfth-century predecessors because of the change to three oarsmen to each bench. Galleys were usually under 40 metres in length but they could exceed 50 metres. The width was usually one-eighth of the length. The rise in the number of rowers had made it possible to build the galley longer, broader and heavier. There were typically about 24 benches to a side, giving a total of 144 oarsmen. There was generally a single mast with a lateen sail, though larger galleys, especially those for the transport of troops, still carried multiple masts. The war galley was not a ship for the open ocean but it did dominate the Mediterranean. There were galleys in northern Europe, copies of Mediterranean galleys, but they remained exclusively warships for fighting on the rivers and along the coast. They were used as far north as Finland, and the Spaniards deployed a squadron in the Caribbean where conditions both of weather and of piracy were similar enough to those in the Mediterranean to make them effective.[8]

The greatest change in the galley came from the introduction of artillery on board. The guns replaced older ballistic devices and took their place at the bow. Guns were already used at sea in the wars between Venice and Genoa in the fourteenth century. Only as guns became more reliable were they put on the majority of galleys. By 1500, a single large gun set along the centre line at the bow was the principal offensive weapon of the galley.[d] These guns were heavy bronze cannon, like those used in sieges on land; they were very expensive and the galley provided the most versatile platform for them. Small guns, as many as six, flanked the large piece. Superstructure disappeared since crews were no longer worried about being higher than the enemy. There was still a small fighting platform above the gun for marines. The addition of heavy guns forward made the ship even more unstable. Artillery changed the value and character of galleys. Large round ships, manoeuvrable and equipped with guns, were almost invulnerable to these light ships. In the early sixteenth century, navies used galleys equipped with cannon to cover landings, to shell fortresses and in general to support amphibious operations. As sailing ships gained more armament, that use declined in importance but not until after 1550. Galleys remained in the fleets of all Mediterranean naval powers to deal with opponents' galleys. Boarding was the usual tactic for victory at sea. Galleys were best suited to the job of making contact with an enemy ship at a lightly defended point and staying long enough to give a boarding party a chance to take the other vessel. With oars for propulsion, galleys could always avoid sailing ships, so only other galleys could effectively neutralise them in naval battles. Galleys were also effective in supplementing the defence of fortified coastal positions. They proved highly effective in the incessant piratical war of attrition fought largely between Christian and Muslim states.[9] So long as the number of guns remained small and galleys had an overwhelming superiority in manoeuvrability over sailing ships, they remained a critical part of Mediterranean naval forces.

Great galleys were driven out of commercial service as improvements in the design of sailing ships made them as efficient in carrying goods. Regular state-sponsored galley service from Venice and from Florence continued throughout the fifteenth century but by the beginning of the sixteenth century these voyages had been sharply curtailed and by mid-century they had disappeared entirely. In the fifteenth century, great galleys carried three lateen sails. Oars were still handled by individual oarsmen. A length of 45 metres was typical. The measurements and design remained much the same as long as great galleys were built at the Venetian Arsenal. They survived longest in voyages from Venice to the eastern Mediterranean. At the end of the fifteenth century, they were still the best carrier for pilgrims going to the Holy Land. So that they could compete with sailing vessels, great galleys were built bigger. By 1500, they had reached capacities of 250 to 300 tons which, given the amount of hold space and methods of measure, probably gave them a payload equivalent to that of a sailing ship of 600 tons.[e] Crews of 200 men or more made them highly defensible but also raised operating costs relative to sailing ships.[10] In part because of government support, in part because of the unique nature of Venetian transport needs in the eastern Mediterranean and in part because of the ability of shipbuilders to expand the capacity of great galleys, this type continued in use well into the sixteenth century; but the success in designing sailing ships in time drove the great galley out of more and more trades. Shipbuilders then turned their attention to building a sailing ship which could retain at least some of the advantageous features of the galley.

The galeass of the first half of the sixteenth century was a large sailing warship, but with oars and with a length-to-breadth ratio like that of a great galley, about 5:1. Because of its larger size it could handle more guns than a galley but retained much of its manoeuvrability. The compromise did not work because the galeass was little more than a big, well-armed but much slower galley. The galeass was clumsy and still had trouble dealing with a warship powered exclusively by sails. Finding crews to man the heavy oars was a constant problem. As sailing ships on the open Atlantic, galeasses left a great deal to be desired. Galeasses could reach 450 tons, making them quite large warships. There were three masts, sometimes four, with lateen sails in the Mediterranean and square sails in the North. Rowers worked on a deck below the full top deck. The latter was reserved for the marines, the cannon and the other missile launchers. The crews were massive, one galeass 47 metres long having a total of 700 men on board. Navies used galeasses in most of the major naval battles of the sixteenth century. King Henry VIII of England considered galeasses a necessary part of his naval armament and had some 15 of them. Of course, the king of France had to have a fleet of galeasses to meet them.[11] For much of the sixteenth century the design of galeasses in northern Europe was little different from that in southern Europe.[f] The type was developed purely because of the demand of governments for a specific kind of warship; based on experience with great galleys and with contemporary sailing ships, builders generated the combined design. The migration of ship carpenters, especially from Italy to northern Europe to work for government shipyards there, guaranteed a consistency of design. Begun in the late thirteenth century, the transfer of shipbuilders at least made the design of certain kinds of warships the same throughout much of Europe. Shipbuilders failed to make the galeass into a viable warship. By the late sixteenth century, sailing ships were better for fighting than were galeasses, just as they were better at carrying cargo than were the similar great galleys.

The history of the caravel, another type originally developed in southern Europe, is rather confusing. The name was first attached to a fishing boat and probably has an Arabic origin, but the exact form of that mid-thirteenth-century fishing boat is unknown. The name may have been used to indicate the type of planking and there is little question that the caravel was, from the first, carvel-built. The Portuguese government, committed by Prince Henry the Navigator to a policy of expansion by sea, needed a ship which would serve for the exploration of the African coast. Explorers used barks of about 25 tons, which had a single mast and may have been very much like earlier Scandinavian and English cargo ships. Explorers also used the *barinel* which was longer and larger than the bark. Neither of these was adequate for the increasingly longer voyages so, by 1440, the caravel joined the squadrons travelling south into the Atlantic from Portugal. From 20 to 30 metres long and 4 to 5 metres wide, they were vessels of 50 tons and more. They carried two masts with lateen sails. Draught was shallow. The caravel was highly manoeuvrable and was able to sail back to Portugal from West Africa despite contrary winds and currents. There was no forecastle on these ships and the small aftercastle was only there to make handling the sails easier. The low sides, sharp ends and lateen rig all created a vessel which could sail closer to the wind than other contemporary European vessels.[g] Carrying capacity was small on the caravel and indeed on all ships used for exploration, so small that they could carry little food for the crews. Such ships had to be able to stay at sea for long periods and could not count on being supplied from ports along the way. The quantity of supplies required was about double that needed for voyages inside Europe. Crews were larger on voyages of

20: Sail Plan of Christopher Columbus's *Nina* as a Lateen Caravel,
and Transformation into a Square Caravel in a Reconstruction by
J.M. Martinez-Hidalgo

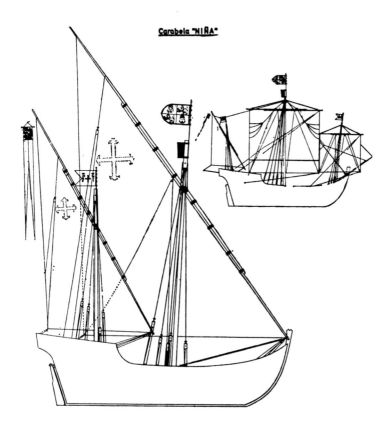

Carabela "NIÑA"

exploration, at least double those on regular trips. Ships of 30 tons, which could carry a payload of more than 22 tons trading in Europe, did not have enough room for the food required for a voyage of exploration.[12] The lack of cargo space in caravels, then, sharply decreased the range of the explorers, but this price had to be paid in order to get the superior handling qualities of the caravel.

In the second half of the fifteenth century, the caravel became larger and also more beamy in order to increase the carrying capacity for each metre of length. Ship carpenters made little sacrifice in manoeuvrability as they modified the design. By 1480, caravels were from 150 to 200 tons. Length-to-breadth ratios also fell, probably into the range of 4:1 and 3:1. The lateen rig was also changed. Yards were made shorter so that they were easier to handle. The yard was set perpendicular to the ship and was held closer to the mast. All these modifications made it possible to come about without having to carry the yard over the masthead. Manpower was not saved, since ships on voyages of discovery always carried big crews, but manoeuvrability was increased. There was a loss in sail area, so a third mast was added to fit a third lateen sail. The new larger version of the caravel, with minor modifications, could be an effective warship. In this new form caravels were also capable of long and profitable voyages on the high seas. They were used in trade from Spain to England and later to the Americas, and they also found a place carrying luxury goods in the eastern Mediterranean. They were faster than earlier sailing ships and there was a major saving in manpower, compared to galleys. In smaller versions, of around 100 tons, caravels were popular also as coasters. Their greatest success, however, came in trade to the Atlantic islands and to West Africa from Iberia.[13] Originally designed for those waters, caravels could efficiently move the growing exports of wine and cane sugar to Europe where demand for those goods rose throughout the fifteenth century.

Despite the fact that Portuguese builders knew about sprit-rig, they retained lateen sails for their caravels. The sprit-rig was more efficient but, after the improvements made in lateen rig in the fifteenth century, the difference had been narrowed. The tradition of using lateen sails was probably not as important a consideration in retaining that rig as the need for larger and heavier masts when any alternative rig was used. For a large spritsail, the long sprit put a strain on any mast. To get enough sail area for an exploring ship, very large masts were needed and masts were already expensive. It was not uncommon to take the masts and spars from a wreck and use them again, since they were so valuable. Moreover, the greatest advantage of the sprit-rig was that it saved man-

power. Since crews had to be large anyway for most voyages by caravels, there was no gain from changing to sprit-rig. Though the caravel
became an effective cargo carrier, the original inspiration for developing the design came from the orders of the Portuguese government
which was striving to promote domestic shipbuilding and design
improvement in order to pursue the possibilities of expansion by sea.

The exploration and indeed the entire programme of the Portuguese
government was made possible by improvements in a related technology, in navigation. Prince Henry the Navigator fully appreciated the
interdependence of ship design and navigation and gave extensive support to research in the latter. The result was the development and
dissemination of the method of sailing by *altura*. The latitude of the
ship was determined by examining the height of the sun at midday.
Earlier sailors had used the Pole Star as their guide but Portuguese
navigators lost sight of that star as they went south along the African
coast and so had to use another approach. By the end of the fifteenth
century, the *altura* method was made easier by the use of more reliable
instruments and declination tables relating height of the sun to degrees
of latitude. Used along with the navigation techniques of the fourteenth
century, which had also been improved, the combination gave a practical system of broad capability, certainly superior to that in contemporary use in the Indian Ocean. By 1500, a Portuguese navigator could
take his ship to the latitude of his destination and then run along that
latitude until he got to the port he wanted, a valuable help in navigating
by dead reckoning. To do this, however, he had to have a grasp of the
theory of astronomical observations for finding positions and he had to
be able to do some mathematics.[14] Arab and Chinese pilots of the
Indian Ocean knew how to take the position of the sun or stars to
derive their own position and they used that information to run down
latitudes. Indeed, they had developed a form of quantitative navigation
well before the Portuguese in the fifteenth century. But western Europeans enjoyed the advantage of a tradition of making charts and using
them on board ship which was not shared in the East. Thus they were
in a better position to visualise and measure their progress as movement
from one cross on a map where latitude and longitude met to another.[h]
By the early sixteenth century knowledge of navigation was well enough
organised to allow for the publication of many guides and tables for
pilots. New books of sailing directions, rutters, were printed, covering
European waters. Though Iberian governments tried to monopolise the
new technology, the information diffused rather quickly throughout
Europe. As a result, some navigators were in a position to choose among

a collection of routes, the decision dependent on where they would expect to find the most favourable wind or currents. In combination with vessels like the caravel, long-distance voyages through unknown waters could be made and, more important, repeated with a high level of accuracy. It was possible to learn how to make such voyages in some way other than by experience. Most navigators for voyages within Europe still relied on only a few aids: the compass in a binnacle-like box, lead and line and a sandglass to measure time. Few sailors had the skills or equipment to use the new navigational methods.[15] Even so, by creating new possibilities, the combination of improvements in technology meant that sailors were in a much better position to exploit natural forces. Once the first voyages of discovery had been made, Europeans could travel along the new routes and establish regular travel. For that task, as for many others inside Europe, they used another type of sailing ship, the type with the greatest versatility.

The full-rigged ship was the great invention of European ship designers in the middle ages. The development of this type marked a major improvement in ships and established the basis for the design of seagoing ships to the nineteenth century and the introduction first of the clipper ship and then of steam power. The full-rigged ship has been called the Atlantic type because it may have been developed by Basque shipbuilders somewhere along the coast of the Bay of Biscay. It is not possible to say who first hit on the idea of building this type but it is true that shipbuilders and shippers from the Atlantic coast of Europe were the ones who adopted it most quickly and who first demonstrated its potential. The full-rigged ship could survive the difficult journeys along that coast and was well suited for making voyages between northern and southern Europe. By the sixteenth century the versatility of the type had made it popular with all European shippers, who used it for all kinds of voyages throughout the world.

For such an important invention, the full-rigged ship on first examination seems quite simple. It was a combination of design features from the cog, as modified by Mediterranean builders, with other features from southern and northern types. The hull planks were placed edge to edge and, like the modified cog it was of full skeleton construction. It had a length-to-breadth ratio a little higher than the cog though, about 3:1 to 3.5:1. Of course, the figure varied. There were through-beams piercing the hull; they supported the two and sometimes three decks. There was a large and high aftercastle running from the stern to the mainmast and a smaller, usually triangular, but still high, forecastle. In fact the forecastle was higher than the aftercastle, the opposite of earlier southern design. To carry the forecastle the forepost was swept up. The sternpost, on the other hand, was straight and at a slight angle to the keel. The ribs were heavy. The bottom may have retained the same kind of flat section around the middle of the ship that appeared on the Bremen cog. The hull tended to be broad at the bow. There was a keelson which also supported the mast. The keel itself was straight. On the sides there were skids as well as wales for protection. On larger ships there was sizeable tumble-home — that is, the breadth of the ship at the deck was significantly less than its breadth at the waterline. The decks could thus carry more weight but the upper parts of the sides were weaker than normal, thus making reinforcing skids all the more necessary.

Control came from a sternpost rudder. There might be a small amount of space between the rudder and the point where the sternpost met the keel, and this was filled with deadwood. With the stern built up there was a hole for the tiller to pass inside to the whipstaff, a common arrangement for all large ships by the sixteenth century. The entire stern was rarely flat. Usually there was a wing transom, a flat section on the upper part of the hull at the top of the rudder. The full square stern, which became more common in the sixteenth century, especially on vessels in southern Europe, did not help control but it did improve carrying capacity.[i] The greatest improvement in handling came from the change in the rig.

Full rig typically included three masts, the fore- and mainmast carrying square sails and the mizzenmast having a lateen. The change to multiple masts was not illogical. There were apparently many experiments with two-masted ships around 1400 but these types were quickly replaced by three-masted vessels. The second mast could be and was stepped either forward or aft of the mainmast. Illustrations survive of both types.[j] Such masts were added to both small and large vessels. But if surviving illustrations and records are a guide, there were surprisingly few two-masted vessels used in Europe in the fifteenth and sixteenth centuries.[16] The addition of one small sail made it necessary to balance that sail with another. So, rather than change the position of the mainmast or redesign the hull, builders simply added a third sail to match the second. It was not necessary that the after- or mizzenmast carry a lateen sail. As late as 1466, a three-masted ship carried all square sails.[k]

By the end of the fifteenth century, yet another sail had been added, slung on.a yard hanging below the bowsprit. The bowsprit had been on ships for 150 years before the spritsail was introduced. It acted as a headsail, like the foresail, giving some pull against the rudder. With a spritsail, the foremast could be moved back from the bow and the fore-

21: Italian Full-rigged Ship, 1470-80

sail could be increased in size without losing control. The spritsail in fact may have been used rarely, only in conditions where manoeuvrability was crucial. The mainmast might be composite — that is, made up of a number of pieces of wood lashed together to get the necessary height and strength. In the South shrouds were still set up with tackles, so there were no ratlines and a ladder just behind the mast was the only way to the top of the mast. Also fore- and mainyards were often two spars fished together. In the sixteenth century those features disappeared, making the southern version even more like its northern counterpart.[17] Lifts were often used for the yards, another sign of the Mediterranean contribution to full rig. In many cases a topsail was added above the mainsail on the mainmast but it was small and made little contribution to the total sail area. The result was the common full rig of the sixteenth century with a spritsail, one square sail on the foremast, two square sails on the mainmast and a lateen mizzen.[l]

The combination rig gave the advantages of both square sails and lateen rig. Though the mainsail was still the principal driving sail in 1500, it was possible to divide square sails, something that could not be done with lateens. Captains could shorten sail or take down some sails in bad weather without having to take down sail and yard. Divisibility, a major advantage with square sails, was increasingly exploited over time. While the mainsail got a little smaller, the other square sails got much bigger. The process was a slow one and had only just got under way by 1550. One method of obtaining some measure of divisibility with lateen sails was to add another on a fourth mast, a bonaventure mizzen aft of the mizzenmast. That extra mast appeared as early as the second quarter of the fifteenth century and as far north as Denmark. By 1500, it was not uncommon both in the Mediterranean and in northern Europe.[m] The sail was usually sheeted to an outlicker, a spar extending from the squared-off top section of the stern,[18] thus making it possible to put the mast close to the stern and give more space to work the sails. It and the other mizzen were often set off centre to give more room to handle the rudder. With the lateen sail, whether one or two, the full-rigged ship was not only more manoeuvrable but also could sail closer to the wind, as little as 80° off the direction of the wind. It could, though to a lesser degree, emulate the Portuguese caravel in being able to get off a lee shore. The square sails, too, were easier to handle, thanks to improvements made in the fourteenth century in the ropes controlling them. With full rig, both propulsion and especially control were markedly better. The full-rigged ship could do more than any of its predecessors and could do so with considerably less risk.

Ship carpenters were building full-rigged ships in the second decade of the fifteenth century but they may have started before then. Dates are based on illustrations which are notoriously late in showing design changes. What the illustrations do show, however, is the rapid change-over in the fifteenth century to the new form of rig. Iberian shipbuilders may have been the leaders in the change. The new type was known by a number of names, the most common of which was carrack, a word of Arabic origin meaning cargo ship; northern Europeans gave most southern vessels that name well into the sixteenth century. Carracks were not essentially different in design from northern full-rigged ships except that they were higher. Less severe winds in the Mediterranean made it possible to increase the upperworks. Southern Europeans called northern full-rigged ships bretons, and also hulks. All the names may well have referred to minor variations in the designs made to deal with certain local or regional needs. Some northern ships were called carvels, and this name certainly referred to the type of hull planking but did not imply any resemblance to the Portuguese caravel.[19] The widespread and rapid adoption, in both southern and northern Europe, of the generic term ship for the full-rigged type, however, reflected its popularity, its versatility and the composite nature of the design.

The state of the market for shipping services made it possible to use the new full-rigged ship very effectively. Even before the Black Death there was something approaching regular trade between northern and southern Europe. As a result of changes in consumption patterns and also access to supplies of alum in the late fourteenth century, Genoese shippers established regular sailings from the Mediterranean to the Low Countries and England. They carried bulk goods. The Venetians and Florentines, using great galleys, exploited the possibilities for selling light and expensive southern and eastern goods in the North. Genoese trade, on the other hand, needed ships which were cheaper to operate for each ton of payload. With fixed and known cargoes and dates of sailings — that is, within a relatively narrow range — the ships for the trade to northern Europe could be built larger. Big Genoese ships, carracks, were well known in the English Channel in the first and second decades of the fifteenth century. As warships, they joined the naval forces of the king of France in fighting the English. By the second half of the fifteenth century Florentine and Venetian shippers also used carracks. Yet for Venice the round ships did not form the overwhelming part of the merchant fleet, as they did at Genoa. The carracks were only marginally less tubby than the cogs which preceded them. If nothing else, they were big, and thus harder to handle and cut down on turnaround time since it took so long to load and unload them. Full rig only partially compensated for these disadvantages. At Venice, by the 1490s, the majority of carracks built for the government were of 1,200 tons. Average tonnage rose throughout the fifteenth century, and in the sixteenth there were many ships of 600 tons in the Venetian merchant fleet — a great change from the Venetian cogs of the fourteenth century which were of 250 to, at most, 400 tons. The Genoese built big carracks much earlier than the Venetians. In the middle of the fifteenth century, Genoese carracks of 500 tons, with an over-all length of almost 40 metres and a breadth of slightly over ten metres, were making direct voyages from the eastern Mediterranean to northern ports. There were larger carracks too, reaching 1,000 and even 1,400 tons. The big carracks were made stronger and were more extensively reinforced. The bows became even more bluff than before and the stern was typically made completely square.[n] The unique size of Genoese ships grew out of their carriage of alum to cloth makers in northern Europe. When the Genoese lost control of supplies of alum, their trade changed to lighter goods and the shipbuilders turned to smaller vessels.[20]

The Genoese chose carvel-built cogs, in the fourteenth century, to move their large cargoes of alum. These cogs were popular because the carrying capacity could be easily augmented, but then a new problem was created. The maximum feasible size for a square sail is 500 square metres. In order to move the biggest ships more sail area was a valuable, if not necessary, addition. Multiple masts and sails provided a simple solution. The full rig allowed carracks to be bigger than cogs. At the same time there was a gain rather than a loss in manoeuvrability. Since trade per person had fallen, or at least was not rising, during the 100 years after the Black Death, cutting shipping costs through increasing ship size was all the more desirable. The goods carried on the big Genoese carracks had higher prices per unit volume than many of the bulk commodities shipped by sea and so they were better able to sustain any increase in charges, thus making it easier to experiment along the Atlantic route, and also increasing the returns to successful experiments. The use of the full-rigged ship made it possible to maintain or increase the volume of trade and at the same time raise profits. The conditions of the first half of the fifteenth century created a low threshold for the adoption of the full-rigged carrack, just as conditions in the fourteenth century had created opportunities for using the cog between southern and northern Europe. Once the full-rigged ship came into general use on that one route, the diffusion of the design throughout the rest of Europe presented few problems.

Spanish shipbuilders built full-rigged ships from the early years of the fifteenth century. Their example, along with that of Italian shipwrights, their reputation for high-quality work and their export of full-rigged ships to northern Europe, contributed to the general adoption of the design there by the end of the fifteenth century. Of course, the simpler single-masted hulk was still used,° but the growth in the absolute volume of commerce after about 1450 increased the output of northern shipyards and made the change to full-rigged ships even more rapid. The new design was suited to smaller vessels, down to 100 tons or less, so the increase in the number of those ships did not slow down the adoption of the new type.[21] The pay-off was greater, of course, in larger vessels. Iberian carracks had no projecting beam-ends and these were later also abandoned in the Mediterranean. It was probably the Iberian form of the carrack that was most commonly seen in the North in the second half of the fifteenth century, and it was on that form that northerners modelled their own full-rigged ships.

In the ports of the German Hanse the full-rigged ship was often called a hulk. It may be that the essential shape was retained from the type developed in the last years of the fourteenth century. But there was a major change in the hull. It was now carvel-built. Apparently, builders in the Low Countries and in Germany were not able to construct carvel hulls immediately. It took them some time to become familiar with the approach. Placing planks edge to edge could not have presented a problem since they already used this design on the hulls of cogs. The source of the trouble may have been a change from a modified version of shell-building long in use in the North to the almost complete skeleton construction typical of the new ships. Shipwrights had to be imported from France to the Low Countries to build the first carvels. Any resistance to the new design in the Baltic was broken down by the unique career of the *Peter of La Rochelle*, a full-rigged French ship of about 700 tons which arrived in Gdansk in 1462 and then remained there because it was deserted by the captain after a controversy over repairs and ownership. Gdansk shippers and the government found uses for the vessel and Gdansk shipbuilders took the opportunity to learn about the type. The first carvel-built three-masted ship was begun at Gdansk in 1473 and large versions were built there after 1488. By the late fifteenth century, then, ship carpenters in the Baltic could and did build the latest type of full-rigged ship, comparable to those from Venice or Genoa in everything but size. There were, of course, minor differences, for example in the fitting of the yards to the masts, in the number and size of wales, in the absence of a through-deck and in other minor features.[22] The ship was, however, in all basic respects the same as its southern counterparts.[p] It relied on internal heavy ribs for strength, and hull planks with edges pushed tightly together and caulking forced in between them for watertightness.

The interest of Gdansk builders and shippers was fed by their need for an economic bulk carrier. Their position was different from the Genoese in that they were handling salt and grain where faster delivery meant little. One voyage a year from the eastern Baltic to the Biscay coast of France or Spain and back was about all that was possible before winter weather prevented sailing. Once such voyages were possible marginal gains in speed meant at best marginal gains in productivity. But Hanse shippers did share with the Genoese a need for bigger ships. The volume of the salt carried east from the Bay of Bourgneuf grew rapidly in the early fifteenth century as the price of Bay salt became competitive with that of locally produced salt in the Low Countries and especially in Germany. The Hanse towns in Prussia were in the best position to exploit the advantages of new larger hulks. Ports to the west soon followed in using the new type. Lübeck, for example, found an immediate use for full-rigged ships in trade to Bergen in Norway. The exchange on that route of grain for fish was a trade well suited to the new type. The largest hulks were still found in towns like Gdansk and Riga, where they reached 300 tons and more. Despite wars and piracy, throughout the fifteenth century that trade continued and expanded. But slowly the nationality of the carriers changed, as Dutch ships replaced those of the Hanse.[23] In part, the success of the Dutch came from their ability to build and effectively to use vessels of the new design.

The goods of Dutch trade were the same as those of Hanse trade. Dutch shippers carried cloth and salt to the Baltic and brought back grain, especially rye. To their exports they added cargoes of herring, caught and packed aboard busses in the North Sea. Bay salt was used to preserve the herring, which created another market for imported salt and gave another reason for the development of an entrepôt trade in salt in the Low Countries. The redistribution gave employment to smaller Dutch ships and fishing boats in the off-season. One problem for Hanse ships was that they had grown too large to visit many harbours in the West, especially in the Low Countries. Dutch builders avoided that difficulty. Their ships tended to be more manoeuvrable and smaller than German hulks. Dutch full-rigged ships did reach 300 tons and more, but the average was probably under 200 tons. The traditional date for the construction of the first skeleton-built ship in the Low

Countries is 1460, though some vessels of the new type may have been built before that date. Local ship carpenters adapted the design to suit local conditions. Dutch ships were known for their ability to sail in any weather, something which could not be said, for example, for Spanish full-rigged ships. By the mid-sixteenth century, the size of the Dutch merchant marine compared favourably with that of any competitors in northern Europe.[24] German Hansards, among others, tried to undermine the competitive advantage of Dutch shippers but failed to do so. Acts of protection generally hurt them more than the Dutch. The Hanseatic League repeatedly prohibited the sale of domestically built ships to foreigners, in an effort to deprive Dutch shippers of hulks. Not all towns observed the embargo and so the policy failed. Moreover, this policy served to promote the expansion of the Dutch shipbuilding industry. A number of German ports at times refused to allow Dutch ships to enter and trade there. Dutch shippers merely changed to smaller ports or did business directly with the growers of grain and the harvesters of wood along the shores of the rivers and inlets of the Baltic.[25] This was feasible because their ships were designed to sail in shallows and estuaries. These Dutch ships were highly versatile and gave Dutch shippers the opportunity to exploit possibilities created by the growth in the volume of commerce in the late fifteenth and the sixteenth century.

Dutch shipbuilders, according to one chronicler, first learned about full-rigged ships from Bretons. Indeed, Breton shipwrights appear to have been responsible, along with Spanish builders, for the interest in this type in western and northern Europe, by producing and using them in relatively large numbers. The Bretons had a ready use for the type in carrying salt to the Low Countries from Brittany. The number of Breton ships in the salt trade rose throughout the fifteenth century. The actions of other governments and the lack of sophisticated business skills in Brittany prevented that growth from continuing in the sixteenth, however. The conditions of harbours and the need for larger ships allowed Bretons to use the new design and incorporate it in smaller ships as well. Around 1500, the average tonnage of the Breton fleet was probably about a hundred; this included coasters of 30 to 35 tons, caravels like those of Portugal of 80 to 110 tons, and full-rigged ships of over 200 tons. The early acceptance of the full-rigged design and its use in a broad range of vessels presumably explains the fact that, by 1500, the Breton merchant fleet boasted a total tonnage four or five times that of Normandy.[26] In each case, in Genoa, in towns of the German Hanse, in Holland and Zeeland and in Brittany, specific trading circumstances made the adoption of full rig advisable and profitable at some point in the course of the fifteenth century. As important as solving the specific transport problems, though, were the general savings which accrued to any shipper using the new type.

Skeleton-building in fifteenth-century northern Europe meant a saving in wood. Since planks did not overlap, as with clinker-building, but were placed edge to edge, less wood was needed for the shell of the ship. The savings which Italian builders found before the eleventh century were still to be had in fifteenth-century northern Europe, and more than compensated for the marginal increase in wood required because the length-to-breadth ratio of full-rigged ships, especially those built in the Low Countries, tended to be higher than for cogs or hulks of the same tonnage. Also, a large skeleton-built ship, above about 300 or 400 tons, was stronger and more reliable than a clinker-built ship of the same size. If strength was to come from internal ribbing, then ribs had to be heavy. By the fourteenth century, clinker-built ships already had an extensive system of heavy oak internal supports along with bulk-heads to separate cargo holds. Over time, builders had put the ribs closer and closer together, almost creating another wall inside the wall of hull planking.[27] So conversion to skeleton-building made no appreciable difference in the quantity of wood needed for internal planking. There may have been a marginal increase in the amount of time builders spent in selecting wood for the frames and ribs, but this, like the building of the edge-to-edge hull itself, was a logical use of the skilled labour which was relatively expensive. The high cost of wood sealed the decision to go over to skeleton-building. The extensive clearing of forests to create arable throughout the thirteenth century had limited supplies of timber. The abandonment by farmers of marginal agricultural land after the Black Death did not lead to a quick recovery in timber supplies from that land. In some places, because of soil erosion, trees could not grow. More important, the replacement rate for trees is slow, especially for the large oak-trees needed for the internal ribs of the now larger ships. So, despite the fall in demand for timber after the Black Death, the price did not collapse because the supply was highly inelastic. Thus any saving in wood was even more attractive for shipbuilders; in northern Europe this meant accepting the southern method of hull construction which lowered timber costs and therefore lowered capital costs to shipping.

This is not to say that clinker-building was totally abandoned or that shipwrights could not build large vessels with overlapping planking; but to build ships the size of Genoese carracks meant extending shell construction rather far, perhaps approaching its technical limits. In the second decade of the fifteenth century, the English navy had to have big ships, in part to transport troops to Normandy for the campaigns of King Henry V and in part to contest control of the Channel with those Genoese carracks in the service of France. A great deal of wood was used, as the example of the English ship *Gracedieu* shows. She was built at Southampton in 1418 by local ship carpenters. The hull had triple clinkering — that is, there were always two layers of hull planking. The keel was more than 38 metres long, the over-all length perhaps as much as 60 metres and the tonnage over 1,400.� She probably had two masts, the second being much smaller than the mainmast. Though the ship was apparently capable of sailing, she must have been hard to handle. The need for transport to carry troops to France disappeared with the English victories in Normandy, so the *Gracedieu* was laid up, never fully fitted out and left to sit tied up along the river.[28] There was seemingly no other possible use for a ship of that design. The *Gracedieu* represented a massive capital expenditure. If nothing else, that ship proved that investment per ton had to fall and the versatility of large ships had to increase. The combination of a change to full skeleton-building and the adoption of full rig met precisely those requirements.

A full-rigged ship needed less labour than its predecessor both in construction and at sea. On the wharf, northern Europeans got the same savings that southern Europeans had earlier come to enjoy. There was a decrease in original work but an increase in repair and caulking, thus lowering the level of skill required — a valuable improvement in the first half of the fifteenth century. As the supply of skilled craftsmen, thanks to the training system, caught up with demand after the middle of the century, ship carpenters' real wages tended to fall. So any increase in the work, caulking and repair that had to be done with the new type of hull was even less crucial. The productivity of ship carpenters increased with the introduction of the brace. That tool made it easier and faster to drill all the holes for nails and treenails. If the brace was too small for large holes, it could be used to make guide holes for bit augers. The brace saved time, since its motion is always positive with no stopping or going back.[29] It raised the productivity of the lowest-paid workers on the wharf and so tended to generate greater equality among shipbuilders.

On board, the adoption of full rig did not increase the manpower requirements. The divisibility of the square sails meant that the same number of men could work more canvas, turning their attention first to one sail and then to another. The newly added lateen sail took more skill to handle but, at least at first, was so small that sailors probably had no trouble with it. The lateen could become rather large before it took more manpower to handle than was needed to raise the mainsail. In fact that threshold was probably never reached. The gain was a more manoeuvrable ship. The result in increased safety, involving a saving in capital reflected by lower insurance rates where insurance was in use, would alone have made the adoption of full rig worth while. But the increase in manoeuvrability also decreased the time spent waiting for the right wind. Big carracks had to spend more time in harbours, loading and unloading, but they spent less time waiting to get in and out of those harbours. Since sailors were paid and fed while on board, the decrease in waiting time meant lower labour costs. The level of piracy was still a primary consideration in the manning ratio of ships. The danger of loss from attack could prevent shippers from fully exploiting the potential labour saving, but the introduction of full rig at least removed the technical constraint on the number of men for each ton shipped. Sources are neither plentiful nor continuous but there is every indication that manning ratios fell throughout the fifteenth and sixteenth centuries. Warships created a special case. The French navy insisted on having one man for each ton of the ship. Small boats and fishing boats could handle only three or four tons of cargo for each crew member. The same ratio held for Genoese carracks in the mid-fifteenth century. In the Baltic, crew sizes were in general relatively small. Defence made a great difference in the size of the crew but, when the Hanse set a minimum manning requirement at about the same time, it still allowed for ten tons per man. For Mediterranean full-rigged ships of the mid-sixteenth century the figure was up to thirteen tons for each man, and that for the largest of cargo ships.[30]

The long-term fall in both capital costs and operating costs was also promoted by the greater flexibility European shipwrights built into full-rigged ships. These men at the same time developed modifications and variations for the new regions where the type was used. The most common modifications came in sail plan. The obvious example was the addition of a second lateen sail on a fourth mast. Though the bonaventure mizzen was especially popular with warships, it was equally common on large merchantmen. The addition of a fourth mast was part of the more general trend of the late fifteenth and the entire sixteenth century towards greater division in the sail plan. The first carracks had sails supplementing the mainsail to help control the ship, and those sails gradually grew in size relative to the mainsail and in the process took on more of the task of propulsion. The foremast became taller, the foresail got bigger and a topsail was added on that mast. The main-topsail became larger relative to the mainsail. Other sails were added on some ships but most of them were later abandoned because they were too small and could be used only irregularly. Those extra bits of canvas were not as important as the development of balance in the rig. The typical result was a square spritsail, two square sails on the fore- and two on the mainmast, and one or two lateen mizzens. There was greater balance in the rig, with the load shared more equally among all sails — a trend started with the introduction of multiple masts.[31] The change in sail plan saved labour only if the absolute size of the mainsail fell. Since the size of ships was increasing, even though the other sails grew relative to the mainsail, its absolute size may not have decreased. Increasing divisibility of sail area continued through a period of rising population when presumably finding sailors was not a pressing problem. Saving labour, then, was not as crucial as was the case previously. But, as always, shippers were interested in lowering costs, and also in keeping up the size of their ships. The recovery of population led to a recovery in grain prices, so more grain found its way into the holds of European ships. With more goods to be moved, shippers were in a better position to exploit larger vessels, and that meant a need for more sail area. If the improved balance of the rig also led to a fall in crew size, the payload could rise without increasing the size of the ship; if this was not enough, then the increase in security made the change worth making. The cost of more equal size of sails was, after all, minimal.

Once Europeans adopted the full-rigged ship, they quickly turned it to a number of different tasks. Of course, it held its place in the bulk trades inside Europe and also in long-distance carriage in Europe. Its success suggested it as the type for the all-water route to the Indies. By the last years of the fifteenth century, the Portuguese had found that the caravel could not carry enough goods for their longer voyages of exploration along the African coast. They started using full-rigged ships and, when the explorer Vasco da Gama opened direct trade from Portugal to India, the carrack quickly became the ship for that trade. Most important, it had the advantage of being big. By the end of the sixteenth century, Portuguese shipwrights were producing the largest wooden ships ever built, exceeding 2,000 tons in some cases. The great distance and the fixed dates of sailing placed intense pressure on carrying capacity. Space on board was for the spices and other luxuries brought back from the East and for the silver carried out there, but also for the people, their food and personal effects, and for the small quantities of trade goods that each sailor was allowed to take. In the sixteenth century, on average 2,400 people left Portugal for the East on the seven

22: Increasing Divisibility of Sail Plan, 1430-1600: (1) c. 1430,
(2) c. 1450, (3) c. 1500, (4) c. 1530, (5) c. 1560, (6) c. 1600

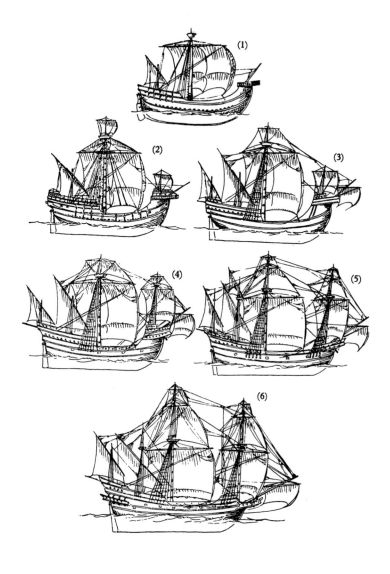

to fourteen ships that sailed out there each year. The port of Lisbon presented no problem. There was no constraint on the draught of the carracks. An English squadron, with a great deal of difficulty, captured one of these giant carracks in the late sixteenth century. The ship impressed the English not only because it was 50 metres long and of 1,600 tons but also because of the great value of the cargo. These ships were highly built up, with aftercastles rising in a series of decks above the three or four full decks, so there was a great deal of space for passengers. They were so high in the water and so big that they were virtually impregnable.[r] Voyages were not pleasant and the death rate among sailors and passengers attests to the crowded conditions and poor hygiene. These Portuguese carracks had the same design as carracks used in Europe, only bigger and with a broader beam and a stempost so sharply curved that it turned back into the ship. Despite the full rig, it was still hard to handle these monsters. The mainsail was massive, carrying two bonnets whenever possible. The Portuguese government tried to limit the size of the ships, finding that carracks of about 600 tons were safer. Finding the right wood for big carracks must increasingly have been a problem. Still, builders and captains continued to opt for the biggest ships. The high value of cargo made the smallest increase in carrying capacity a source of a sharp increase in revenue. Overloading added to the risk. Just a small amount of sloppy caulking could in these circumstances lead to a massive loss. Even so, in 1582, one commentator said it was safer to go by ship from Goa to Lisbon than from Genoa to Barcelona. These ships, 1,000 tons by the mid-sixteenth century, even at that date could not visit most northern European ports on account of their deep draught. There was some question whether such a ship could get through the Sound.[32] The full-rigged design made trade with the East Indies by sea viable and profitable. The situation was similar for other emerging long-distance trades outside Europe. Not incidentally, the use of the carrack on voyages to India increased the use of full-rigged ships within Europe. For example, Portugal had to import copper from northern Europe for trade to west Africa. Portuguese merchants also needed to market their spices in the North. For that carriage along the Atlantic coast of Europe they used carracks, though not as large as those going to the Indies.

The full-rigged ship could also be used for exploration. In fact, most early voyages, in uncharted and often dangerous waters over long distances, were made in ships built for the common trades of western Europe. Virtually none of the ships was designed for exploration and in fact they were often poor examples of European cargo ships. The most famous example is Columbus' *Santa Maria*, used on his first voyage to the New World. The greater potential capacity meant that larger crews might be carried. More important, though, was the fact that smaller versions of full-rigged ships, like the *Santa Maria*, with higher length-to-breadth ratios than the carracks and relatively larger lateen sails, were capable sailing ships. They could not match caravels in manoeuvrability and that type was still popular on such voyages. Columbus used two of them in 1492.[s] Full-rigged ships used for exploration were small, rarely exceeding 100 tons. They carried castles but those were small too. The type was also used in the first tentative trading voyages to the New World. Once trading relationships had been established, size increased.[33]

The caravel also changed in the course of its use on voyages of exploration. The *caravela redonda* had a length-to-breadth ratio of just over 3:1, compared to 7:1 for earlier caravels. The change increased capacity, but the heavier hull needed more sail area to move it. For long reaches, like that made by Columbus across the Atlantic, captains re-rigged their caravels, putting a square sail on the mainmast, thus leading to a type with something very similar to full rig, square sails on the fore- and mainmasts and a lateen mizzen. The lack of castles, the gentle small curve of the stempost and the cut of the hull still made it a caravel.[t] It was in that form that the caravel came to be known and copied in northern Europe. In the sixteenth century, the Portuguese caravel took on its classic form. There was a foremast raked slightly forward with one and often two square sails and then two or three other masts, each with a lateen sail. It could never achieve the size of the carrack but it was better going to windward and faster. The manning ratio was about the same, since manpower was needed to handle the lateen sails. Though used in the Mediterranean and along the Atlantic coast, that style of caravel was popular only in Portugal,[34] probably because it made an effective cargo ship for trading to the coast of Africa and the Atlantic islands, more economical than its smaller predecessor which was completely lateen-rigged. It could also be used as a warship but for that job full-rigged ships were much preferred.

Another technical change external to shipbuilding promoted the adoption of the full-rigged ship. Guns had been in use on land and sea for some time before 1400 but it was not until the late fifteenth and sixteenth centuries that they were made large enough, accurate enough and reliable enough to assume an important place on ships. The change affected the design and use of galleys but it affected sailing ships much more. Galleys with guns were effective warships, as they had been

23: The *Nao Santa Maria* of
Columbus: Hull Lines and Sail
Plan in a Reconstruction by
J.M. Martinez-Hidalgo

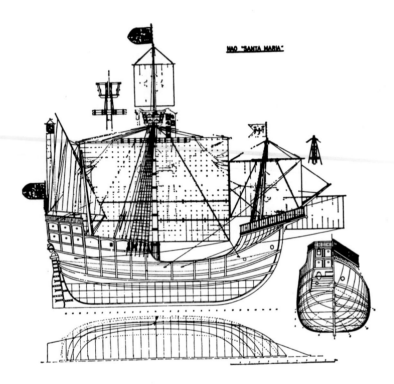

NAO "SANTA MARIA"

24: *Caravela Redonda* fitted as a Warship, from a Sixteenth-century Dutch Illustration

previously. Sailing ships with enough guns and handled properly could be effective warships against all opponents, and this was new. The first guns were small and used as anti-personnel weapons, therefore, like all other projectile launchers, gaining an advantage from height above the water. They were light enough to be fitted in the castles. The carrack's over-all size, high freeboard and very high castles recommended it as a warship. Moreover, it was well suited to this use of light guns. The major step was the introduction on board of heavy artillery of cast bronze, the type used for sieges on land. So they would not make the ship unstable, the guns were placed in the middle of the ship, in the waist. Ports, like those used for handling cargo, were cut in the top wale, thereafter called the gunwale. The square stern was also a likely place to put some of the lighter guns. On larger ships, by the 1530s, guns were placed on the lower deck, keeping down the centre of gravity, and the hull was pierced with rows of gunports. These heavy pieces were as much to scare the enemy as to pierce his hull. Rates of fire were very low and guns and gunners were inaccurate. In the first half of the sixteenth century, it was still expected that fighting would come down to boarding, so small guns were retained to clear the decks of enemy ships. As early as 1513, however, a ship was sunk by enemy gunfire. The Portuguese fought the first sea battles which were decided by guns and not by boarding in the Indian Ocean in the early years of the sixteenth century. Heavy guns implied some changes in the design of ships. The tumble-home of the sides was increased to take the weight of the cannon. The greatest change was the more rapid adoption of carvel-building. With that type of construction it was easier and less dangerous to pierce the hull with gunports.[35] The ship was also less vulnerable to gunfire since the source of strength was internal rather than external. Moreover, the interior system of ribs was better able to support the heavy artillery. In 1550, there was still no strict division between warships and cargo ships but, because of the improvements in guns, shipbuilders were already moving in that direction.

The use of guns on board led governments to promote the change to skeleton-building and the adoption of the carrack design. It also led governments to exploit the limits of the new type. In the first three decades of the sixteenth century, there was almost a craze for the construction of the largest possible warships for the kings of northern Europe. Even the Portuguese did not escape, despite the fact that they already had cargo ships of unprecedented size. The possession of a great ship became a matter of prestige for kings, more important to them than the fighting qualities of the ship. They typically demanded massive ships with high castles and extensive armament. To move these vessels more and more canvas was added. Four masts were necessary. Three square sails on each of the two forward masts were typical and in some cases a fourth and even a fifth sail were added on the mainmast.[u] The mizzenmasts carried topsails on the largest French ship, which also had a fifth mast. There was a tennis court on board too. Rated at 1,500 tons, that ship demonstrated all the problems with such vessels. The crew was massive, at least 500 men just to sail her and then another 1,300 to 1,500 soldiers. She was not highly seaworthy and after one voyage was caught in a storm and blown over on her side. It proved impossible to right her and she was broken up. As warships, in general, these ships were not highly serviceable but, with their ever-increasing size, reaching 74 metres and more in length, they were built in response to the actions of other rulers rather than out of a desire to have an effective warship. The city of Lübeck built such a ship too, merely because the king of Sweden had one. Except for rare appearances in battle and in ceremonies, these ships stayed, well guarded, in harbour.[36] Even if these ships could sail, there was little for them to do and the massive investment was unproductive. If the kings, in their demand for ever more impressive ships, proved anything, it was that sail area could be divided effectively. The only limit was the amount of manpower available to handle the sails. The royal ships also showed the technical and economic disadvantages of the overextension of the carrack design.

The changes in warships from 1400 to 1500 had more direct and obvious effects on European governments and society than did the introduction of full rig on cargo ships. Unfree men worked the oars of European galleys for the first time. When men refused to accept the heavier work at a price the state could afford, governments began by putting petty criminals on board; thus they divested the job of any status it may have had, no volunteers could be found at any price and rowers became exclusively men who had not chosen the task.[37] Uninhibited by concern for the humanity of subjects, governments freely impressed rowers for the galleys, using it also as punishment for political and religious opponents or as a place for prisoners of war. The labour problems of the fifteenth century, the lack of interest in pulling the big oars already obvious on pilgrim galleys in the fifteenth century, the increasing power of the European states and the pressing need to maintain fleets of war galleys in the Mediterranean, made impressment a necessity. Though it may have been undertaken with reluctance in some cases, the use of forced labour under miserable conditions as punishment reflected and contributed to the new relationship between the state and its subjects.

There was a change at the same time in the kind of men needed on board sailing ships. The general tendency towards the production of specialised warships – for example, the development of the galeass and the conversion to carracks with guns on board – meant that sailors had to be able to handle ships and also to handle guns in battle. Thus not only the quality but also the range of skills required of sailors on those warships was increased. Training sailors to use the light artillery and hand guns of the fifteenth and sixteenth centuries was relatively simple. Indeed, it was much simpler than training archers. Handling the heavy guns in the waist required a great deal more skill. Guns were unreliable because of the quality of contemporary casting techniques. The unpredictability of cannon made gunners into artists rather than technicians knowing how to get the most out of their own guns. Their skill and their bravery – guns often exploded when fired – gave gunners a unique status, far above that of sailors and marines, and higher incomes. Gunners were part of a specialised and privileged profession, which eroded as guns became more reliable and more predictable after the mid-sixteenth century.

For governments it was no longer possible just to convert cargo ships to warships. Throughout much of the fifteenth century, as in the fourteenth century, obtaining warships merely meant hiring cargo ships and putting soldiers on board with, at most, minor modifications to the superstructure. The change in ships forced a change in the form of naval administration. All governments had to develop permanent yards for the construction and maintenance of warships. The prototype naval yard, the Arsenal at Venice, itself had to expand buildings and workforce. Governments had to have facilities to support a permanent force of warships, though that force could be small. They had to have facilities for the impressment or hiring of crews and the modification and supply of merchant ships used for war. Governments, therefore, had to develop methods of oversight of all these operations and of the increased budgets of the navies. The office of admiral had appeared in the twelfth century. Originally a financial officer, by 1200 the title was associated with a naval commander. The office was usually temporary and, when it was more permanent in the fourteenth and fifteenth centuries, admirals had been responsible only for handling legal problems associated with shipping. From the sixteenth century, however, the admiral's occasional task of calling out the fleet changed to a permanent function, which in turn created a need for a stable and continuing staff of officers. Navies had to have a bureaucracy and, by the second half of the sixteenth century, many European admiralties were exactly that. If nothing else, these people were needed to deal with the work generated by larger naval forces. The sailors of the king even got something like uniforms, thus creating more work for the new bureaucrats. The position and the responsibilities of these men were increasingly subject to strict regulation.[38] Many states had war fleets before the sixteenth century but, from then on, like Venice, and the Byzantine Empire before it, all states had to have a navy, with all the continuing apparatus that went with it.

Governments in the fifteenth and early sixteenth centuries became involved even more in shipbuilding and in more phases of the whole process of designing, selling and building ships. Improvements in ship design had fed, and continued to feed, the rising absolute and relative income of states, thus giving governments the ability to mobilise the capital needed for projects which were beyond the scope of individuals. The building of giant warships was not as economically important in this as the launching and promotion of certain trades. Venice and Florence subsidised the galley trade to Flanders. Iberian states followed similar practice in the organisation and development of trade to the New World and to India. Both the Portuguese and the Spanish governments accepted the job of training pilots for the voyages. They also supplied ships, men, ship repair facilities, protection for traders and many other services to make the trade profitable and successful. In northern Europe the kings of Sweden, among others, invested in the building and operation of ships to promote trading activity by native merchants.[39] The result of such promotions, in the long run, was generally to raise state incomes. The increasing volume of trade and the way it was directed, promoted and supported by governments, all placed at the disposal of monarchs more ready money. The process, which became clear in the second half of the fourteenth century, became more obvious and more pronounced over the fifteenth and sixteenth. Certainly, monarchs recognised this fact and so turned themselves more vigorously to the promotion of shipping and shipbuilding.

In general, the drift towards government involvement in shipping became a rush by the sixteenth century. With the introduction of full-rigged ships and guns on board those full-rigged ships, the importance of sea power was even more appreciated as a source for political power and for economic power, which amounted to the same thing. Governments became more conscious of economic policy in general and increased the mass of legislation on trade, and especially trade at sea. For example, the Iberian governments at various times set manning ratios and maximum and minimum tonnages for ships in their trades to the East and West Indies. In some cases legislation was passed to guarantee defensibility, in some cases to guarantee access to certain ports. The result of legislation and of regulation of the shipbuilders themselves, was to limit what they could do. In fact, those rules could in extreme cases cause changes in the rules of construction.[40] Certainly, the minute regulation of manning, armament and so on forced minor adjustments. Having contributed to the development of more effective governments interested in shipbuilding, the shipbuilding industry became a subject for direction by those governments, whose promotion of change in ship design took a number of different forms. There were direct subsidies in the form of rebates on customs duties or cash payments to men who built and used the kinds of ships the government wanted. The Venetian state needed big ships to fight the Turks in the fifteenth century but the capital requirement was too high and the returns too low for any citizen or group of citizens. So the government gave cash subsidies to anyone undertaking the building of such ships. The policy cost less than if the government itself built the ships. The private owners used them in commerce but, since they were Venetian, the government could seize them and use them as warships when necessary. The simplest solution to the problem of having cargo ships large enough and with enough superstructure to be effective warships was to offer a bounty for ships over a certain size.[41] That device stretched both the finances and the administrative skills of most governments. Shipbuilding also received an indirect subsidy from governments in the general promotion of shipping. Rules which required that ships on certain routes had to be of native construction might hurt the trade but gave domestic shipbuilders a protected market for a certain type of ship. Governments could and did make such rules, not only because they had the power but also because shipbuilders had shown throughout the fifteenth century an increasing ability to design craft suited to specific jobs. Thus the economic losses from such protection decreased. It may well be that governments, by their regulation and protection of shipbuilding, slowed the response on the part of designers to the economic needs of shippers but, in the process, governments introduced their own limitations, pressures and direction on the development of ship design.

For smaller vessels the most prominent change in the fifteenth and sixteenth centuries was the diversification and specialisation in design, which led directly to the greater specialisation of workers in shipping. Specialisation was by no means complete but at least it was possible in some cases, for example, for a fisherman to be exclusively a fisherman.

Greater concentration of effort in a specific job was an obvious source of increased output from workers. Probably more significantly, at the same time there was an increase in the specialisation of ports. Certain harbours became centres for a certain type of ship or for certain types of shipping. The resources of the area and the location of industry also contributed to the specialisation of ports. If only by cutting turnaround time, a saving was made. The improved design of smaller vessels also led to a significant growth in short-haul shipping throughout Europe. As a result, more ports and more regions could count on economic water-borne transport service and on greater frequency of that service. As population grew, settlement spread out and was not as concentrated in certain cities or districts as otherwise would have been the case. The better service made possible the survival and indeed the prosperity of a large number of towns of the second and even third rank. Large ports and cities did emerge as centres of long-distance commerce served by the new bigger full-rigged ships. But at the same time there were, around those cities, many coastal towns and villages which acted to supply them and formed a market for goods off-loaded at the large ports. The growth in the total volume of trade and the use of special-ised coasters generated an expansion in those smaller ports. Using fore-and-aft rig, those vessels could approach the labour productivity of big carracks. By making more frequent voyages, they might also approach the capital productivity. They opened a wider range of trading possibilities, since in some cases and on some routes it was not econom-ically feasible to use vessels of full-rig design, even if they were scaled down to 100 tons. In any case, the smaller size meant a fall in the required initial investment. Entry by new shippers was made much easier. This was most noticeable in northern Europe. The tendency from the mid-fifteenth century on, then, was back to a broad base of investment and of participation in the ownership of vessels. It was obscured by the success of large ships and certain very wealthy merch-ants who exploited monopolistic privileges. But in all likelihood there were more shippers, both absolutely and relatively, in the sixteenth century than in the fourteenth.

The adoption of the full-rigged ship, along with other design improve-ments in larger vessels, made possible the voyages of discovery. In many cases they were not actually discoveries, since Europeans already knew about and had travelled to the places. Scandinavians had visited North America and Italian merchants, in the thirteenth century, had kept up an active overland trade with China and India. What was novel in the fifteenth and sixteenth centuries was the discovery of new routes which by that time could be exploited commercially. Ships were seaworthy enough to make voyages along the trade routes and to make them consistently. Not incidentally, shipbuilders thus had a reason to keep on building the new types of ships. The success of Europeans in Asia and America had complex origins and was by no means based solely on the quality of the vehicle they used. The commitment of governments to exploration and exploitation of the discoveries for political and religious reasons and the ability of Europeans effectively to coerce resident populations with guns certainly made trade with these areas safer and more profitable for the Europeans. However, expansion was based on commerce and exploiting the potential for commerce. It was the profit from trade which was responsible for the existence of the European colonies or rather trading posts, for the continued interest of European merchants, shippers and shipbuilders and for the continued interest and support of the ventures by European states. It is easy to overestimate the short-term economic and cultural effects of the discoveries on Europe, but it is much easier to underestimate the long-term effects. Similarly, it is easy to underestimate the effects of the opening of viable commercial connections on Asia and the Americas. The full-rigged ship did not create the discoveries but it did make them feasible and did allow for the first steps to be made in integrating the trading relationships of large regions of the world.

By 1550, significant steps had already been taken towards the integration of the diverse local and regional economies within Europe. From the mid-fifteenth to the mid-sixteenth century, sailing ships from the Atlantic and northern Europe expanded their activities in the Mediterranean. Along the Atlantic coast, direct voyages were being made from Portuguese salt ports to the eastern Baltic. Dutch shippers travelled to Reval and Gdansk in the East and to Iberia in the South. The lower cost of transport implicit in the carrack and related types allowed long-distance intra-European trade to increase in volume and in value. The greater over-all efficiency in the economy and the growth it implied also meant a greater interdependence of the economies of all parts of Europe. The extensive expansion of European trade, typified by the discoveries, also made possible, and indeed created pressure for, an intensive expansion of commerce within Europe.

The increase in trade brought with it a rise in the absolute number of merchants. There was also an increase in their relative number. As a larger percentage of the total population, the group became more important politically. That position was positively enhanced by their access to the technology of the most productive sector of the economy.

Within the kingdoms of western and northern Europe, merchants, shippers and shipowners took on more of the attributes and the political position which had for some time been enjoyed by their counterparts in the Italian merchant republics. Economic growth and the character of investment in shipping worked to decrease the differences in income among merchants. There were still some merchants who were much richer than the great majority. The differences that remained illustrate a certain division of labour among merchants, with men specialising in a certain type of trade or along certain routes. That division was even more acute on board ship. On larger vessels, given the size of the crews, differentiation of task and greater regimentation were necessary. A hierarchy of status became typical. The lowest men in that hierarchy sold their strength for a fixed wage. There was increasing hostility between the sailors and the skippers, their bosses. For example, legal sanctions were established against the collective action of sailors to raise wages.[42] The rise in the number of smaller vessels, however, prevented such sharp distinctions within crews from becoming commonplace.

The success of shipbuilders in the fifteenth and sixteenth centuries enhanced their social and economic position, but the change was most noticeable for men who had the skill to design the newest types of vessels. There was the beginning of a distinction between the designer and the builder, a division not complete even in the twentieth century. By the sixteenth century, however, the designer was a man who could do something more than form wood. It was an advantage for him to know how to read and write and even to have some simple mathematical skills. The success of experiments with ships led to further experimentation, which, combined with improvements in navigation, led to a much wider interest in practical knowledge. Scholars and humanists turned their attention to shipbuilding, admittedly only rarely, as a worthy topic of investigation. The actions of governments, their interest in standardisation and the improvements in the skill and literacy of ship designers, generated the first efforts by those men to give some order to their knowledge. They wrote the first treatises on shipbuilding, but only for a limited audience. The major goal was to reduce at least some of their knowledge to mathematical formulae so that other skilled craftsmen could imitate their work. It is clear from the treatises that these men did not, and perhaps simply could not, transform their acquired knowledge to an easily transferable body of information.[43] Treatises could not be used as effective tools of learning. That is why northerners, to imitate superior Italian skill, simply imported Italian shipwrights.

At the same time, though. Europeans established institutions for the teaching of shipbuilding and ship design. Most men still learned by observation and imitation of a master, without the intermediary of the written word. That handicraft tradition was institutionalised in guilds of ship carpenters. The fifteenth century saw a rapid expansion of guilds for all types of trades in a response to the need to train new men. Shipbuilding did not escape but ship carpenters' guilds were different from industrial guilds. Instead of acting to suppress competition, they rather directed competition towards improvements in the design of the product. By giving certificates on completion of a training period and completion of a masterpiece, in some cases they also made ship carpenters more mobile, thus aiding the diffusion of techniques as the skilled craftsmen could travel more freely from place to place. The success of guilds as promoters of technical change and of education varied from town to town and from region to region,[44] but the effect, especially in northern Europe, was on the whole positive, as the development of new designs for smaller ships, the diffusion of those designs and the more rapid pace of technical change in the second half of the sixteenth century, bear witness.

NOTES

1. Dorothy Burwash, *English Merchant Shipping, 1460-1540* (University of Toronto Press, Toronto, 1947), p. 142. L. Denoix, 'Caractéristiques des Navires de l'Epoque des Grandes Découvertes', *TCHM*, V, pp. 139-40. G. V. Scammell, 'English Merchant Shipping at the End of the Middle Ages: Some East Coast Evidence', *Economic History Review*, second series, XIII (1960-61), pp. 332-4.
2. G. Asaert, *Westeuropese scheepvaart in de middeleeuwen*, pp. 101-3. Jacques Bernard, *Navires et Gens de Mer à Bordeaux (vers 1400–vers 1550)* (SEVPEN, Paris, 1968), pp. 237-41. Dorothy Burwash, *English Merchant Shipping, 1460-1540*, pp. 103-17, 124-7, 140. Walther Vogel, *Geschichte der deutschen Seeschiffahrt*, pp. 498-507. Wendy R. Childs, *Anglo-Castilian Trade in the Later Middle Ages* (Manchester University Press, Manchester, 1977), pp. 158-9.
3. A. Anthiaume, *Cartes marines, constructions navales, voyages de découverte chez les Normands 1500-1650* (Ernest Dumont, Paris, 1916), vol. II, pp. 280-8, 292-6, and *Le Navire Sa construction en France et principalement chez les Normands* (Ernest Dumont, Paris, 1922), pp. 160-4, 204-9. Jehan Banse, 'Les Corporations des Constructions Navales dans Le Port de Fécamp', in *Le Corporatisme Ancien de Construction Navale en France* (Académie de Marine, Paris, 1939), pp. 155-7. Harold A. Innis, *The Cod Fisheries, The History of an International Economy* (University of Toronto Press, Toronto, 1954), pp. 16-21, 40-2.
4. R. C. Anderson, 'Jal's "Memoire No. 5" and the Manuscript "Fabbrica di Galere" ', *MM*, XXXI (1945), p. 165. William A. Baker, *Sloops and Shallops* (Barre Publishing Co., Barre, 1966), pp. 14-24. Fernand Braudel and Ruggiero Romano, *Navires et Marchandises à l'entrée du Port de Livourne (1547-1611)* (Librairie Armand Colin, Paris, 1951), pp. 39, 109. Jacques Heers, 'Types de

Navires et Spécialisation des Trafics en Méditerranée à la Fin du Moyen Age',
pp. 107-8. Marco Bonino, 'Lateen-rigged medieval ships', pp. 18-21.
      5. J. van Beylen, *Schepen van de Nederlanden Van de late middeleeuwen
tot het einde van de 17e eeuw* (P.N. van Kampen en Zoon N.V., Amsterdam,
1970), pp. 127-9, 134-9, 141-6, 175-81. Dorothy Burwash, *English Merchant
Shipping, 1460-1540*, pp. 127-8, 136-40. G. C. E. Crone, *Onze Schepen in de
Gouden Eeuw* (P. N. van Kampen en Zoon N. V., Amsterdam, 1943), pp. 156-63.
H. A. H. Boelmans Kranenburg, 'Zeescheepvaart in Zuid-Holland 1400-1550',
Zuid-Hollandse Studiën XI (1965), pp. 225-35. Alan Moore and R. Morton
Nance, 'Round-Sterned Ships', *MM*, I (1911), pp. 105-9, 293. Both the hoeker
and the buss were given round sterns at the end of the sixteenth century.
      6. J. van Beylen, *Schepen van de Nederlanden*, pp. 121-4. O. Buyssens,
'Antverpia Mercatorvm Emporivm Actvm 1515(?)', *MAB*, VI (1952), pp. 190-1.
Bernhard Hagedorn, *Die Entwicklung der wichtigsten Schiffstypen*, pp. 92-6.
      7. J. van Beylen, *Schepen van de Nederlanden*, pp. 11-12, 183-5. Richard
Lebaron Bowen, Jr, 'The origins of fore-and-aft rigs', pp. 160-2. Joseph Needham,
Science and Civilisation in China, vol IV, part III, pp. 588-9, 606, 614-15.
      8. M. Garnier, 'Galères et Galéasses à la fin du Moyen Age', *TCHM*, II,
pp. 38-42. G. P. B. Naish, 'Ships and Shipbuilding', in Charles Singer *et al.* (eds),
A History of Technology, vol. III (Oxford University Press, London, 1957),
pp. 471-2. Alberto Tenenti, *Cristoforo Da Canal La Marine Vénitienne avant
Lépante* (SEVPEN, Paris, 1962), pp. 29-30. *HSUA*, pp. 208-10.
      9. J. van Beylen, *Schepen van de Nederlanden*, pp. 4-5. The use of guns on
ships came much slower in northern Europe. The first instance in Flanders was in
1365. Guns were first used in the northern Low Countries in 1396. Also see John
F. Guilmartin, 'The Early Provision of Artillery Armament on Mediterranean War
Galleys', *MM*, LIX (1973), pp. 258-80, and *Gunpowder and Galleys Changing
Technology and Mediterranean Warfare at Sea in the Sixteenth Century*
(Cambridge University Press, Cambridge, 1974), pp. 37-41, 59-62, 74-83.
      10. R. C. Anderson, 'Italian Naval Architecture about 1445', *MM*, XI (1925),
p. 144. F. C. Lane, *Navires et Constructeurs à Venise*, pp. 13-21, 25-9, 129-32,
222-3, 'Venetian Naval Architecture about 1550', p. 144, and *Venice*, pp. 337-53.
Michael E. Mallett, *The Florentine Galleys in the Fifteenth Century*, pp. 40-63,
144-51. Jules Scottas, *Messageries Maritimes de Venise XIVe et XVe siècles*,
pp. 70-83, 137-83, 209-32. E. G. R. Taylor, *The Haven-Finding Art*, pp. 143-5.
Alberto Sacerdoti, 'Note Sulle Galere Da Mercato Veneziane Nel XV Secolo',
Studi Veneziani (1962), pp. 80-6.
      11. Romola and R. C. Anderson, *The Sailing-Ship*, pp. 131-3. A. Anthiaume,
*Cartes marines, constructions navales, voyages de découverte chez les Normands
1500-1650*, pp. 280-2. M.Garnier, 'Galères et Galéasses à la fin du Moyen Age',
pp. 43-4. *HSUA*, pp. 211-12. R. C. Anderson, 'Henry VIII's "Great Galley" ',
MM, VI (1920), pp. 274-81.
      12. G. Asaert, *Westeuropese scheepvaart in de middeleeuwen*, pp. 105-7.
J. Ferreira David, 'Aperçu Historique des Types de Navires à Travers les Siècles et
l'Influence des Navires Ibériques sur la Construction Naval Européenne', *TCHM*,
V, pp. 153-5. L. Denoix, 'Caractéristiques des Navires de l'Epoque des Grandes
Découvertes', pp. 142-4. Quirino da Fonseca, *A Caravela Portuguesa e a priori-
dade téchnica da Navegacoes Heniquinas* (Imprensa da Universidade, Coimbra,
1934), pp. 597-9, 619. Edgar Prestage, *The Portuguese Pioneers* (A. and C. Black,
London, 1933), pp. 331-2.
      13. Wendy R. Childs, *Anglo-Castilian Trade in the Later Middle Ages*, p. 159.
Huguette and Pierre Chaunu, *Séville et l'Atlantique (1504-1650)* (Librairie
Armand Colin, Paris, 1955), vol. VI, part 1, table 12E. R. Morton Nance, 'Caravels',
MM, III (1913), pp. 267-9. J. H. Parry, *The Establishment of the European*

Hegemony, 1415-1715 (Harper and Row, New York, 1961), pp. 24-5.

14. L. Denoix, 'Les Problèmes de Navigation au Début des Grandes Découvertes', pp. 136-9. E. G. R. Taylor, *The Haven-Finding Art*, pp. 123-8, 154-83. D. W. Waters, 'Science and the Techniques of Navigation in the Renaissance', in Charles S. Singleton (ed.), *Art, Science, and History in the Renaissance* (The Johns Hopkins Press, Baltimore, 1967), pp. 201-8. See also D.W. Waters, *The Art of Navigation in England*, pp. 455-96. J.H. Parry, *Discovery of the Sea*, pp. 172-90.

15. Joseph Needham, 'Abstract of Material Presented to the International Maritime History Commission at Beirut', *TCHM*, VIII, pp. 143-6. M. A. Clos-Arceduc, 'La Genèse de la Projection de Mercator', *TCHM*, III, pp. 143-5. W. E. May, *A History of Marine Navigation*, pp. 119-25. D. W. Waters, *The Art of Navigation in England*, pp. 46-57, and *The Rutters of the Sea* (Yale University Press, New Haven, 1967). Samuel Eliot Morison, *The European Discovery of America The Southern Voyages A.D. 1492-1616* (Oxford University Press, New York, 1974), pp. 174-7.

16. H. H. Brindley, 'Note: Mediaeval Two-Masters', *MM*, X (1924), pp. 215-16. H. H. Brindley and Alan Moore, 'Square-Rigged Vessels with Two Masts', *MM*, VII (1921), pp. 194-8. Alan Moore, 'Accounts and Inventories of John Starlyng, Clerk of the King's Ships to Henry IV', *MM*, IV (1914), p. 173, and 'Rig in Northern Europe', *MM*, XLII (1956), pp. 9-11, 14-15. R. Morton Nance, 'The Ship of the Renaissance', pp. 189-90.

17. H. H. Brindley, 'Early Reefs', *MM*, IV (1920), pp. 77-85, and 'Mediaeval Ships', *MM*, II (1912), pp. 130-4, 172. The last illustration of reef-points is from 1528. They did not reappear until the late seventeenth century. T. C. Lethbridge, 'Shipbuilding', in Charles Singer *et al.* (eds), *A History of Technology*, vol. II (Oxford University Press, London, 1956), p. 587. José Maria Martinez-Hidalgo, *Columbus' Ships* (Barre Publishers, Barre, 1966), pp. 59-61.

18. R. C. Anderson, 'Note: Danish Drawings of Fifteenth-Century Ships', *MM*, XXIII (1937), p. 108. J. van Beylen, *Schepen van de Nederlanden*, p. 3. R. Morton Nance, 'Some Old-Time Ship Pictures VII A Batch of Carracks', *MM*, IV (1914), p. 281.

19. R. C. Anderson, ' "Carvel" and "caravel" ', *MM*, XXVIII (1932), p. 189. Jacques Bernard, *Navires et Gens de Mer à Bordeaux (vers 1400-vers 1550)*, pp. 359-68. O. Buyssens, 'Antverpia Mercatorvm Emporivm Actvm 1515(?)', p. 181. He wants to say that a carvel had a sharper bow than a carrack and a flat stern. This is probably correct for many uses of the word carvel in the Low Countries. J. van Beylen, *Schepen van de Nederlanden*, pp. 6-8. Bernhard Hagedorn, *Die Entwicklung der wichtigsten Schiffstypen*, pp. 42-3, 74-5. *AB*, p. 292. English shipyard ledgers at the end of the fifteenth century include 'carvell nayles' for the first time to distinguish them from the old 'clinchnayl'.

20. R. C. Anderson, 'Italian Naval Architecture about 1445', pp. 149-50. A. Anthiaume, *Le Navire*, pp. 153-5. W. Brulez, 'The Balance of Trade of the Netherlands in the Middle of the 16th Century', *Acta Historiae Neerlandica*, IV (1970), p. 34, says that Antwerp in the mid-sixteenth century imported 16,000 tons of alum annually. The figure is misleading since volume had undoubtedly increased since the early fifteenth century and it does not represent total alum imports in northern Europe. Still, even if the Genoese were shipping half that amount north in 1425, it would have required about twelve carracks of over 600 tons. Jacques Heers, *Gênes au XVe Siècle*, pp. 273-6, and 'Types de Navires et Spécialisation des Trafics en Méditerranée à la Fin du Moyen Age', pp. 111-14. R. Morton Nance, 'Some Old-Time Ship Pictures VI A Group of Florentines', *MM*, III (1913), pp. 238-44. F.C. Lane, *Navires et Constructeurs à Venise*, pp. 43-4, 94-102, 222-8.

21. L. Denoix, 'Caractéristiques des Navires de l'Epoque des Grandes Découvertes', p. 14. R. Morton Nance, 'The Ship of the Renaissance', pp. 283-4, and 'Some French Carracks', *MM*, IX (1923), pp. 131-2. G. La Roërie, 'More About the Ship of the Renaissance', *MM*, XLIII (1954), pp. 181-4. Wendy R. Childs, *Anglo-Castilian Trade in the Later Middle Ages*, pp. 160-1. She found a rise in the average size of ships to the 1460s, and then a fall.

22. H. H. Brindley, 'A Ship of Hans Burgkmair', *MM*, III (1913), pp. 81-4. Bernhard Hagedorn, *Die Entwicklung der wichtigsten Schiffstypen*, pp. 58-68; another potential source for the change to full-rigged design came from the orders from Italians for ships to be built in Gdansk – they chose that port presumably because of the availability of wood and of cargoes for the maiden voyage west and south. R. Morton Nance, 'A Hanseatic Bergentrader of 1489', *MM*, III (1913), pp. 161-7. Otto Lienau, 'Danziger Schiffahrt und Schiffbau in der zweiten Hälfte des 15. Jahrhunderts met 7 Bildtafeln', *Zeitschrift des Westpreussichen Geschichtvereins*, LXX (1930), pp. 77-9, 82. Dagmar Waskönig, 'Bildliche Darstellung des Holks im 15. und 16. Jahrhundert', pp. 143-61.

23. Arthur Agats, *Der Hansische Baienhandel*, pp. 35-6, 64-75, 94-105. E. Daenell, *Die Blütezeit der Deutschen Hanse* (Georg Reimer, Berlin, 1905), vol. I, pp. 433-5, vol. II, pp. 345-50. Niels-Knud Liebgott, 'A wooden Norwegian calendar of 1457 with ship graffiti Problems relating to the source value of primitive representations of ships', *IJNA*, II (1973), pp. 156-7. Presumably it was the Hansards who introduced the full-rigged ship to Scandinavia. Walther Vogel, *Geschichte der deutschen Seeschiffahrt*, pp. 356-9, 495. Konrad Fritze, *Am Wendepunkt der Hanse* (VEB Deutscher Verlag der Wissenschaften, Berlin, 1967), pp. 63-81.

24. G. C. E. Crone, *Onze Schepen in de Gouden Eeuw*, pp. 11-14. W. S. Unger, 'De Hollandsche Graanhandel en Graanhandelspolitiek in de Middeleeuwen', *De Economist* (1916), pp. 260, 339-48. Bernhard Hagedorn, *Die Entwicklung der wichtigsten Schiffstypen*, pp. 56-8, 67-8. A. R. Bridbury, *England and the Salt Trade in the Later Middle Ages*, pp. 78-101, 118-27. W. Brulez, 'The Balance of Trade of the Netherlands in the Middle of the 16th Century', pp. 26-30. Grain imports from the Baltic by the 1560s had reached over 100,000 tons annually. This meant a sizeable demand for Dutch ships. The salt trade made similar demands on capacity.

25. Ernst Baasch, *Beiträge zur Geschichte des deutschen Seeschiffbaues und der Schiffbaupolitik*, pp. 2-8, 214-15, 268-71. F. L. Carsten, *The Origins of Prussia* (The Clarendon Press, Oxford, 1954), pp. 117-34. E. Daenell, *Die Blütezeit der Deutschen Hanse*, vol. I, pp. 265-75, vol. II, pp. 377-88, and 'Holland und die Hanse im 15. Jahrhundert', *Hansische Geschichtsblätter*, IX (1903), pp. 3-41.

26. Jacques Bernard, *Navires et Gens de Mer à Bordeaux (vers 1400–vers 1550)*, pp. 363-5, 519. Henri Touchard, *Le Commerce Maritime Breton à la fin du Moyen Age* (Les Belles Lettres, Paris, 1967), pp. 261-3, 319-25, 378-80.

27. G. D. van der Heide, 'Oudheidkundig Onderzoek in de Voormalige Zeebodem', *Mededelingen van de Nederlandse Vereniging voor Zeegeschiedenis*, XVII (1968), p. 25. Friedrich Jorberg, 'Beiträge zum Studium des Hanseschiffes', *Zeitschrift der Vereins für Lübeckische Geschichte und Altertumskunde*, XXXV (1955), pp. 65-6.

28. R. C. Anderson, 'The Bursledon Ship', *MM*, XX (1934), pp. 158-70. The ship has been the object of more than one archaeological excavation. It now lies in the mud of the Hamble River where it settled after burning in 1439. J. R. Claridge, 'Joinery of Medieval Hulls, c. 1450', *MM*, XLV (1959), pp. 78-9. Michael E. Mallett, *The Florentine Galleys in the Fifteenth Century*, p. 259. L. G. C. Laughton, 'The Great Ship of 1419', *MM*, IX (1923), pp. 83-7.

M. W. Prynne, 'Henry V's Grace Dieu', pp. 122-6, and 'Note: The Dimensions of the *Grace Dieu* (1418)', *MM*, LXIII (1977), pp. 6-7. W. J. Carpenter Turner, 'The Building of the *Gracedieu, Valentine* and *Falconer* at Southampton, 1416-1420', *MM*, XL (1954), pp. 55-72, and 'The Building of the *Holy Ghost of the Tower*, 1414-1416, and her Subsequent History', *MM*, XL (1954), pp. 270-81.

29. W. L. Goodman, *The History of Woodworking Tools*, p. 175. Henry C. Mercer, *Ancient Carpenters' Tools*, p. 205. Lynn White, Jr, *Medieval Technology and Social Change* (Oxford University Press, Oxford, 1962), p. 112.

30. E. Daenell, *Die Blütezeit der Deutschen Hanse*, vol. II, p. 355. L. Denoix, 'Caractéristiques des Navires de l'Epoque des Grandes Découvertes', pp. 141-3. Jacques Heers, *Gênes au XVe Siècle*, p. 301. Harold Innis, *The Cod Fisheries*, pp. 19-21, 47-8. Charles De La Roncière, *Histoire de la Marine Française*, vol. II, pp. 456-7. M. J. Tadić, 'Le Port de Raguse et sa flotte au XVIe siècle', *TCHM*, II, pp. 15-16.

31. G. La Roërie, 'More about the Ship of the Renaissance', pp. 191-2. Alan Moore, 'Rig in Northern Europe', pp. 11-13.

32. E. W. Bovill, 'The *Madre De Dios*, the taking of a carrack', *MM*, LIV (1968), pp. 129-52. C. R. Boxer (ed.), *The Tragic History of the Sea, 1589-1622*, Hakluyt Society Publications, series II, CXII (Cambridge University Press, Cambridge, 1959), pp. 1-5, 17-25, 55, 115-16, and *The Portuguese Seaborne Empire* (Hutchinson, London, 1969), pp. 206-19. L. Denoix, 'Caractéristiques des Navires de l'Epoque des Grandes Découvertes', pp. 145-6. Bernhard Hagedorn, *Die Entwicklung der wichtigsten Schiffstypen*, pp. 75-6. C. L. Kingsford, 'The Taking of the Madre De Dios. Anno 1592', in Naval Miscellany, vol. II, *Publications of the Navy Records Society*, XL (1912), pp. 85-121. Vitorino Magalhães Godinho, *L'Economie de L'Empire Portugais aux XVe et XVIe Siècles* (SEVPEN, Paris, 1969), pp. 665-77.

33. J. H. Parry, *The Age of Reconnaissance*, pp. 67-8. A. Anthiaume, *Le Navire*, pp. 213-18. C. H. Haring, *Trade and Navigation between Spain and the Indies in the Times of the Hapsburgs* (Harvard University Press, Cambridge, Mass., 1918), pp. 261-3. José Maria Martinez-Hidalgo, *Columbus' Ships*, pp. 8-9, 24-39, 51-61, 87-90.

34. R. C. Anderson, 'Ship-Paintings in the Alhambra', *MM*, LI (1965), pp. 1-6. L. Denoix, 'Caractéristiques des Navires de l'Epoque des Grandes Découvertes', pp. 144-5. Quirino da Fonseca, *A Caravela Portuguesa*, pp. 313-28, 606-9. José Maria Martinez-Hidalgo, *Columbus' Ships*, pp. 99-100. Alan Moore, 'Rig in Northern Europe', p. 15. R. Morton Nance, 'Caravels', pp. 267-71.

35. Romola and R. C. Anderson, *The Sailing-Ship*, pp. 121-2, 127-30. Guns firing from the waist certainly date from the 1480s in northern Europe and probably earlier. Arne Emil Christensen, 'Lucien Basch: Ancient wrecks and the archaeology of ships A comment', p. 141. John F. Guilmartin, *Gunpowder and Galleys*, pp. 157-75. L. G. C. Laughton, 'Hull Protection', *MM*, XXVI (1940), pp. 55-60. *HSUA*, pp. 227-30. R. Morton Nance, 'The Ship of the Renaissance', pp. 288-9. Peter Padfield, *Guns at Sea* (H. Evelyn, London, 1973), pp. 19-33.

36. A. Anthiaume, *Le Navire*, pp. 211-17. Bernhard Hagedorn, *Die Entwicklung der wichtigsten Schiffstypen*, pp. 68-72. Michel Mollat, *Le Commerce Maritime Normand*, pp. 343-5, 464-5.

37. F. C. Lane, *Navires et Constructeurs à Venise*, p. 27. Venice, because of a long tradition, was the last state to give up free rowers on its galleys. See also F. C. Lane, *Venice*, pp. 366-9. Alberto Tenenti, *Cristoforo Da Canal* (SEVPEN, Paris, 1962).

38. C. S. L. Davies, 'The Administration of the Royal Navy under Henry VIII: the Origins of the Navy Board', *English Historical Review*, LXXX (1965), pp. 268-88. Henry Kitson, 'The Early History of Portsmouth Dockyard, 1496-1800',

MM, XXXIII (1947), pp. 256-7. Charles De La Roncière, *Histoire de la Marine Française*, vol. II, pp. 454-9. Armand Le Hénaff, *Etude sur L'Organisation Administrative de La Marine sous L'Ancien Régime et la Révolution*, pp. 30-8, 51. M. Oppenheim, *A History of the Administration of the Royal Navy*, pp. 28-86.
39. Fernand Braudel, *The Mediterranean and the Mediterranean World, in the Age of Philip II* (Collins, London, 1972) (first French edition, 1949), pp. 449-50. Carl Ekman, 'Skeppet Svanens resa till Holland år 1546', *Sjöhistorisk Årsbok* (1951-52), pp. 163-6. C. H. Haring, *Trade and Navigation between Spain and the Indies*, pp. 21-35. Archibald R. Lewis, 'The Medieval Background of American Atlantic Development', in Benjamin W. Labaree (ed.), *The Atlantic World of Robert G. Albion* (Wesleyan University Press, Middletown, Conn., 1975), pp. 37-8.
40. Lawrence A. Clayton, 'Ships and Empire: The Case of Spain', *MM*, LXII (1976), pp. 239-44. E. Daenell, *Die Blütezeit der Deutschen Hanse*, vol. II, pp. 342-5. Bernhard Hagedorn, *Die Entwicklung der wichtigsten Schiffstypen*, pp. 53-4. C. H. Haring, *Trade and Navigation between Spain and the Indies*, pp. 262-76. M. J. Tadić, 'Le Port de Raguse et sa flotte au XVIe siècle', p. 15. Iberian governments were not alone in fixing maximum tonnages for ships.
41. E. M. Carus-Wilson, *The Overseas Trade of Bristol in the later Middle Ages* (Merlin Press, London, 1937), no. 192. Eli Heckscher, *Mercantilism* (edited by E.R. Söderlund, translated by M. Shapiro) (George Allen and Unwin Ltd, London, 1955), vol. II, pp. 34-6. F. C. Lane, *Navires et Constructeurs à Venise*, pp. 99-105; for much of the sixteenth century the government simply built the big ships itself since the subsidy programme did not yield adequate results. Charles De La Roncière, *Histoire de la Marine Française*, vol. I, p. 245, vol. II, p. 465. Michel Mollat, *Le Commerce Maritime Normand*, pp. 34, 464-5. M. Oppenheim, *A History of the Administration of the Royal Navy*, pp. 88, 167-8.
42. G. Asaert, *Westeuropese scheepvaart in de middeleeuwen*, pp. 123-9. Dorothy Burwash, *English Merchant Shipping, 1460-1540*, p. 166. G. V. Scammell, 'Shipowning in the Economy and Politics of early modern England', *Historical Journal*, XV (1972), pp. 406-7.
43. R. C. Anderson, 'Italian Naval Architecture about 1445', pp. 135-63, and 'Jal's "Memoire No. 5" and the Manuscript "Fabbrica di Galere" ', pp. 160-7. F. C. Lane, *Navires et Constructeurs à Venise*, pp. 59, 82-9, and 'Venetian Naval Architecture about 1550', pp. 24-49. Gerhard Timmerman, 'Das Eindringen der Naturwissenschaft in das Schiffbauhandwerk', *Deutsches Museum, Abhandlungen und Berichte*, XXX, 3 (1963), pp. 10-14. Walther Vogel, 'Ein neuentdecktes Lehrbuch der Navigation und des Schiffbaues aus der Mitte des 16. Jahrhunderts', *Hansische Geschichtsblätter*, XVII (1911), pp. 370-4.
44. A. Anthiaume, *Le Navire*, pp. 175-7. Ernst Baasch, *Beiträge zur Geschichte des deutschen Seeschiffbaues und der Schiffbaupolitik*, pp. 271-3. Paul Augustin-Normand, 'Introduction', in *Le Corporatism Ancien de Construction Navale en France* (Académie de Marine, Paris, 1939), pp. 5-12. Karl-Friedrich Olechnowitz, *Der Schiffbau der Hansischen Spätzeit* (Verlag Hermann Böhlaus Nachfolger, Weimar, 1960), pp. 67-95. Richard W. Unger, 'Regulations of Dutch Shipcarpenters in the Fifteenth and Sixteenth Centuries', *Tijdschrift voor Geschiedenis*, LXXXVII (1974), pp. 503-20.

NOTES TO ILLUSTRATIONS

a. Romola and R. C. Anderson, *The Sailing-Ship*, p. 110. Claude Farrère, *Histoire de la Marine Française*, p. 42. R. Morton Nance, 'The Ship of the Renaissance', *MM*, XLI (1955), p. 294. Marco Bonino, 'Lateen-rigged medieval ships', pp. 18-20.

b. G. Asaert, *Westeuropese scheepvaart in de middeleeuwen*, p. 42, 103. Richard Lebaron Bowen, Jr, 'The origins of fore-and-aft rigs', p. 189. J. van Beylen, 'Zelandiæ Descriptio', *MAB*, X (1956-57), pp. 99, 103-4, 106, 108, 110. Siegfried Fliedner, ' "Kogge" und "Hulk" ', no. 35.

c. G. Asaert, *Westeuropese scheepvaart in de middeleeuwen*, pp. 74-5. Richard Lebaron Bowen, Jr, 'The origins of fore-and-aft rigs', pp. 162, 165. O. Buyssens, 'Antverpia Mercatorvm Emporivm Actvm 1515(?)', *MAB*, VI (1952), pp. 172-3, 175, 196, 200. Bernhard Hagedorn, *Die Entwicklung der wichtigsten Schiffstypen*, plate XXVI. R. Morton Nance, 'A Fifteenth Century Trader', *MM*, I (1911), pp. 65-7. Björn Landström, *The Ship*, nos. 314-17.

d. Romola and R. C. Anderson, *The Sailing-Ship*, p. 115. Lionel Casson, *Illustrated History of Ships and Boats*, nos. 69, 87-8, 91-2, 118, 144. Claude Farrère, *Histoire de la Marine Française*, pp. 65, 69, 85, 95. Björn Landström, *The Ship*, nos. 319-22, 329, 331. *HSUA*, pp. 208, 218-19. G. La Roërie and J. Vivielle, *Navires et Marins*, vol. I, pp. 81, 92-3, 95-6, 101.

e. Romola and R. C. Anderson, *The Sailing-Ship*, p. 114. R. C. Anderson, 'Italian Naval Architecture about 1445', *MM*, XI (1925), p. 144. G. Asaert, *Westeuropese scheepvaart in de middeleeuwen*, p. 59. O. Buyssens, 'Antverpia Mercatorvm Emporivm Actvm 1515(?)', pp. 172-3, 175, 177, 199. Lionel Casson, *Illustrated History of Ships and Boats*, no. 95. Claude Farrère, *Histoire de la Marine Française*, p. 62. Björn Landström, *The Ship*, no. 323. R. Morton Nance, 'The Ship of the Renaissance', p. 182. G. La Roërie and J. Vivielle, *Navires et Marins*, vol. I, pp. 90, 94, 257. *HSUA*, pp. 211, 215. E. G. R. Taylor, *The Haven-Finding Art*, figure V.

f. Romola and R. C. Anderson, *The Sailing-Ship*, pp. 132-3. Lionel Casson, *Illustrated History of Ships and Boats*, no. 142. Claude Farrère, *Histoire de la Marine Française*, pp. 53, 94. Björn Landström, *The Ship*, nos. 327, 334-8. R. Morton Nance, 'The Ship of the Renaissance', p. 286. G. La Roërie and J. Vivielle, *Navires et Marins*, vol. I, p. 99. *HSUA*, pp. 211-12, 222-3.

g. Romola and R. C. Anderson, *The Sailing-Ship*, p. 124. G. Asaert, *Westeuropese scheepvaart in de middeleeuwen*, p. 108. Siegfried Fliedner, ' "Kogge" und "Hulk" ', nos. 39-40. Björn Landström, *The Ship*, nos. 267-9, 274, 276, 277. José Maria Martinez-Hidalgo, *Columbus' Ships*, pp. 20-1.

h. Lionel Casson, *Illustrated History of Ships and Boats*, no. 115. Claude Farrère, *Histoire de la Marine Française*, pp. 66-7, 72, 89, 90, 93. José Maria Martinez-Hidalgo, *Columbus' Ships*, p. 65. G. La Roërie and J. Vivielle, *Navires et Marins*, vol. I, plate XV. *HSUA*, pp. 217, 223. E.G.R. Taylor, *The Haven-Finding Art*, figures IX, XI, XVIII, XIX.

i. *AB*, no. 203. G. Asaert, *Westeuropese scheepvaart in de middeleeuwen*, p. 112. Paul Heinsius, *Das Schiff der Hansischen Frühzeit*, plate II, no. 4. Björn Landström, *The Ship*, nos. 249-53, 255, 256, 265, 270. José Maria Martinez-Hidalgo, *Columbus' Ships*, between p. 52 and p. 53. R. Morton Nance, 'The Ship of the Renaissance', pp. 282, 284, and 'Some Old-Time Ship Pictures VI A Batch of Carracks', *MM*, IV (1914), pp. 279-80.

j. Romola and R. C. Anderson, *The Sailing-Ship*, plate V. L. Arenhould, 'Note: Ancient German Ships', *MM*, III (1913), p. 313. G. Asaert, *Westeuropese scheepvaart in de middeleeuwen*, pp. 95, 130. H. H. Brindley, 'Mediaeval Ships', *MM*, I (1911), p. 72, and 'Note: Mediaeval Two-Masters', *MM*, X (1924), opposite p. 215. Lionel Casson, *Illustrated History of Ships and Boats*, no. 105. Siegfried Fliedner, ' "Kogge" und "Hulk" ', no. 36. Claude Farrère, *Histoire de la Marine Française*, pp. 15, 19, 35, 62. Björn Landström, *The Ship*, nos. 246-8, 257-60. Alan Moore, 'Rig in Northern Europe', p. 10. R. Morton Nance, 'The Ship of the Renaissance', pp. 189, 192. G. La Roërie and J. Vivielle, *Navires et Marins*, vol. I, pp. 209, 217, 237, 271. *HSUA*, pp. 219, 237. Dagmar Waskönig, 'Bildliche

Darstellung des Holks im 15. und 16. Jahrhundert', p. 154.

k. Björn Landström, *The Ship*, no, 254. Romola and R. C. Anderson, *The Sailing-Ship*, p. 119, no. 75. G. Asaert, *Westeuropese scheepvaart in de middeleeuwen*, pp. 33, 94. Claude Farrère, *Histoire de la Marine Française*, p. 42. Siegfried Fliedner, ' "Kogge" und "Hulk" ', no. 37. Bernhard Hagedorn, *Die Entwicklung der wichtigsten Schiffstypen*, plate XVIII. José Maria Martinez-Hidalgo, *Columbus' Ships*, between p. 52 and p. 53. Dagmar Waskönig, 'Bildliche Darstellung des Holks im 15. und 16. Jahrhundert', pp. 148, 150.

l. *AB*, no. 204. Romola and R. C. Anderson, *The Sailing-Ship*, p. 122. G. Asaert, *Westeuropese scheepvaart in de middeleeuwen*, pp. 95, 110. Lionel Casson, *Illustrated History of Ships and Boats*, n. 107. G. S. Laird Clowes, *Sailing Ships*, part II, plate IV. Claude Farrère, *Histoire de la Marine Française*, pp. 58-9. Bernhard Hagedorn, *Die Entwicklung der wichtigsten Schiffstypen*, plate XXI. Kenneth Harrison, 'The King's College Chapel Window Ship', *MM*, XXXIV (1948), p. 14. Siegfried Fliedner, ' "Kogge" und "Hulk" ', no. 29. Björn Landström, *The Ship*, nos. 262, 263, 264, 266. Alan Moore, 'Rig in Northern Europe', p. 11, and 'Some XV Century Ship Pictures', *MM*, V (1919), opposite pp. 16 and 17. R. Morton Nance, 'The Ship of the Renaissance', p. 288, and 'Some Old-Time Ship Pictures I The Kraeck of W̄Ā', *MM*, II (1912), pp. 225-32.

m. Romola and R. C. Anderson, *The Sailing-Ship*, p. 127. R. C. Anderson, 'Note: Danish Drawings of Fifteenth-Century Ships', *MM*, XIII (1937), p. 108, and 'Ship-Paintings in the Alhambra', *MM*, LI (1965), p. 2. J. van Beylen, 'Zelandiae Descriptio', p. 88. O. Buyssens, 'Antverpia Mercatorvm Emporivm Actvm 1515(?)', p. 199. G. Asaert, *Westeuropese scheepvaart in de middeleeuwen*, pp. 63, 71, 97. Lionel Casson, *Illustrated History of Ships and Boats*, nos. 109-10. Claude Farrère, *Histoire de la Marine Française*, pp. 71, 85. Björn Landström, *Sailing Ships*, nos. 208, 210-12, and *The Ship*, nos. 271, 278-80. Alan Moore, 'Rig in Northern Europe', pp. 12-13. R. Morton Nance, 'The Ship of the Renaissance', pp. 285, 293, 'Some French Carracks', *MM*, IX (1923), opposite p. 131, and 'Some Old-Time Ship Pictures VII A Batch of Carracks', pp. 280-1. G. La Roërie and J. Vivielle, *Navires et Marins*, vol. I, pp. 200, 254, 270. G. Nesbitt Wood, 'Note: Church Painting of a 16th-Century Great Ship', *MM*, LVIII (1972), opposite p. 134.

n. Romola and R. C. Anderson, *The Sailing-Ship*, p. 120. R. C. Anderson, 'Italian Naval Architecture about 1445', p. 149. G. Asaert, *Westeuropese scheepvaart in de middeleeuwen*, p. 82. O. Buyssens, 'Antverpia Mercatorvm Emporivm Actvm 1515(?)', p. 192. Lionel Casson, *Illustrated History of Ships and Boats*, nos. 102-4, 106. Claude Farrère, *Histoire de la Marine Française*, p. 57. Bernhard Hagedorn, *Die Entwicklung der wichtigsten Schiffstypen*, plate XX. Paul Heinsius, *Das Schiff der Hansischen Frühzeit*, p. 200. José Maria Martinez-Hidalgo, *Columbus' Ships*, pp. 42-3. R. Morton Nance, 'The Ship of the Renaissance', pp. 190-1, 289, 'Some Old Time Ship Pictures VI A Group of Florentines', *MM*, III (1913), pp. 239-41, and 'Some Old-Time Ship Pictures VII A Batch of Carracks', pp. 275-8. G. La Roërie and J. Vivielle, *Navires et Marins*, vol. I, pp. 213, 219, 224, 226-7, 230. *HSUA*, p. 219.

o. Romola and R. C. Anderson, *The Sailing-Ship*, p. 97, plate IV. G. Asaert, *Westeuropese scheepvaart in de middeleeuwen*, pp. 27, 69, 78, 80, 93, 100, 112-13, 131, 133. H. H. Brindley, 'Mediaeval Ships', *MM*, I (1911), opposite p. 131, 196. Lionel Casson, *Illustrated History of Ships and Boats*, no. 94. Claude Farrère, *Histoire de la Marine Française*, pp. 22, 26-7, 34, 36-7, 42-3, 45, 49, 56, 82. Siegfried Fliedner, ' "Kogge" und "Hulk" ', nos. 16-17, 19, 31. Bernhard Hagedorn, *Die Entwicklung der wichtigsten Schiffstypen*, plate XIX. José Maria Martinez-Hidalgo, *Columbus' Ships*, pp. 28, 38. G. La Roërie and J. Vivielle, *Navires et Marins*, vol. I, pp. 204-5, 218, 273, plate X.

p. Romola and R. C. Anderson, *The Sailing-Ship*, plates VI, VII. G. Asaert, *Westeuropese scheepvaart in de middeleeuwen*, pp. 86, 96, 98. H. H. Brindley, 'Mediaeval Ships', *MM*, I (1911), p. 74. and 'A Ship of Hans Burgkmair', *MM*, III (1913), opposite p. 81. Lionel Casson, *Illustrated History of Ships and Boats*, nos. 108, 112-13. G. S. Laird Clowes, *Sailing Ships*, part I, plate IX, part II, plate III. Claude Farrère, *Histoire de la Marine Française*, pp. 40, 68. Siegfried Fliedner, ' "Kogge" und "Hulk" ', nos. 28, 32, 38. Paul Heinsius, *Das Schiff der Hansischen Frühzeit*, plate XIV, no. 30. *HSUA*, p. 237. R. Morton Nance, 'A Hanseatic Bergentrader of 1489', *MM*, III (1913), opposite p. 16. G. La Roërie and J. Vivielle, *Navires et Marins*, vol. I, pp. 256, 259, plate XII. Dagmar Waskönig, 'Bildliche Darstellung des Holks im 15. und 16. Jahrhundert', pp. 144, 146, 148, 157, 159.

q. *HSUA*, pp. 227-8, 239.

r. Lionel Casson, *Illustrated History of Ships and Boats*, no. 117. Björn Landström, *The Ship*, nos. 282-4. José Maria Martinez-Hidalgo, *Colmbus' Ships*, pp. 45-6. Dagmar Waskönig, 'Bildliche Darstellung des Holks im 15. und 16. Jahrhundert', p. 160.

s. Siegfried Fliedner, ' "Kogge" und "Hulk" ', no. 41. José Maria Martinez-Hidalgo, *Columbus' Ships*, pp. 6, 11, 14, 16, 50, between 52 and 53, 88, 91. G. La Roërie and J. Vivielle, *Navires et Marins*, vol. I, pp. 238-41, 243-6, 248-9. Björn Landström, *The Ship*, nos. 272, 273.

t. Romola and R. C. Anderson, *The Sailing-Ship*, p. 130. G. Asaert, *Westeuropese scheepvaart in de middeleeuwen*, p. 107. Lionel Casson, *Illustrated History of Ships and Boats*, no. 111. Claude Farrère, *Histoire de la Marine Française*, p. 39. Björn Landström, *Sailing Ships*, no. 225, and *The Ship*, nos. 275, 290. José Maria Martinez-Hidalgo, *Columbus' Ships*, pp. 22, 24. Alan Moore, 'Rig in Northern Europe', p. 15.

u. Romola and R. C. Anderson, *The Sailing-Ship*, p. 131, plate VIII. Lionel Casson, *Illustrated History of Ships and Boats*, nos. 116, 121. G. S. Laird Clowes, *Sailing Ships*, part I, plate VIII. Claude Farrère, *Histoire de la Marine Française*, opposite p. 80. Bernhard Hagedorn, *Die Entwicklung der wichtigsten Schiffstypen*, plate XXIII. Björn Landström, *The Ship*, nos. 293-5. *HSUA*, pp. 240-1. G. La Roërie and J. Vivielle, *Navires et Marins*, vol. I, p. 229, plate XI.

6 WARSHIPS, CARGO SHIPS AND CANNON: 1550-1600

The second half of the sixteenth century was marked by revolts within many established states of western Europe, in the Netherlands, Spain and France. Other states tried to exploit that internal instability. The conflict which resulted was international. The addition of a religious dimension to that of civil conflict and to international political competition made the fighting more bitter, if that were possible. The conditions offered freebooters more opportunites to pursue their own interests in the name of some higher authority. Political connections extended to the eastern Mediterranean and the Ottoman Turks participated in the international struggles. The defeat handed the Turks at Lepanto (1571) by a combination of Spanish, Venetian, Genoese and Papal forces at least temporarily neutralised them as a naval force. By the end of the sixteenth century, through military and naval success and more often through attrition and exhaustion, a certain political stability had been reintroduced. By a series of truces the major powers at least allowed a breathing space in the protracted wars, which meant also a breathing space for commerce. Trade, even during truces, did not escape its proper function as a weapon of state policy. The monarchs of

Illustration above: A four-masted warship carrying two lateen mizzens and heavy guns in the waist, seal of Michael Stanhope, Vice-Admiral of Suffolk, 1540.

Europe and their advisers were devoted to political success, an integral part of which was the enrichment of the state. Given the way politicians perceived their function, political and economic conflict with other states was inevitable.

The evolution in the design of ships in the second half of the sixteenth century followed the pattern laid down over the previous hundred years. The potential of the full-rigged ship was regularly tested. Innovation continued at all levels, from the rig on the smallest of inland vessels to the hull design of the largest of seagoing ships. The variety of types and designs continued to grow throughout Europe and for all sizes of craft. The most significant improvements came from specialised design. For the largest ships, major steps were taken in distinguishing ships for violence from ships for trade. The Dutch fluyt, first built in the last decade of the sixteenth century, was designed as a cargo ship. Meanwhile, the galleon, developed originally in Venice but later used extensively by states on Europe's Atlantic seaboard, became in the course of the sixteenth century the prototype for the ships-of-the-line of later navies. By 1600, cargo ships were easily distinguished from warships. The division between the two types over the seventeenth and eighteenth centuries led to great savings for the world economy. While the basis for that distinction was laid in the half-century after 1550, it was a part of the more general trend of specialisation and elaboration of earlier inventions. Small ships and boats went through much the same process and perhaps show equally graphically the pressures on sixteenth-century shipbuilders and how they reacted to those pressures.

The increase in specialisation and variety among smaller ships and boats applied also to those intended for fighting. In the Netherlands, for example, various types were adopted or developed for engagements and patrol work along the rivers and lakes by both sides in the revolt which began there in 1568. Galleys similar to those of the Mediterranean were built in many coastal and river towns. Dutch builders also produced sailing gunboats, crompsters. Based on the flat-bottomed inland boat with a sharply turned-up prow, this boat made a stable gun platform. The fore-and-aft rig made it manoeuvrable. It still had shallow draught, despite the heavy artillery on board. Though they were not large ships, crompsters could carry 100 men or more. They offered exactly the advantages of galleys — good ships for coastal patrol and defence, well suited to amphibious operations.[1] There were also small seagoing ships. For carrying cargo, two-masted vessels of from 50 to 100 tons became more common in European waters. They were designed to fill the gap between the full-rigged ship and the single-masted coastal and inland vessel. These two-masters with two, three or four square sails were also capable of making transatlantic voyages. For smaller vessels, for those usually used on inland waters, Dutch builders added another new feature, leeboards. An oval plank on each side of an almost flat or flat-bottomed sailing ship could be lowered to keep the boat from going to leeward. These leeboards acted like the later centre-board or took the place of a keel for many types which had to be built with shallow draught.[a] The European version was probably based on the Chinese use of a similar device.[2] Leeboards gave even more manoeuvrability and reliability to inland craft. They also allowed shipbuilders further to differentiate such vessels by function, even to the point of adjusting the length-to-width ratio of the leeboards.

Dutch shipbuilding is only the most extreme example of the increase in design specialisation. Shipwrights throughout Europe perfected many types as they and the users of ships clarified their goals and needs. As a result of the use of galleys for fighting, Venice had long been required to produce two kinds of ships, one for war and the other for trade. There were also differences between cargo and warships in the Viking era. In the second half of the sixteenth century, the same distinction between the two types came to apply to all sailing ships. The principal type of vessel in use for long-distance trade, the full-rigged ship, was subjected to that same drive by builders to make the design fit the job. This is not to say that cargo ships could not or did not become involved in fighting or that fighting ships could not or did not carry cargo, but the substitution of the two types, still common in the fifteenth century, no longer prevailed. By 1600, shipwrights were building warships for government and cargo ships for merchants who had no other goal than to carry goods at the lowest possible cost. The evolution of the sailing warship and its success led to changes in the oldest of European warships, the galley.

The increase in the size of galleys and the rise in weight because of the use of increasingly heavy guns led to a change in the rowing arrangement, to get more pull on the oars. Around 1550, earlier for some states and later for others, the trio of oars for each bench, with one man pulling on each oar, was replaced by a single oar, the three men all pulling together on it. All the rowers were at the same level, so each handled the oar at a different angle. The rowers on one thwart had to co-ordinate among themselves as well as with all the other groups of oarsmen. The oars were very heavy, more than 50 kilograms including the iron counterweight sunk into the handle. The oars had to pivot on the outrigger, which itself was very strong, taking the weight of the oars

25: Galley Rowed *a scaloccio* and a Mediterranean Warship of the
Mid-Sixteenth century, from an Engraving by Pieter Breugel the Elder

and also gangways for fighting marines. It was impossible for the man furthest inboard to row seated. Rowers since the thirteenth century, and before, rose and then pushed themselves back to throw all of the strength of their thighs and torsos into the stroke, thus giving a short and choppy stroke which caused the ship almost to leap through the water. The action was accentuated even more when builders experimented first with four and later with five men to a bench. The original purpose of the change to rowing *a scaloccio* was, after all, to put more men on the oars. The rowers at the extremes added little to the pull of the oar, the one very cramped and the other almost running to keep up with the motion of the oar.

Galleys became bigger, rising to 170 tons with over-all lengths of some 45 metres and a width of seven metres. The number of benches remained the same, about 25 to a side. If there were only three rowers to an oar, then the crew size remained the same, but a rise to five rowers on each oar meant a 67 per cent rise in the total. The complement of 75 to 100 sailors and marines grew during the period. Under oars these galleys could do seven knots for brief periods, say in the middle of a battle. For longer pulls of some two hours the speed would have been little over four knots. These galleys were used as fighting ships in the Caribbean and off the coast of the Netherlands in the sixteenth century but their principal theatre of operations was, as always, the Mediterranean. There were variations in design from state to state, depending on the availability of rowers and guns and the type of war the states expected to fight. The rise in crew sizes increased manning problems. Fortunately, the change in the rowing arrangement did alleviate one problem. Only one of the rowers, the man furthest inboard on each oar, had to be skilled. He had to know how to row and was responsible for co-ordinating the effort of the men on his oar with the pulling of the rest of the crew. As to the other men, their function was just to supply muscle power and literally any man, even unwilling and weak, could do that. There was a high correlation between the use of slaves and the new rowing arrangement. In fact, the shortage of qualified oarsmen may have been the cause for the mid-sixteenth-century change in rowing. One critical result was a rise in costs because of the increasingly large crew; this, combined with the rising costs of food to feed the men on board, led to galleys being used increasingly for defensive purposes and much closer to home. Even before the change in rowing, Mediterranean states had difficulty paying the cost of maintaining galley fleets. For some states, by 1600, the cost was almost prohibitive.[3]

Galeasses, the design intended to combine the best of the sailing ship and the galley, were the heavy units of Mediterranean fleets. They too suffered a change in the rowing arrangement which made for even larger crews. The northern European version largely disappeared in the second half of the sixteenth century, while its Mediterranean counterpart showed some different design features. Venetian galeasses were, like the merchant galleys from which they derived, capable sailing ships. They were bigger than the standard war galleys, rising to 55 metres in length and 12 metres in width. They had 25 or 26 banks of oars to a side, with perhaps six rowers to each oar.[b] In the last two decades of the sixteenth century, the galeass, like the galley, was superseded in the Mediterranean by sailing warships, vessels which by that time could deploy more firepower, more effectively, than could oared ships.

The development of the full-rigged warship began early in the sixteenth century. The introduction of heavy artillery, combined with the widespread use of full rig, dictated the need for a novel design. Pressed by this imbalance in technologies, shipbuilders turned to the combination of features from known types to get an efficient warship. The development of the galleon produced the warship that governments demanded. First built in the Venetian Arsenal, the great galleon was really a full-rigged sailing ship, and there lay its success. The name is confusing since it was also used for ships very similar to the galeass. By the middle of the century the galleon was about as long as a great galley but was wider, giving it a length-to-breadth ratio of under 4:1. It was, then, much narrower than other full-rigged ships. It was lower than the carrack, with a beak-head which showed its galley ancestry, and which served to break the waves before they reached the small forecastle. It was also a solid base for the bowsprit. The aftercastle was still sizeable and fully built into the hull. It included the half-deck which ran up to the mainmast. Because of the narrow build of the hull and the lack of extensive superstructure, the galleon did not have the deep draught of the carrack but it did not ride high in the water. It was much easier to handle than the carrack. Range was not sacrificed, since there was still a sizeable space in the hold for food for the crew. The sides tended to be straight. As fighting strength came from the guns, there was a good deal of internal strengthening and displacement was increased fore and aft to support the weight of the guns there. There were two or three decks and guns were arranged in one or two tiers on the decks. The ship was propelled by the standard complement of sails, with four masts on the larger galleons. Topgallants, square sails on the main- and foremasts above the topsails, were often added. There might in some rare cases be royals above the topgallants, thus giving even greater divisibility of sails. The sails served to give much of the control, since the sternpost rudder was hard to handle and ineffective in heavy weather. By 1550, the type had spread to other parts of Europe, and Spanish, French and English shipwrights built galleons of the same design. There were variations and continuing experiments with the type. French galleons, for example, stayed small — about 100 tons — and were often used for work close to shore. Broadside armament, speed, greater handling qualities and her strength from internal ribs and external wales made contemporaries look on the galleon as a warship.[c] Tonnage did not reach the figure for the carrack, but galleons of 500 to 800 tons were not uncommon,[4] and very large crews could be carried — one man for each ton of capacity or slightly more. The men were there to fight but they also served as a pool of labour to handle the increased number of sails.

It was the galleon in its various modifications which drove the galley from its position as the most important fighting ship in the Mediterranean. Naval battles with sailing ships, long a feature of the Atlantic and northern European waters, also became typical in the Mediterranean after the introduction of the galleon and, more important, of more and cheaper guns. The quality of guns and gunpowder and of naval gunnery in general was still far from ideal but guns improved during the sixteenth century, thus increasing the effectiveness of the broadside fire of the galleons.

Reliable iron guns cost much less to make and were much easier to handle than their bronze predecessors. Gunners lost their privileged position, their higher status and incomes, as it became possible to train most sailors to fire the new weapons. With increased firepower and the improved handling qualities of sailing ships, tactics changed, at least for the weaker opponent, from boarding to standing off and firing cannon. In the 1580s, there was a large influx into the Mediterranean of English and Dutch sailing ships equipped with more guns. Their vessels proved highly effective for piracy, at which oared ships had previously excelled. It was in precisely these last years of the sixteenth century that heavily armed sailing warships drove oared vessels from their dominance of Mediterranean naval forces. Mediterranean navies had tried using broadside armament before, around 1500, but it proved ineffective because of the small numbers of guns and slow rates of fire.[5] It was the northern Europeans who solved those problems and so it was they who came, over time, to dominate the dangerous trades in the Mediterranean and long-distance trades outside Europe.

The campaign of the Spanish Armada in 1588 demonstrated that, at sea, fighting was to be between fleets of ships firing guns. The plan of King Philip II of Spain to land troops in England failed for a number of reasons, including the weather, but certainly a principal cause of the English success in preventing any landing, or for that matter any co-ordination of Spanish efforts, was the manoeuvrability of their ships. Their galleons were smaller, faster, easier to handle than the Spanish and Portuguese warships and so the English were able to deploy their guns more effectively.[d] It was clear from 1588 that seapower would depend on that ability to use guns, making the low, narrow galleon of 500 tons or slightly more the best option for European navies.[6] The massive carracks, like those built for the kings of Europe in the first half of the sixteenth century, had lost their value. The massive fighting ships were expensive and had a bad tendency to sink easily. The English warship *Mary Rose* went down in the middle of the century because inexperience with using guns led her to heel over and water rushed in through the gunports which no one had thought to close. The *Gustavas Vasa* sank in Stockholm harbour on her maiden voyage in 1628 when there was a sudden strong wind.[e] She was unstable when built and the addition of heavy guns increased the problem. The *Vasa* was not a massive carrack but the loss did show the great liability of warships even in the seventeenth century. Since with heavy guns large ships could be sunk by almost any properly handled warship, the logical response of naval shipbuilders was to design for handling qualities, internal strength with thicker timbers and maximum firepower. The galleon supplied those requirements and, though large galleons could be built — 1,000 tons and more — such concentration of investment was rare. The galleon was not the only warship built in the second half of the sixteenth century. Heavily armed four-masted ships, really large carracks, still participated in sea battles. With or without guns, they were also used for commerce.[f] The engravings and paintings by Pieter Breugel the Elder of ships and battles from the 1550s are accurate reproductions of the large warships of the Mediterranean and the Low Countries. His representations of galleys are equally trustworthy.[g] The sailing warships of many of Breugel's works show the tendency towards longer vessels, straighter sides and greater reliance on internal rather than external support. Coming at the middle of the century, the prints include some transitional carracks which already had galleon features. At the same time, the works show the degree of diffusion of certain northern and southern rigging techniques.[7]

Galleons also made good cargo ships. They were costly to operate because of the size of the crew and the expensive guns. On the other hand, they were highly defensible. Thus galleons were limited to use on dangerous trade routes where the value of goods per unit volume was high enough to cover the costs. On short voyages they might face competition from galleys but even there, by the end of the sixteenth century, the galleon could effectively compete, with its larger carrying capacity and therefore presumably lower cost for each ton shipped. For dangerous long-distance trades there was no question about the superiority of this type of sailing ship. The galleon found a place in traffic to the New World from Seville in Spain since the back cargo was silver. As silver production rose in the New World and as other states sent naval forces to try and capture the silver shipments, the number of galleons in the New World fleets rose. The increase in the average tonnage of ships going to the New World throughout the sixteenth century indicated not only a rising volume of trade but also greater opportunities for the use of the galleon. The design yielded greater advantages in the range of about 500 tons than in smaller versions. This is not to say that smaller sailing ships were not designed in imitation of the galleon. The New World trade was not the only trade where galleons found a place. Exchange of luxuries, including the carriage of silver, between Iberia and the Low Countries brought galleons to northern European ports. Northern Europeans, on their first trading ventures to the East Indies, used ships very like the Spanish galleons which sailed to the Americas.[8] The similarity in goods and in the expected dangers suggested the use of the same ship type.

The change to smaller and more manoeuvrable warships was a lesson not lost on pirates. Piracy was always a problem for European commerce. In the latter middle ages and throughout the sixteenth century, piracy usually rose out of political conflict, since privateering and piracy were hard to distinguish. Piracy was more profitable if there was a state to support the robbers, to offer them sanction, a base of operations and a market for captured ships and goods. There was apparently some constraint on these men which kept them from unrestrained piracy, from acting indiscriminately without some excuse granted them by a belligerent power. Since there was usually a number of belligerent powers at any one time, they generally chose to act as privateers with some legal sanction. Government efforts to suppress piracy always proved unsuccessful − that is, except in a few rare instances where all parties agreed to join together in stopping the practice. In many cases governments used piracy as a method of carrying on undeclared war. The pirate fleets served as a source of trained men and warships in times of war, a source which could then be used as an official navy. Their ships had manning ratios of three tons for each man, or less, while cargo ships would operate generally at ten tons per man, or more. With their ships built narrow and light and with some light guns on board, pirates could pursue, catch and take most cargo ships.[9] The addition of the guns, even if light, made the pirate ship much more productive. Crews still had to be large and so labour costs did not fall, but success in seizing cargo ships increased. If only by intimidating the commercial vessel with firepower, the pirate ship could better its chances. After all, pirates were not interested in sinking ships but only in capturing them for the goods on board. The increased power of pirate ships was combined with a general rise in the total volume of commerce and therefore a rise in the potential quantity of goods for the pirates to steal. More profitable piracy drew more investment and more sailors.

The threat from pirates meant that cargo ships had to better their defences. There was an increase in piracy in the Mediterranean in the sixteenth century, not just because of the operations of corsairs from Algiers. Northern Europeans and Turks were equally willing to exploit the new opportunities, thus giving even greater impetus to Mediterranean shippers to adopt ships like the galleon. English merchants trading to the Levant ordered heavy, well-armed highly defensible merchantmen from English shipbuilding yards so that they could make the long voyage through the Mediterranean unhindered. Not incidentally, the use of such types also gave them the possibility of becoming privateers or pirates if the opportunity presented itself. The cargoes of the Levant trade were valuable enough to support the higher cost of freight in these defensible ships and the charges were high since manning ratios were 5 to 4.5 tons for each crewman. Piracy, or rather privateering, was a business highly organised by a small group of investors exploiting the potential created by shipbuilders.[10] Once ship design made that kind of privateering venture possible, piracy spread to the New World where similar trade patterns and geography and the importation of European political conflicts combined to generate circumstances much like those in the Mediterranean. Whether for privateering or for navies, galleons became the fighting ships of Europe.

The specialised cargo ship was the product of a series of design changes throughout the sixteenth century. The progression was most obvious in Holland where shipbuilders first tested the extremes of design for a purely cargo-carrying vessel. Dutch trade was principally with the Baltic where ships went for grain to bring to the storehouses of Amsterdam for redistribution to western and southern Europe. For that traffic and for shorter voyages in the North Sea, Dutch builders

26: Boyer (left) and Netherlands Cargo Ship Showing Many Features of the Later Fluyt, from a Mid-sixteenth-century Engraving by Pieter Breugel the Elder

produced a series of low-cost carriers. The first to emerge was the boyer which gained widespread popularity in those trades in the 1560s and 1570s. Like its successors, it sacrificed speed and a large crew for cargo space. The boyer started as a flat-bottomed low vessel of shallow draught in the fifteenth century or earlier. In the sixteenth century it was made into a seagoing vessel. Sides were built up, it became larger and the rig was expanded. Though there were variations, the usual arrangement seems to have been two masts, the mizzen having a lateen and the mainmast carrying two square sails and a spritsail. Another sail was often hung from the forestay,[h] giving a combination of both square and fore-and-aft rig which made the ship highly manoeuvrable. Moreover, it took only a few men to handle the rig. The length-to-breadth ratio was better than 3:1, with lengths reaching 20 metres and more. There was a deck to protect cargo. Boyers of about 100 tons were most common, though they could be as small as 50 and as large as 130 tons. Boyers were capable of long voyages but they were most popular for short runs in the North and Baltic Seas. The manning ratio was among the best of any cargo ship, rising to 20 tons for each man.[11] The *vlieboot* tended to replace the boyer after the 1570s because it was even better designed for bulk carriage. It was also two-masted with one mast carrying a spritsail, but in this case each mast carried two square sails. It had a square built-up stern, broad beam and very shallow draught. These boats were small, rarely exceeding 100 tons. With its sizeable cargo space from the hull design and its combination of sails, it was the leading medium and small bulk carrier of the last years of the sixteenth century. It was superseded by a ship of even more efficient design.

The *fluit* grew out of the experience of builders with other bulk carriers. A date of 1595 has been given for the invention of the fluyt by a Dutch ship carpenter at the town of Hoorn, north of Amsterdam. This new ship may have been a marked improvement over its predecessors, but cargo ships with many features of the fluyt were certainly built before that date. Pieter Breugel, in one of his engravings, shows a cargo ship alongside a boyer which looks much like the fluyt of the seventeenth century.[i] Obviously, builders were making incremental progress towards the final fluyt design, not established until the second decade of the seventeenth century. The English called fluyts flyboats, which suggests that the fluyt and *vlieboot* were closely related. The unique features of the fluyt included a high length-to-breadth ratio — 4:1 in 1595 and higher in the following years, rising to 5:1 and even 6:1 — shallow draught, light upperworks aft and none forward, and a low centre of gravity. The bottom was nearly flat, the hold large and almost square. The posts were close to vertical to give an even more box-like spacious hold. Bows were bluff and almost bulging. Usually there was a full deck. Given the form of the hull, it was a good sailer even to windward. The rig had a square sail on the foremast, two square sails on the mainmast and a lateen mizzen with a square mizzen topsail along with a spritsail under the bowsprit. The arrangement was common on full-rigged ships. The fluyt rarely added more canvas and in fact often dropped the topsails. Pole-masts were also used on some versions so that the work of handling the sails could be done from the deck. Most sailing ships of the second half of the sixteenth century had detachable topmasts so that the topsail and all its spars could be taken in in bad weather, thus saving valuable masts, creating greater flexibility and making for greater potential sail area. For the fluyt, however, sail area was far from maximised. It had shorter masts and spars and smaller sails than, for example, on galleons of comparable size. The fluyt was slower as a result, but builders did not design the fluyt for speed. The goal was to minimise costs. Pulleys and tackles were also extensively used for control of the sails, thus also keeping down the size of the crew. The stern was rounded, a return to the tradition of the sailing ships of the Low Countries before 1450. There was extensive tumble-home which gave the wing transom a taper, with the upper decks, if there were any, much narrower than the main deck. This design cut wind resistance and, along with the round stern, improved handling. It must have been difficult to bend the large planks to fit the great curves of the stern. Builders used as much pine as possible in construction, since it was easier to work and also made the fluyt even lighter.[12] The final result was a slow, light ship, with good handling qualities which could be and were traded off for smaller crews. It was specifically designed for the Dutch trades in salt, herring and grain and offered the lowest cost transport available for those goods, thus keeping delivered prices down and increasing the size of the market. Since the Dutch could move these goods in fluyts for less than could their competitors, the result was more trade in Dutch ships. The available data on Baltic trade in the late sixteenth and seventeenth centuries confirm the success of the fluyt.[13]

The fluyt rarely carried guns and, when it did, the armament was small. Given its slowness and light build, it was not worth much in a fight. It was primarily for use in the Baltic where piracy was at a minimum. Fluyts could in some cases be defensible. On rare occasions they were even used for piracy. The Baltic was not always a peaceful sea and fluyts found employment along the Atlantic seaboard and even in the

West Indies, both areas well known for danger from freebooters. For these voyages and for trips to the Mediterranean, shippers chose modified and better-armed fluyts. More important in those trades was the protection offered by convoys. In the fifteenth and sixteenth centuries, as shipbuilders produced specialised cargo ships, governments began to organise the convoys arming ships to sail with and protect the relatively defenceless vessels. In the Low Countries the process began with the herring busses, built as fishing boats with no consideration for defence. As shipyards produced more efficient cargo ships, the need for protecting them, especially in time of war, became a pressing problem. By 1600, northern European governments had accepted the responsibility for defending shipping. Fishermen and shippers had to pay for the service, usually by a levy based on the duration of the voyage and the tonnage of the ship. It was the government admiralties, though, which built the warships and organised the convoys. The pinnass, square-sterned, full-rigged and heavily armed, was a standard ship for that work. The term was used rather loosely in the sixteenth century but, by 1600, it typically meant a vessel of over 50 tons, fast and intended for defence. Smaller versions were rowed and the sleekness of the sailing warships may have earned them the name. Since ships had been made more efficient by the design changes, the cost of state-organised convoys could be more easily sustained. Governments were glad to offer protection to valuable shipping and at the same time find a way to cover the cost of operating their warships. The increased vigour of governments in organising convoys and supplying protection served to push back even more the constraints on shipbuilders. They could go further in building specialised low-cost bulk carriers — that is, except for ships trading in difficult waters such as the Mediterranean and the West Indies, but even here the convoy system kept some slower, lighter, less well-armed ships in service.

Convoys worked to decrease the flexibility of seaborne commerce, tying skippers to specific routes and sailing dates. Convoys could only move as fast as the slowest ship. But technical changes more than compensated for the loss in flexibility. Southern methods of navigation were slowly introduced in the North. Improvements in aids to navigation in northern Europe attest to the rise in long-distance trade between North and South. Moreover, there were advances in the equipment used. A ship's position could be more easily and more accurately determined, thanks to improvements in the compass and the quadrant. Better projections made it possible to navigate a great circle course with contemporary charts. The appearance of trigonometry tables for use by sailors made it easier to resolve courses. Moreover, by the end of the sixteenth century, along with printed rutters of an increasing variety, navigators in the Atlantic and the North Sea had charts available to them as good as any for the Mediterranean. They were less expensive too, thanks to low-cost copper engraving developed in the Netherlands.[14]

More important to over-all efficiency than improvements in navigation were the decisions by builders and shipowners to use ships of less than maximum size. While wooden cargo ships could be built up to 2,000 tons, it was found that the optimal size was significantly less, somewhere between 300 and 500 tons. Especially with the fluyt, this kept down crew size and meant shippers could offer more varied services for the fluctuating demand for transport. Small vessels, those of under about 100 tons, tended to disappear from long-distance trade, as did the giants. The great ships had always presented problems, with their long turnaround times. The advantage had been in the lower cost for each ton shipped, implied by the great carrying capacity. The improvements in the fluyt, by cutting the manpower needs, had erased any of that saving. There were no advantages to be gained from the larger scale implied by big carracks. With shorter turnaround time and easy handling, the fluyt of 300 to 500 tons could also compete favourably with small ships, taking away at least part of their advantage in being able to make more trips each year. By decreasing labour costs and increasing the return on investment, the fluyt established an optimal size for a specialised cargo ship. In the process it brought more diversity to trade routes and to trade goods.

By the end of the sixteenth century, ship design had reached something of a plateau. Until the late eighteenth century, there was little change in the design of warships or of larger cargo carriers. The galleon emerged as the ship-of-the-line, while the rig and hull design were modified to give greater speed and reliability without increasing crew size. Much more significant advances were made with small craft, now increasingly limited to short hauls along coasts and on inland waters. What savings were made in the cost of shipping goods by sea over the seventeenth and eighteenth centuries came not from design changes but rather from changes in political and economic conditions which allowed shippers to exploit the design improvements of the fifteenth and sixteenth centuries.[15] The division between cargo ship and warship among sailing vessels was certainly made by 1600. The economic bulk carrier needed for the expansion of European commerce had been created in the fluyt. The greater ability to move bulk goods was reflected in the invasion of the Mediterranean by northern European ships in the last

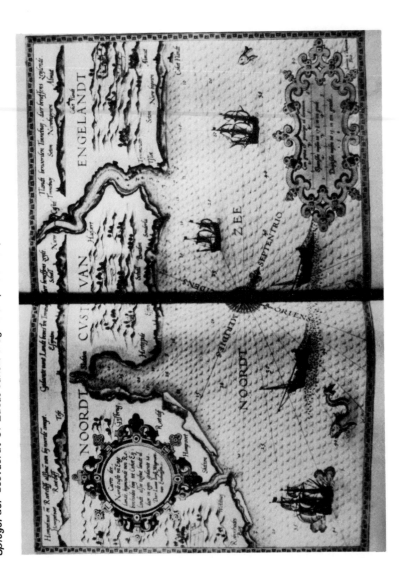

27: Herring Busses Fishing off the English North Sea Coast, from the *Spiegel der zeevaerdt* of Lucas Jansz. Waghenaer, 1584-85.

decade of the sixteenth century. Crop failures led to a famine in the Mediterranean and Dutch, along with German and English, traders exploited the opportunity by carrying grain to southern ports in sharply increased quantities. The bulk carriers provided valuable services both to and within the Mediterranean. English shippers with large and defensible cargo ships, more effective than small local ships, had already made a place for northern shippers, and for that matter pirates, in the Mediterranean. The great volume of trade between the North and the South, however, was in the bulk goods exported from northern Europe in Dutch fluyts, demonstrating to all Europeans the superior qualities of Dutch bulk carriers. Recognising this fact, shippers from throughout Europe bought ships from Dutch yards.[16] The success of Dutch shipbuilders reflected not only their own skill at designing ships for a specific purpose but also the general rise in the volume of trade in bulk goods. The situation of the fourteenth century was reversed. The South still ran a balance of payments surplus with the North, exports being of higher total value than imports. But now the Mediterranean was importing a larger volume of goods than it exported. Mediterranean producers were faced with the problem of finding a bulk cargo to fill the holds of those slow cargo ships from northern Europe for their return voyage. Almost any back cargo would do in order to cut the cost of the total trip. It even proved worth while to carry Italian marble back to the North. But then Dutch ships, rather than go in ballast, carried bricks to the Baltic and even to the East Indies. Carrying cargoes of such low value was possible, under the right circumstances, because of the efficiency embodied in the specialised fluyt.

Shipbuilders in the second half of the sixteenth century faced the same general and pervasive pressure to lower the price of their finished product while maintaining, or preferably increasing, its quality. Builders certainly became better able, over time, to deal with designs and design features. That kind of learning was combined with the fuller exploitation of previously developed improvements, such as the more divided sail plan, to increase the security of ships. Perhaps the better sail arrangement and their own confidence with skeleton-building allowed shipwrights to cut down on the massive amount of wood used in hulls and ribs, thus creating a saving in capital as well as in the labour used in construction. The design of the fluyt also demonstrated the advantage of keeping the ship light, at least where cargo vessels were concerned. It was not, of course, possible with warships.

The question of capital costs became more pressing in the sixteenth century, as, for the first time, European shipbuilders had some serious problems with supplies of raw materials. While in the late fourteenth and fifteenth centuries wood prices probably remained firm, in the sixteenth century wood prices rose sharply. In some cases, builders could not get the right type of wood at all. The big pieces of oak for keels, ribs and knees and the tall pine for masts had to be of just the right size and shape. Shipbuilders in the Low Countries always had to import their wood. As the sixteenth century progressed, they had to look further afield. Supplies were harder to find in England and in France, so builders there had to import more of their wood, both as timber and as cut and prepared lumber. The wood came principally from the Baltic and from Norway. Shipbuilders could not just walk into the forest to select what they needed. They had to rely on a long chain of merchants and shippers to get them the right kind of wood. Wood was not the only raw material that had to be imported. For example, hemp for rope, tar and pitch all had to be brought into western Europe, and the principal sources were in the North, in Scandinavia and in lands bordering the Baltic. This created an expanding trade in such materials and, with it, a greater demand for ships. But the increase in the total production of ships was much less important to builders than obtaining the quantity and the kind of wood they needed at a price that would keep them competitive. As the wood had to travel great distances, first by road or river and then by sea, the possibility of interruption of supply and of price increases was greater. In the fifteenth and even more in the sixteenth century, as farmers cleared land in Poland and Russia to raise grain, they generated timber for export. The process of colonisation meant short-term abundance of supplies but also meant a long-term migration of sources eastward and northward.[17] Merchants, especially those from Holland, by organising the trade and by finding efficient ships, were able to contain increases in the delivered price of wood and to a great degree maintain security of supplies to western Europe.

In southern Europe, in Iberia and along the northern shores of the Mediterranean, the situation was much more critical. The change in ship design towards higher ratios of length-to-breadth increased the demand for wood — especially hardwood for planking — for each ton of carrying capacity built. With the fluyt, the rise to a ratio of 6:1 meant a sharp rise in the amount of wood needed, and southern European builders were handicapped in imitating the design because of shortages of wood. Importing wood from the Baltic and Scandinavia was expensive. German shippers from Gdansk and Königsberg still found a lively and growing market for their wood in Spain and Portugal in the fifteenth and sixteenth centuries. The rising price served to keep transport costs down as a percentage of delivered cost. Despite this fact and improvements in ships, it was apparently never economically advisable to carry wood for shipbuilding into the Mediterranean in large quantities. Supplies of wood there were shrinking. Indiscriminate cutting had, over time, led to soil erosion on islands in the Adriatic and on the mainland. Forests did not replace themselves. All the easily accessible wood had been used and so the cost of bringing trees from the hills and mountains drove up the price of timber. Recognising the problem, governments, and especially the Venetian government, embarked on programmes of forest management to protect limited and decreasing supplies. Their principal goal, however, was to assure themselves of sufficient wood to build warships. Venice made officers of the Arsenal responsible for overseeing the cutting and use of trees. By effectively depriving private shipbuilding yards of wood, the government doomed them to collapse. The process of importing shipbuilding wood in finished form was thus accelerated. Completed ships from northern Europe were brought in, not only because of their superior design but also because northern builders had access to wood, at prices below those faced by their Mediterranean counterparts. States in southern Europe were driven to find alternative sources of ships. The Portuguese government considered having all its ships for trade to the Indies and the New World built in Gdansk. Both Spain and Portugal developed shipbuilding yards in their colonies. The growing local market, the availability of labour but, most important, the abundant supplies of timber recommended the decision. The Portuguese found that carracks for the trade to India built in Goa of local teak were better and more reliable than those built in Lisbon.[18] Over time, Indian-built ships constituted a larger share of the Portuguese merchant marine. Colonial yards in the Americas and the Philippines made similar inroads in Spanish shipping.

Technical change in ship design in the sixteenth century worked against builders short of wood. Shipwrights in the South could not follow the Dutch in building their vessels lighter. Pirates and the continuing war of attrition made trading in the Mediterranean dangerous, so ships had to be heavy and strong. In the case of these designers, it proved impossible to develop a technology which could overcome the loss of the shipbuilders' principal raw material, wood. The generally rising price of wood created pressure for design improvement throughout Europe. The price increases created a threshold of technical change which was needed to continue building ships. The threshold was low enough in northern Europe and especially in Holland for builders to overcome the problem. They were rewarded with the largest share of the European market for bulk-carrying cargo ships. In the Mediterranean, existing technologies and political conditions combined to make the price threshold too high and builders withdrew to work on smaller craft or on warships on which governments by fiat removed price constraints. As with Muslims in tenth-century Egypt, the lack of wood in adequate quantities and at a less than prohibitive price led to the decline of shipbuilding in Italy and Iberia. No technical change was made to counter the decline and the decline itself decreased the chances for innovation. The downturn was self-reinforcing.

Since northern European ships came to spend more time in warm waters in the sixteenth century, shipbuilders were pressed to find a solution to attacks on hulls by the shipworm. It was an old problem in the Mediterranean. The Roman practice of covering the hull with paint and wax may well have continued throughout the middle ages. The waters of the Caribbean were as bad or worse than those of the Mediterranean and sixteenth-century Spanish builders tried methods such as the long-abandoned Roman one of covering the hull with a layer of lead sheathing. The covering was later changed to copper, perhaps to decrease the weight, but, as it also increased the price, the method was rarely used. In any case, such additions had to damage the handling qualities of the ship. In the North, the typical solution was to add another hull, a sheathing of thin planks over the true hull with a layer of tar and oakum or horsehair between the two. If the shipworm attacked the outer layer, at least those boards could be replaced with less danger and less cost. No solution was foolproof. Shipbuilders had the same type of problem with dry rot, a fungus which attacked the wood and spread through the timbers of the hull unless caught in time.[19] For neither of the two problems was there anything like a systematic study of the causes or the potential cures. Obviously, with all solutions there was a trade-off and most of those suggested or tried by ship carpenters were discarded simply because they cost too much — that is, unless governments insisted on the solution as, for example, with the use of copper sheathing. The failure to find an answer to attacks either of the shipworm or of dry rot gave ship carpenters more repair work. Bad planks were torn out and replaced if the trouble was discovered in time. The failure to deal effectively with those problems kept up capital costs throughout the middle ages. In the sixteenth century, the situation became more critical because of the rising price of wood. The penalty was greatest for southern European shippers, since they traded in regions at home and in the East and West Indies where the shipworm thrived. In this case also, southern shipbuilders failed to overcome an immediate and obvious problem, thus creating another advantage for northern Europeans.

Shipbuilders in the second half of the sixteenth century faced increased pressure to expand their range of knowledge. The appearance of the first treatises on shipbuilding in the fifteenth century indicated that ship design had to some degree changed character. With the introduction of full-scale skeleton construction on all large ships, builders had to approach the job of designing and setting up the vessel in a different way. The effect was greatest in northern Europe where shell construction had protected builders from the problem into the fifteenth century. The compromise of southern European shipwrights, by which one or three ribs were set up and connected by wales and the remaining ribs cut to fit, retained some of the uncertainty, as well as difficulties in handling the ribs common to shell construction. By the late sixteenth century, ship designers were drawing all the ribs and lines of the entire ship before they laid down the keel. Not only did they have a better idea of what they would end up with, but they also cut out all the internal framing in place and then simply added the hull planking. This method was faster and easier, especially for large vessels, but it meant that ships had to have plans and builders had to use not only simple mathematics but also compass and ruler to make the scale drawing of the vessel. At least that was the approach in one case. Mathew Baker, the master shipwright to Queen Elizabeth I of England, in a short and confusing treatise on shipbuilding, showed how drawings could and should be used.[j] His drawings gave the shape of the section amidships and, for that matter, throughout much of the vessel. Shape was defined by a series of arcs and circles and proportional relationships.[20] The same type of information could be obtained from models of ships. In the late sixteenth century, buyers of ships, especially governments, began to insist on scale models before agreeing to buy the vessel. The model could in fact be a drawing on paper as well as a replica in wood. The replica had the advantage of giving the shape of the rib. Builders took the shape by pressing a flexible lead rod against the outside of the model. By no means did all shipwrights approach their job in this way, but builders of larger ships, and especially builders of warships, increasingly relied on some kind of systematically developed, preconceived and fixed design executed before the keel was laid down. Shipwrights still imitated past success — a common approach — but at least, in the course of the sixteenth century, the ability to imitate previous experiment had improved and a basis was laid for the evolution of systematic and transferable techniques. Treatises contained more vulgarised mathematics and borrowings from writers who dealt with questions of buoyancy in a more abstract way. Such works were more easily available. The first book on shipbuilding was published at Mexico City in 1587. Included were plans, a model of a ship and illustrations and directions for a number of other jobs associated with shipbuilding, such as making sails.[21]

None of these changes made shipbuilding a formal or systematic science. Certainly, the improvements in approach and in diffusion of information helped shipwrights to deal with technical changes already made. They allowed more builders to use the new techniques and increased the opportunities for further improvements as more men tried their hand at using models in designing and building. But shipbuilders still could not predict the major attributes of the ship before launching. It was not until late in the seventeenth century that anyone could say beforehand with any accuracy what the draught of a ship would be. Shake-down cruises were still a necessity because the hull often had to be filled out in certain places to make the ship seaworthy. The experience with the *Vasa* showed the degree of inaccuracy in ship design. Builders retained a notion that the hull should be something like a mackerel or some other relatively long fish on the simple understanding that if the fish moved well through the water then a ship of similar design logically would do so too. Despite such thinking, it is clear that, by the late sixteenth century, some European shipbuilders were applying more sophisticated techniques to the whole problem of designing ships. Shipwrights like Mathew Baker found themselves employed by governments on a permanent or semi-permanent basis for the production of warships. The situation of the Venetian Arsenal in the fourteenth century became widespread. Shipwrights working for governments had a greater incentive to develop systematic approaches to design. Since much of the pressure came from the governments, the change in approach was most noticeable and the need to learn much greater for the builders of warships. Only slowly did learning encroach on the handicraft tradition of the building of cargo ships.

Though there were problems with obtaining and maintaining supplies of wood for shipbuilding, labour appears to have been relatively abundant. The continued growth of population in the second half of the sixteenth century, despite some checks here and there, supplied the necessary pool of unskilled workers for the industry. Migration to the cities brought even more potential workers close to the sites of shipbuilding yards. The need for unskilled workers had increased relatively because ships were bigger. More muscle power was needed to raise those large frames. For skilled labour the ship carpenters' guilds, to be found in most major ports by the second half of the sixteenth century, continued to train new men. These would-be ship carpenters were drawn by the expectation of rising incomes, rising if not because of higher wage rates at least because of more regular work with the greater demand for ships and therefore for shipbuilders' services. Guilds of ship carpenters did not attack the problem of formal training to teach men to deal with the new methods in the trade, to make models and understand written works on shipbuilding.

The results of design change in the second half of the sixteenth century formed a microcosm of the effects of technical improvements in the design and building of ships over the years from 600 to 1600. The same sectors of the economy enjoyed the advantages of lower transport costs, and similar economic opportunities were pursued in those sectors. As was to be expected, European governments found the pressures on them and the opportunities for them similar to those created by earlier design changes. After all, design change followed a similar pattern over the 1,000 years. Builders were devoted to lowering the cost of shipping goods, no matter what or who those goods might be. At the same time, the structure of demand had changed at various times so that shipwrights, in response to those demand changes, had attacked one aspect of the general problem and then another. Throughout, however, the greatest demand they faced and their greatest success was with the movement of bulk goods. It was here that waterborne transport enjoyed a competitive advantage which land transport could overcome only with great difficulty and only in certain highly specific circumstances. By no means did builders ever abandon building ships for carrying luxuries. Indeed, in many cases, competition from land transport created yet another pressure on shipbuilders to refine and improve the designs of such carriers. But with moving bulk goods, the opportunity to supply a ready market almost invariably existed. By retaining many designs, by borrowing from designs of smaller or different types of vessels as occasions arose and by supplying ships in the quantity and type to fulfil the needs — both immediately perceived and less obvious — of shippers, shipbuilders, over time, generated the potential for lower-cost bulk transport. The potential was embodied in the design of their ships. The cheaper shipping services made possible world-wide economic connections, on a continuing basis. The lower-cost bulk carrier also opened the door to regular reliance on distant suppliers for all kinds of goods, including luxuries, since over great distances that type of ship proved efficient in handling them too.

Falling transport costs could and did lead to specialisation in production by region. Commercial agriculture was practised ever more widely. Farmers did not produce necessities for their own consumption but rather relied on ships to bring them those goods to exchange for their own output. This led logically to the more intensive exploitation of land in agricultural districts far removed from centres of consumption. It also led to the problems inherent in the complete reliance on one product. While agriculture became more specialised by region, industry became less tied to a specific location. As shipping costs became a smaller portion of the delivered price of raw materials, industries could move those supplies over greater distances to the point of manufacture, with no increase in costs. In general the potential fall in the cost of moving goods, and especially bulk goods, allowed for a greater distribution of productive activities and of population. Moreover, that possibility was enhanced by the greater flexibility of transport by sea.

With improvements in ships and in the ways of building them, shipwrights enjoyed the higher status and buoyant incomes which reflected the better quality of their work. Shipbuilders were now technologists and, though they were not exactly the equivalent of engineers, they could still expect to receive something of the same kind of recognition. Shipbuilders not employed by governments still had to combine a large number of skills. They were not only designers but also skilled artisans working on the ships and businessmen with all the problems of raising capital and finding and paying workers. The capital requirements of builders increased, if slowly, throughout the sixteenth century. Owners of shipbuilding wharves, in 1600, were still typically shipwrights – that is, with the exception of government shipyards. If those men wanted to build larger ships, they had to have slipways, which meant investment in floor planking, capstans, chains and other apparatus. Owners also had to supply more tools and a shed for the tools, along with sheds to protect some of their wood. Shipbuilders had to become even more skilled to continue to design ships. All these forces combined to generate a greater distinction and a more unequal income distribution among builders. The differentiation was not sharp nor was it extreme – that took some time to emerge – but the rising capital requirements of shipbuilding, both physical and human, established a basis for setting certain builders apart from other ship carpenters. This situation was less true among merchants. The boom in commerce of the sixteenth century served to make more merchants wealthy. On the other hand, on board ship the distinction between the captain, now himself more of an employee than an employer and shipowner, and the seamen who worked under him continued to grow.

The expansion of trade, and the establishment of new trading relationships made possible by the lower shipping costs, brought greater diffusion of business methods. The most obvious example is the use of marine insurance which, throughout the fifteenth and sixteenth centuries, spread from Italy to Iberia, France and northern Europe. Southern European merchants living in the North set up markets in insurance and after some delay northern Europeans took up the practice themselves. Partnership arrangements to build and operate ships effectively spread risks in the North, as elsewhere, and worked to retard the diffusion of marine insurance. But the increasing volume of trade, the size of ships and their greater reliability which brought down insurance premiums made the practice common by the late sixteenth century.[22] At the same time in northern Europe merchants increasingly used factors, agents and correspondents. The methods of the Mediterranean of the twelfth and thirteenth centuries were widely imitated by 1600. The establishment of trading posts by Europeans in the New World, in south and southeast Asia also served to spread those Italian techniques. In northern Europe the bulk character of trade had slowed the diffusion of those business methods for many years but the development of bulk carriers of optimum size, which in turn meant a greater flexibility of transport, served to create something more like the commercial conditions of the twelfth- and thirteenth-century Mediterranean which made it worthwhile to imitate the already well-established Italian practices.

The specialisation of cargo ships and warships placed certain constraints on European governments. Power, the ability of the state and the dynasty to impose its will on other states, depended on guns, including guns on board ships, if effectively deployed. In order to pay for the guns, states needed the kind of money which, in the sixteenth century, could only be obtained from trade. Government administration continued to expand in order to maintain naval forces and to deal with the growing regulations of trade. Among those duties was the collection of taxes. The promotion of trade and its control by government was intended to enhance state power. The growing volume of trade, increased by the lower cost of waterborne transport, created an even larger stream of income for the state to tap. The organisation, control and direction of trade to the East Indies and the New World by Spain and Portugal was only the extreme example of a pattern repeated in the rest of Europe. In principle, governments, with rare exceptions, looked on commerce with the same eye. The apparatus of government legislation, which was later to be called the mercantile system, was set

276 Warships, Cargo Ships and Cannon: 1550-1600

up to take advantage of the potential created by, among other things, improvements in ship design.

Of course, not all social change was a result of the technical improvements in transportation and especially of improvements in shipping. From 600 to 1600, trade was always a small proportion of total economic activity. The origins of social change are multiple, technical change being only one source. Ship design changed slowly, much too slowly to be at the base of the complex mass of adjustments made in European society over the 1,000 years. Yet the temptation still exists to credit design improvements in ships with making a significant contribution to many of the social changes in that period. This temptation comes from the pervasive nature of the effects of changes in the cost and nature of shipping services. The results of design improvements unquestionably reached a broad spectrum of society. Shipbuilders provided capital goods to the most productive sector of the European economy. The effectiveness of shipbuilders in improving their products, therefore, was crucial to what economic growth there was.

The catalogue of design changes is lengthy. It is easy to see the changes as an unbroken line of incessant and relentless improvement, leading to the galleon and the fluyt of the late sixteenth century. Of course this is a gross exaggeration. The impression is created by foreshortening the developments of a millennium, by concentrating on the most significant changes, especially those in larger ships, and by generally ignoring any loss of technology. The major changes are the ones most easily documented and those subjected in the past to the most extensive study. But small improvements, the obscure and almost arcane minor adjustments, could be and were the source of significant productivity changes, generating, in the long run, over-all savings of sizeable proportions. In the absence of extensive quantitative material on the cost of shipping goods, however, the economic contribution of design changes will never be known to a high degree of accuracy. Still, it is possible to estimate, within a relatively narrow range, the potential increases in productivity of both labour and capital for many design improvements.

The ability of economic circumstances to induce technical innovation is an open question, and will undoubtedly remain so for some time. There is the same problem with the relationship between the economy, and more specifically factor costs, and improvements in ship design in the middle ages. Evidence from marine archaeology has increased sharply our knowledge of the boats and ships built in classical and medieval Europe. Marine ethnology, the study of ship design as evidence about local and indigenous culture, has shown the survival until very recently in many parts of Europe of designs from centuries past. The impression from study in both fields suggests strongly that, at any time between 600 and 1600, shipbuilders throughout Europe had at their disposal a broad range of designs. In small boats especially, ship carpenters apparently knew about and were familiar with many very distinct possibilities of how to go about their job. While in larger craft, at any point in time, the variety was much more restricted, the potential existed of scaling up and modifying any of the designs of smaller ships. While shipwrights could try new ways of building ships, it was always much simpler to do what they had been doing all along. They had to have reasons and very good ones to take on a new design.

Forces external to shipbuilding from 600 to 1600 were often such as to give shipbuilders a reason for trying something new. Usually those forces were apparently economic. In the fifth and sixth centuries, it seems that the high level of skill typical of Roman shipwrights was lost and many sophisticated techniques had to be abandoned. That retrogression, the opposite of technological advance, also seems to have been the result of economic forces. The shipbuilders of the early middle ages lost Roman techniques but in another sense they chose a different way to build their ships, a simpler and less expensive way to move the smaller volume of goods in trade. So even apparent decline in skill was a result of conscious choice based on economic circumstances. Builders borrowed or adapted designs over the years when faced with specific difficulties. Always they were confined by past practice but always they did respond in some way to external pressure. Their efforts were not always successful and the continuing problem of what to do about wood supplies was often dealt with but never completely solved.

If there was one single effect of all the changes, great and small, in the design of European ships over the millennium to 1600 it was greater specialisation. It was true of the ships and the shipbuilders as well. By no means was the process complete by the end of the period nor for that matter were there no specialised ship types in the early middle ages. But in 1600 there were more full-time shipbuilders than ever before, men whose entire efforts were devoted to a single profession. There were more ships relegated to specific duties and able to earn more because they had design features specific to those duties. Ships on the average became bigger over the millennium and were of more specialised design, even though they were larger.

Demand conditions and factor prices were the two pressures between which shipbuilders found themselves. Intermittently, they also had to deal with the dictates of political authorities. Those were the forces which shaped their decisions on design change. The greater professionalisation of shipbuilders, the increasing volume of work and thus growing opportunities for experiment made them better able, over time, to solve the problems of buyers. The pace of technical advance did quicken, especially in the fifteenth and sixteenth centuries. At the same time, though, that pace could slow if the economic conditions acted to deter innovation. In each century, in each decade, shipbuilders had to deal, above all, with the costs of materials and labour and with the immediate needs of shippers. The unique set of circumstances, economic and political, which prevailed in Europe from the seventh to the seventeenth century, led shipbuilders to make a series of technical advances which, over time, yielded greater efficiency in moving goods. The process was not a simple one nor was it entirely in one direction. It did lead to conditions in which the shipbuilding industry could and did respond more directly and fully to demands. It did lead to a reliance on innovation or variation in design to deal with changing circumstances. The process ultimately became self-reinforcing, as success led to greater experiment. Over the entire 1,000 years, though, it is often hard to see any trend in the great variety of products which came from European shipyards. Finally, however, there emerged the most versatile, durable and efficient warships and cargo ships produced anywhere in the world. Ship carpenters proved themselves, over the long term, above all capable of responding to the external forces which pressed on them. It was precisely that technical responsiveness which formed the base of the long-term economic success of European shipbuilders and the men who used their products.

NOTES

1. L. Th. Lehmann, 'Use and construction of galleys in the Netherlands', *Mededelingen van de Nederlandse Vereniging voor Zeegeschiedenis*, XXXVI (1978), pp. 11-23. G. C. E. Crone, *Onze Schepen in de Gouden Eeuw*, pp. 98-104, 149-50. R. H. Boulind, 'The Crompster in Literature and Pictures', *MM*, LIV (1968), pp. 3-17.
2. William A. Baker, 'Gosnold's *Concord* and Her Shallop', *AN*, XXXIV (1974), pp. 236-40. Edward Bowness, 'Some Drawings of Old Ships', *MM*, XLII (1956), pp. 323-7. Edwin Doran, Jr, 'The Origins of Leeboards', *MM*, LIII (1967), pp. 39-51. Alan Moore, 'Rig in Northern Europe,' pp. 14-15.
3. William L. Rodgers, *Naval Warfare under Oars, 4th to 16th Centuries* (United States Naval Institute, Annapolis, 1939), pp. 230-6. Randal Gray, 'Spinola's Galleys in the Narrow Seas, 1599-1603', *MM*, LXIV (1978), pp. 71-83; the defence preparations made by the English and Dutch in the face of the threat

from Spinola's galley flotilla show that contemporaries still thought them effective warships even in northern waters. John F. Guilmartin, *Gunpowder and Galleys*, pp. 69-72, 108-11, 196-232. Lionel Casson, *Illustrated History of Ships and Boats*, pp. 118-19. F. C. Lane, *Venice*, pp. 373-4. In the seventeenth century, on the largest Venetian flagships there were eight men to each oar, an extreme case.

4. William A. Baker, 'The Arrangement and Construction of Early Seventeenth-Century Ships', *AN*, XV (1955), p. 265. Tom Glasgow, Jr, 'The Shape of the Ships that Defeated the Spanish Armada', *MM*, L (1964), pp. 177-8. F. C. Lane, *Navires et Constructeurs à Venise*, pp. 47-8, and 'Venetian Naval Architecture about 1550', pp. 27, 39. Charles De La Roncière, *Histoire de la Marine Française*, vol. II, pp. 471-2. Josip Luetić, 'Dubrovački Galijun Druge Polovini XVI. Stoljeća [The Galleon of Dubrovnik in the Second Half of the sixteenth century], *Anali Historijskog Instituta Jugoslavenske, Akademije Znanosti I Umjetnosti U Dubrovniku*, VI-VII (1959), pp. 129-41. G. P. B. Naish, 'Ships and Shipbuilding', pp. 480-4.

5. Peter Padfield, *Guns at Sea*, pp. 37-45. John F. Guilmartin, *Gunpowder and Galleys*, pp. 35-9, 83-93, 272-3. James A. Williamson, *The Age of Drake* (A. and C. Black, London, 1938), pp. 253-4, 261-80. J. E. G. Bennell, 'English Oared Vessels of the Sixteenth Century', *MM*, LX (1974), pp. 9-26, 169-71.

6. Literature on the campaign of the Spanish Armada is extensive. The best summary is Garrett Mattingly, *The Defeat of the Spanish Armada* (Jonathan Cape, London, 1959). D. W. Waters, *The Elizabethan Navy and the Armada of Spain*, National Maritime Museum, Greenwich, Monographs and Reprints, 17 (1975). C. H. Haring, *Trade and Navigation between Spain and the Indies*, pp. 226, 275-6.

7. O. Buyssens, 'De Schepen bij Pieter Breugel de Oude Proeve van Identificatien', *MAB*, VIII (1954), pp. 159-91. H. Arthur Klein (ed.), *Graphic Worlds of Peter Bruegel the Elder* (Dover Publications, Inc., New York, 1963), pp. 51-5. G. La Roërie, 'More About the Ship of the Renaissance', pp. 186-8; Breugel's works were based on the paintings of a Portuguese artist of the first half of the sixteenth century so the date of 1556-60 for the ship studies may be misleading. I am indebted to T. Iain Gunn-Graham of the University of Alberta for pointing out many of the features of these ships.

8. Huguette and Pierre Chaunu, *Séville et l'Atlantique (1504-1650)*, vol. VI, part 1, table 12E. C. H. Haring, *Trade and Navigation between Spain and the Indies*, pp. 263-5. *HSUA*, pp. 256-7.

9. Fernand Braudel, *The Mediterranean and the Mediterranean World in the Age of Philip II*, pp. 129-30, 866-80. J. Craeybeckx, 'De Organisatie en de Konvooiering van de Koopvaardijvloot op het Einde van de Regering van Karel V', *Bijdragen voor de Geschiedenis der Nederlanden*, III (1949), pp. 194-5. C. L'Estrange Ewen, 'Organized Piracy Round England in the Sixteenth Century', *MM*, XXXV (1949), pp. 29-33. *HSUA*, p. 256.

10. Kenneth R. Andrews, *Elizabethan Privateering During the Spanish War, 1585-1603* (Cambridge University Press, Cambridge, 1964), pp. 102, 217-31. Fernand Braudel, *The Mediterranean and the Mediterranean World in the Age of Philip II*, pp. 288, 305, 886-7. Ralph Davis, 'England and the Mediterranean, 1570-1670', in F. J. Fisher (ed.), *Essays in the Economic and Social History of Tudor and Stuart England* (Cambridge University Press, Cambridge, 1961), pp. 117-37. Alberto Tenenti, *Piracy and The Decline of Venice 1580-1615* (University of California Press, Berkeley, 1967), pp. 3-86.

11. J. van Beylen, *Schepen van de Nederlanden*, pp. 123-5. Bernhard Hagedorn, *Die Entwicklung der wichtigsten Schiffstypen*, pp. 82-92. Alan Moore, 'Rig in Northern Europe', pp. 13-14. G. V. Scammell, 'Manning the English Merchant Service in the 16th Century', *MM*, LVI (1970), p. 132. R. E. J. Weber, 'Note: The

Hollanse Hulck', *MM*, LIX (1973), p. 298.

12. J. van Beylen, *Schepen van de Nederlanden*, pp. 42, 101-9. Bernhard Hagedorn, *Die Entwicklung der wichtigsten Schiffstypen*, pp. 92-117. R. Morton Nance, 'The Ship of the Renaissance', pp. 294-7. Richard W. Unger, 'Dutch Ship Design in the Fifteenth and Sixteenth Centuries', *Viator*, IV (1973), pp. 387-411.

13. Aksel E. Christensen, *Dutch Trade to the Baltic About 1600* (Martinus Nijhoff, The Hague, 1941). Pierre Jeannin, 'Le Tonnage des Navires utilisés dans la Baltique de 1550 à 1640 d'après les sources Prussiennes', *TCHM*, III, pp. 45-63.

14. D. Gernez, 'Lucas Janszoon Wagenaer: A Chapter in the History of Guide-Books for Seamen', *MM*, XXIII (1937), pp. 190-7, and 'The Works of Lucas Janszoon Wagenaer', *MM*, XXIII (1937), pp. 332-50. D. W. Waters, 'Science and the Techniques of Navigation in the Renaissance', pp. 231-2, and *The Art of Navigation in England*, pp. 497-500. W. E. May, *A History of Marine Navigation*, pp. 14-19, 123-8. A. W. Lang, *Seekarten der südlichen Nord- und Ostsee* (Deutsches Hydrographisches Institute, Hamburg, 1968).

15. F. C. Lane, 'Progrès technologiques et productivité dans les transports maritimes de la fin du Moyen Age au début des Temps modernes', p. 302. Gary M. Walton, 'Sources of Productivity Change in American Colonial Shipping, 1675-1775', *Economic History Review*, second series, XX (1967), pp. 67-78.

16. Fernand Braudel, *The Mediterranean and the Mediterranean World in the Age of Philip II*, pp. 226, 621-36. Fernand Braudel and Ruggiero Romano, *Navires et Marchandises à l'entrée du Port de Livourne (1547-1611)*, pp. 49-56, 99. J. H. Kernkamp, 'Scheepvaart- en Handelsbetrekkingen met Italië Tijdens de Opkomst der Republiek', in *Economisch-Historische Herdrukken* (Martinus Nijhoff, The Hague, 1964), pp. 199-234. F. C. Lane, *Navires et Constructeurs à Venise*, p. 108. David Parker, 'The Social Foundation of French Absolutism 1610-1630', *Past and Present*, 53 (1971), p. 85. At La Rochelle he says that any ship over ten tons was imported from the Dutch Republic. A. P. Usher, 'Spanish Ships and Shipping in the Sixteenth and Seventeenth Centuries', in *Facts and Factors in Economic History* (Harvard University Press, Cambridge, 1932), pp. 193-5.

17. Marian Malowist, 'L'approvisionnement des ports de la Baltique en produits forestiers pour les constructions navales aux XVe et XVIe siècles', in *TCHM*, III, pp. 25-40. Otto Röhlk, *Hansisch-Norwegische Handelspolitik im 16. Jahrhundert* (Karl Wacholtz, Neumünster i. H., 1935), p. 30.

18. C. R. Boxer (ed.), *The Tragic History of the Sea, 1589-1622*, pp. 3-5. Gervasio de Artiñano Y de Galdácano, *La Arquitectura Naval Española*, pp. 128-9. Konrad Häbler, *Die Geschichte der Fugger'schen Handlung in Spanien* (Emil Feber, Weimar, 1897), pp. 35-7. F. C. Lane, *Navires et Constructeurs à Venise*, pp. 98-9, 107, 203-6, and 'Venetian Shipping during the Commercial Revolution', *American Historical Review*, XXXVIII (1933), pp. 234-7. Robert Mantran, 'L'écho de la bataille de Lépante à Constantinople', *Annales (ESC)*, XXVIII (1973), p. 402; the Ottoman Empire may have also had a system of forest management to guarantee supplies of wood for warships. Ernst Schäfer, 'Internationaler Schiffsverkehr in Sevilla (San lucar) auf Grund einer spanischen Schiffahrtsstatistik vom Ende des 16. Jahrhunderts', *Hansische Geschichtsblätter*, LIX (1934), pp. 172-3.

19. J. van Beylen, *Schepen van de Nederlanden*, pp. 42-3. Tom Glasgow, Jr, 'Sixteenth-Century English Seamen Meet a New Enemy The Shipworm', *AN*, XXVII (1967), pp. 177-84. C. H. Haring, *Trade and Navigation between Spain and the Indies*, pp. 277-8. F. Moll, 'The History of Wood-Preserving in Shipbuilding', *MM*, XII (1926), pp. 357-60.

20. Wescott Abell, *The Shipwright's Trade* (Cambridge University Press, Cambridge, 1948), pp. 28-36. Ernst Baasch, *Beiträge zur Geschichte des deutschen Seeschiffbaues und der Schiffbaupolitik*, pp. 34-9. Arne Emil Christensen,

'Lucien Basch: Ancient wrecks and the archaeology of ships A comment', p. 143. He does not agree about the development of the skeleton form of construction. G. P. B. Naish, 'Ships and Shipbuilding', p. 488.
21. J. van Beylen, *Schepen van de Nederlanden*, pp. 31-6. L. Denoix, 'Caractéristiques des Navires de l'Epoque des Grandes Découvertes', pp. 141-2. Olaf Hasslöf, 'Main Principles in the Technology of Ship-Building', in O. Hasslöf, H. Henningsen, A. E. Christensen (eds), *Ships and Shipyards, Sailors and Fishermen, Introduction to Maritime Ethnology* (Rosenkilde and Bagger, Copenhagen, 1972), pp. 59-68. Diego Garcia de Palacio, *Instruccion Nautica para Navegar*, Colleccion de Incunables Americanos, VIII (Ediciones Cultura Hispanica, Madrid, 1944). Vernon D. Tate, 'The Instruction Nauthica of 1587', *AN*, I (1941), pp. 191-5. Gerhard Timmerman, 'Das Eindringen der Naturwissenschaft in das Schiffbauhandwerk', pp. 15-16.
22. L. A. Boiteux, *La Fortune de Mer*, pp. 89-114. Jelle C. Riemersma, 'Trading and shipping associations in 16th century Holland', p. 332.

NOTES TO ILLUSTRATIONS

a. H. H. Brindley and Alan Moore, 'Square-Rigged Vessels with Two Masts', *MM*, VII (1921), figures 1-5. Björn Landström, *The Ship*, nos. 396-7. Alan Moore, 'Rig in Northern Europe', p. 14.

b. *HSUA*, pp. 209, 246. Björn Landström, *The Ship*, nos. 324-6, 328, 330, 332, 333. Randal Gray, 'Spinola's Galleys', *MM*, LXIV (1978), p. 73. See also Chapter 5, d. and f.

c. Romola and R. C. Anderson, *The Sailing-Ship*, pp. 128-9, 138. R. C. Anderson, 'Ship-Paintings in the Alhambra', p. 3. Björn Landström, *The Ship*, nos. 286-8, 291, 292, 307, 310-12. R. Morton Nance, 'The Ship of the Renaissance', pp. 291, 296. G. La Roërie and J. Vivielle, *Navires et Marins*, vol. I, pp. 253, 274, 275.

d. Romola and R. C. Anderson, *The Sailing-Ship*, p. 136. Lionel Casson, *Illustrated History of Ships and Boats*, nos. 122-3. G. S. Laird Clowes, *Sailing Ships*, part I, plate X, part II, plate V. Björn Landström, *The Ship*, nos. 302, 304.

e. Björn Landström, *The Ship*, no. 357, and *Sailing Ships*, nos. 262-5. *HSUA*, pp. 233, 242-3, 248-9.

f. Romola and R. C. Anderson, *The Sailing-Ship*, pp. 126, 137. Bernhard Hagedorn, *Die Entwicklung der wichtigsten Schiffstypen*, plate XXIV.

g. Romola and R. C. Anderson, *The Sailing-Ship*, p. 134. Lionel Casson, *Illustrated History of Ships and Boats*, nos. 119-20. Claude Farrère, *Histoire de la Marine Française*, p. 96. Bernhard Hagedorn, *Die Entwicklung der wichtigsten Schiffstypen*, plate XXV. Björn Landström, *Sailing Ships*, nos. 228-9, and *The Ship*, nos. 196, 297. *HSUA*, p. 246. R. Morton Nance, 'The Ship of the Renaissance', p. 295. G. La Roërie and J. Vivielle, *Navires et Marins*, vol. I, pp. 97, 260-1, 263, plates XII, XIV.

h. J. van Beylen, 'Zelandiae Descriptio', p. 97. Bernhard Hagedorn, *Die Entwicklung der wichtigsten Schiffstypen*, pp. 82, 84-5, 94-5.

i. Romola and R. C. Anderson, *The Sailing-Ship*, p. 135. O. Buyssens, 'De Schepen bij Pieter Breugel de Oude Proeve van Identificatien', *MAB*, VIII (1954), pp. 181-3. Bernhard Hagedorn, *Die Entwicklung der wichtigsten Schiffstypen*, pp. 74, 96. Björn Landström, *The Ship*, nos. 298, 362, 363. R. Morton Nance, 'The Ship of the Renaissance', p. 294.

j. G. S. Laird Clowes, *Sailing Ships*, part I, plate XII. Björn Landström, *The Ship*, nos. 299-301, 303. *HSUA*, p. 244. G.La Roërie and J. Vivielle, *Navires et Marins*, vol. I, pp. 265, 267.

BIBLIOGRAPHY

Journals

The American Neptune, Salem, Mass., 1941-
Handels- og Søfartsmuseum Pâ Kronborg, Årbog, Helsinor, 1942-
The International Journal of Nautical Archaeology and Underwater Exploration, London, 1972-
Marine Academie van België, Mededelingen (Académie de Marine de Belgique, Communications), Antwerp, 1950-
The Mariner's Mirror, Cambridge, 1911-
Sjøfartshistorisk Årbok, Norwegian Yearbook of Maritime History, Bergen, 1965-
Sjøhistorisk Årsbok, Stockholm, 1940-

Books and Articles

(*indicates books also cited for their illustrations)

Abell, W., *The Shipwright's Trade* (Cambridge University Press, Cambridge, 1948)
Agats, A., *Der Hansische Baienhandel* (Carl Winter's Universitätsbuchhandlung, Heidelberg, 1904)
Ahrweiler, H., *Byzance et la Mer La Marine de Guerre La Politique et les Institutions Maritime de Byzance au VIIe – XVe Siècles* (Presses Universitaires de France, Paris, 1966)
Åkerlund, H., *Fartygsfynden i den Forna Hamnen i Kalmar* (Almquist & Wiksells Boktryckeri AB, Uppsala, 1951)
—, *Nydamskeppen En Studie I Tidig Skandinavisk Skeppsbyggnadskonst* (Sjöfartsmuseet, Gothenburg, 1963)
*Anderson, Romola and R. C., *The Sailing-Ship* (George G. Harrap and Co. Ltd, London, 1926)
Andersson, T. and K. I. Sandred (eds), *The Vikings* (Uppsala University, Uppsala, 1978)
Andrews, K. R., *Elizabethan Privateering During the Spanish War, 1585-1603* (Cambridge University Press, Cambridge, 1964)
Anthiaume, A., *Cartes marines, constructions navales, voyages de découverte chez les Normands 1500-1650*, 2 vols (Ernest Dumont, Paris, 1916)

——, *Le Navire Sa construction en France et principalement chez les Normands* (Ernest Dumont, Paris, 1922)

*Antoniadis-Bibicou, H., *Etudes d'histoire maritime de Byzance A propos du 'Theme des Caravisiens'* (SEVPEN, Paris, 1966)

——, 'Problèmes de la marine byzantine', *Annales (ESC)*, XIII (1958)

Asaert, G., *Westeuropese scheepvaart in de middeleeuwen* (Unieboek, Bussum, 1974)

Augustin-Normand, P., 'Introduction', in *Le Corporatisme Ancien de Construction Navale en France* (Académie de Marine, Paris, 1939)

Baasch, E., *Beiträge zur Geschichte des deutschen Seeschiffbaues und der Schiffbaupolitik* (Lucas Gräfe und Sillem, Hamburg, 1899)

Bacon, E. M., *Manual of Navigation Laws* (A. C. McClurg and Co., Chicago, 1912)

Baker, W. A., *Sloops and Shallops* (Barre Publishing Co., Barre, Mass., 1966)

Banse, J., 'Les Corporations des Constructions Navales dans Le Port de Fécamp', in *Le Corporatisme Ancien de Construction Navale en France* (Académie de Marine, Paris, 1939)

van Bastelaer, R., *Les estampes de Peter Bruegel l'ancien* (G. Van Oest et Co., Brussels, 1908)

Bathe, B. W., *Seven Centuries of Sea Travel from the Crusaders to the Cruises* (Barrie and Jenkins, London, 1972)

Beaver, P. A., *A History of Lighthouses* (The Citadel Press, Seacaucus, New Jersey, 1973)

Berkenvelder, F. C., 'Frieslands handel in de late Middeleeuwen', *Economisch-Historisch Jaarboek*, XXIX (1963), pp. 136-87

Bernard, J., *Navires et Gens de Mer à Bordeaux (vers 1400–vers 1550)*, 3 vols (SEVPEN, Paris, 1968)

van Beylen, J., *Schepen van de Nederlanden Van de late middeleeuwen tot het einde van de 17e eeuw* (P. N. van Kampen en Zoon, N. V., Amsterdam, 1970)

Binswanger, H. P., 'A Microeconomic Approach to Induced Innovation', *Economic Journal*, LXXXIV (1974), pp. 940-58

Boeles, P. C. J. A., *Friesland tot de Elfde Eeuw* (Martinus Nijhoff, The Hague, 1927)

Boiteux, L. A., *La Fortune de Mer, le Besoin de Sécurité et les Débuts de l'Assurance Maritime* (SEVPEN, Paris, 1968)

Boxer, C. R. (ed.), *Further Selections from The Tragic History of the Sea, 1559-1565*, Hakluyt Society Publications, series II, CXXXII (Cambridge University Press, Cambridge, 1968)

——, *The Portuguese Seaborne Empire* (Hutchinson, London, 1969)

— (ed.), *The Tragic History of the Sea, 1589-1622*, Hakluyt Society Publications, series II, CXII (Cambridge University Press, Cambridge, 1959)

Bratianu, G. I., *Recherches sur Le Commerce Génois dans la Mer Noire au XIIIe Siècle* (Librairie Orientaliste Paul Guethner, Paris, 1929)

Braudel, F., *The Mediterranean and the Mediterranean World in the Age of Philip II* (translated by Sian Reynolds), 2 vols (Collins, 1972; first French edition, London, 1949)

— and Ruggiero Romano, *Navires et Marchandises à l'entrée du Port de Livourne (1547-1611)* (Librairie Armand Colin, Paris, 1951)

Bréhier, L., 'La Marine de Byzance du VIIIe au XIe Siècle', *Byzantion*, XIX (1949), pp. 1-16

Bresc, H. *et al.*, *Studi di storia navale*, Centro per la storia della tecnica in Italia, Pubblicazioni, IV, 7 (1975)

von Breydenbach, B., *Bevaerden tot dat heilighe grafft* (E. Reuwich, Mainz, 1488)

Bridbury, A. R., *England and the Salt Trade in the Late Middle Ages* (The Clarendon Press, Oxford, 1955)

*Brøgger, A. W. and Haakon Shetelig, *The Viking Ships, Their Ancestry and Evolution* (Dreyers Forlag, Oslo, 1971; first Norwegian edition, 1950)

Brooks, F. W., *The English Naval Forces 1199-1272* (University of Manchester Press, Manchester, 1932)

—, 'William de Wrotham and the Office of Keeper of the King's Ports and Galleys', *English Historical Review*, XL (1925), pp. 570-9

*Bruce-Mitford, R. L. S., *The Sutton Hoo Ship Burial A Handbook* (The Trustees of the British Museum, London, 1968)

Brulez, W., 'The Balance of Trade of the Netherlands in the Middle of the 16th Century', *Acta Historiae Neerlandica*, IV (1970), pp. 20-48

—, 'De zoutinvoer in de Nederlanden in de 16e eeuw', *Tijdschrift Voor Geschiedenis*, LXVIII (1955), pp. 181-92

Bull, E., *Leding* (Steenske Forlag, Oslo, 1920)

Burwash, D., *English Merchant Shipping, 1460-1540* (University of Toronto Press, Toronto, 1947)

Byrne, E. H. *Genoese Shipping in the Twelfth and Thirteenth Centuries* (The Mediaeval Academy of America, Cambridge, 1930)

de Capmany, A., *Memorias Historicas sobre la marina Commercio y artes de la antigua ciudad de Barcelona*, 5 vols (Antonio de Sancha, Madrid, 1779-92)

Carsten, F. L., *The Origins of Prussia* (The Clarendon Press, Oxford, 1954)

Carus-Wilson, E. M., 'The Effects of the acquisition and of the loss of Gascony on the English wine trade', *Bulletin of the Institute of Historical Research*, XXI (1947), pp. 145-54

Casado Soto, J. L., 'Arquitectura naval en el Cantabrico durante el siglo XIII', *Altamira* (Santander, 1975), pp. 23-56

Casson, L., *The Ancient Mariners Seafarers and Sea Fighters of the Mediterranean in Ancient Times* (Victor Gollancz Ltd, London, 1959)

*——, *Illustrated History of Ships and Boats* (Doubleday and Co., Inc., Garden City, New York, 1964)

——, 'Sailing', in Carl Roebuck (ed.), *The Muses at Work, Arts, Crafts and Professions in Ancient Greece and Rome* (MIT Press, Cambridge, Mass., 1969)

*——, *Ships and Seamanship in the Ancient World* (Princeton University Press, Princeton, 1971)

Chaunu, Huguette and Pierre, *Séville et l'Atlantique (1504-1650)*, 8 vols (Librairie Armand Colin, Paris, 1955)

Cheyette, F. L., 'The Sovereign and the Pirates, 1332', *Speculum*, XLV (1970), pp. 40-68

Childs, W. R., *Anglo-Castilian trade in the later Middle Ages* (Manchester University Press, Manchester, 1977)

Christensen, A. E., *Dutch Trade to the Baltic About 1600* (Martinus Nijhoff, The Hague, 1941)

——, 'La Foire de Scanie', *Société Jean Bodin, Recueils*, V (1953), pp. 241-66

*——, 'Scandinavian ships from earliest times to the Vikings', in *HSUA*, pp. 159-80

——, *Scheepvaart van de Vikingen* (DeBoer Maritiem, Bussum, 1977)

Cipolla, C. M., *Guns and Sails in the Early Phases of European Expansion 1400-1700* (Pantheon Books, New York, 1965)

*Clowes, G. S. L., *Sailing Ships, Their History and Development*, 2 parts (His Majesty's Stationery Office, London, 1948)

Craeybeckx, J., 'De Organisatie en de Konvooiering van de Koopvaardijvloot op het Einde van de Regering van Karel V', *Bijdragen voor de Geschiedenis der Nederlanden*, III (1949), pp. 179-208

Crone, G. C. E., *Onze Schepen in de Gouden Eeuw* (P. N. van Kampen en Zoon, N. V., Amsterdam, 1943)

Crumlin-Pedersen, O., *Das Haithabuschiff, Berichte über die Ausgrabungen in Haithabu*, Bericht 3, Schleswig-Holsteinisches Landesmusem für Vor- und Frühgeschichte (Karl Wacholtz Verlag, Neumünster, 1969)

—, *Traeskibet Fra Langskib til fregat* (Traebranchens Oplysiningsrad, Copenhagen, 1968)

—, 'The Viking Ships of Roskilde', in *Aspects of the History of Wooden Shipbuilding*, The National Maritime Museum, Greenwich, Maritime Monographs and Reports, 1 (1970), pp. 7-23

*—, 'The Vikings and the Hanseatic merchants: 900-1450', in *HSUA*, pp. 181-204

Daenell, E., *Die Blütezeit der Deutschen Hanse*, 2 vols (Georg Reimer, Berlin, 1905)

—, 'Holland und die Hanse im 15. Jahrhundert', *Hansische Geschichtsblätter*, IX (1903), pp. 3-41

Davies, C. S. L., 'The Administration of the Royal Navy under Henry VIII: the Origins of the Navy Board', *English Historical Review*, LXXX (1965), pp. 268-88

Davis, R., 'Merchant Shipping in the Economy of the Late Seventeenth Century', *Economic History Review*, second series, IX (1956), pp. 59-65

—, 'England and the Mediterranean, 1570-1670', in F. J. Fisher (ed.), *Essays in the Economic and Social History of Tudor and Stuart England* (Cambridge University Press, Cambridge, 1961), pp. 117-37

DeRoover, F. E., 'Early Examples of Marine Insurance', *Journal of Economic History*, V (1945), pp. 172-200

DeWeerd, M. D. and J. K. Haalebos, 'Schepen voor het Opscheppen', *Spiegel Historiael*, VIII, 7/8 (July-August 1973), pp. 386-97

Diffie, B. W., *Prelude to Empire Portugal Overseas before Henry the Navigator* (University of Nebraska Press, Lincoln, 1960)

Doehaerd, R., 'Méditerranée et économie occidentale pendant le haut Moyen Age', *Cahiers d'histoire mondiale*, I (1954), pp. 571-93

*Dolley, R. H., 'The Warships of the Later Roman Empire', *Journal of Roman Studies*, XXXVIII (1948), pp. 47-53

Dollinger, P., *La Hanse* (Editions Montaigne Aubier, Paris, 1964)

*van Doorninck, F., 'Byzantium, mistress of the sea: 330-641', in *HSUA*, pp. 133-58

van Driel, A., *Tonnage Measurement: Historical and Critical Essay* (Government Printing Office, The Hague, 1925)

Dufourcq, C.-E., *L'Espagne Catalane et Le Maghrib aux XIIIe et XIVe Siècles* (Presses Universitaires de France, Paris, 1966)

—, *La Vie Quotidienne dans les Ports Méditerranéens au Moyen Age* (Hachette, Paris, 1975)

Ebel, E., 'Kaufman und Handel auf Island zur Sagazeit', *Hansische Geschichtsblätter*, XCV (1977), pp. 1-26

Eickhoff, E., *Seekrieg und Seepolitik zwischen Islam und Abendland Das Mittelmer unter Byzantischer und arabischer Hegemonie (650-1040)* (Walter De Gruyter & Co., Berlin, 1966)

*Ellmers, D., *Frühmittelalterliche Handelsschiffahrt in Mittel- und Nordeuropa* (Karl Wacholtz Verlag, Neumünster, 1972)

*——, 'Keltischer Schiffbau', *Jahrbuch Römisch-Germanischen Zentralmuseums Mainz*, XVI (1969), pp. 73-122

Engelbrecht, W. A. *Schets der Historische Betrekkingen Portugal-Nederland* (Martinus Nijhoff, The Hague, 1940)

Ewe, H., *Schiffe Auf Siegeln* (VEB Hinstorff Verlag, Rostock, 1972)

Fahmy, A. M., *Muslim Sea-Power in the Eastern Mediterranean from the Seventh to the Tenth Century A.D. (Studies in Naval Organisation)* (Tipografia Don Bosco, London, 1950)

*Farrère, C., *Histoire de la Marine Française* (Flammarion, Paris, 1962)

Fenwick, V. *et al.*, *Three Major Ancient Boat Finds in Britain*, National Maritime Museum, Greenwich, Maritime Monographs and Reports, no. 6 (1972)

Fliedner, S., 'Die Bremer Kogge', *Hefte des Focke-Museums, Bremen*, II (1964)

——, 'Der Fund einer Kogge bei Bremen im Oktober 1962', *Mededelingen van de Nederlandse Vereniging voor Zeegeschiedenis*, VII (1963), pp. 4-17

*——, ' "Kogge" und "Hulk" Ein Beitrag zur Schiffstypengeschichte', in *Die Bremer Hanse-Kogge Fund Konservierung Forschung* (Verlag Friedrich Röver, Bremen, 1969), pp. 39-126

Da Fonseca, Q., *A Caravela Portuguesa e a prioridade téchnica da Navegações Heniquinas* (Imprensa da Universidade, Coimbra, 1934)

Fritze, K., *Am Wendepunkt der Hanse Untersuchungen zur Wirschafts- und Sozialgeschichte wendische Hansestädte in der ersten Hälfte des 15. Jahrhunderts* (VEB Deutscher Verlag der Wissenschaften, Berlin, 1967)

Fryde, E. B., 'Anglo-Italian Commerce in the Fifteenth Century: some evidence about profits and the balance of trade', *Revue Belge de Philologie et d'Histoire*, L (1972), pp. 345-55

Galdácano, G., *La Arquitectura Naval Española (en Madera)* (for the author, Madrid, 1920)

Godinho, V. M., *L'Economie de L'Empire Portugais aux XVe et XVIe Siècles* (SEVPEN, Paris, 1969)

Goitein, S. D., *Letters of Medieval Jewish Traders* (Princeton University Press, Princeton, 1973)

——, *A Mediterranean Society The Jewish Communities of the Arab World*

as Portrayed in the Documents of the Cairo Geniza, vol. I, Economic Foundations (University of California Press, Berkeley, 1967)
——, *Studies in Islamic History and Institutions* (E. J. Brill, Leiden, 1966)
*Goodman, W. L., *The History of Woodworking Tools* (G. Bell and Sons Ltd, London, 1964)
Goutalier, R., 'Privateering and Piracy', *The Journal of European Economic History*, VI (1977), pp. 199-213
*Greenhill, B., *Archaeology of the Boat* (A. and C. Black Ltd, London, 1976)
Guilmartin, J. F., *Gunpowder and Galleys Changing Technology and Mediterranean Warfare at Sea in the Sixteenth Century* (Cambridge University Press, Cambridge, 1974)
Haasum, S., *Vikingatidens Segling och Navigation* (Scandinavian University Books, Stockholm, 1974)
Habakkuk, H. J., *American and British Technology in the Nineteenth Century: the Search for Labour-Saving Innovations* (Cambridge University Press, Cambridge, 1962)
Häbler, K., *Die Geschichte der Fugger'schen Handlung in Spanien* (Emil Felber, Weimar, 1897)
*Hagedorn, B., *Die Entwicklung der wichtigsten Schiffstypen bis ins 19. Jahrhundert* (Verlag von Karl Curtis, Berlin, 1914)
Halldin, G. (ed.), *Svenskt Skeppsbyggeri En Översikt av Utvecklingen Genom Tiderna* (Allhems Förlag, Malmö, 1963)
Harbitz, G. P. *et al.*, *Der Norske Leidangen* (Sjøforsvarets Overkommando, Oslo, 1951)
Haring, C. H., *Trade and Navigation between Spain and the Indies in the Times of the Hapsburgs* (Harvard University Press, Cambridge, 1918)
Hasslöf, O., 'Main Principles in the Technology of Ship-Building', in O. Hasslöf, H. Henningsen, A. E. Christensen (eds), *Ships and Shipyards, Sailors and Fishermen, Introduction to Maritime Ethnology* (Rosenkilde and Bagger, Copenhagen, 1972)
Heckscher, E., *Mercantilism* (edited by E. F. Söderlund, translated by M. Shapiro), 2 vols (George Allen and Unwin Ltd, London, 1955)
Heers, J., *Gênes au XVe Siècle Activité économique et problèmes sociaux* (SEVPEN, Paris, 1961)
——, *L'Occident aux XIVe et XVe Siècles* (Presses Universitaires de France, Paris, 1963)
van der Heide, G. D. H., 'Oudheidkundig Onderzoek in de Voormalige Zeebodem', *Mededelingen van de Nederlandse Vereniging voor Zeegeschiedenis*, XVII (1968), pp. 21-6

290   *Bibliography*

*Heinsius, P., *Das Schiff der Hansischen Frühzeit* (Verlag Hermann Böhlaus Nachfolger, Weimar, 1956)

Hewitt, H. J., *The Black Prince's Expedition of 1355-1357* (Manchester University Press, Manchester, 1958)

——, *The Organization of War under Edward III 1338-62* (Manchester University Press, Manchester, 1966)

Holwerda, J. H., *Dorestad en Onze Vroegst Middeleeuwen* (A. W. Sijthoff's Uitgeversmij, N. V., Leiden, 1929)

Hourani, G. F., *Arab Seafaring in the Indian Ocean in Ancient and Early Medieval Times* (Princeton University Press, Princeton, 1951)

Howse, D. and M. Sanderson, *The Sea Chart* (David and Charles, Newton Abbot, 1973)

Humbla, Ph., 'Bjorke-båten från Hille socken', *Från Gästrikland* (1949), pp. 5-30

—— and L. von Post, 'Galtabäcksbåten och Tidigt Båtbyggeri I Norden', *Göteborgs Kungl. Vetenskaps- och Vitterhets-Samhäles Handlingar*, V, A, 6, 1 (1937)

Innis, H. A., *The Cod Fisheries, the History of an International Economy* (University of Toronto Press, Toronto, 1954)

James, M. K., 'The Fluctuations of the Anglo-Gascon Wine Trade during the Fourteenth Century', in E. M. Carus-Wilson (ed.), *Essays in Economic History*, vol. II (St. Martin's Press, New York, 1962), pp. 125-50.

Jamison, E., *Admiral Eugenius of Sicily His Life and Work* (Oxford University Press, London, 1957)

Jankuhn, H., 'Der Fränkisch-friesische Handel zur Ostsee im frühen Mittelalter', *Vierteljahrschrift für Sozial- und Wirtschaftsgechichte*, XL (1953), pp. 193-243

——, *Haithabu: Ein Handelsplazt der Wikingerzeit*, 4th expanded edition (Karl Wachholtz Verlag, Neumünster, 1963)

Jellema, D., 'Frisian Trade in the Dark Ages', *Speculum*, XXX (1955), pp. 15-36

Jorberg, F., 'Beiträge zum Studium des Hanseschiffes', *Zeitschrift des Vereins für Lubeckische Geschichte und Altertumskunde*, XXXV (1955), pp. 57-70

Joris, A., 'Transports et voies de communications au moyen âge', *Cahiers de Clio*, XXIII (1970), pp. 27-40

Kernkamp, J. H., 'Scheepvaart- en Handelsbetrekkingen met Italië Tijdens de Opkomst der Republiek', in *Economisch-Historische Herdrukken* (Martinus Nijhoff, The Hague, 1964), pp. 199-234

Kingsford, C. L., 'The Taking of the Madre De Dios Anno 1592', in

Naval Miscellany, II, *Publications of the Navy Records Society*, XL (1912), pp. 85-121

Klein, H. A. (ed.), *Graphic Worlds of Peter Bruegel the Elder* (Dover Publications, Inc., New York, 1963)

van Konijnenburg, E., *Shipbuilding from Its Beginnings*, 3 vols (The Permanent International Association of Congresses of Navigation, Brussels, 1913)

Kranenburg, H. A. H. Boelmans, 'Zeescheepvaart in Zuid-Holland 1400-1550', *Zuid-Hollandse Studiën*, XI (1965), pp. 200-62

Kreutz, B. M. 'Mediterranean Contributions to the Medieval Mariner's Compass', *Technology and Culture*, XIV (1973), pp. 367-83

——, 'Ships, Shipping and the Implications of Change in the Early Medieval Mediterranean', *Viator*, VII (1976), pp. 79-109

Krieger, K.-F., *Ursprung and Wurzeln der Rôles D'Oléron* (Böhlau Verlag, Cologne, 1970)

*Landström, B., *Sailing Ships in words and pictures from papyrus boats to full-riggers* (Doubleday and Co., Inc., Garden City, New York, 1969)

*——, *The Ship* (Allen and Unwin, London, 1961)

Lane, F. C., 'The Crossbow in the Nautical Revolution of the Middle Ages', in D. Herlihy *et al.* (eds), *Economy, Society and Government in Medieval Italy, Essays in Memory of Robert L. Reynolds* (Kent State University Press, Kent, 1969), pp. 161-72

——, 'The Economic Meaning of the Invention of the Compass', *American Historical Review*, LXVIII (1963), pp. 605-17

——, *Navires et Constructeurs à Venise pendant la Renaissance* (SEVPEN, Paris, 1965)

——, 'Progrès technologiques et productivité dans les transports Maritimes de la fin du Moyen Age au début des Temps modernes', *Revue Historique*, 510 (1974), pp. 277-302

——, 'Tonnages, Medieval and Modern', *Economic History Review*, second series, XVII (1964), pp. 213-33

——, 'Venetian Merchant Galleys, 1300-1334: Private and Communal Operation', *Speculum*, XXXVIII (1963), pp. 179-205

——, 'Venetian Shipping during the Commercial Revolution', *American Historical Review*, XXXVIII (1933), pp. 219-39

——, *Venice A Maritime Republic* (Johns Hopkins University Press, Baltimore, 1973)

Lang, A. W., *Seekarten der südlichen Nord- und Ostsee Ihre Entwicklung von den Anfängen bis zum Ende des 18. Jahrhunderts* (Deutsches Hydrographisches Institut, Hamburg, 1968)

La Roncière, C. de, *Histoire de la Marine Française*, 5 vols (Librairie Plon, Paris, 1909-20)

Le Hénaff, A., *Etude sur L'Organisation Administrative de La Marine sous L'Ancien Régime et la Révolution* (Librairie de la Société du Recueil Sirey, Paris, 1913)

Lehmann, L. Th., 'Use and construction of galleys in the Netherlands', *Mededelingen van de Nederlandse Vereniging voor Zeegeschiedenis*, XXXVI (1978), pp. 11-26

Lethbridge, T. C., 'Shipbuilding', in Charles Singer *et al.* (eds), *A History of Technology*, vol. II (Oxford University Press, London, 1956), pp. 563-88

Le Tourneau, R., *The Almohad Movement in North Africa in the Twelfth and Thirteenth Centuries* (Princeton University Press, Princeton, 1969)

Lewis, A. R., 'The Medieval Background of American Atlantic Development', in Benjamin W. Labaree (ed.), *The Atlantic World of Robert G. Albion* (Wesleyan University Press, Middletown, Conn., 1975), pp. 18-39

—, *Naval Power and Trade in the Mediterranean A.D. 500-1100* (Princeton University Press, Princeton, 1951)

—, 'Northern European Sea Power and the Straits of Gibraltar, 1031-1350 A.D.', in William C. Jordan *et al.* (eds), *Order and Innovation in the Middle Ages: Essays in Honor of Joseph R. Strayer* (Princeton University Press, Princeton, 1976), pp. 139-64

—, *The Northern Seas, Shipping and Commerce in Northern Europe A.D. 300-1100* (Princeton University Press, Princeton, 1958)

Lewis, M., *The History of the British Navy* (Penguin Books, Harmondsworth, 1957)

—, *The Navy of Britain A Historical Portrait* (George Allen and Unwin Ltd, London, 1948)

Lindqvist, S., *Gotlands Bildsteine*, 2 vols (Kungl. Vitterhets Historie och Antikvitets Akademien, Stockholm, 1952)

Lineau, O., 'Danziger Schiffahrt und Schiffbau in der zweiten Hälfte des 15. Jahrhunderts met 7 Bildtafeln', *Zeitschrift des Westpreussischen Geschichtvereins*, LXX (1930), pp. 69-83

Lopez, R. S., 'The Evolution of Land Transport in the Middle Ages', *Past and Present*, 9 (1956), pp. 17-29

Luetić, L., 'Dubrovački Galijun Druge Polovini XVI. Stoljéca' [The Galleon of Dubrovnik in the Second Half of the Sixteenth Century], *Anali Historijskog Instituta Jugoslavenske, Akademije Znanosti I Umjetnosti U Dubrovniku*, VI-VII (1959), pp. 129-41

Luzzatto, G., *An Economic History of Italy from the Fall of the Roman Empire to the beginning of the Sixteenth Century* (translated by Philip Jones) (Routledge and Kegan Paul, London, 1961)

McGrail, S. and E. McKee, *The Building of the Replica of an Ancient Boat: The Gokstad Faering*, 2 parts, National Maritime Museum, Greenwich, Maritime Monographs and Reports, no. 11 (1974)

*McKee, A., 'The influence of British naval strategy on ship design: 1400-1850', in *HSUA*, pp. 225-52

Mallett, M. E., *The Florentine Galleys in the Fifteenth Century with The Diary of Luca di Maso degli Albizzi Captain of the Galleys 1429-1430* (The Clarendon Press, Oxford, 1967)

Mansfield, E., *The Economics of Technological Change* (W. W. Norton and Co., Inc., New York, 1968)

Mantran, R., 'L'écho de la bataille de Lépante à Constantinople', *Annales (ESC)*, XXVIII (1973), pp. 396-405

Marques, A. H. DeO., *History of Portugal*, 2 vols, second edition (Columbia University Press, New York, 1976)

——, 'Navigation entre la Prusse et le Portugal au début du XVe siècle', *Vierteljahrschrift für Sozial- und Wirtschaftsgeschichte*, XLVI (1959), pp. 477-90

*Marsden, P., 'Ships of the Roman period and after in Britain', in *HSUA*, pp. 113-32

*Martinez-Hidalgo, J.M., *Columbus' Ships* (Barre Publishers, Barre, 1966)

Mattingly, Garrett, *The Defeat of the Spanish Armada* (Jonathan Cape, London, 1959)

May, W. E., *A History of Marine Navigation* (G. T. Foulis and Co. Ltd, Henley-on-Thames, 1973)

*Mercer, Henry C., *Ancient Carpenters' Tools Illustrated and Explained with the Implements of the Lumberman, Joiner and Cabinetmaker in Use in the Eighteenth Century* (The Bucks County Historical Society, Doylestown, Penns., 1960)

Miskimin, H. A., *The Economy of Early Renaissance Europe, 1300-1460* (Prentice-Hall, Inc., Englewood Cliffs, NJ, 1969)

Moll, F., *Das Schiff in der Bildenden Kunst* (Kurt Schroeder, Bonn, 1929)

*——, 'Der Schiffbauer in der Bildenden Kunst', *Deutsches Museum, Abhandlungen und Berichte*, II, 6 (1930), pp. 153-77

Mollat, Michel (ed.), *Le Navire et l'économie maritime, XVe–XVIIIe siècle*, *TCHM*, I

—— (ed.), *Le Navire et l'Economie maritime, Moyen-âge au XVIIIe siècle principalement en Méditerranée*, *TCHM*, II

— (ed.), *Le Navire et L'Economie Maritime du Nord de L'Europe du Moyen Âge au XVIIIe siècle*, TCHM, III

— (ed.), *Les Sources de l'histoire maritime en Europe du Moyen Age au XVIII siècle*, TCHM, IV

— (ed.), *Les Aspects Internationaux de la Découverte Océanique aux XVe et XVIe siècles*, TCHM, V

— (ed.), *Océan Indien et Méditerranée*, TCHM, VI

— (ed.), *Sociétés et Compagnies de Commerce en Orient et dans l'Océan Indien*, TCHM, VIII

—, *Le Commerce Maritime Normand à la Fin du Moyen Age* (Librairie Plon, Paris, 1952)

Morison, Samuel Eliot, *The European Discovery of America The Northern Voyages A.D. 500-1600* (Oxford University Press, New York, 1971)

—, *The European Discovery of America The Southern Voyages A.D. 1452-1616* (Oxford University Press, New York, 1974)

—, *Portuguese Voyages to America in the Fifteenth Century* (Harvard University Press, Cambridge, 1940)

Müller-Wille, M., *Das Bootkammergrab von Haithabu* (Karl Wachholtz Verlag, Neumünster, 1976)

Mumford, L., *Technics and Civilization* (Harcourt, Brace and Co., New York, 1934)

Munro-Smith, R., *Applied Naval Architecture* (Longmans Green and Co. Ltd, London, 1967)

Naish, G. P. B., 'Ships and Shipbuilding', in Charles Singer *et al.* (eds), *A History of Technology*, vol. III (Oxford University Press, London, 1957), pp. 471-500

Needham, J., *Science and Civilisation in China*, vol. IV, *Physics and Physical Technology*, part III, Civil Engineering and Nautics (Cambridge University Press, Cambridge, 1971)

Nicolas, L., *Histoire de la Marine Française* (Presses Universitaires de France, Paris, 1961)

Olechnowitz, K., *Der Schiffbau der Hansischen Spätzeit* (Verlag Hermann Böhlaus Nachfolger, Weimar, 1960)

*Olsen, O. and O. Crumlin-Pedersen, 'The Skuldelev Ships, A preliminary report on an underwater excavation in Roskilde Fjord, Zealand', *Acta Archaeologica*, XXIX (1958), pp. 161-75

*—, 'The Skuldelev Ships (II)', *Acta Archaeologica*, XXXVIII (1967), pp. 73-174

Oppenheim, M., *A History of the Administration of the Royal Navy and of Merchant Shipping in Relation to the Navy* (John Lane the Bodley Head, London, 1896)

Padfield, P., *Guns at Sea: a history of naval gunnery* (H. Evelyn, London, 1973)

de Palacio, D. G., *Instruccion Nautica para Navegar*, Colleccion de Incunables Americanos, VIII (Ediciones Cultura Hispanica, Madrid, 1944)

Papadopoulos, S. A., *The Greek Merchant Marine (1453-1580)* (National Bank of Greece, Athens, 1972)

Parker, D., 'The Social Foundation of French Absolutism 1610-1630', *Past and Present*, 53 (1971), pp. 67-89

Parry, J. H., *The Age of Reconnaissance* (New American Library, New York, 1963)

—, *Discovery of the Sea* (Weidenfeld and Nicolson, London, 1975)

—, *The Establishment of the European Hegemony, 1415-1715* (Harper and Row, New York, 1961)

Penrose, B., *Travel and Discovery in the Renaissance, 1420-1620* (Harvard University Press, Cambridge, Mass., 1952)

Periz-Embid, F., 'Navigation et commerce dans le port de Séville au bas moyen âge', *Le Moyen Age*, I (1969), pp. 263-89, 479-502

Peterson, M. L., 'Traders and privateers across the Atlantic: 1492-1733', in *HSUA*, pp. 253-80

Phillips, A., *Technology and Market Structure: A Study of the Aircraft Industry* (D. C. Heath and Co., Lexington, Mass., 1971)

Platt, C., *Medieval Southampton: the port and trading community A.D. 1000-1600* (Routledge, London, 1973)

Prestage, E., *The Portuguese Pioneers* (A. and C. Black Ltd, London, 1933)

Prestwich, M., *War, Politics and Finance under Edward I* (Faber and Faber Ltd, London, 1972)

Renouard, Y., 'L'exportation des vins gascons', *Histoire de Bordeaux*, vol. III (Fédération historique de Sud-Ouest, Bordeaux, 1965)

Riemersma, J. C., 'Trading and shipping associations in 16th century Holland', *Tijdschrift voor Geschiedenis*, LXV (1952), pp. 330-8

Rodgers, W. L., *Naval Warfare under Oars, 4th to 16th Centuries* (United States Naval Institute, Annapolis, 1939)

La Roërie, G., 'Introduction à une histoire du navire', *Annales (ESC)*, XI (1956)

*— and J. Vivielle, *Navires et Marins de la rame à l'hélice*, 2 vols (Editions Duchartre et van Buggenhoudt, Paris, 1930)

Röhlk, O., *Hansisch-Norwegische Handelspolitik im 16. Jahrhundert* (Karl Wachholtz Verlag, Neumünster i. H., 1935)

Rohwer, B., *Der friesische Handel im frühen Mittelalter* (Robert Noske, Leipzig, 1937)

Rosenberg, N., 'The Direction of Technological Change: Inducement Merchanisms and Focusing Devices', *Economic Development and Cultural Change*, XVIII (1969), pp. 1-24

——, 'Factors Affecting the Diffusion of Technology', *Explorations in Economic History*, X (1972), pp. 3-34

——, 'Science, Invention and Economic Growth', *Economic Journal*, LXXXIV (1974), pp. 90-108

Runyan, T. J., 'Ships and Mariners in Later Medieval England', *The Journal of British Studies*, XVI (1977), pp. 1-17

Sacerdoti, A., 'Note Sulle Galere Da Mercato Veneziane Nel XV Secolo', *Studi Veneziani*, (1962), pp. 80-105

Samuelson, P., 'A Theory of Induced Innovation along Kennedy-Weisäcker Lines', *Review of Economics and Statistics*, XLVII (1965), pp. 343-56

Scammell, G. V., 'English Merchant Shipping at the End of the Middle Ages: Some East Coast Evidence', *Economic History Review*, second series, XIII (1960-61), pp. 327-41

——, 'Shipowning in the Economy and Politics of early modern England', *Historical Journal*, XV (1972), pp. 385-407

*Scandurra, E., 'The Maritime Republics: Medieval and Renaissance ships in Italy', in *HSUA*, pp. 205-24

Schäfer, E., 'Internationaler Schiffsverkehr in Sevilla (San lucar) auf Grund einer spanischer Schiffahrtsstatistik vom Ende des 16. Jahrhunderts', *Hansische Geschichtsblätter*, LIX (1934), pp. 143-76

Schmookler, J., *Invention and Economic Growth* (Harvard University Press, Cambridge, 1966)

Schnall, U., 'Bemerkungen zur Navigation auf Koggen', *Jahrbuch der Wittheit zu Bremen*, XII (1977), pp. 137-48

Scottas, J., *Messageries Maritimes de Venise XIVe et XVe siècles* (Société d'Editions Géographiques, Maritimes et Coloniales, Paris, 1938)

Shetelig, H. and F. Johannessen, *Kvalsundfundet og Andre Norske Myrfund av Fartøier* (John Griegs Boktrykkeri, Bergen, 1929)

Skov, S., 'Et Middelalderligt Skibsfund fra Eltang Vig', *Sætryk af Kuml, Årbog fur Arkæologisk Selskab* (1952), pp. 65-83

Stenton, F. M., 'The Road System of Medieval England', *Economic History Review*, VII (1936), pp. 1-21

*Taylor, E. G. R., *The Haven-Finding Art A History of Navigation from Odysseus to Captain Cook* (Abelard-Schuman Ltd, New York, 1957)

Tenenti, A., *Cristoforo Da Canal La Marine Vénitienne avant Lépante* (SEVPEN, Paris, 1962)
—, *Piracy and the Decline of Venice 1580-1615* (translated by B. and J. Pullan) (University of California Press, Berkeley, 1967)
*Thorvildsen, K., *The Viking Ships of Ladby* (The National Museum, Copenhagen, 1967)
*Throckmorton, P., 'Romans on the sea', in *HSUA*, pp. 65-86
Timmerman, G., 'Das Eindringen der Naturwissenschaft in das Schiffbauhandwerk', *Deutsches Museum, Abhandlungen und Berichte*, XXX, 3 (1963), pp. 5-53
Touchard, H., *Le Commerce Maritime Breton à la fin du Moyen Âge* (Les Belles Lettres, Paris, 1967)
UNESCO, *Underwater Archaeology a nascent discipline* (UNESCO, Paris, 1972)
Unger, R. W., 'Dutch Ship Design in the Fifteenth and Sixteenth Centuries', *Viator*, IV (1973), pp. 387-411
—, 'Regulations of Dutch Shipcarpenters in the Fifteenth and Sixteenth Centuries', *Tijdschrift voor Geschiedenis*, LXXXVII (1974), pp. 503-20
Unger, W. S., 'De Hollandsche Graanhandel en Graanhandelspolitiek in de Middeleeuwen', *De Economist* (1916), pp. 243-69, 337-86, 461-507
Usher, A. P., 'Spanish Ships and Shipping in the Sixteenth and Seventeenth Centuries', in *Facts and Factors in Economic History* (Harvard University Press, Cambridge, 1932), pp. 189-213
Verlinden, C., *The Beginnings of Modern Colonization* (translated by Yvonne Freccero) (Cornell University Press, Ithaca, NY, 1970)
Vogel, W., *Geschichte der deutschen Seeschiffahrt*, vol. I (Georg Reimer, Berlin, 1915)
—, 'Ein neuentdecktes Lehrbuch der Navigation und des Schiffbaues aus der Mitte des 16. Jahrhunderts', *Hansische Geschichtsblätter*, XVII (1911), pp. 370-4
Walton, G. M., 'Sources of Productivity Change in American Colonial Shipping, 1675-1775', *Economic History Review*, second series, XX (1967), pp. 67-78
Waskönig, D., 'Bildliche Darstellung des Holks im 15. und 16. Jahrhundert', *Altonaer Museum Jahrbuch*, VII (1969), pp. 139-66
Waters, D. W., *The Art of Navigation in England in Elizabethan and Early Stuart Times* (Hollis and Carter, London, 1958)
—, *The Elizabethan Navy and the Armada of Spain*, National Maritime Museum, Greenwich, Monographs and Reports, no. 17 (1975)

——, *The Rutters of the Sea The Sailing Directions of Pierre Garcie*
(Yale University Press, New Haven, 1967)

——, 'Science and the Techniques of Navigation in the Renaissance', in
C. S. Singleton (ed.), *Art, Science, and History in the Renaissance*
(The Johns Hopkins Press, Baltimore, 1967), pp. 187-237

van der Wee, H., *The Growth of the Antwerp Market and the European
Economy*, 2 vols (Publications Universitaires, Louvain, 1963)

White, L. T., Jr, 'The Diffusion of the Lateen Sail', *Medieval Religion
and Technology Collected Essays* (University of California Press,
Berkeley, 1978), pp. 255-60

——, *Medieval Technology and Social Change* (Oxford University Press,
Oxford 1962)

Williamson, J. A., *The Age of Drake* (A. and C. Black, London, 1938)

Winter, H., *Das Hanseschiff im ausgehenden 15. Jahrhundert (Die letzte
Hansekogge)* (VEB Hinstorff Verlag, Rostock, 1961)

——, *Die Katalanische Nao von 1450 nach dem Modell im Maritiem
Museum Prins Hendrik in Rotterdam* (Robert Loef, Magdeburg,
1956)

——, *Die Kolumbusschiffe* (Robert Loef Verlag, Magdeburg, 1944)

INDEX

INVENTORY 1983